William Blakemore Lyon

Forged in Genocide

Africa in Global History

Edited by
Joel Glasman, Omar Gueye, Alexander Keese and
Christine Whyte

Volume 9

William Blakemore Lyon

Forged in Genocide

Migrant Workers Shaping Colonial Capitalism in Namibia, 1890–1925

DE GRUYTER
OLDENBOURG

Berlin, Humboldt-Universität zu Berlin, Department of Asian and African Studies, dissertation, 2022, title: Namibian Labor Empire: Genocide, Migrant Labor, and the Origins of Colonial Capitalism in South West Africa, 1892–1925.

The publication of this work was supported by the Open Access Publication Fund of Humboldt-Universität zu Berlin.

HUMBOLDT-UNIVERSITÄT ZU BERLIN

Gedruckt mit Unterstützung der Gerda Henkel Stiftung, Düsseldorf.

GERDA HENKEL STIFTUNG

ISBN 978-3-11-137465-9
e-ISBN (PDF) 978-3-11-137491-8
e-ISBN (EPUB) 978-3-11-137503-8
ISSN 2628-1767
DOI https://doi.org/10.1515/9783111374918

Library of Congress Control Number: 2024935946

Bibliographic information published by the Deutsche Nationalbibliothek
The Deutsche Nationalbibliothek lists this publication in the Deutsche Nationalbibliografie; detailed bibliographic data are available on the internet at http://dnb.dnb.de.

Cover image: Swakopmund: Hafengebiet/Holzlandungsbrücke, „Krujungens“, unknown author, *Bildarchiv der Deutschen Kolonialgesellschaft, Universitätsbibliothek Frankfurt am Main, Photo: A_00H_1229.*
Typesetting: Integra Software Services Pvt. Ltd.
Printing and binding: CPI books GmbH, Leck

MIX Papier | Fördert gute Waldnutzung FSC® C083411

www.degruyter.com

Acknowledgements

While the end product is my own, the following book would have never occurred without unbelievable support, advice, and guidance from so many in my life. I will attempt to list a few who have assisted me in my journey here. First and foremost, my wife, Melanie has been the best of supporters since this project first took shape in 2017. I would surely not have gotten here without her. The same goes for my family and in particular my mom Kim who believed in me from the beginning. Also, my brother Blake, grandmother Karine, my dad Mike, along with aunt Laura, uncle Rob, and cousins Kelly and Grace.

I have also had the privilege of good friends who are also colleagues that have helped me immeasurably along the way to this book becoming a reality. They include Bernie Moore, Tristan Oestermann, Michael Mhindu, Christian Williams, Tarminder Kaur, Marie Muschalek, Ana Carolina Schveitzer, Kai Herzog, Stephanie Quinn, Julia Rensing, Alina Oswald, Lennart Bolliger, Lea Börgerding, Oscar Broughton, Friedrich Ammerman, Joachim Zeller, Heiko Wegmann, Luisa Schneider, Luregn Lenggenhager, Bayron Van Wyk, Hergen Junge, Armin Owzar, and so many others.

All the conference participants over the years who have given me feedback, advice, or simply had a good chat with me about possible ideas were also helpful in this work. Those at the archives I have visited have assisted me above and beyond their duties, especially those at the National Archives of Namibia where I have spent so much time.

A special thanks to all those at Basel University who let me join writing workshops and history conferences. I have received so much good feedback and assistance from your community. Also, the amazing support from all those at Basler Afrika Bibliographien, with Dag Henrichsen being a very important advisor in my work. Of course, I am deeply grateful to the Nakatana family for giving me a home away from home in Namibia. The same goes for John Mackay in South Africa.

There are also many wonderful and wise researchers and professors in Southern Africa, the USA, and Europe that have given me phenomenal advice and ideas over the years. Those include Britta Schilling, Baz Lecocq, Cassandra Mark-Thiesen, Charles van Onselen, Cristof Dejung, Frederick Cooper, Giorgio Miescher, Gregor Dobler, Jeremy Silvester (rest in peace), Kletus Likuwa, Lorena Rizzo, Marion Wallace, Martha Akawa, Martin Kalb, Napandulwe Shiweda, Nina Kleinöder, Reinhard Kößler, Robert Gordon, Robert Trent Vinson, Steven Press, Sylvanus Job, Ushe Kufa, Ellen Ndeshi Namhila, Werner Hillebrecht, Henry Dee, and the entire re:work community at Humboldt University. Of course, none of this would have been possible without the oversight of my PhD supervisors Andreas Eckert and Julia Tischler.

https://doi.org/10.1515/9783111374918-202

You always supported me and helped me work out the challenges I faced in my research. It was very much appreciated.

Additionally, I am thankful to the staff and those connected with the publishing house De Gruyter who took on this book project, including Rabea Rittgerodt, Jana Fritsche, and my anonymous peer reviewers for their invaluable feedback. Further, to ensure this book could be read by any and all who are interested, I am grateful to the Gerda Henkel Stiftung and Humboldt-Universität for providing me with open access funding.

Going far back in my 'career,' I want to thank Mr. Rose at Jesuit Highschool for always being my number one supporter as a history nerd. The same goes for my great uncle Rixford Snyder (rest in peace), who was the only historian in my family, as well as the teachers at St. Michaels. Thank you so much for believing in me when I was young. I know there are many I have forgotten in these brief lines, and if you do not see your name in this but helped me along the way, my apologies and know that I certainly appreciate all your help.

William Blakemore Lyon

Contents

Acknowledgements —— V

Abbreviations —— XI

Glossary —— XIII

Introduction —— 1
Research Questions —— **6**
Trends and Interventions in Relevant Literature —— **8**
Methodology and Sources —— **12**
Structure and Chapter Overview —— **17**

1 Colonial Contact Zones: Power, Politics and Labor at Early Work Sites in German South West Africa, 1892–1903 —— 19
Early South West Africa from a Regional and German Imperial Perspective —— **23**
SWACO Expedition to the Otavi Mines, 1892–1894 —— **27**
Swakopmund as Entrepôt —— **42**
Between Ship and Shore: Early Swakopmund Longshore Workers —— **42**
Building Swakopmund's Mole —— **49**
Constructing the Swakopmund-Windhoek Railway Line —— **58**

2 The Human Infrastructure of the Namibian War: Origins of the 'Namibian Labor Corridors' in War and Genocide, 1904–1908 —— 69
The Failure of the European Labor Corridor: An Italian Job? —— **75**
Construction of the Otavibahn, 1904–1905 —— **75**
From Italy to South West Africa —— **76**
Work, Strikes and Italian Interactions with Herero Forced Labor —— **78**
Macaroni and Cheap Wine: A Day in the Life —— **82**
Repercussions from Windhoek to Rome and Berlin —— **88**
The West African Labor Corridor: Supplying the German War Effort —— **89**
The Kru at Sea —— **92**
Ship Life —— **96**
On Shore: Port of Swakopmund's Free and Un-free Labor Force —— **104**
The South African Labor Corridor: Wagon Drivers as Essential Workers of the Colonial Army in German South West Africa —— **114**
The 'Labor Question' in Southern Africa and the Outbreak of War in 1904 —— **115**

Auxiliary Labor Demand, Recruitment, and Experiences in German South West Africa — **118**
Cape Wagon Drivers' Perspectives on Concentration Camps and Forced Labor in GSWA — **126**
War's End and the Colonial Workforce's Transformation — **130**

3 Workers from the North: The Ovambo Labor Corridor, 1905–1914 — 132
Ovambos in the Settler Region and the Northern Polities — **135**
Why Go South? Going on Contract and the Process of Labor Recruitment — **139**
Journey South to the Settler Region — **151**
On Contract in the Settler Zone — **162**
The Diamond Mines — **162**
The Itere affair: A Death in the Diamond Fields — **170**
The Tsumeb Mine — **173**
The General Strike of 1910 — **180**
Life Beyond Work — **181**
Religion — **182**
Social and Personal Life — **185**
Housing, Health, and Provisions — **191**
The Trip Back North — **196**
Conclusion — **201**

4 Privileged but Precarious West and South African Migrants: Labor Elite and Entrepreneurs, 1908–1914 — 202
Defining African Migrant Elite in German South West Africa — **205**
GSWA's 'Colonial logistics': The Role of the Military and Private Enterprise in Train Line Construction, 1905–1912 — **207**
From Military Auxiliaries to Railway Construction Workers — **212**
Cape Worker Recruitment and Individual Organized Migration — **213**
Response of the South African Government to Cape Worker Migration — **216**
The Construction of the Southern Line (Südbahn), 1905–1909 — **219**
The Construction of the Windhoek-Keetmanshoop Line (Nord-Südbahn), 1910–1912 — **224**
The Karibib to Windhoek Wide-Gauge Line, the Wilhelmstal Massacre, and its Repercussions, 1910–1911 — **228**
Religion, Social Life, and Sport amongst the South African Labor Elite of GSWA — **240**

Wealthy West African Entrepreneurs and Skilled Workers — **244**
Pieter Dares and Kru in the Post-war GSWA Colonial Economy — **246**
Alfred Kulivo and Togolese Entrepreneurs in the Colonial Ports — **249**

5 The End of the 'Namibian Labor Corridors': War, Pandemic, Unions, and Garveyism, 1914–1925 — 261
The First World War and South African Rule in South West Africa — **263**
The Cameroonian Exiles: Women as the Backbone of a Small but Tenacious West African Community in GSWA — **265**
The Fall of the Kru Labor Elite and Challenges Under South African Rule — **270**
The Early SWA Labor Regime and 'Native Affairs' Under South African Rule — **273**
A Pandemic Arrives: Spanish Influenza — **279**
Economic Challenges lead to New Solutions: Industrial and Commercial Workers' Union (ICU) and the United Negro Improvement Association (UNIA) in South West Africa — **282**
The End of the 'Namibian Labor Corridors' — **290**

Conclusion — 292

Figures — 297

Tables — 301

Primary Sources — 303

Bibliography — 309

Name Index — 323

Subject Index — 325

Abbreviations

BAB	*Basler Afrika Bibliographien*
BArch	*Bundesarchiv – Berlin-Lichterfelde*
BArch-MA	*Bundesarchiv – Militärarchiv*
BADKGUBFM	*Bildarchiv der Deutschen Kolonialgesellschaft, Universitätsbibliothek Frankfurt am Main*
CA	Cape Town Archive Depot in Cape Town
CDM	Consolidated Diamond Mines
DKEBBG	*Deutsche Kolonial-Eisenbahn-Bau- und Betriebsgesellschaft*
DKGfSWA	*Deutsche Kolonialgesellschaft für Südwestafrika*
DKZ	*Deutsche Kolonialzeitung*
DSWAZ	*Deutsch-Südwestafrikanische Zeitung*
ELCRN	Archives of the Evangelical Lutheran Church in Windhoek
GLH	Global Labor History
GSWA	German South West Africa
ICU	Industrial and Commercial Workers' Union
JSAS	Journal of Southern African Studies
KBG	*Koloniale Bergbaugesellschaft*
Km	Kilometer
LZ	*Lüderitzbuchter Zeitung*
M	Meter
NAF	National Archives of Finland
NAN	National Archives of Namibia
NASA	National Archives of South Africa in Pretoria
NES	Native Estate Files
OFS	The Orange Free State
OMEG	*Otavi Minen- und Eisenbahn-Gesellschaft*
OPO	Ovamboland People's Organisation
POW	Prisoner of War
RMG	Rhenish Mission Society
SAR	South African Railways
SSS	Scientific Society Swakopmund
STDs	Sexually transmitted diseases
SWA	South West Africa
SWACO	The South West African Company
SWAPO	South West Africa People's Organisation
UNIA	United Negro Improvement Association and African Communities League
VDM	*Vereinigte Diamanten Minen*
VdR	*Verhandlungen des Reichstages*
VEM	Archive of the Vereinigte Evangelische Mission
WA	Windhuker Anzeiger
WN	*Windhuker Nachrichten*
WWI	World War I

https://doi.org/10.1515/9783111374918-204

Glossary

Baster An ethnic group in Namibia (often associated with Rehoboth) descended from white European men and black African women, usually of Khoisan origin, but occasionally also enslaved women from the Cape, who resided in the Dutch Cape Colony in the eighteenth century.

Cape Coloured A person of mixed ethnic descent (in South Africa) from the Western Cape, speaking Afrikaans or English as their first language, and typically not a follower of Islam.

Cape Worker A term for non-white South African laborers in GSWA from the Western and Eastern Cape in the late nineteenth and early twentieth centuries.

Ovambo A people of Southern Africa, sharing a similar culture and typically speaking dialects of the Oshivambo language. At the end of the nineteenth and early twentieth centuries most were living in a variety of polities in northern present day Namibia and southern Angola. Many polities were ruled by monarchs but not all.

Kru A people from Western Africa, most from the Kru Coast of Liberia, with a long tradition of work in the maritime industry. In the early twentieth century, many communities were to be found throughout West Africa including in towns like Monrovia and Free Town.

Transkei A region in the Eastern Cape of South Africa, largely home to Xhosa peoples.

Ciskei A region in the Eastern Cape of South Africa, largely home to Xhosa peoples.

Police Zone / Settler Region The settler-occupied regions of southern and central Namibia.

Baaiweg The word used to define the two important roads, often used by wagons, between the coast and the interior in Namibia. In central Namibia this road is between Walvis Bay/ Swakopmund and Windhoek. In southern Namibia this road was between Lüderitzbucht and Keetmanshoop.

Kaptein Cape Dutch word for Captain, chief, leader

Bigman A highly influential individual in a community.

Red Line The boundary between the settler region and the areas to the north.

Schutztruppe German colonial military forces.

Veld Open, uncultivated country or grassland in Southern Africa.

Black/White Both are categorizations used by the GSWA and SWA colonial states, denoting separate legal, political, and economic categories. Those categorized as white (*Weiß*) benefited from essentially all aspects of colonial rule. Those categorized as black (*Farbige/Schwarz*) or Coloured (this was a category in South African but not in GSWA) were subjugated to a variety of obstacles, some small and some immense, that had a very large role in typically forcing those labelled as 'non-white' into roles below 'whites' in colonial society.

European/African These terms have a large amount of crossover with the terms above. European includes those from the European continent or with heritage from the European continent. The term is often synonymous with 'white' for the 1892 to 1925 period. African in this book will include all individuals from Africa or with African heritage that were not considered 'white' within colonial society. This will include those labelled 'black,' and individuals of mixed-race ancestry as they were, within the confines of early colonial society in Namibia, almost always labelled as 'non-white.'

https://doi.org/10.1515/9783111374918-205

Introduction

In April 2022, colleagues and I went to the desert coastal town of Lüderitz in Southern Namibia for work. Our group of three having met up in Bloemfontein South Africa, had driven west in our *bakkie* (pickup truck) to the Northern Cape Province. From there we continued north across the Orange River, which, following good rains, was filled to the brim, to arrive in Namibia. One night in Lüderitz, after a day of writing, we drove our *bakkie* south of town to Radford Bay, near the train tracks heading east into the desert. We parked and got out to see the full moon illuminate the placid shores where in the daytime you could come across flamingos feeding in the shallows. In the evening the bay was calm and the craggy hills going east were covered in a ghostly silver light. Not too far between where we stood were the train tracks, built during the era of German colonialism, and near the rails one could see large sand mounds dotting the area. Many were unmarked graves of workers dating to around 1905, including forced laborers that had died during the colonial war and the genocide waged by the German colonizers against the Herero and Nama. Yet, even in the present era, the echoes of that colonial past reverberated through the daily arrival of diesel freight trains laden with ore from manganese mines, reinforcing the enduring importance of this colonial infrastructure to the local Namibian economy.

It was in this desolate port town that we felt the spirits of the past come to life. Along these very train tracks in 1908, a migrant worker from South Africa, Zacharias Lewala, stumbled upon diamonds in the desert. This chance discovery ignited a diamond rush in German South West Africa (GSWA), beginning an economic mining boom and consequent flood of migrant workers to the expanding diamond fields around Lüderitzbucht.[1] In the aftermath of the genocide, the region, sparsely populated, relied heavily on the labor of migrants, who became the backbone of the colony's economy. In the following pages I seek to unravel the mysteries of migrant workers' lives across colonial Namibia, exploring their identities, origins, and the profound impact they had on the country's history to the modern day.

This book traverses the skies of historical inquiry, spanning large structural examinations of colonialism, capitalism, and politics to the intimate landscapes of individual perspectives and life experiences. Much like a bird, the narrative sometimes perches attentively, capturing the intricacies of a single day in a person's life. At other times, it takes wing, rising to provide broader regional, conti-

1 This book primarily uses the term 'South West Africa' for the period in Namibia from the South African occupation in 1915 until independence in 1990. However, colonial Namibia is at times used instead of South West Africa or German South West Africa.

https://doi.org/10.1515/9783111374918-001

nental, or even global contexts. This approach allows readers to understand the significance of details across multiple scales. Regardless of the shifting lenses of inquiry, the heart of the book remains the individual migrants themselves. The following three life stories give a small glimpse into the types of lives around which the book revolves.

In 1914, Petrus Klaas, a Cape Coloured migrant laborer from South Africa, had been employed since June of the previous year as a diamond washer for the large mine *Koloniale Bergbaugesellschaft* (KBG).[2] He died of electrical shock following an accident related to the power line supplying the central wash. His estate included £1/9/4 cash, three pairs of wool socks, one pillow, two pairs of shoes with laces, three shirts, one beanie, one hat, two soccer jerseys, five shirt collars, four neckties, one pair of gloves, two skirts, one belt, one scarf, two packets of sugar, and two cans (likely of food).[3]

About five months after Petrus started his contract, Amkanga, from the Ovambo polity Ovambadja, in the far north of the colony that was beyond formal German control, started to work at another diamond mine in the area, the *Vereinigte Diamanten Minen* (VDM).[4] He had been working just over five months at VDM's *Schmidtfeld* mine when he came down with tuberculosis and was sent to a 'native hospital.'[5] After 52 days of illness, Amkanga succumbed and died in late May of 1914. His estate included about 3/- in cash, one sack of old clothing, one steel suitcase with two blankets, four pieces of cloth, one harmonica, and what the colonial bureaucracy labelled as "diverse Ovambo items." He was survived by Chango, a potential brother and colleague who at the time of Amkanga's death was also in the hospital.[6]

---

2 The spelling of 'coloured' is intentional as it reflects the Southern African ethnic identification 'Cape Coloured.'

3 NAN (National Archives of Namibia), BLU [011] B.G.L Band 5, Estate of Petrus Klaas 9654/137; As this study spans both the German and South African colonial period in Namibia, and includes comparisons across the African continent and the world, I have converted all currency in the book into British pounds. Marks have been converted using the "historical currency converter," developed by Rodney Edvinsson, Stockholm University, available at https://www.historicalstatistics.org/Currencyconverter.html, update January 10, 2016.

4 On the Various Ovambo polities, see Harri Siiskonen, *Trade and Socioeconomic Change in Ovamboland, 1850–1906* (Helsinki: SHS, 1990), 136–243; Martti Eirola, *The Ovambogefahr: The Ovamboland Reservation in the Making: Political Responses of the Kingdom of Ondonga to the German Colonial Power, 1884–1910* (Rovaniemi: Ponjois-Suomen Historiallinen Yhdistys, 1992), 77–149.

5 These were hospitals for black individuals and people of a mixed background who were not legally classified as white according to the colonial administration. These hospitals were in general much worse in quality than those for whites in colonial Namibia.

6 NAN, BLU [011] B.G.L Band 5, Estate of Amkanga 1740.

In the four years following Petrus and Amkanga's death, the First World War (WWI) wrought its destruction and eventually came to an end. During the conflict, GSWA was invaded by the South African army and came under military occupation.[7] The diamond mines, which had temporarily shut down during the war, again became operational. One worker at the KBG, where Petrus had previously been employed, was George Hannes, a West African Kru migrant worker from River South, Grand Bassa County, Liberia. He had been in the colony since before the war and was accompanied by his brother Myer Hannes who worked at the Pomona Mine. In the wake of WWI, a global pandemic known as Spanish influenza, decimated populations around the world, and in 1918 it came to colonial Namibia. Around March of 1919, George also came down with Spanish flu and eventually passed away. His estate was approximately £1/13- and we don't have evidence of his personal belongings. The money would likely go to Myer who would eventually take the money to their mother, Mary Hannes, back in Liberia.[8]

Petrus, Amkanga, and George were more than just laborers employed in South West Africa's diamond mines. They were members of a large and diverse cohort of migrant workers who journeyed to the settler region, also known as the "Police Zone," in colonial Namibia.[9] This book aims to investigate the origins, growth, and role of migratory labor in Namibia between 1892 and 1925. I posit that migrant workers became central to the regional workforce by the early twentieth century, and examining their stories is key to a deeper investigation of the economic, political, and military history of early colonial Namibia. Further, while migrants came from diverse locations and backgrounds, bringing them into one study with a regional focus on Namibia contextualizes their importance as part of a larger labor recruitment system built up and expanded under German colonialism both during and following war and genocide. Migrant workers examined in this book primarily engaged in mining, wagon and train transport, port infrastructure, and railway construction. Some pursued various other jobs connected to expanding urban economies ranging from restaurant waiters to bank clerks to

---

7 The South African military occupation of Namibia lasted from the South African military occupation of the colony in 1915 until the declaration of colonial Namibia as a Class C Mandate in 1920. In the book I also refer to this period in Namibia as the 'martial law period.'

8 NAN, NES [004], Estate of George Hannes 5753/510.

9 The so-called "Police Zone" covers the central and southern region of German occupied Namibia. The zone was established by the German colonial government as a precaution against the spread of the cattle disease rinderpest, which affected much of sub-Saharan Africa in the late nineteenth century. The Police Zone failed as a disease barrier but was maintained as a geographical designation by both the German and South African colonial states. It primarily defines the area of white settler colonialism, see Giorgio Miescher, *Namibia's Red Line: The History of a Veterinary and Settlement Border* (New York: Palgrave Macmillan, 2012), 69–100.

assistants at bookstores, especially within settler towns. Others established their own businesses.

The majority of these migrants secured employment through written contracts or verbal agreements between individual workers or representatives of worker groups and their employers. Some arrived independently in search of work opportunities, while others faced coercion. A small minority were subjected to forced labor. It's important to note that the majority, though not all, of the migrant labor force in colonial South West Africa during this era followed a circular employment pattern. Local workers are integrated into the study as far as their interactions with migrant labor are concerned. Their position in the colonial economy often differed from that of most migrants, as they frequently engaged in ad hoc work or were prisoners of war forced into labor. By 1904, the majority of labor migrants were primarily recruited from specific regions I refer to as the 'Namibian Labor Corridors.' These corridors encompassed three recruitment areas: one in West Africa, another in South Africa, and the third along the border between Namibia and Angola (see Figure 1 below).

Migrants from West Africa originated from the small port towns along the Kru coast, as well as Kru communities in the Liberian capital, Monrovia, and Freetown in the British colony of Sierra Leone. There were also smaller numbers of non-Kru West Africans in the colony who came from Togo, Cameroon, and the Gold Coast. South African migrants comprised Cape Coloureds, Xhosa, and Zulu, with the primary recruitment areas being the Western and Eastern Cape. Finally, the largest of these three corridors in terms of overall recruitment was located in northern Namibia and southern Angola. Workers from this region predominantly belonged to the Ovambo polities, with the Oukwanyama and Ondonga groups being the most notable participants.

The chronological scope of this book begins in 1892, coinciding with the establishment of the German port of Swakopmund, facilitated by West African labor. After examining the early economic and infrastructural evolution of the region, the work delves into the transformation of labor dynamics within colonial Namibia from 1904 to 1908. This period was a clear turning point in the colony regarding labor, marked by the outbreak of the German war and genocide against the Herero and Nama peoples. The beginning of this conflict prompted a significant exodus of local African laborers from their workplaces, as the majority returned to their respective home communities.

Migrant laborers, who numbered only a few hundred prior to the war, mainly working in construction and port jobs, would soon swell in their ranks to arrive in the thousands. These workers swiftly became central to the wage labor workforce in the Police Zone of Namibia. Their initial roles as auxiliaries for the German military and as workers in railway and port construction expanded, es-

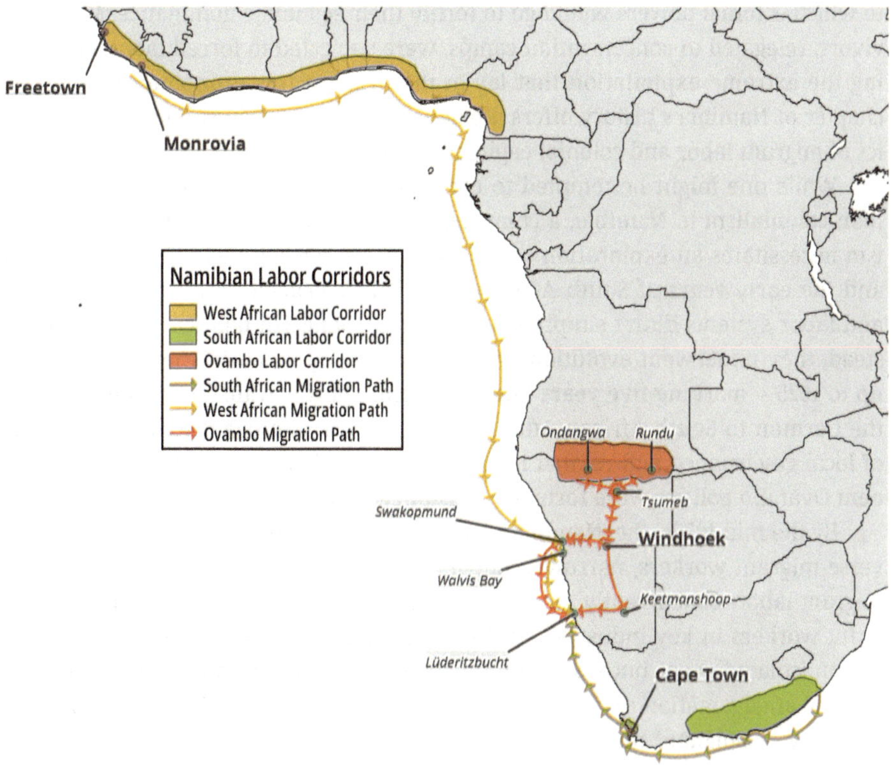

Figure 1: The 'Namibian Labor Corridors' 1892–1914 (Cartography by Bernard C. Moore).

pecially after the discovery of diamonds, as they became pivotal within many industries of the colony.

This rapid transition and reliance on migrant laborers begs the question: What makes the capitalism during this period uniquely 'colonial'? I posit that the essence of 'colonial capitalism' in pre-WWI Namibia is intricately tied to the fusion of colonial governance, economic imperatives, and labor dynamics. The term 'colonial capitalism' in this study encapsulates an economic system that was not merely shaped by market forces but was structured and maintained using colonial governance, laws, and practices. These colonial structures, in turn, facilitated the strategic integration of migrant labor, ensuring that the colony's economic mechanisms operated in tandem with colonial objectives.

The brutal legacy of the Herero and Nama genocide further accentuates the intertwined nature of racial ideologies and economic imperatives under colonial capitalism. The lands and resources seized from the massacred Herero and Nama were directly co-opted into the colonial economic framework, revealing the lengths to which colonial powers would go to fortify their economic dominance. Many survivors, relegated to concentration camps, were subjected to forced labor, epitomizing the extreme exploitation that lay at the heart of this economic system. This chapter of Namibia's history offers a poignant backdrop against which the dynamics of migrant labor and colonial capitalism must be assessed.

While one might be tempted to conclude the narrative with the end of German colonialism in Namibia, a comprehensive understanding of colonial capitalism necessitates an exploration of the transitional period during World War One and the early years of South African rule. This is crucial because the economic and labor systems didn't simply vanish with a change in political leadership. Instead, they underwent evolution and adaptation. My analysis, therefore, extends up to 1925 – marking five years after the formal power transfer in Namibia from the German to South African Administration. It's a significant juncture in terms of local governance and related labor dynamics as it's the year the last independent Ovambo polities were formally subsumed under colonial rule.

By the mid-1920s, the 'Namibian Labor Corridors,' which once encompassed diverse migrant workers, narrowed down, centering almost exclusively on Ovambo migrant labor. Concurrently, in this period of the 1920s, the overall number of migrant workers in key industries, including mining, decreased. This reduction was not an isolated event but was symptomatic of a broader economic slump and the gradual amalgamation of the Namibian economy with the dominant South African economy. A poignant manifestation of this shift was the waning diversity among the labor force. Migrants who had previously contributed to the colonial economy under German rule found their distinct backgrounds blurring. The overarching colonial system, now under South African control, sought to fit these diverse narratives into predefined racial categories, reshaping identities and labor relations in the process.

Research Questions

Given this complex backdrop of shifting labor dynamics and the interplay of diverse colonial influences in Namibia, it becomes imperative to delve deeper into the undercurrents of these changes. This leads us to some critical research questions that not only seek to understand the role of Namibia in the broader African labor landscape but also explore the intricate human stories and socio-economic factors behind the migration patterns of this era.

One of the overarching questions I pose is: What role did German colonial Namibia serve as a labor nexus in early twentieth-century Africa? Investigating the associated recruitment networks provides fresh insights into the connections between the African German colonial empire and other African colonies, as well as independent nations like Liberia. To address this, I examine two labor recruitment catchments – one rooted in West Africa and the other in Southern Africa (encompassing migrants from both South Africa and the Ovambo polities) – that converged in Namibia. What specific elements of the early Namibian colonial economy influenced individuals from these catchments to migrate to the region? And how did conditions in their native regions shape their decisions?

Shifting to a more Namibian centric focus, what does examining such a diverse group of workers bring to our understanding of the region? As will be explored in this book, I posit that integrating all migrant work into one study is necessary to understand the societal and economic changes in the region. Such a broad lens gives us a more holistic examination of early twentieth-century Namibian history that can often, because of the genocide, be bifurcated into the categories of victim (Herero, Nama, etc) and culprit (German / colonizer). The often-polarized perspectives related to these categories are complicated when integrated into this study of migrants to the region, who as we will see had their own complex views related to war, genocide, and societal change in the first decades of the 1900s in Namibia. In the last section of this study, I will examine how economic loss suffered by certain migrants during the First World War led to their growing participation in politics, and anti-colonial movements during the first decade of South African control of Namibia. By exploring both migrant involvement in unions as well as Garveyism in the 1920s, can we expand our understanding of local Southern African adaptations of global networks and worker centered movements?

The following chapters not only traverse these global, continental, and regional themes but also highlight the individual. This includes what everyday life was like for migrants, and if a discrepancy existed for them in the colony under German and early South African rule. Expanding on that theme, what could this tell us about the German colonial labor regime and whether the system largely continued unchanged or transformed after the First World War? Included in the process of answering these questions will be explorations of what work itself entailed, as well as pay, provisions, transport, and a variety of details regarding ordinary life. In doing so, I am engaging with what Frederick Cooper labelled the "nitty-gritty of labour."[10]

---

10 Frederick Cooper, "Back to Work: Categories, Boundaries and Connections in the Study of Labour," in *Racializing Class, Classifying Race: Labour and Difference in Britain, the USA and Africa*, ed. Peter Alexander and Rick Halpern (London: Palgrave Macmillan, 2000), 213.

Trends and Interventions in Relevant Literature

By engaging the aforementioned questions, I position this book at the cross sections of Global Labor, African Migration, and Namibian historiographies. In doing so, I intend to partially address some blind spots in the history of the genocide, as well as the often-ethnocentric labor histories of Namibia (mainly focused on the Ovambo) using the concept of global labor history. Early Namibian history, in particular during the period of German South West Africa, has a modern historiography largely defined by genocide.[11]

Beginning this focus in the last decades was the anthology *Genocide in German South-West Africa: The Colonial War of 1904–1908 and its Aftermath.*[12] With sections by a variety of authors, the editors Joachim Zeller and Jürgen Zimmerer brought in a modern era of critical analysis regarding the genocide. Later Jürgen Zimmerer and others argued for a more direct connection between the genocide in Namibia and the later Holocaust in Europe.[13] This argumentation has been met with its fair share of criticism in drawing what many see to be a tenuous line between the two genocides, and for not delving further into a deep analysis of primary sources. However, such authors have been important for the historiography of genocide, German empire, and perhaps most importantly public discourse in Namibia and Germany.

Historical debates often revolve around the 1904 to 1908 genocide in German colonial Namibia, creating a vortex that pulls Namibian history toward German historiography. This not only diminishes the event's significance within the broader scope of African history but also overshadows the profound impact of the 75 years of South African colonial rule post-1915 over the nation that emerged as independent Namibia in 1990.[14] I aim to reposition the 1904 to 1908 genocide at the heart of an African history, viewing it through the prism of evolving labor practices, migra-

---

11 Drechsler and Bley were some of the first to analyze in depth the genocidal nature of the war in GSWA, see Helmut Bley, *Namibia under German Rule* (Windhoek: Namibia Scientific Society, 1996); Horst Drechsler, *Let Us Die Fighting: The Struggle of the Herero and Nama against German Imperialism (1884–1915)* (London: Zed, 1980).

12 Jürgen Zimmerer and Joachim Zeller, *Genocide in German South-West Africa: The Colonial War of 1904–1908 and Its Aftermath* (Monmouth: Merlin Press, 2008).

13 Jürgen Zimmerer, *Von Windhuk nach Auschwitz? Beiträge zum Verhältnis von Kolonialismus und Holocaust* (Münster: LIT Verlag, 2011); David Olusoga and Casper W. Erichsen, *The Kaiser's Holocaust: Germany's Forgotten Genocide and the Colonial Roots of Nazism* (London: Faber and Faber, 2011).

14 A variety of scholars have pushed against this; see Dag Henrichsen et al., "Rethinking Empire in Southern Africa," *Journal of Southern African Studies* 41, no. 3 (2015): 431–435; Jeremy Silvester, ed., *Re-Viewing Resistance in Namibian History* (Windhoek: UNAM Press, 2015); the work of Emtion, and local demographics during the German era and its aftermath.[15] This research brings the genocide period into the limelight of Namibian labor studies. It juxtaposes the workforce conditions during the genocide with those of other settler colonies, like the Americas and Australia, where genocidal practices unfolded. In doing so, I aim to integrate the Namibian genocide into the broader economic fabric of nineteenth-century settler colonialism.

Labor studies in Namibia have long been conflated with politics.[16] This is often connected with the fact that many individuals who played a large role in Namibian independence, were previously migrant laborers or closely associated with fellow freedom fighters who were.[17] Relatedly, much of the literature on Namibian labor focuses both on migrant workers under South African colonialism and has a teleological bent pointing towards the liberation struggle and eventual Namibian independence.[18] Lastly, works tend to focus on either the German, or

mett was also groundbreaking, see Tony Emmett, *Popular Resistance and the Roots of Nationalism in Namibia, 1915–1966* (Basel: Schlettwein, 1999).

15 For earlier work on forced labor during the genocide, see Jan-Bart Gewald, "The Issue of Forced Labour in the Onjembo: German South West Africa 1904–1908," *Itinerario: Journal of Imperial and Global Interactions* 19, no. 1 (1995): 97–104; Kim Sebastian Todzi, *Unternehmen Weltaneignung: der Woermann-Konzern und der deutsche Kolonialismus 1837–1916*, Hamburger Beiträge zur Geschichte der kolonialen Globalisierung (Göttingen: Wallstein Verlag, 2023).

16 Bernard C. Moore et al., "Balancing the Scales: Re-Centring Labour and Labourers in Namibian History," *Journal of Southern African Studies* 47, no. 1 (2021): 1–16.

17 Kaire Mbuende, *Namibia, the Broken Shield: Anatomy of Imperialism and Revolution* (Malmö: Liber, 1986); Peter H. Katjavivi, *A History of Resistance in Namibia* (James Currey Publishers, 1988); Zed Ngavirue, *Political Parties and Interest Groups in South West Africa (Namibia): A Study of a Plural Society* (Basel: Schlettwein, 1997); Sam Nujoma, *Where Others Wavered: The Autobiography of Sam Nujoma* (London: Panaf Books, 2001); Ellen Ndeshi Namhila, *Kaxumba kaNdola: Man and Myth: The Biography of a Barefoot Soldier* (Basel: Basler Afrika Bibliographien, 2005).

18 Regina Strassegger, "Die Wanderarbeit der Ovambo während der deutschen Kolonialbesetzung Namibias. Unter besonderer Berücksichtigung der Wanderarbeiter auf den Diamantenfeldern in den Jahren 1908 bis 1914" (PhD thesis, Graz, Karl-Franzens-Universität Graz, 1988); Ndeutala S. Hishongwa, *The Contract Labour System and Its Effects on Family and Social Life in Namibia: A Historical Perspective* (Windhoek: Gamsberg Macmillan, 1992); Richard Moorsom, "Underdevelopment and Labour Migration: The Contract Labour System in Namibia," (Bergen, Norway: Chr. Michelsen Institute, 1997); Gretchen Bauer, *Labor and Democracy in Namibia: 1971–1996* (Athens: Ohio Univ. Press, 1998); Allan D Cooper, "The Institutionalization of Contract Labour in Namibia," *Journal of Southern African Studies* 25, no. 1 (1999): 121–138; Kletus Muhena Likuwa, *Voices from the Kavango: A Study of the Contract Labour System in Namibia, 1925–1972.* (Basel: Basler Afrika Bibliographien, 2020); Kletus Muhena Likuwa and Napandulwe Shiweda, "Okaholo: Contract Labour System and Lessons for Post Colonial Namibia," *Mgbakoigba: Journal of African Studies* 6, no. 2 (2017): 26–47; Lovisa Tegelela Nampala, *Infrastructures of Migrant Labour in Colonial Ovamboland, 1915 to 1954* (Basel: Schlettwein, 2023); Lovisa T. Nampala and

the South African period, and in doing so at times exempt important continuations that bled from one era to the other. The following chapters, in examining the migrant workforce as a totality from the 1890s to the early South African colonial period, underlines the cosmopolitan nature of many work sites in early colonial Namibia, and how those diverse communities interacted with one another and influenced local society and the economy.

In the context of labor migration across the African continent, Namibia has largely been overlooked or briefly mentioned in relation to other regions. More dominant labor systems, such as the plantation economies in West and East Africa, as well as the mines of West and Southern Africa, have traditionally dominated scholarly discourse. By juxtaposing labor flows in Namibia with the labor systems of Southern and West Africa, I argue for a richer and more comprehensive understanding of African migrant labor dynamics in the early twentieth century. While Namibia under South African colonial rule post-WWI might be viewed as a periphery of the South African Union, its stature under prior German control was different. As the cornerstone of the German overseas empire and its only true settler colony, Namibia saw substantial investment in its colonial economy, evidenced by its rapid expansion from 1908 onward and the influx of migrants, both recruited and independent. Thus, by focusing on the 'Namibian Labor Corridors' in a single study, we gain deeper insights into the expansive German economic and labor systems in Africa.

Global labor history (GLH) has developed new avenues for studying labor in the Global South, and scholars in the last few years have laid the groundwork to further pursue this field in the context of Namibia.[19] By engaging in GLH, this book interprets Namibian history through trans-imperial, and global lenses to move beyond the "methodological nationalism" that has defined much classical labor history.[20] Utilizing the analytical structure of GLH, I aim to add to literature

---

Vilho Shigwedha, *Aawambo Kingdoms, History and Cultural Change: Perspectives from Northern Namibia* (Basel: Schlettwein, 2006).

19 Stefano Bellucci and Andreas Eckert, ed., *General Labour History of Africa: Workers, Employers and Governments, 20th–21st Centuries* (Woodbridge: James Currey, 2019); Marcel van der Linden and Jan Lucassen, *Prolegomena for a Global Labour History* (Amsterdam: International Institute of Social History, 1999); Karin Hofmeester and Marcel van der Linden, ed., *Handbook Global History of Work* (München: De Gruyter Oldenbourg, 2017); Andreas Eckert and Marcel van der Linden, "New Perspectives on Workers and the History of Work: Global Labor History," in *Global History, Globally: Research and Practice around the World*, ed. Sven Beckert and Dominic Sashsenmaier (London; New York: Bloomsbury, 2018), 145–162; Moore et al., "Balancing the Scales: Re-Centring Labour and Labourers in Namibian History."

20 Marcel van der Linden, "Globalizing Labour Historiography – The IISH Approach" (working paper, Amsterdam: International Institute of Social History, 2002), 1.

focusing on the Global South that contributes to the re-defining of the working class beyond the European sphere.[21] To do this I decenter the 'classical worker' in Namibia, such as mine or union labor, and integrate it into a larger definition of who are considered laborers (children and women) and what I include as forms of labor (ranging from sex work, to clothing washers, to expedition guides). Further, by utilizing a relatively broad definition of which laborers and what form of labor fit into this study, it adds to a more nuanced and contextualized analysis of the more conventional worker type (young men) and forms of labor, which fit in similar traditional industrial labor categories (mining, railway construction). I posit that by looking at this diversity of workers we can actually better understand the development of colonial capitalism in Namibia. While GLH is essential to the structure of this book, my project draws upon a rich lineage of research that focuses on the everyday lives of Africans in colonial contexts. Among these influences, the work of Charles van Onselen stands out as particularly impactful. His detailed and vivid examinations of workers and their lives have thus been essential for the development of this project.[22]

One intersecting theme that travels across the many historiographical debates I have referenced is the discussion regarding free versus unfree labor. This topic has been one of the key elements in bringing two central topics in African studies, labor history and the history of slavery, into dialogue with one another.[23] Scholarship within GLH has been essential in this and has helped to show the spectrum within the free versus unfree debate.[24] Importantly, many scholars engaged in the debate have concluded that the lines between these two extremes are often blurred.[25] Contributing to this, my book examines a wide variety of work along that spectrum and analyzes their coexistence throughout the 1892 to

21 Marcel van der Linden, *Workers of the World: Essays Toward a Global Labor History* (Leiden: Brill, 2008).

22 Charles van Onselen, *Chibaro: African Mine Labour in Southern Rhodesia 1900–1933* (London: Pluto Pr, 1980); Charles van Onselen, *New Babylon, New Nineveh: Everyday Life on the Witwatersrand 1886–1914* (Johannesburg: Jonathan Ball, 2001).

23 Tom Brass and Marcel van der Linden, *Free and Unfree Labour: The Debate Continues* (Bern: Peter Lang, 1997); Marcel van der Linden, "The Promise and Challenges of Global Labor History," *International Labor and Working-Class History* 82 (2012): 61.

24 van der Linden, *Workers of the World*, 10–11; Sven Beckert and Dominic Sashsenmaier, ed. *Global History, Globally: Research and Practice around the World* (London; New York: Bloomsbury, 2018), 202; Andreas Eckert, "Why All the Fuss about Global Labour History?," in *Global Histories of Work*, ed. Andreas Eckert (Berlin: De Gruyter Oldenbourg, 2016), 3–22.

25 Adam McKeown, "Global Migration, 1846–1940," *Journal of World History* 15, no. 2 (2004): 1846–1940; Carolyn Brown and Marcel van der Linden, "Shifting Boundaries between Free and Unfree Labor: Introduction," *International Labor and Working-Class History*, no. 78 (2010): 4–11.

1925 period in colonial Namibia. This will include showing how the relative freedom of workers could and did shift, for example from working as a contract laborer on a railway construction project in the 1890s, to being pushed into forced laborer as war broke out in 1904. Also, in examining the complexity of the lives of laborers in the colony, we see that autonomy could vary drastically depending on factors such as employer, overseer, wealth, skin color, politics and beyond. To engage in the various historical fields above, the project has utilized a wide array of methodological tools and diverse sources.

Methodology and Sources

Alltagsgeschichte (history of everyday life) guides my research, enabling the exploration of workers' daily lives in the larger context of labor trends in Namibia. In having a central focus on everyday life, a goal is to go beyond a "sharp dichotomy opposing objective, material, structural, or institutional factors to subjective, cultural, symbolic, or emotional ones."[26] The details of individuals' experiences foregrounds their unique life trajectories and varying degrees of agency as historical actors.[27] Building on the work of Alf Lüdke and Geoff Eley by investigating forms of "microhistory," I hope to emphasize more of the ambiguities and contradictions of ordinary people's perceptions and behavior as they actually live their lives.[28] Compared to research on settler communities, there is limited *Alltagsgeschichte* focused on migrant workers in early colonial Namibia – a gap this study aims to address.

In the subsequent chapters, this book employs Christian De Vito and Anne Gerritsen's micro-spatial historical method, an approach that integrates micro-

26 Hans Medick and David Warren Sabean, ed., "Introduction," in *Interest and Emotion: Essays on the Study of Family and Kinship* (Cambridge: Cambridge University Press, 1984), 2.
27 A focus on life trajectories of workers as well as an analysis of African labor within a global context are important elements of this project which were influenced by the goals of re:work or IGK Work and Human Life Cycle in Global History research institute at Humboldt University; see Andreas Eckert and Jürgen Kocka, "Mission and Themes – Work and Life Course as Historical Problems. Perspectives of the International Research Center 'Re:Work,'" accessed March 22, 2021, https://rework.hu-berlin.de/mission-and-themes.html.
28 Geoff Eley, "Foreward," in *The History of Everyday Life: Reconstructing Historical Experiences and Ways of Life*, ed. Alf Lüdtke, trans. William Templer (Princeton: Princeton University Press, 1995), x; Alf Lüdtke, "'Alltagsgeschichte': Verführung Oder Chance? Zur Erforschung Der Praxis Historischer Subjekte," *Göttinger Jahrbuch*, 1986, 183–200.

analysis with spatial awareness.[29] This strategy allows for a flexible, localized analysis that spans distinct geographical settings: from the intricacies of Namibia to the broader contexts of West and Southern Africa. Rather than being confined by localized boundaries, implementation of this methodology allows for the research to weave disparate threads of information into a comprehensive tapestry that reflects the dynamic interplay between various contexts. The book delves deep into the migration patterns of not just people, but also material goods and evolving concepts. Key themes of trans-locality and entanglement are underscored, serving to bridge both proximate and expansive connections, thereby challenging traditional demarcations between the global and the local. Integral to the successful implementation of these innovative research methods has been a meticulous analysis of credible and relevant sources.

Central to this project is the *Namibian Worker Database*, constructed specifically for this project.[30] It is a collection of data on more than 1,000 workers made up of essentially unutilized African estate files: documenting the possessions, dependents, and circumstances relating to workers' death. The material making up the database is primarily from the 'Native Estate Files' (NES) held at the National Archives of Namibia. The NES contain information on all non-white workers who died working in Namibia from 1917 to 1951.[31] The *Namibian Worker Database* integrates over 4,000 pages of material from these files. Below (see Figure 2) we can see an example of a page from the NES file of Tango Mifango, an Ovambo man from Oukwanyama who died in 1918 of Spanish influenza.

The NES were marked for destruction by the apartheid South African government in the 1970s based on the supposition that the estates of non-white workers were of no historical importance, only escaping their planned fate through bureaucratic disregard. More than two decades after Namibian independence, the Native Estate Files were rediscovered by Ellen Ndeshi Namhila of the University of Namibia.

29 Christian G. De Vito and Anne Gerritsen, ed., *Micro-Spatial Histories of Global Labour* (Cham: Palgrave Macmillan, 2018), 2.

30 Lyon, William Blakemore. "Namibian Worker Database." CSV, Data set. Berlin: edoc-Server Open-Access-Publikationsserver der Humboldt-Universität, 2024. https://doi.org/10.18452/28347.

31 In this study, the term 'non-white' is employed as a reflection of the historical nomenclature and conceptual framework of the colonial and apartheid eras. Recognizing the contentious nature of the term, which historically grouped a vast diversity of racial and ethnic groups under one floating classification, it's used here with both caution and specificity. Although 'non-white' evokes divisions reminiscent of apartheid's artificial racial categories, it remains a concept deeply embedded in the legislation, psyche, and daily realities of colonial rule. This work uses 'non-white' not to perpetuate racial divisions but to engage critically and historically with a term that was significant during the period under study.

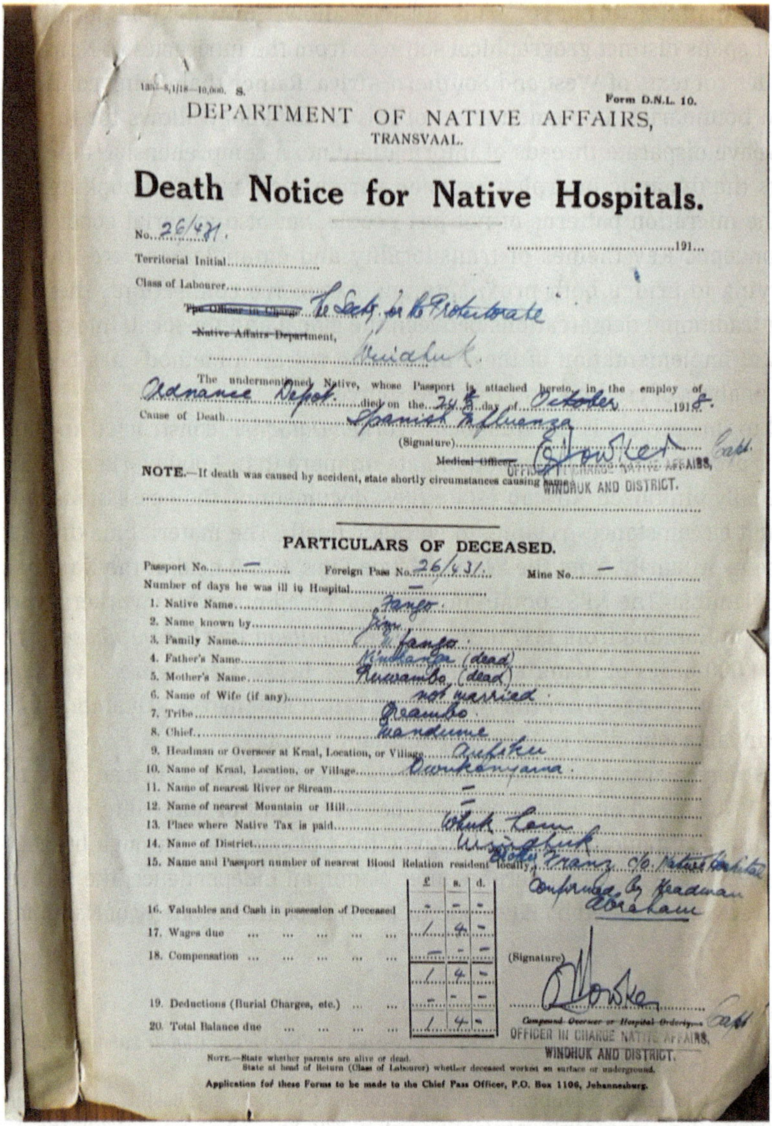

135–8/1/18—10,000. S. Form D.N.L. 10.

DEPARTMENT OF NATIVE AFFAIRS,
TRANSVAAL.

Death Notice for Native Hospitals.

No. 26/471. ....191...

Territorial Initial..........

Class of Labourer..........

~~The Officer in Charge~~ The Secty. for the Protectorate

~~Native Affairs Department~~,

Windhuk.

The undermentioned Native, whose Passport is attached hereto, in the employ of Ordnance Depot died on the 24th day of October 1918.

Cause of Death Spanish Influenza

(Signature)..........

~~Medical Officer~~ OFFICER IN CHARGE NATIVE AFFAIRS, WINDHUK AND DISTRICT. Capt.

NOTE.—If death was caused by accident, state shortly circumstances causing same.

....

PARTICULARS OF DECEASED.

Passport No. — Foreign Pass No. 26/431. Mine No. —

Number of days he was ill in Hospital —

1. Native Name Tango.
2. Name known by Jim
3. Family Name Mifango.
4. Father's Name (dead)
5. Mother's Name (dead)
6. Name of Wife (if any) not married.
7. Tribe Ovambo.
8. Chief Mandume
9. Headman or Overseer at Kraal, Location, or Village
10. Name of Kraal, Location, or Village Oukwanyama.
11. Name of nearest River or Stream —
12. Name of nearest Mountain or Hill —
13. Place where Native Tax is paid
14. Name of District Windhuk
15. Name and Passport number of nearest Blood Relation resident locally

	£	s.	d.
16. Valuables and Cash in possession of Deceased	–	–	–
17. Wages due	1	4	–
18. Compensation	–	–	–
	1	4	–
19. Deductions (Burial Charges, etc.)	–	–	–
20. Total Balance due	1	4	–

(Signature)..........

~~Compound Overseer or Hospital Orderly~~ OFFICER IN CHARGE NATIVE AFFAIRS, WINDHUK AND DISTRICT. Capt.

NOTE.—State whether parents are alive or dead.
State at head of Return (Class of Labourer) whether deceased worked on surface or underground.

Application for these Forms to be made to the Chief Pass Officer, P.O. Box 1106, Johannesburg.

Figure 2: Estate File of Tango Mifango from the Ovambo Oukwanyama Polity. Note the cause of death is 'Spanish Influenza.' Files like this make up the majority of the Namibian Worker Database source material.[32]

32 NAN, NES [003], 135/443, Estate File of Tango Mifango.

The size of the files in total is vast with over 11,000 individual estates.[33] A group of NES have been supplemented by similar files from the German colonial period in creating the *Namibian Worker Database.* While colored by colonial record keeping, these files give us a view into the lives of African workers in early Namibian history. Data points comprise the monetary value of their estates upon death, personally held items, their place of origin, ethnicity, employer, work location, cause of death, start of contract, date of death, and number of days spent in hospital. Almost all files include information entered on pre-printed forms, making the data relatively uniform and therefore more comparable. This material is rather unique in the colonial Namibian archives, as information on Africans' individual lives is often lacking, unless in relation to their labor for industry and farming, methods of control, or traditional leadership affairs.

The *Namibian Worker Database* is supplemented by a diverse blend of written, photographic, and oral sources. Written sources encompass colonial records, missionary letters, contemporary books and magazines, newspapers from both Europe and Africa, business quarterly reports, and individual's ego documents. In examining colonial archives, this book heeds Namhila's counsel to read "against the grain."[34] This method involves critically interpreting dominant narratives to unearth information and voices that have been obscured, marginalized, or deliberately silenced. Engaging with these various written sources, this work primarily draws from German and English materials, but also incorporates texts in Italian, Cape Dutch, Oshiwambo, and French.

Furthermore, photographs are not simply supplemental to the written record in this project; they are central to it. Embracing a 'pictorial turn,' I accord photographs equal interpretive value as other sources, drawing inspiration from the seminal work on Namibian visual history, *The Colonizing Camera.*[35] Gesine Krüger has posited that images should not be relegated to the sidelines, but instead should be at the very core of historical analysis.[36] This contrasts with the conventional approach where they merely serve as illustrative backdrops to textual insights. While photographs provide rich, nuanced narratives, especially in contexts where written

---

33 Ellen Ndeshi Namhila, *Native Estates: Records of Mobility across Colonial Boundaries* (Basel: Basler Afrika Bibliographien, 2017), xii.

34 Namhila, *Native Estates*, 49.

35 Wolfram Hartmann, Jeremy Silvester, and Patricia Hayes, ed., *The Colonising Camera: Photographs in the Making of Namibian History* (Cape Town: University of Cape Town Press, 1999).

36 Gesine Krüger, "Writing in Images: Aspects of Mission Photography in Southern Africa," in *Hues between Black and White: Historical Photography from Colonial Namibia 1860s to 1915*, ed. Wolfram Hartmann (Windhoek: Out of Africa Publishers, 2004), 241–242.

accounts are scant or biased, it's crucial to confront the challenges they present, particularly when stemming from colonial contexts.

The very nature of photography during the colonial era raises questions of representation, intention, and gaze. I am aware of the pitfalls of relying too heavily on these images without a critical lens. My position, as a modern researcher, comes with its own set of biases and preconceived notions that can influence my interpretation of these images. However, rather than viewing these photographs merely as 'slides of reality', my analysis, inspired by Brent Harris, treats them as intentional acts of communication and representation.[37] This means delving deep into the intricate dynamics between the photographer, the subject, and the eventual audience while also acknowledging the aspects that might forever remain obscured or misrepresented due to the colonial lens. The methodology is particularly useful in segments focusing on forced and Ovambo laborers. In such contexts, written records from the laborers themselves are often sparse or entirely absent. By utilizing photographs, this research aims to humanize and give voice to the experiences of the men, women, and children depicted. To further enrich this approach, select photos were presented to interviewees. This not only triggered personal memories but also allowed for re-interpretation and recontextualization, offering a more holistic view that moves beyond the limiting colonial lens.

The interviews of ancestors of migrants and employers, which I have conducted in Namibia have not only served a role in the project in terms of photographic interpretation, but they also enhance and add details which are at times lacking in archival records. As has been seen in recent Namibian historiography, such as Kletus Muhena Likuwa's *Voices from the Kavango*, effectively utilizing oral accounts adds new and essential dimensions to the experiences of Africans during the colonial period.[38] My project employs the theoretical framework laid out by Elizabeth Tonkin, which does not treat oral testimony "as the repository of facts and errors of facts" but rather as interpretations from the perspective of the colonized.[39] These sources allow for contemporary Namibian views on the origins of contract labor to be heard while also helping to examine the system's societal impact via cultural memory.

---

37 Brent Harris, "Photography in Colonial Discourse: The Making of ‚the Other' in Southern Africa, c. 1850–1950," in *The Colonising Camera*, ed. Wolfram Hartmann, Jeremy Silvester, and Patricia Hayes (Cape Town: University of Cape Town Press, 1999), 20.

38 See Likuwa, *Voices from the Kavango.*

39 Elizabeth Tonkin, *Narrating Our Pasts the Social Construction of Oral History* (Cambridge: Cambridge University Press, 1999), 12.

The various sources were collected and examined over many months through extensive and wide-ranging field research conducted in Southern Africa, Europe, and North America between 2017 and 2022. While the following work utilizes a wide array of sources and methodologies for analysing them, the structure was kept relatively simple.

Structure and Chapter Overview

This book embarks on a journey through the evolution of Namibia's labor from 1892 to 1925, underpinned by the intricate dynamics of three pivotal migrant labor corridors. We begin with the late nineteenth century, where the foundational structures of colonial labor and infrastructure development were taking root. In the opening chapter, 'Colonial Contact Zones: Power, Politics and Labor at Early Work Sites in German South West Africa, 1892–1903,' we delve into the nascent phases of interactions between local societies, migrant workers, and German imperialists at seminal work sites. Although this chapter relies on limited worker-centered sources due to archival limitations, it is instrumental in laying the groundwork for subsequent chapters, offering invaluable insights into the antecedents of Namibia's labor dynamics.

Progressing to the second chapter, 'The Human Infrastructure of the Namibian War: Origins of the 'Namibian Labor Corridors' in War and Genocide, 1904–1908,' the lens sharpens its focus on the labor dynamics during the tumultuous wartime years, especially against the backdrop of the Herero and Nama genocide. The pivotal events of this period elucidate the intersection of German imperial ambitions, African resistance, and labor intricacies.

In the third chapter, 'Workers from the North: The Ovambo Labor Corridor, 1905–1914,' attention pivots to the Ovambo labor corridor. The period, marked by significant mining developments, saw the Ovambo labor segment emerge as the center of the colonial economy, elucidating not just the known facets of labor, but also lesser-explored dimensions of child and women laborers.

Chapter four, 'A Precarious African Labor Elite: South and West Africans, 1908–1914,' navigates through the labor landscapes of West and South Africans in Namibia. This chapter presents a dichotomy where these laborers, despite their 'elite' economic stature, grappled with the racial realities of the colonial society, culminating in events like the tragic Wilhelmstal massacre.

The narrative arc concludes in the fifth chapter, 'From War to Workers' Rights: Namibia under South African Mandate, 1914–1925,' chronicling the culmination of the 'Namibian Labor Corridor' recruitment system amid global and local upheavals, from WWI to the Spanish influenza pandemic, and the shift in colonial governance to South Africa. This chapter also foregrounds the emergence of pivotal labor movements and the eventual decline of the West and South African labor corridors.

In weaving these narratives together, this book not only chronicles the multifaceted journey of Namibia's labor history from 1892 to 1925 but also illuminates the profound ways in which migrant laborers shaped the socio-economic and cultural tapestry of Namibia, leaving an indelible mark on its historical landscape and offering a lens through which we can reexamine colonial legacies and their enduring impact on modern African societies.

1 Colonial Contact Zones: Power, Politics and Labor at Early Work Sites in German South West Africa, 1892–1903

This chapter explores the role of work sites in German South West Africa from 1892 to 1903, focusing on three pivotal locations: the mines in the Otavi region, the harbor of Swakopmund, and the railway line connecting Swakopmund to Windhoek. These sites were 'contact zones' where hundreds of workers from diverse backgrounds converged – making them hubs of activity at the colonial frontier characterized by extreme weather, vast expansiveness, and a sparse population.[1] I have taken the 'contact zone' concept from Mary Louise Pratt but modify it to explore spaces where diverse groups sometimes found mutual accommodation, diverging from Pratt's focus on conflict and inequality. Further, following Giorgio Miescher's notion, the frontier at which these contact zones existed, was not merely a boundary but a nexus of interaction between the existing local societies and the encroaching colonial settlement.[2] In line with Martin Legassick's analysis, these frontiers became arenas where identities overlapped and power was negotiated.[3] At the heart of these negotiations were the fluid relationships between African headmen and chiefs, and the colonial employers/administrators.

Thus, the 'colonial contact zones' scrutinized in this chapter emerge not only as geographic locales but also as lenses through which to examine the labor relations that signal broader economic, infrastructural, and socio-political shifts. Events and developments that originated at these sites often had a far-reaching impact, influencing the wider colony. Economic change in late-nineteenth century GSWA included growing acceptance of contract labor in African societies.[4] Far from being passive figures, traditional leaders played a crucial role in recruiting and retaining workers, as well as shaping working conditions. Further, within many local African societies, including the Herero, nobles at the end of the nine-

1 Mary Louise Pratt, *Imperial Eyes: Travel Writing and Transculturation* (London: Routledge, 2009), 6.

2 Miescher, *Namibia's Red Line*, 8.

3 Martin Legassick, "The Frontier Tradition in South African Historiography," in *Economy and Society in Pre-Industrial South Africa*, ed. Shula Marks and Anthony Atmore, vol. 12 (London: Longman Group, 1972), 44–79.

4 For an explanation of how labor, including both contract and migrant are defined and utilized in this book, see my Introduction.

https://doi.org/10.1515/9783111374918-002

teenth century had their children work for settlers in positions viewed as important. These jobs ranged from foreman to nursemaid and were sometimes seen as a sign of prestige, locating their families clearly within the status of elites.[5] In making such an analysis, this chapter draws connections with works such as Cassandra Mark-Thiesen's scholarship on colonial Ghana, emphasizing the agency of African leaders in the colonial labor context.[6]

The trend towards increasing acceptance of contract labor accelerated as external pressures, including colonial confiscation of Herero cattle, and in 1896 to 1897 an outbreak of the rinderpest epizootic, which killed up to 95 percent of Herero herds – central to their economic and societal stability – drastically impacted Herero communities.[7] Additionally, seized Herero lands were increasingly given to settler farmers by concession companies and the colonial state.[8] Shifts in local economic incentives, societal norms, land ownership as well as violence and drought would drive large numbers of people into the ranks of the colonial contract labor workforce. The need of the colonial economy for contract labor not only led to more local recruitment, but also expanding numbers of workers from beyond the settler region. This period lay the foundations for the later exponential rise in migrant labor.

Work sites were also microcosms of land-use and infrastructural trends occurring across the colony. The three locations of examination are part of the first expansive physical manifestations of German colonialism in South West Africa. Laying train tracks across huge swaths of 'formerly' African-owned land, building settlements out of the desert on the coast, and mining deep into rock formations at Otavi and Tsumeb altered the land itself on a previously unseen scale. As the German colonial endeavors reshaped the landscape of South West Africa, they simultaneously set the stage for profound shifts in the local social fabric, pulling African communities into the orbit of colonial economics and labor demands.

---

5 Bley, *Namibia under German Rule*, 89.

6 Cassandra Mark-Thiesen, *Mediators, Contract Men, and Colonial Capital: Mechanized Gold Mining in the Gold Coast Colony, 1879–1909* (Rochester: University of Rochester Press, 2018), 145–157.

7 On the German government's confiscation of Herero cattle in the 1890s, see Drechsler, *Let Us Die Fighting*, 88; regarding the rinderpest in Namibia and its affect on Herero cattle and society, see Gary Marquardt, "Open Spaces and Closed Minds : A Socio-Environmental History of Rinderpest in South Africa and Namibia, 1896–1897" (PhD thesis, Madison, University of Wisconsin-Madison, 2007), 124–125; Jan-Bart Gewald, *Herero Heroes: A Socio-Political History of the Herero of Namibia 1890–1923* (Oxford: James Currey, 1999), 110; B.T. Mokopakgosi, "German Colonialism in Microcosm: A Study of the Role of Concessionaire Companies in the Development of the German Colonial State in Namibia, 1890–1915" (PhD thesis, University of London, 1988), 272.

8 Drechsler, *Let Us Die Fighting*, 92.

Amidst these changes, local Africans began to engage in contract work – whether by individual choice, communal influence, or sheer necessity – to complement their traditional livelihoods of farming, hunting, and trading. This work in turn provided related pay and provisions. Politically, the hiring and employment of contract labor in early-1890s GSWA was characterized by colonial, military and company representatives finding middle ground with African leaders and laborers regarding work conditions. However, in the mid- and especially late-1890s, these conditions deteriorated. Inadequate provisions and water at work sites became more commonplace, and employers often violated contracts and kept workers on the job beyond agreed-upon timelines. Some workers pushed back against the increasingly difficult conditions through complaints to headmen, abandonment of work sites and strikes. Worsening work conditions also mirrored other factors in German-Herero relations, such as German soldiers' frequently violent sexual engagements with Herero women.[9]

While local Africans grappled with the worsening conditions of their contract work, the German empire's engagement with GSWA was entering a new phase, marked by substantial investments in the colony's infrastructure, mining ventures, and settler farming. The South West African Company (SWACO), for instance, raised £15,000 in working capital for the Otavi mining venture from 1892 to 1894.[10] The completion of the Swakopmund-Windhoek Trainline in June 1902 and the Swakopmund mole in February 1903 involved costs of £708,035 and £122,310, respectively.[11] Moreover, despite the impending war in January 1904, the Otavi Minen- und Eisenbahn-Gesellschaft (OMEG) had already earmarked £905,095 for the early phases of the Otavi Bahn.[12]

Agriculturally, the settler farmer population tripled between 1899 and 1903, encouraged by a colonial fund that provided £14,677 in farm loans by 1903.[13] This growth in settler population, coupled with a pervasive anti-Herero sentiment among the new settlers in major towns like Windhoek, heightened fears of an African uprising and the endorsement of violent measures.[14]

---

9 Wolfram Hartmann, "Urges in the Colony. Men and Women in Colonial Windhoek, 1890–1905," *Journal of Namibian Studies: History Politics Culture* 1 (2007): 65–66.

10 Horst Drechsler, *Südwestafrika unter deutscher Kolonialherrschaft: Die großen Land- und Minengesellschaften* (Stuttgart: Steiner, 1996), 86–87.

11 Gerhardus Pool, *Eisenbahnen in Deutsch-Südwestafrika, 1897–1915*, ed. Rolf-Reinhard Henke, trans. Kuno Budack (Windhoek: Namibia Wissenschaftliche Gesellschaft, 2009), 63; "Die Mole," *Deutsch-Südwestafrikanische Zeitung* (DSWAZ), 7 (February 12, 1903): 5.

12 Bundesarchiv, Abt. Potsdam, RKolA Nr. 1660, Bl. 38, Notiz Golinellis betr. OMEG, s.d. in Drechsler, *Die großen Land- und Minengesellschaften*, 215.

13 Drechsler, *Let Us Die Fighting*, 113–114.

14 Bley, *Namibia under German Rule*, 38–39.

The extensive investments and demographic expansion not only solidified the German empire's presence in GSWA but also set in motion a series of geopolitical shifts.

These developments played a role in precipitating the conditions that would eventually lead to the Namibian War. Against this backdrop, this chapter seeks to unravel the intricate connections between the establishment of work sites, the dynamics of labor, and their collective impact on the colony's geopolitics leading up to the conflict starting in 1904. It probes the factors that necessitated increased reliance on migrant laborers and examines the changing local dynamics that paved the way for such a transition.

In the period from the 1890s to 1903, the colonial work sites employing contract labor included a mix of local workers, including Herero, Damara, Nama, and San peoples. Work by locals encompassed a variety of tasks from sharing knowledge of local mineral outcrops to driving wagons between work sites and the coast. Additionally, women and children were also at the work sites often doing the essential work of cleaning, cooking, and assisting contracted male labor.

As for migrant laborers, who over time would increase in number and proportion of the overall workforce, the majority came from the Ovambo polities in the north of the colony. The two largest polities made up the greatest proportion of workers, i.e., Oukwanyama and Ondonga. Men from the various Ovambo polities, in particular traders, hunters, raiders, and smiths, had a centuries-old history of traveling south to the Hereroland region: or what during colonial times became known as the 'settler region' (Police Zone) – of central and southern South West Africa. Trips could last from only a few days, to in the case of some smiths, years.[15] Perhaps most well-known is travel primarily by the Ndonga to the Otavi region for trade with San in exchange for copper, which Ndonga smelted and used for making tools and jewelry.[16] In relation to the work sites of the 1890s and early 1900s, those Ovambo on contract were part of a growing movement of young men coming south. Many were pressured by changes in Ovambo societies, where in the wake of rinderpest and colonial capitalist penetration, colonial currency played an increasingly important role. In allowing young men to earn wages and bring home pay from waged labor in the south, migrant labor provided a new avenue for them to attain a place in society in the polities.[17] Ovambo

15 Siiskonen, *Trade and Socioeconomic Change in Ovamboland, 1850–1906*, 229–230.

16 Eirola, *The Ovambogefahr*, 43–44; Ilse Schatz, *Tsumeb zu O.M.E.G.'s Zeiten* (Namibia: S.N. Publishing Company, 1997), 2–3.

17 Meredith McKittrick, "The 'Burden' of Young Men: Property and Generational Conflict in Namibia, 1880–1945," *African Economic History* 24 (1996): 122–123.

men would eventually make up a large portion of workers at all three of the work sites examined in this chapter.

Migrants instrumental in the development of Swakopmund, which lacked a natural harbor, included West African Kru from Liberia and Sierra Leone, who worked as longshoremen.[18] Their efforts were crucial in transferring goods and people from ship to shore.[19] The construction of the mole and railway attracted additional workers from South Africa, particularly Cape Coloured, various European residents, and Boers from the Cape Colony fleeing the South African War (1899–1902).[20] However, legislation at the time in cities like Cape Town, restricted the number of black South African migrants. Europeans, mainly Germans and English, were also recruited for their engineering and labor skills.

As the nineteenth century waned, the fabric of South West Africa was increasingly interwoven with contract labor, pivotal in shaping places like Swakopmund and increasingly vital to the colonial economy. This labor force, from Herero train line construction workers to Kru longshoremen and Ovambo miners, underscored the demographic shifts and economic imperatives of the time. The subsequent pages will expand on these developments, situating GSWA within the broader regional dynamics and German imperial ambitions of the era. A panoramic view of this complex colonial and regional landscape sets the stage for a deeper dive into the specific case studies that illuminate the period up until 1904.

Early South West Africa from a Regional and German Imperial Perspective

Prior to 1884, German aspirations for formal overseas imperial holdings were limited. Nevertheless, a subset of private individuals, primarily businessmen and entrepreneurs, advocated for the German empire to annex territories that could offer protections to their overseas ventures. One such individual was Adolf Lüderitz, a tobacco merchant from Bremen. In 1882, Lüderitz ventured to the southern coast at Angra Pequena, in what would become South West Africa. Here, he

18 Ludwig Sander, *Geschichte der Deutschen Kolonial-Gesellschaft für Südwest-Afrika: von ihrer Gründung bis zum Jahre 1910; in zwei Bänden*, vol. 1 (Berlin: Reimer, 1912), 100.

19 Verhandlungen des Reichstages (VdR), Bd.: 128. 1892/93, 55. Sitzung, 01.03.1893, Reichskanzler Graf von Caprivi, 1359.

20 'Vom Südafrikanischen Kriegsschauplatz', DSWAZ, 01.01.1902, 1.

erected warehouses and, through largely dubious treaties, secured extensive tracts of land and mineral rights from local Nama leaders. Facing financial constraints, Lüderitz sought imperial protection from Germany. His initial appeals were unsuccessful; however, the looming threat of selling his assets to the British compelled Chancellor Bismarck to incorporate Lüderitz's territories into the German empire by April 1884.[21] This acquisition marked the inception of German South West Africa.

In the subsequent decade, German intervention in its nascent colony was minimal. Nevertheless, the 1890s marked a period of notable shifts, underscored by a surge in infrastructure and economic investment. This period saw developments that echoed the colonial expansions of its neighbors, with the proliferation of railways and mining under British dominion in regions like Rhodesia and Bechuanaland – what we now know as Zimbabwe, Zambia, and Botswana. Regional scholars have observed that such hallmarks of colonial extraction capitalism – railways, mines, and other infrastructural advancements – precipitated deep-seated changes within indigenous societies.[22] Distinctively, though, while British undertakings were part of an extensive imperial settler scheme, German South West Africa was emerging as a unique case in the German empire; by the mid-1890s, it became the sole settler colony within the overseas possessions. Evidence of this transformation is reflected in the 1899 census, which recorded a population of 2,872 white settlers in GSWA, with Germans comprising 1,879 of that number – amounting to approximately 63 percent of all white settlers across the German colonies.[23]

GSWA's central role at the cross-section of German imperialism and settler colonialism developed in contrast to the other colonies of the empire where German settlement was relatively minimal.[24] The reasons for small settler populations in other German colonies varied. Limiting environmental factors existed in

21 Gewald, *Herero Heroes*, 31.

22 Jon Lunn, *Capital and Labour on the Rhodesian Railway System: 1888–1947* (Basingstoke: Macmillan, 1997), 1; Gordon Pirie, "Railways and Labour Migration to the Rand Mines: Constraints and Significance," *Journal of Southern African Studies* 19, no. 4 (1993): 729; Barbara Ntombi Ngwenya, "The Development of Transport Infrastructure in the Bechuanaland Protectorate 1885–1966," *Botswana Notes and Records* 16 (1984): 73–74.

23 Kaiserlichen Statistischen Amt, ed., "XVIII. Die Schutzgebiete," *Statistisches Jahrbuch für das Deutsche Reich.* 1899 (1900): 215.

24 Sebastian Conrad, *German Colonialism: A Short History* (Cambridge: Cambridge University Press, 2012), 38–41.

the tropical colonies of West Africa, which were declared 'unsuitable for white settlement.[25] As for German East Africa, unfavorable economic factors and uprising largely dashed the dreams of cotton plantations and settlement.[26] Colonial policy itself limited settlement in German Samoa via Governor Solf's guiding principle of *salvage colonialism* and its ethnographically driven goals of 'preserving' local customs and society.[27] Similarly unsuited to colonial settlement was the German Navy's 'model' colony Kiatschou in China, which was intended as a 'German' variant of Britain's Hong Kong with an emphasis on trade. By 1913 of a total population of 55,700 in Kiatschou, only 2,700 were non-Chinese.[28] In contrast to the majority of the empire, colonial and economic policy by the mid-1890s in German South West Africa promoted settlement. By 1893, a speech in the German Reichstag by chancellor Caprivi made clear that German settlement, mining, and business ventures in GSWA would be supported by military and police presence to ensure the protection of colonial expansion from local African polities such as the various groups of Herero and Nama in the settler region.[29]

The 1890s in GSWA coincided with an abandonment of chancellor Bismarck's previously endorsed 'flag follows business' blueprint of colonialism in the colony. This strategy posited that early private corporate investment in the colonies would result in 'colonialism on the cheap', led by concessionaire companies.[30] While early German financiers were found for concessionaire companies like the Deutsche Kolonialgesellschaft für Südwestafrika (DKGfSWA) in the 1880s, by the following decade many were disillusioned with the potential to get returns on their investments in GSWA. Conversely, a number of British and South African businessmen and bankers had years of experience investing in the region, includ-

25 D.E.K. Amenumey, "German Administration in Southern Togo," *The Journal of African History* 10, no. 4 (October 1969): 633; Horst Gründer, *Geschichte der deutschen Kolonien*, 7th ed. (Paderborn: Ferdinand Schöningh, 2018), 139, 154.

26 Thaddeus Sunseri, "The Baumwollfrage: Cotton Colonialism in German East Africa," *Central European History* 34, no. 1 (2001): 46–49.

27 George Steinmetz, *The Devil's Handwriting: Precoloniality and the German Colonial State in Qingdao, Samoa, and Southwest Africa*, Chicago Studies in Practices of Meaning (Chicago: University of Chicago Press, 2007), 355–358; Matthew Fitzpatrick, "Population Policy and the Plantation Economy in German Samoa" (paper presented at the conference Colonial Capitalism in Action: The New Social and Economic History of German Colonialism, Hamburg, Germany, May 5–6, 2021), 14.

28 Gründer, *Geschichte der deutschen Kolonien*, 216, 221.

29 Adam A. Blackler, "From Boondoggle to Settlement Colony: Hendrik Witbooi and the Evolution of Germany's Imperial Project in Southwest Africa, 1884–1894," *Central European History* 50, no. 4 (2017): fn. 62.

30 Mokopakgosi, "German Colonialism in Microcosm," 73.

ing beyond their own colonial possessions. Many also had a higher financial risk tolerance and wished to invest in the neighboring German colony. Therefore, the failure to attract enough new capital from Berlin led to the policy of 'better English than no capital'. While this birthed new ventures such as the South West African Company, which we will later discuss, there were also risks involved in this new policy. This became clear when the failure of the Jameson raid in 1895 highlighted that British capital – in particular connected to Cecil Rhodes who also controlled a large amount of SWACO shares during this period – *did* pose a threat to non-British colonies and settler polities that impeded British imperial and economic expansion in Southern Africa.[31] This was regardless of whether they were Boer Republics or the German colony of South West Africa.

In the midst of this evolving landscape, the German colonial government intensified its foothold in German South West Africa through heightened investment, the deployment of more imperial troops, and expanding its colonial bureaucracy. This escalation is quantified by the substantial increase in German Imperial grants for GSWA, which soared from an annual average of £12,715 between 1889–1893 to £129,193 between 1894–1898.[32] The transition from a concessionary company-led model to more direct imperial control marked a pivotal shift in the colony's administration, ushering in an era of labor-intensive construction projects. This shift underscored the burgeoning reliance on contract labor, which became an increasingly important segment of the colonial economy during this transformative period.

The rising German imperial involvement in local colonial affairs, in conjunction with copper findings in the area around Otavi by the mid-1890s, and lastly the debilitating effects of rinderpest on ox-wagon transport were catalysts for the expansion of infrastructure at Swakopmund and the railway to connect it with Windhoek. These necessitated growing numbers of contract laborers, and when local recruitment could not fulfill demand or did not possess the right skill sets, long-distance migrant labor was sought after. By the early years of the twentieth century, increased state intervention, particularly in construction projects, alongside the escalating reliance on contract labor, emerged as the twin pillars underpinning the infrastructural and economic expansion of German colonialism in GSWA. To delineate this landscape, we begin with the Otavi experimental mines, a case study that illuminates the intricate power relations between companies, local Africans, and the colonial government. This examination will reveal some of

31 Drechsler, *Die großen Land- und Minengesellschaften*, 8–9.

32 Mokopakgosi, "German Colonialism in Microcosm," 116, Table 1. SWA Budget Estimates, 1886–1914 (M).

the early manifestations of colonial labor on a worksite and set the stage for understanding the subsequent evolutions in GSWA.

SWACO Expedition to the Otavi Mines, 1892–1894

The earliest of the three colonial work sites explored in this chapter which attracted migrant labor was the copper mine at Otavi. While the first modern iteration was opened in the late nineteenth century, the region had, as previously mentioned, a very long history as a mine worked by local San and visiting Ovambo. While lacking industrial tools, the Ovambo and San techniques were effective for surface mining. An observation from the 1892 to 1893 exploratory mission to Otavi mentioned the following:

> The Bushmen and Ovambos, having no mining implements but hard sharp pointed sticks, first cleaned out the soil from these pits, and picked the small pieces of copper from it; afterwards removing the rock between the pits where the veins are rich, by levering the small cracks made by sudden changes in temperature, until the whole mass is removed . . . the Bushmen and Ovambo workers have been so assiduous in their labour that there is scarcely any copper left in the small veins penetrating the surface limestone rock.[33]

In addition to the Ovambo who were still visiting the region in the late nineteenth century for trade with San, the area was also inhabited by the Nama and Damara. By the 1860s the Otavi region, which was well endowed with water, was also increasingly visited by the cattle herding Herero who were expanding their territory northward. In the 1870s heavy conflict erupted for control of the region. For the Herero and their growing cattle herds, which increasingly necessitated more and better grazing land, Otavi offered prime real estate. During the Herero move into the region, local Damara were increasingly pushed into their service. As observed in 1889 by missionary Eich of the Rhenish Missionary Society, Damara groups who had fled the Waterberg region attempting to avoid suppression under the Herero in the 1870s were later forced to be herders for them.[34] These cattle herds were very large with thousands of cows per day drinking from the well at Okombahe near Otavi.[35] It was into this contested atmosphere, where the German colonial

33 BArch (*Bundesarchiv – Berlin-Lichterfelde*) R 1001/1482, Matthews to the Company. Otavi Mines, Enclosure to his Letter of the 11.03.1893, 54.

34 Waterberg is about 200 km to the south of Otavi.

35 Dag Henrichsen, *Herrschaft und Alltag im vorkolonialen Zentralnamibia: das Herero- und Damaraland im 19. Jahrhundert* (Basel: Basler Afrika Bibliographien, 2011), 17.

state played essentially no role, that the South West Africa Company sent an expedition to 'its' concession in the northern half of the colony in 1892.

The founding of SWACO in 1892 marked the beginning of a pivotal expedition, significantly funded by South African and British capital, which constituted 86 percent of the initial investment. Envisioned as an Anglo-German enterprise, SWACO's investors would gradually become more German.[36] One of the initial acts of the company was securing the Damaraland Concession (see Figure 3 below), which was controlled by Sir Donald Currie, a prominent British shipping magnate and investor. Currie's 'Damaraland-Company, Limited' had previously acquired the concession from Robert Lewis in 1890, who had arranged a mining agreement with Herero leader Kamaharero in the Otavi region as early as 1883.[37]

The German government, eager to see the concession utilized more effectively, sanctioned the transfer to SWACO on the condition that £15,000 of the capital be earmarked for regional expeditions.[38] These ventures included a geological survey at Otavi, led by mining engineer Matthew Rogers – which will be the focus of this section – and a reconnaissance for a potential railway line connecting SWACO's concession to the coast, headed by railway engineer David Angus. This strategic move by SWACO signified the waning of the *Deutsche Kolonialgesellschaft für Südwestafrika*'s monopoly, which had until then dominated but had shown economic stagnation.[39]

---

36 Mokopakgosi, "German Colonialism in Microcosm," 203 f.n. 34; William Blakemore Lyon, "The South West Africa Company and Anglo-German Relations, 1892–1914" (Master's thesis, Cambridge University, 2015), 39–51.

37 Bernard C. Moore, "Namibia Report on Concession Companies up to 1920," ERC Project, Political Economy of African Development (Windhoek, Namibia, 2021), 17–18; Herbert Jäckel, *Die Landgesellschaften in den deutschen Schutzgebieten. Denkschrift zur Kolonialen Landfrage* (Jena: Verlag von Gustav Fischer, 1909), 199.

38 Drechsler, *Die großen Land- und Minengesellschaften*, 86.

39 Mokopakgosi, "German Colonialism in Microcosm," 251; Drechsler, *Die großen Land- und Minengesellschaften*, 88–89; DKGfSWA had been founded by German bankers, industrialists and politicians in the 1880s with exclusive monopoly rights over minerals in the colony, with the support of colonial department of the foreign office; see Drechsler, 1–29.

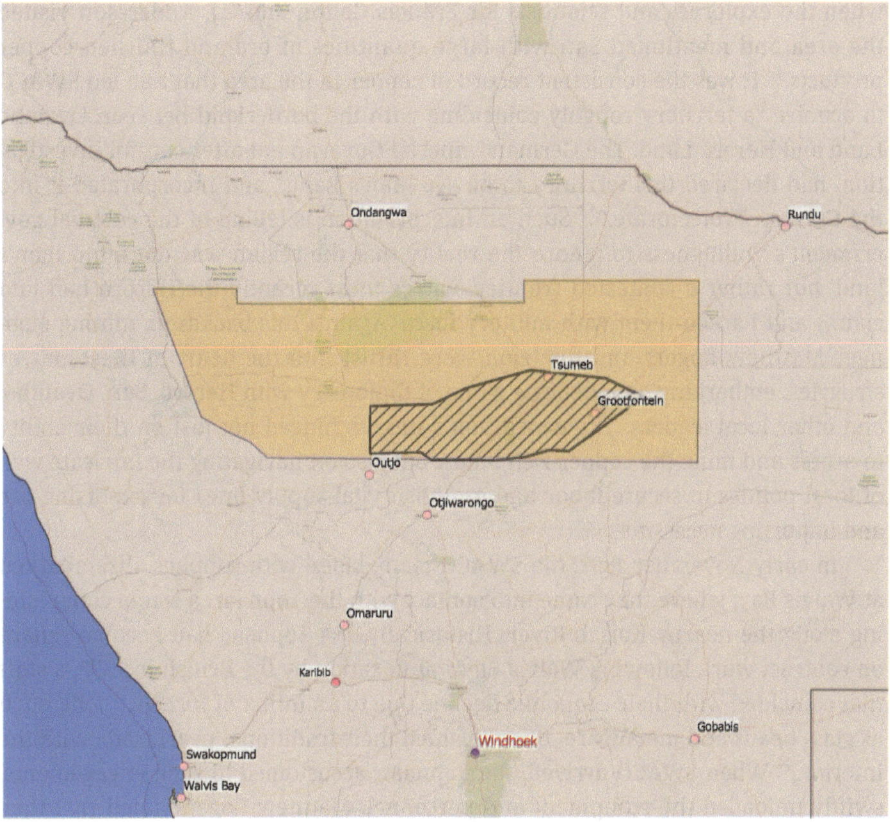

Figure 3: Approximate Boundaries of Concession Zone of the South West Africa Company, Ltd. The diagonal lines represent the area which had land concession rights as well. The yellow color represents mining and prospecting rights.[40]

The expedition to Otavi, as referenced in a letter from SWACO to its shareholders, followed an unrelated previous 1890 expedition to the area by a mining engineer named Mr. Hoefer who had been working for Sir Donald Currie.[41] While Hoefer had only been in Otavi for a few days, he had confirmed the presence of substantial copper oxides. Such observations by Europeans went as far back as 1851,

40 Figure 16: Approximate Boundaries of Concession Zone of the South West Africa Company, Ltd. from Moore, "Namibia Report on Concession Companies up to 1920," 53.

41 Richard A. Voeltz, "The European Economic and Political Penetration of South West Africa, 1884–1892," *The International Journal of African Historical Studies* 17, no. 4 (1984): 632–634.

when the explorers and scientists Sir Francis Galton and C.J. Andersson visited the area and mentioned San with large quantities of ore and finished copper products.[42] It was the consistent record of copper in the area that had led SWACO to acquire "a territory roughly coinciding with the borderland between Ovambo Land and Herero Land. The German Imperial Government after careful investigation, had declared this territory to be 'No Man's Land', and incorporated it into the German Protectorate."[43] Such an interpretation is telling of the colonial government's willingness to ignore the reality that the region was not a 'no man's land' but rather a contested frontier, where most recently the Herero had laid claims and backed them with military force. Against this backdrop, mining engineer Matthew Rogers and his team were thrust into the heart of these power struggles, embarking on a delicate game of diplomacy with Herero, San, Ovambo, and other local leaders. The expedition's success hinged not just on their ability to access and mine the copper-rich lands, but also on navigating the intricate web of local politics to secure labor and establish vital supply lines for exporting ore and importing necessities.

In early November 1892, the SWACO team, laden with supplies, disembarked at Walvis Bay, where they came into contact with the Topnaar, a Nama clan residing along the nearby Kuiseb River. Historically, the Topnaar had become reliant on contract work following Walvis Bay's annexation by the British in 1878, a shift that coincided with their economic decline due to an influx of foreign goods, such as glass beads and metalware, that devalued their traditional pearl trade with the interior.[44] When SWACO arrived, the Topnaar, accustomed to such engagements, swiftly unloaded the equipment and personnel. Matthew Rogers noted that they were promptly paid double to hasten their work throughout the night.[45] By No-

42 Francis Galton, *The Narrative of an Explorer in Tropical South Africa: Being an Account of a Visit to Damaraland in 1851* (London: John Murray, 1853), 223.

43 The University of Manchester, John Rylands University Library, 19th Century British Pamphlets, Foreign and Commonwealth Office Collection, To the shareholders of the South-West Africa Company, Limited., 07.04.1893, 5–6.

44 Henrichsen, *Herrschaft und Alltag im vorkolonialen Zentralnamibia*, 21–22, 74; For more on relations between Topnaar and whalers in particularly from the USA, see Felix Schürmann, "Ships and Beaches as Arenas of Entanglements from Below: Whalemen in Coastal Africa, c. 1760–1900," *InterDisciplines. Journal of History and Sociology* 3, no. 1 (2012): 36–37; For a more general overview of trade and relations between coastal peoples in Namibia and Europeans from the late 18th century to the beginning of German colonialism, see Jill Kinahan, *Cattle for Beads: The Archaeology of Historical Contact and Trade on the Namib Coast*, vol. 14 (Windhoek, Namibia: Namibia Archaeological Trust, 2000), 16–19.

45 BArch, R 1001/1482, Letter No. 1, Mr. Matthew Rogers to the Company, Walfish Bay, 01.11.1892, 1–2.

vember 11, the expedition had organized its supplies, wagons, and cattle and had contracted six Topnaar men to manage the livestock. These men were bound by a contract that promised the majority of their wages upon safe return to Walvis Bay, a strategic decision by Rogers to ensure their commitment for the duration of the journey.[46]

Accompanied by Topnaar and around 20 English miners, the expedition would make its long journey, over 595 kilometers, by ox-wagon, to Otavi. The journey was exceedingly difficult with early challenges such as waterless desert weakening oxen and sand temporarily bringing wagons to a standstill. But the journey was interspersed with small pleasures, including for the Topnaar workers. On the first night, as the expedition camped in the desert separating the coast from the interior, the group came across a European trader who sold the workers Eau de Cologne, which they drank and became intoxicated on.[47] While Rogers mentions the event to criticize workers for not being able to do their work afterwards, it also highlights restrictive British and German colonial policies on trade and consumption and the repercussions for local people. Both colonial governments outlawed the selling of alcohol to Africans, likely meaning that events such as this were not uncommon as a way for people to indulge.

Before we examine the work that would take place at the mines, one event is of particular value to understand the expedition and its relation to the power dynamics of 1892 GSWA: the negotiations that took place during travel through the interior with the Herero Chief Manasse Tjiseseta at Omararu. While permission to travel to the Damaraland concession for prospecting had already been given by the German colonial authorities in GSWA, their permission counted for almost nothing on the ground. Therefore, upon reaching Karibib, about 300 kilometers inland, the group delivered a letter to chief Manasse Tjiseseta. Tjiseseta in turn sent an escort comprising of headmen, including his own nephew and heir apparent, to bring them to his seat of power at Omaruru, 65 kilometers to the north.[48]

The negotiations both resulted in receiving permission to enter the territory as well as gave keen insight of Herero perspectives of the Germans and prospective colonial business endeavors in the colony. In writing of the negotiations with Tjiseseta, railway engineer David Angus who was present wrote:

> "All I ask is permission to go up to Otavi to look over the mines; we cannot take away with us the mines; also to see which is the best way to construct a railway to the coast." He (Tjiseseta) said "If I let you go forward to Otavi, will you promise me that whenever I write you a

46 BArch, R 1001/1482, Letter No. 2, Mr. Matthew Rogers to the Company, Usakhos, 11.11.1892, 4.
47 BArch, R 1001/1482, Letter No. 2, Mr. Matthew Rogers to the Company, Usakhos, 11.11.1892, 6.
48 BArch, R 1001/1482, Letter No. 3, Mr. Matthew Rogers to the Company, Omaruru, 26.11.1892, 12.

> letter asking you to return, that you will do so, and in a friendly way, and come straight to me and hear the reason I have recalled you?" We promised him we would do as he had asked. The Chief said "I will give you some of my big men to go with you, as some of my people are friendly, like myself, but some may cause you trouble, and these men I send can explain matters to you." ". . . So I accepted his offer with thanks. You say, Chief, that with your permit we can go all over your land and to many places you have never visited, and that the permit shall be written so we can show it to your Brother Chief Samuel Maharero if we should meet him?" -Ans: "Yes, I grant you this if you are an English Company and not allied with the Germans. But if you are allied with the Germans you must go back to the Bay at once, and you will tell me upon your return whether the land is rich or poor."[49]

The chief made perhaps his most direct statement as to his relation to the land, SWACO, and the Germans: "This is our country! We are the owners of it! We do not want war! We are for peace. We have been cheated many times before; but now our eyes are opened, and when once you could buy our land with a bottle of whiskey or a suit of clothes, that time is all gone by."[50] This declaration from Tjiseseta not only underscored his stance on land ownership and intentions for peaceful relations but also foregrounded the broader issue of language as a contentious point. The Europeans' general lack of language skills or effective translation often led to misunderstandings with local communities. This communication challenge, which would become a recurrent complication at work sites like the Otavi mines, was starkly highlighted during these negotiations, where the language barrier was explicitly acknowledged and confronted. The dialogue continued:

> Chief: Did you understand the people at Karibib?
>
> Angus: No; because I did not understand the language.
>
> Chief: What language did they speak?
>
> Angus: Damara.
>
> Chief: How did you think they drove you from the water, if you did not understand the language?
>
> Angus: My native boys interpreted for me, and also said we could not have water at Etiro.
>
> Chief: Where are the people that interpreted for you?
>
> Angus: In the village.

---

49 BArch, R 1001/1480, Letter No. 3, Mr. G.H. Copeland to the Company, Omaruru, 26.11.1892, 9–10.

50 BArch, R 1001/1480, Letter No. 3, Mr. G.H. Copeland to the Company, Omaruru, 26.11.1892, 10.

Chief: It may be a small thing to the master, but a big thing to me, that strangers coming into the land for the first time should be stopped. Why did you not bring the interpreters? Would it not be better to bring the interpreters to the Chief?

Angus: I did not know they could be required.[51]

Following the granting of permission by Tjiseseta, a company representative on the expedition, G.H. Copeland laid out his perspective on the state of affairs in the region: "The Germans at present only command at the mouth of the Swakop and at Windhoek. Here a German permit is not worth the paper it is written on. For instance, Messrs. Duft and Bülow (German colonial commissioners in GSWA) dare not try to enforce a German law or command here with the natives, but they do with the Europeans."[52] Reiterating where the real power lay, Copeland urged the SWACO board: "My last word is – "Write that letter to Chief Tjiseseta by all means."[53] As interpreted in SWACO's correspondence and the words of Tjiseseta, local African leaders in central Namibia of the early 1890s remained in a decisive position of power compared to the few German administrators located at a handful of fortified locations. Furthermore, leaders such as Tjiseseta and Maharero were clear eyed about the possible ramifications of increasing concessions made to Europeans, in this case regarding land usage.

The expedition after having been granted permission by Manasse Tjiseseta to continue to the interior sent Angus and Copeland to visit Herero Paramount Chief Samuel Maharero at Okahandja, who confirmed previous permission granted by Tjiseseta, while Matthews and his team of miners continued to Otavi. Matthews on the final leg of the journey to the mine observed that all "classes and sexes" of Damara, San and Herero encountered along the way often ask for tobacco. Similar to the European expedition members, with the exception of Matthews himself, smoking was a treasured pastime.[54] What such notes confirm is that by the early 1890s European traders in the region were not an uncommon sight for locals, and indeed many looked to take advantage by making requests of these visitors passing through their lands. The SWACO group was perceived as a potential resource for luxury commodities.

Once at Otavi by the beginning of 1893, the team built huts that emulated local building technology – as wood for European-style housing was in short sup-

51 BArch, R 1001/1480, Mr. Matthew Rogers to the Company (Enclosure to his Letter), Copy of Proceedings at meeting of the Raad, to which we were summoned on Tuesday, 22.11.1892, 15.

52 BArch, R 1001/1480, Letter No. 3, Mr. G.H. Copeland to the Company, Omaruru, 26.11.1892, 11.

53 BArch, R 1001/1480, Letter No. 3, Mr. G.H. Copeland to the Company, Omaruru, 26.11.1892, 13.

54 BArch, R 1001/1482, Letter No. 5, Mr. Matthew Rogers to the Company, Otavi Mines, Damaraland, 27.12.189, 30.

ply – and took advantage of wooden poles, small branches and interlaced long grass. Over time, with enough supplies, larger western style buildings and storage were also constructed. The area was inhabited by a variety of people including San, Damara, Nama and Herero. While the Herero chiefs Tjiseseta and Maharero lay claim to the region, it was often Nama that held power on the spot according to SWACO. The previous granting of mining rights to SWACO was contested by a variety of leaders. Upon arrival, a San chief and the expedition's local guide and prosperous werf owner with Griqualand roots, Johannes Kruger, pressured the expedition for payments to be granted mining rights. Further, as SWACO asked for local insights as to where test shafts should be dug, both Kruger and SWACO's translators, Mr. Getzen and his wife, requested payment in return. As months passed, claims of control over the area shifted, and in April 1893 visiting Nama voiced consternation at local Damara leaders who had granted permission to SWACO, even threatening war against the Damara as a result. Other visiting and local Africans occasionally asked for tobacco, traded livestock in exchange for finished Western goods, or sought Western medicine when sick. An item of contention was ammunition and firearms, frequently requested by many but which the expedition chose to not sell, this to local people's clear chagrin. While many Europeans could easily sell firearms to Africans and regularly did, regardless of British or German laws, the expedition likely did not sell them both out of fear of them potentially being used against them, as well as to keep themselves within the legal bounds of the Germans, who had given them the initial permission to travel into the colony.

Arriving at Otavi in early 1893, the team constructed huts using local building techniques, utilizing wooden poles, branches, and interlaced long grass due to the scarcity of wood for European-style housing. As resources became available, they also built larger Western-style structures. The region was home to diverse groups: San, Damara, Nama, and Herero. Herero chiefs Tjiseseta and Maharero claimed sovereignty over the area, yet SWACO observed that it was often the Nama who exerted immediate authority.[55]

The legitimacy of SWACO's mining rights, previously granted, was challenged by various local leaders. San chief Johannes Kruger, the expedition's local guide with Griqualand roots and a prosperous werf, demanded payments for mining access upon the team's arrival. The requests for compensation extended to SWACO's own translators, Mr. Getzen and his wife, when consulted on potential mining sites. By April 1893, the dynamic of control had evolved; visiting Nama leaders

55 BArch, R 1001/1482, Letter No. 22, Mr. Matthew Rogers to the Company, Soomep, Damaraland, 16.12.1893, 114.

expressed outrage at Damara authorities for authorizing SWACO's operations, even threatening war, although tensions would eventually ease.[56]

Interactions with locals were varied: some traded livestock for Western goods or sought Western medical aid, while others expressed frustration at the expedition's refusal to sell firearms. The SWACO company board had stipulated that payments to local people were contingent on the identification of ore-rich sites. Nevertheless in order to maintain the peace, certain leaders, including Maharero, were eventually compensated regardless of what they did or did not provide.[57] Despite numerous hurdles, work moved forward. Rogers characterized the initial phase as follows:

> In my opinion we are in an unenviable position in these mountains. Whatever we do is looked on with suspicion. Our work will be carried on practically under protest, as the natives are not solicitous we should remain here, and it is not to be wondered at, as they think our very presence and work will perhaps take from them the means by which they have hitherto earned a livelihood, and they have not sufficient foresight to see if mining is carried on by us we shall be able to employ them.[58]

Mine shafts dug by the expedition punctuated the landscape around Otavi, but it was in Tsumeb where the earth yielded the most promise, hinting at the wealth of copper that would eventually support a significant industrial mining operation. Tsumeb not only presaged the greatest potential but also became the epicenter of labor for the 1892 to 1894 expedition, employing the largest number of workers. It was Johannes Kruger who first guided the team to this favorable site. Recollecting his initial impressions, Matthew Rogers narrates:

> I have been holding places of trust in mining for the past 24 years; have visited various countries of the world, inspecting mines, mineral outcrops, and prospecting for minerals; have been associated with the minerals, gold, silver, tin, copper and lead; but in the whole of my experience, I have never seen such a sight as was presented before my view at Soomep [sic. Tsumeb], and I very much doubt if I shall ever see such another in any other locality.[59]

56 BArch, R 1001/1482, Diary of Mr. Matthew Rogers, 09.04.1893, 35.

57 Mokopakgosi, "German Colonialism in Microcosm," 352.

58 BArch, R 1001/1482, Letter No. 6, Mr. Matthew Rogers to the Company, Otavi Mines, Damaraland, South West Africa, 21.01.1893, 32–33. The Company documents incorrectly refer to Mr. Kruger as 'Creiger' and Mr. Getzen as 'Jetzen'. For more information on Kruger see Jeremy Silvester and Jan-Bart Gewald, ed., *Words Cannot Be Found: German Colonial Rule in Namibia: An Annotated Reprint of the 1918 Blue Book*, Sources for African History, v. 1 (Leiden, NL ; Boston, USA: Brill, 2003), 243.

59 BArch, R 1001/1482, Letter No. 6, Mr. Matthew Rogers to the Company, Otavi Mines, Damaraland, South West Africa, 21.01.1893, 37.

Figure 4: The 12-meter tall malachite hill (green hill) of Tsumeb. Although this photo was supposedly taken in the early 1900s, it may very well date from the early 1890s as Rogers did have a Kodak camera that may have been repaired during mining operations.[60]

Mining near this imposing outcrop, often referred to as the 'green hill' (See Figure 4 above) because of its malachite content, began as the earlier Otavi site was eventually abandoned. Tsumeb, similar to the other test mine shafts, was occasionally beset with work stoppages as local leaders, including the Herero chiefs Kambazembi and Maharero, tried to leverage their position over the mine in return for regular payments, sending big men representatives to oversee the operation. One event in particular threatened to permanently shutter operations: the 1893 raid by the German military commander Curt von François on the Hornkranz fortress of the Witbooi Nama chief Hendrik Witbooi, located about 120 kilometers southwest of Windhoek. This ruthless raid, whereby women and children were killed, left African leaders in the north of the colony very wary of the continued presence of the SWACO expedition. questioned whether SWACO were accomplices to the German

60 The 12-meter-tall malachite hill (green hill) of Tsumeb, ca. 1905, Tsumeb Museum, Unknown author, Public domain, via Wikimedia Commons, https://commons.wikimedia.org/wiki/File:1905_Tsumeb_Malachithuegel.JPG.

administration and rumors whirled of impending German attacks.[61] A local leader by the name of Kambatoni, with Nama and Herero followers, convinced that the expedition was German, shut down the mine. It was only reopened following the receipt of letters from Herrero chiefs reinstating permission. Kambazembi wrote: "My dear White-men, I really wish to impress on you the fact that the country really is our own, and no other tribes have any right in our country, and what rights you have are given by us."[62] A separate letter from Maharero went even further, chastising Rogers for listening to leaders in the Otavi area, such as Kambatoni or Kruger: "You will listen to everyone that comes and says, "This is my place. I am captain." Now, I forbid you to listen – even unto death."[63] To help paper over this conflict, Kambatoni was eventually given a stipend of £3 per month to ensure he would in his own right allow for mining to continue.[64]

While the ever-fluctuating relations between African leaders and mine management were an important barometer of the state of the mining community's affairs, it was the miners and laborers – the majority Africans hired to supplement the small English workforce – that were most directly connected to the mine's successes and failures. Let us examine what their work and daily lives entailed as well as the series of strikes, likely the first documented in Namibian history as pointed out by Robert Gordon, that contributed to the eventual end of operations in 1894 of the first SWACO mining operation.[65]

In a dispatch dated May 1893, Rogers offered insights into the labor situation at the mining sites, noting, "[w]e are employing some native labour at a minimum wage per day to assist us, as well as testing the possibility of their being brought to do mining work."[66] While the team engaged local workers for mining tasks, traditional activities such as hunting and the setting of bush fires – a San and Damara tactic to drive game and possibly summon rains – persisted in the vicinity of the camps. These fires, however, were a source of contention for the Europeans, who found them detrimental to the grazing pastures needed for their

61 BArch, R 1001/1482, Letter No. 15 Mr. Matthew Rogers to the company. Otavi Mines, Damaraland, 29.07.1893, 81.

62 BArch, R 1001/1482, Letter from Chief Kamabethembie to Matthew Rogers, Enclosure to Mr. Matthew Rogers' Letter No. 18, Waterberg, 09.1893, 103.

63 BArch, R 1001/1482, Letter from Paramount Chief Samuel Maharero to Matthew Rogers, Enclosure to Mr. Matthew Rogers' Letter, No. 18, Okahanja, 15.09.1893, 102.

64 BArch, R 1001/1482, Letter No. 16 Mr. Matthew Rogers to the company. Otavi Mines, Damaraland, 01.08.1893, 89.

65 Robert J. Gordon, "A Note on the History of Labour Action in Namibia," *South African Labour Bulletin* 1, no. 10 (1975): 7.

66 BArch, R 1001/1482, Letter No. 12, Mr. Matthew Rogers to the Company, Otavi Mines, Damaraland, 18.05.1893, 65.

oxen.[67] Concurrently, the ancient trade routes remained active as Ndonga men from the Ovambo polities continued their customary excursions to extract surface-level silicate copper for transport back to their homelands.[68] Life around the mines was not solely about labor; it also encompassed social and leisure pursuits, some introduced by the SWACO team.

Holidays brought a special atmosphere to the work sites including on Christmas of 1893. A SWACO letter mentions: "The European force . . . playing tennis" and "a number of sports were got up for the natives, and prizes to the winners distributed. They seem to appreciate this very much; everything was new to them, and the various amusements were engaged in with gusto . . . ." Also mentioned were fireworks launched in celebration that scared the African community. In a rather cruel description of how Rogers and the other Europeans perceived Africans at the camp, "it was amusing to hear of men, women and children leaving their huts, and scampering off into the bush; such was their fear that they did not return for the whole night."[69] Obviously these men, women and children were horrified of the fire and thunderous booms of fireworks, which they had doubtfully experienced previously.

For all those living in the community around the mine, conditions could be challenging, including outbreaks of disease at the Otavi location.[70] Rogers' diary pointed out that Africans were particularly susceptible to fevers in comparison to Europeans, who in turn were suffering in large number from gastrointestinal issues. The digestive problems were blamed on too much cornmeal, which according to Matthew, irritated "the lining of the bowels" and "[t]he mining force indirectly grumble at having so much corn . . . ."[71] As for the differences in who was catching fevers, the diary notes that many Africans in the camp would hunt and came from 'fever districts,' likely where malaria-infected mosquitos could be found.[72] Moreover, exacerbating factors among Africans at the camp existed such as higher-density housing with traditional cohabitation including extended family and tribal members. Further, food given to the African workforce was often inadequate because it was divided amongst the local community. Types of work also played a role, for example fetching water or washing clothes for the mine, likely

67 BArch, R 1001/1482, Diary of Mr. Matthew Rogers, 05.05.1893, 42.

68 BArch, R 1001/1482, Diary of Mr. Matthew Rogers, 24.05.1893, 45.

69 BArch, R 1001/1482, Letter No. 26, Mr. Rogers to the Company, Soomep, Damaraland, 20.01.1894, 123.

70 BArch, R 1001/1482, Letter No. 12, Mr. Matthew Rogers to the Company, Otavi Mines, Damaraland, 18.05.1893, 68.

71 BArch, R 1001/1482, Diary of Mr. Matthew Rogers, 25.04.1893, 39.

72 BArch, R 1001/1482, Diary of Mr. Matthew Rogers, 23–25.04.1893, 38–39.

undertaken by local women at standing bodies of water where mosquitos bred. Labor such as this was essential to the continuation of daily life surrounding the mining operations. 'Informal' work however was often not reported in company documents, but it was rather mine related jobs for adult males with regular pay and rations that were typically mentioned.

Work given to African men varied with occasional details given in documents, for example two men, one San and another Nama, who operated a mining windlass.[73] Rations for workers as reported in July of 1893, consisted of "five pounds of meat per day, together with a little meal, one-and-a-half pannikins (a small tin cup) of coffee, and two pannikins of sugar per week . . . they divide them among so many of their friends that they soon feel hungry, and ask for more, especially as they are now required to do regular duty daily."[74]

As roles expanded and the size of the African work force grew, Rogers noted the potential influence they could have over operations:

> [T]he employment of native labour is done under great risk. If an accident occurs (and accidents will happen under the most careful management), we shall be held responsible and shall have to pay heavy damages in some way or other, if not with our lives. To employ all Europeans brings us under the stigma of wishing to strengthen our position for hostile purposes.[75]

But as opposed to an accident, demands for better pay were a major factor behind a brewing strike. Perhaps foretelling of the coming conflict, a large fire burned down the company's storage building in mid-December of 1893 and though there was no firsthand evidence of how the blaze began, one theory by Rogers was that it was set by disgruntled Damara.[76]

The strike was a broad effort spanning the ethnic spectrum of African workers with a central demand focusing on increased pay. One group of organizers were the Herero headmen at the worksite – two sent by Maharero and two by Kambazembi – that were being paid the same rate as other African laborers and jobbers at 20 shillings (20/-) per month (they also received 'additional presents' as headmen). This was actually less than the 30/- per month paid to those assisting the white miners. These headmen joined Nama chiefs (at the mine to dock pay from Damara when they received it) and Ovambo workers to organize a strike to demand higher wages. The action began the morning of December 1st with those

73 BArch, R 1001/1482, Diary of Mr. Matthew Rogers, 12.05.1893, 43.

74 BArch, R 1001/1482, Diary of Mr. Matthew Rogers, 02.07.1893, 52.

75 BArch, R 1001/1482, Letter No. 15, Mr. Matthew Rogers to the Company, Otavi Mines, Damaraland, 29.07.1893, 83.

76 BArch, R 1001/1482, Letter No. 22, Mr. Matthew Rogers to the Company, Soomep, Damaraland, 16.12.1893, 112.

not involved either convinced to join or threatened with large cudgels and yelling to ensure they could not start work.

Those who did not join the strike, according to Rogers, came to his quarters and he wrote: "I did not wish to force them, but if they cared to work I would protect them."[77] The manager went to the mine with those wishing to work and stood between them and the strikers. This led to an escalation and a headmen representative of Kambazembi gouged Rogers' eye with a finger. Rogers in response threatened to use his revolver and would not change his policy. He retreated to his office to write a letter to Kambazembi and after seeing his determination, the Nama and Ovambo workers abandoned the strike. The remaining Herero eventually repented to Rogers and requested he not send the letter to Kambazembi, which he did not.

While the strike ended without any real resolution, Matthew Rogers understood the problems amongst the workforce: "Money and food questions have always been difficult ones to solve here. As I have frequently remarked, the food our men get is ample for themselves but there is always a large following surrounding them, that, doubtless, when divided amongst so many, is not sufficient." He goes on to highlight an additional issue connected to visiting merchants doing business with the workers: "The traders' price for clothing is so high here, that scarcely a single article can be purchased for less than £ 1 . . . . Indeed, when food and everything is taken into consideration the average pay per native must be £ 4 per month."[78]

The grounds of the strike were clearly understood by Matthew Rogers. His threat to use tribal power structures as a tool to reprimand chiefs' headmen at the mine served as a method of control that forced the organizers of the strike to fold. Their fellow countrymen then followed. But the persisting labor problems were clear: "There is still, however, an under-current feeling, and they may break out again at any time . . . ."[79] Only a few days after the first strike a second one emerged with a central focus around provisions. Additionally, external pressures were increasing: Ovambo had raided nearby Johannes Kruger's werf taking livestock and killing five men. Further, waggoners arriving at the mine from Omaruru reported Damara all along the route demanding money and goods. The future of the operation looked to be in the balance.

77 BArch, R 1001/1482, Letter No. 22, Mr. Matthew Rogers to the Company, Soomep, Damaraland, 16.12.1893, 115.

78 BArch, R 1001/1482, Letter No. 22, Mr. Matthew Rogers to the Company, Soomep, Damaraland, 16.12.1893, 115.

79 BArch, R 1001/1482, Letter No. 22, Mr. Matthew Rogers to the Company, Soomep, Damaraland, 16.12.1893, 115.

The underlying assumption by management was that although the mine was within the confines of local African social, political, and military boundaries, which clearly threatened the continuation of the expedition, the mine's African workforce should accept colonial extractive mining conceptions of work, pay and provisions. These equated to a primarily all adult male workforce with no dependents and importantly in a subservient role to Europeans. Rogers explained his perceptions of what the rolling strike and external situation meant for the company's position in writing: "Our difficulties now appear to have taken a more critical form. Before, our enemies were from without, now they are from within the camp, and being so much farther away we are more isolated . . . a report is prevalent, the Ovambos being displeased at our being here, are coming in force to make war on us." Lastly, in pointing out the precarious situation for the mine he again reiterates that if German soldiers were sent to guard the site the supply road would certainly be cut off and conflict would likely ensue.[80]

The second iteration of the strike focusing on food would last days. It was led by the Topnaar that had been hired at Walvis Bay, who were very influential amongst the African worker community. Rogers would not concede to the worker demands. SWACO rather laid off all the striking workers and hired in their place local Damara and San who would work.[81] As a result, the strikers left Tsumeb for their homes. Others who had not been directly involved in the strike were rehired but according to Rogers the company "could not tolerate these strikes, and if they ceased work again they must not expect to return any more."

By March of 1894, the mineral loads at Tsumeb and surrounding mines was of a quality that given global copper prices and the costs of labor and transport to the coast, continued mining was not profitable until transport infrastructure and/or mechanization was improved.[82] The first iteration of the SWACO Tsumeb mine was shut down. A later 1900 to 1901 expedition, under Christopher James came back to Tsumeb with 33 miners but by August of 1901 the operation would also be shuttered. The costs outweighed the profits. James stated: "I therefore propose to discard this low-grade ore and leave it for some future time when the country shall be more developed and prosperous and permit of it being profitably worked."[83] Even-

80 BArch, R 1001/1482, Letter No. 23, Mr. Matthew Rogers to the Company, Soomep, Damaraland, 20.12.1893, 117.

81 BArch, R 1001/1482, Letter No. 26, Mr. Rogers to the Company, Soomep, Damaraland, 20.01.1894, 121.

82 BArch, R 1001/1482, Letter No. 31, Mr. Rogers to the Company, Tsumeb, Damaraland, 24.03.1894, 138.

83 Paul Gerhard Söhnge, *Tsumeb, a Historical Sketch* (Windhoek: Committee of the S.W.A. Scientific Society, 1976), 24.

tually, as will be explored later in this book, the outcrops at Tsumeb would become a profitable venture with the construction of a railway to transport the ore to the coast as well as large scale industrial smelting and mining infrastructure.

In the early 1890s, the mining expedition could not foresee the transformative changes awaiting the communities of central Namibia in the years to come. The local influence on the initial mining operations had cast doubt on the project's viability. Although there were no successful strikes, it was speculated that military action by local chieftains against SWACO might have compelled changes in the African workers' compensation and provisions. Instead, SWACO adeptly exploited divisions within and among African communities – such as those between chiefs and headmen, and among Herero, Ovambo, Nama, and Damara groups – to retain control over its labor force. Subsequent reports from the Otavi region indicated that aside from the rising global commodity prices and improved local relations, the development of robust infrastructure was critical for Tsumeb's profitability. The late 1890s and early 1900s indeed saw the introduction of long-distance train infrastructure and the diminishing authority of African polities in central GSWA.

Yet, for Tsumeb's ore to reach global markets, a functioning port was essential. The British-controlled Walvis Bay would not integrate with German colonial networks, necessitating the establishment of a German-operated harbor. This infrastructural need set the stage for the founding of Swakopmund and the construction of its harbor and mole.

Swakopmund as Entrepôt

Between Ship and Shore: Early Swakopmund Longshore Workers

That Swakopmund became a colonial town, port, primary transit and trade hub in the central region of German South West Africa was not a predestined fate. As a potential port location, it most notably lacked a natural harbor. An event that highlighted some of the settlement's more challenging attributes, was the 1884 German Navy's visit to the mouth of the Swakop river (an ephemeral stream) following the founding of the colony.[84] The cannon boat *Wolf*, which had been in Hong Kong and was heading back to the metropole with a navy flotilla, was given

84 Swakopmund derives from the word "Tso-axaub-ams" in the Nama and Damara language Khoekhoegowab. Tsoaxaub translates to "Swakopriver" and "ams" to mouth. Mbenzi, Petrus Angula. "Renaming of Places in Namibia in the Pre-Colonial, Colonial and Post-Colonial Era: Colonising and Decolonising Place Names." *Journal of Namibian Studies* 25 (2019): 83.

a 'special mission' on its return voyage. It was to partake in a challenging maneuver: anchoring off the windswept and sandy coast north of British Walvis Bay and to send surf boats to row through the breakers to land equipped with a German imperial flag and pole. Having received news of the upcoming event, the small German community of about ten people at Walvis Bay; including German missionaries, merchants and a hotel owner, travelled north around 30 kilometers to watch. However, extremely difficult surf conditions and the resulting delays meant that the crowd had left before the landing actually occurred. With no audience, the German flag was raised, and as had previously transpired at 'Angra Pequena' (Lüderitzbucht) in the south, the region was declared a *Schutzgebiet* or 'protectorate' of the German empire.[85]

From the mid-1880s to the early-1890s, the desolate area where the seasonal Swakop river met the sea would remain largely uninhabited. Ships coming to supply the central region of the colony in the early years would often offload at Walvis Bay or 55 kilometers south at Sandwich Harbor, which unlike Walvis, was within the German protectorate. But by 1889, this alternative location was largely sanded in and could only be accessed by ships' pinnaces.[86] As the colony's capacity to supply the north lay at the mercy of British willingness to allow ships to utilize Walvis Bay, the necessity of establishing a port in the region under German control was clear. This was made more acute in 1892 as the German military increasingly needed resupply in its attempt to defeat Hendrik Witbooi and his troops. Up until that point, Magistrate Cleverly at Walvis Bay had the capacity to hold up German supplies, which he had done in the early 1890s, angering German military commander Curt von François.[87]

Options as to where a port could be built were in short supply. Along the entire coastline from Mossamedes in southern Angola to the border with northern South Africa, there were, with the exceptions of Walvis Bay and Lüderitzbucht, no good natural harbors.[88] Despite these geographic challenges, a location for a coastal 'port' would be chosen (see Figure 5 below).

---

85 'Erinnerung an die Gründung und Flaggenhissung in Swakopmund 1884', *Deutsche Kolonialzeitung* (DKZ), 33, 14.08.1909, 1.

86 Hermann Ortloff, *Die Landungsverhältnisse an der Küste Deutsch-Südwestafrikas* (Berlin: Verlag von Dietrich Reimer, 1902), 29–30; Sander, *Geschichte der Deutschen Kolonial-Gesellschaft für Südwest-Afrika*, 1: 30–31.

87 TNA, CO 879/34/4, African (South), no. 407, 'State of Affairs Walfish Bay' Jun. 8 and Jun. 14, 1893, quoted in Martin Kalb, "Water, Sand, Molluscs: Imperial Infrastructures, the Age of Hydrology, and German Colonialism in Swakopmund, Southwest Africa, 1884–1915," *Environment and History* 26, no. 2 (2020): 185; Curt von François, *Deutsch-Südwest-Afrika, Geschichte der Kolonisation bis zum Ausbruch des Krieges mit Witbooi (April 1893)* (Berlin: D. Reimer, 1899), 157.

88 Sander, *Geschichte der Deutschen Kolonial-Gesellschaft für Südwest-Afrika*, 1: 30.

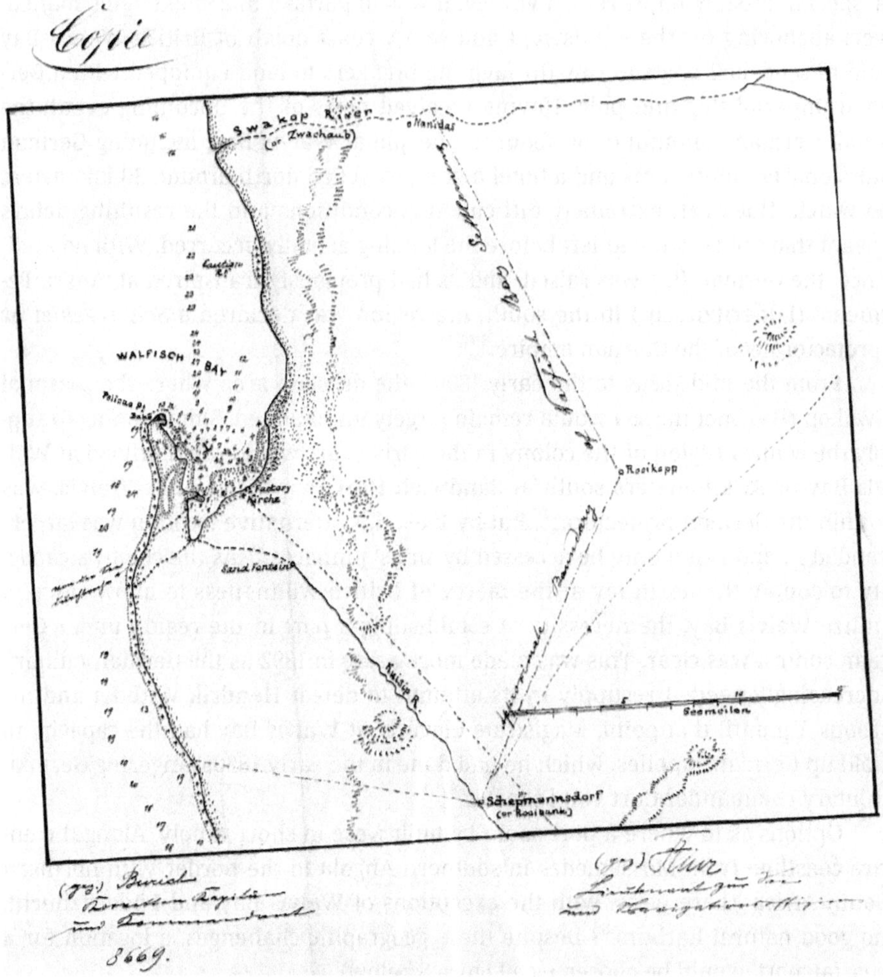

Figure 5: Map showing Walvis Bay and the Swakop River to the north.[89]

Under the guidance of Curt von François in August of 1892, the gunboat SMS *Hyäne* anchored one and a half kilometers off the coast of the Swakop river and

89 BArch R 1001/1863, Häfen an der südwestafrikanischen Küste Juni 1886 – Sept. 1895, Anlage zu IV 2015, Inhalt + Plan, 25.

confirmed that the location could be used as a landing place for the colony.[90] By January of 1893, the cruiser SMS *Falke* would return and offload soldiers, West African Kru longshoremen, and supplies to man a small coastal outpost. The foreman of the Kru workforce, a Liberian from Monrovia with many years' experience working as a steamer boat steersman on the Guinean coast, told the ship captain that there was no such favorable landing place in Guinea.[91] Shortly after the station was established, the Kru who had come from a tropical homeland, were relieved of their duty as they were suffering from the cold coastal climate. They were replaced by eleven German sailors who served both as police and provided signal service. Additionally, ships such as those of the shipping company *Woermann-Linie*, which would eventually dominate trade at Swakopmund, employed up to 150 Kru onboard who assisted with offloading.[92]

The actual process of longshore work at the new settlement would often occur as follows: Steamers would offload goods and people into surf boats approximately 500 to 1,000 meters (m) from the shore. Surf boats were approximately 8m long, 2.3m wide and could hold up to 1.7 tons. To get to shore they were manned by rowers and sometimes assisted by tugboats. About 100–200m from the shore were the most dangerous waves that often came into the boat, leaving crew and payload soaked. A typical *Woermann-Linie* steamer with a 1,800 to 2,300 ton loading capacity, a tugboat and eight surf boats, would take approximately ten to fourteen days to unload.[93] But before such an operation was to become common practice, the government first wished to have a test run.

An early success was the unloading of *Woermann-Linie*'s troop transport steamer 'Marie Woermann'. Conducted in late August of 1893, within 25 hours, 135 passengers, 100 tons of freight and cattle were unloaded without major problems. Much of the labor was conducted by Kru who were commonly hired to work on European and American Men-of-War that operated along the Atlantic African coast, including German military vessels, to conduct a variety of tasks including man surf boats and offload supplies.[94] The much quicker timeline than the previ-

90 BArch R 1001/1863, Häfen an der südwestafrikanischen Küste, Abschrift Kommando S.M. Kanonenboot „Hyäne", St. Paul de Loanda, 20.08.1892, 38–39. Also see 'Die Deutsche Siedlung in Deutsch-Südwestafrika', DKZ, 13, 10.12.1892, 175.

91 VdR, Bd.: 136. 1893/94, Berlin 1894, Aktenstück Nr. 48 (Denkschrift über das ost und Südwestafrikanische Schutzgebiet.), Landungsstelle an der Swakop-Mündung, 351.

92 BArch, R 1001/1865a Hafenanlage in Swakopmund, Woermann-Linie während des Aufstandes, 4.

93 Wilhelm Ortloff, *Erläuterungsbericht zum Entwurf für eine Hafenanlage in Swakopmund, Jahresbericht über die Entwickelung der Deutschen Schutzgebiete im Jahre 1898/1899, Beilage zum Deutschen Kolonialblatt 1900*, 146.

94 George E Brooks, *The Kru Mariner in the Nineteenth Century: An Historical Compendium* (Newark: Liberian Studies Association in America, 1972), 1.

ously mentioned average, compiled in 1899, was likely do to the much smaller payload of this 1893 test. A report in the Reichstag concluded that: "Swakopmund is a usable anchoring and landing place."[95]

During a trip to Walvis Bay and Swakopmund, a visitor named Dr. Kaerger chronicled a three-day journey in late September of 1893. Upon his arrival at the German outpost of Swakopmund, he encountered a modest assembly of two non-commissioned officers, seven sailors, and a handful of settlers. Among these settlers were the Unglaubes, a father-son duo who eked out a living repairing wagons and guns. Their dwelling, nestled within a sand dune and shored up by driftwood, featured a tin roof and was uniquely marked by a whale rib arching over the entrance. Driftwood, relics of shipwrecks accumulated over the ages, along with whalebones – remnants of the region's past frequented by European and American whalers – littered the beach nearby.[96] Amidst these vestiges of maritime history, other settlers had taken up temporary residence, some with wagons freshly ravaged by Witbooi raids, indicating their resolve to stay despite recent conflicts.[97] Additionally, Swakopmund was home to a nondescript government tin hut, a storeroom for drinking water and provisions, overseen by station chief Franz Joseph von Bülow.

While a ragtag operation, the military at Swakopmund had a simple purpose devised by von François: to offload ships when they came, store and protect their supplies when necessary, provide drinking water, and then help to facilitate transport inland. In his recollections, Dr. Kaerger also highlighted some of Swakopmund's redeeming traits. It had a preferable depth off the coast, allowing for larger ships to approach closer than at the British sister location to the south.[98] It also had relatively easily accessible drinking water and decent pasture for cattle one kilometer (km) inland at Nonidas. Lastly, there was a direct path to the interior along the Swakop valley.[99]

In its first years, Swakopmund would remain relatively stagnant. Beyond its small *Schutztruppe* station, a handful of tin houses, a 'store,' a few settlers, and a dozen or so Nama and Damara people, there was not much to be found. Compared to the community at Walvis with its 30 whites and about 125 Nama Topnaar in

---

95 VdR, Bd.: 136. 1893/94, Berlin 1894, Aktenstück Nr. 48 (Denkschrift über das Ost- und Südwestafrikanische Schutzgebiet.), Landungsstelle an der Swakop-Mündung, 351.

96 This pair were some of the only settlers at Swakopmund in 1893, see Kurd Schwabe, *Mit Schwert und Pflug in Deutsch-Südwestafrika* (Berlin: Ernst Siegfried Mittler und Sohn, 1899), 112.

97 Kaerger, 'Drei Tage in Südwestafrika', DKZ, 12, 7.10.1893, 151.

98 Kaerger, 'Drei Tage in Südwestafrika', DKZ, 12, 7.10.1893, 151.

99 These attributes compared favorably to Walvis Bay, whereby for example drinking water needed to be imported from Cape Town even by 1895, and Walvis Bay cattle were brought to the German area around Nonidas for grazing; see VdR, Bd.: 141. 1894/95, Berlin, 1895, Aktenstück Nr. 89 (Denkschrift, betreffend das Südwestafrikanische Schutzgebiet.), 494.

nearby Sandfontein, life was monotonous.[100] Furthermore, difficult surf during unloading would occasionally cause tragedy. For example, the DKGfSWA representative Dr. Rhodes, reported that in 1895 during heavy seas a surf boat off of Swakopmund capsized killing all sailors on board with the exception of one.[101] Despite occasional extreme surf conditions, and a search for other alternatives, such as Rock bay 16 km to the north, by 1895 the decision to keep the German colonial port at Swakopmund had been made official.[102] Expansion to this point was confined by limited commerce, which began to change in 1896. In that year the DKGfSWA, followed by the government and various trading houses at Swakopmund, re-employed Kru longshoremen from Liberia to replace the sailors. DKGfSWA also secured a deal with the *Woermann-Linie* to add a regular shipping route between Germany and the colony, including Swakopmund, six times a year.[103]

Kru longshoremen laboring in the cold sea could often fall ill, and in the case of choppy surf potentially risk injury or drowning. Adding to the challenges, fog would regularly shroud the landing site, necessitating the use of bells for signaling both on the beach and on steamers offshore to keep surf boats going in the right direction.[104] A contemporary account by Margarethe von Eckenbrecher, a German settler who arrived at Swakopmund in early 1902, gives us a glimpse into what working as a longshoreman at Swakopmund entailed. She was taken from her ship, *Woermann-Linie*'s *Eduard Bohlen*, to shore by Kru workers via surf boats.

> I admired the skill of the Kruboys, who, with the greatest certainty and cold-bloodedness, put their oars in the waves and made rapid progress. But when I saw the colossal wave up close it either seemed as tall as a house or to create a deep abyss, I couldn't stop from getting goosebumps . . . . We shot forward like an arrow through the breakers, and with a tremendous heave, the bow of the boat was on the sand as the stern rose high. A few Kaffirs from the shore had already come out to us and before I knew their intentions, one had me on his back and carried me to dry land.[105]

---

100 VdR, Bd.: 141. 1894/95, Berlin, 1895, Aktenstück Nr. 89 (Denkschrift, betreffend das Südwestafrikanische Schutzgebiet.), 494.

101 Sander, *Geschichte der Deutschen Kolonial-Gesellschaft für Südwest-Afrika*, 1: 97; Schwabe, 'Von der Südwestafrikanischen Eisenbahn', DKZ, 10, 04.12.1897, 501.

102 Sander, 1: 82–83.

103 Sander, 1: 100; BArch, R 1001/1865a Hafenanlage in Swakopmund, Woermann-Linie während des Aufstandes, 3.

104 Schwabe, 'Von der Südwestafrikanischen Eisenbahn', DKZ, 10, 04.12.1897, 500.

105 Margarethe von Eckenbrecher, *Was Afrika mir gab und nahm: Erlebnisse einer deutschen Ansiedlerfrau in Südwestafrika* (Berlin: E.S. Mittler & Sohn, 1907), 42. Translation to English by W.B. Lyon.

The account by Margarethe of a ship-to-shore trip underscores the perils inherent in each journey, dangers that were compounded over time by the damp climate, leading to health risks. Werner Haak, a soldier who arrived in German South West Africa in September of 1904, attested to the severity of these conditions: "They have hard work over there, the whole day in water, where it is hardly 13 degrees [Celsius], and you must work in heavy surf; many die from pneumonia . . . ."[106]

Yet, the lives of the Kru in Swakopmund extended beyond their arduous labor. Max Rudolf Uth, a businessman present from 1902 to 1903, captured a slice of life in his recounting of a Sunday morning, where he interacted with two Kru men known by their given aliases Thomas and Monkey – names once capriciously bestowed by Western ships. Such names, often intended to be demeaning, were reclaimed with pride, becoming symbols of status and experience among Kru communities.[107] Uth's narrative continued, highlighting the Kru's perspective on the local hardships: He notes their critical view, expressed in Pidgin English, of the destitute local Africans scavenging for leftovers in the white populations' food conserves amidst a backdrop of rinderpest and malaria.[108] The Kru derogatorily labeled these individuals 'kaffern'. Monkey was a handsome playboy, who only dressed in white and was always struggling with debt. Fine clothing like his, and in particular suits were of central importance in the social life of Kru in GSWA.[109] Additionally, wearing high-end European apparel upon returning to their home communities in West Africa to highlight their successes was a common tradition. His fellow Kru colleague, Thomas came from the humid tropical forest, likely the Kru coast of Liberia.[110] It was there that he left his faithful bride, whom he missed dearly. Contrasting Monkey's fast paced lifestyle, Thomas was adamantly saving his earnings with the goal of returning to her. Upon arrival home after work abroad, it was a typical practice for Kru to get married or to take an additional wife if they were already married.[111] In Thomas' down time, he drew pictures of

---

106 Werner Haak, *Tagebuchblätter aus Südwest-Afrika* (Berlin: Boll & Pickardt, 1906), 12. Translation to English by W.B. Lyon.

107 Brooks, *The Kru Mariner in the Nineteenth Century*, 28; Jeffrey Gunn, "Homeland, Diasporas and Labour Networks: The Case of Kru Workers, 1792–1900" (Ph.D. thesis, Toronto, York University, 2019), 90–91.

108 Already by the 1830s, pidgeon English was widespread in West Africa and commonly spoken by Kru; see Brooks, *The Kru Mariner in the Nineteenth Century*, 21.

109 William Blakemore Lyon, "From Labour Elites to Garveyites: West African Migrant Labour in Namibia, 1892–1925," *Journal of Southern African Studies* 47, no. 1 (2021): 44.

110 Brooks, *The Kru Mariner in the Nineteenth Century*, 59; Jane Martin, "Krumen 'Down the Coast': Liberian Migrants on the West African Coast in the 19th and Early 20th Centuries," *The International Journal of African Historical Studies* 18, no. 3 (1985): 408–410.

111 Brooks, *The Kru Mariner in the Nineteenth Century*, 60.

steam ships.[112] Yet before these observations, in the late 1890s, there was concern over whether Swakopmund would retain its West African labor force post-contract, casting doubt on the port's future efficacy as a commercial nexus. The Kru workforce was indispensable; without them, the settlement's role as a transit and trade hub would be jeopardized.

In 1897, the Liberian government, began to increase barriers to Europeans hiring Kru for work abroad. This was likely an attempt by Monrovia to increase pressure in order to collect more taxation from the recruitment.[113] For Swakopmund in particular, reports of many Kru deaths because of bad working conditions likely influenced increasing difficulty in recruitment for work in GSWA.[114] As Kru labor became more challenging to hire and could not realistically be replaced by other workers because of their unique skill sets, the German colonial department needed a solution. They were able to propose and then have the Reichstag approve, an initial £12,228 to begin construction of a mole with the intention to make the loading and unloading of ships at the port feasible without the necessity for Kru labor.[115]

Building Swakopmund's Mole

In early August 1899 at a well-attended and lively cabaret at Ludwigs' ballroom in Klein-Windhoek, Hans Beck from Munich, 'the Hercules at the end of the century', was a fan favorite and a few of his songs were even printed in the *Windhoeker Anzeiger* (WA). One went like this:

> A couple of old Africans sit on the beach of Swakopmund
>
> One of them has a heavy heart. His face shows it clearly, He scratches his copper nose.
>
> The other asks: What's wrong with you today? Then he quickly has another drink and laments his sorrow:
>
> "Do you know, Jonny, what I dreamed: I saw a harbor causeway, it was so long, so wide, so solid, you could walk to the steamer. You didn't have to get wet anymore."
>
> The Kru stayed in Monrovia. Landing was no trouble in beautiful Southwest Africa.[116]

---

112 Max Rud. Uth, *Im Sattel und Ochsenwagen: Erlebnisse und Beobachtungen in Deutsch-Südwest-Afrika* (Fulda: Uth, 1907), 15–16.

113 Starting in the middle of the nineteenth century, Monrovia had begun to impose increased taxation on Kru migrant laborers; see Gunn, "Homeland, Diasporas and Labour Networks," 234–235.

114 Sander, *Geschichte der Deutschen Kolonial-Gesellschaft für Südwest-Afrika*, 1: 112;

115 VdR, Bd.: 159. 1897/98, Berlin, 8. Sitzung, Aloys Fritzen (Düsseldorf), 11.12.1898, 144.

116 Local-Nachrichten, *WA*, 17.08.1899, 3. Translation to English by W.B. Lyon.

While Hans Beck's song projected what the settler community was thinking onto Africans, it gives us a view into themes occupying settler society at the time. His other songs of the evening covered topics like farmers with cattle dying of rinderpest, a future where they could sell livestock utilizing the not yet complete Swakopmund-Windhoek railway, and lost dreams and yearning for the homeland. As the quoted song above highlights, settlers also fantasized, and likely Kru as well due to the very dangerous work, about a mole at Swakopmund allowing for much safer and efficient loading and offloading at the port. In addition to Kru recruitment bottlenecks, the port's inadequacy had been laid bare starting in 1897 with the large increase in imports related to the construction of the Swakopmund-Windhoek railway.[117] There were instances whereby ship captains, facing long offloading delays, ordered wooden supplies for the train line construction pushed overboard to float to the beach to be collected.[118]

As the century was nearing its end, the funds that had already been approved the previous year by the Reichstag had not yet translated into construction. The mole project proposal was still awaiting approval from the government. Then on the August 29th, 1899, another tragedy struck and a Kru worker for the *Woermann-Linie* ship, the 'Marie Woermann', drowned in the surf at Swakopmund. His death was a tipping point. The *Woermann-Linie*'s local representative wrote to the German foreign office stating: "The residents of Swakopmund, in view of the incessant accidents, urgently request a speedy approval of the mole construction."[119] By the second of September 1899 the foundation stone was laid.

The construction was initially led by hydraulic engineer Hermann Friedrich Ortloff as highlighted in detail in the work of Martin Kalb.[120] Ortloff would arrive from Germany accompanied by approximately eighty workers, including twenty that had worked with him previously. Additionally, 160 European workers were hired from Cape Town. These included Russians, Finns, Swedes, English, Germans, and Dutch. There was also a good number of Slovenians. Throughout the project there were on average 75 whites employed.[121] According to Orloff, while

117 Wilhelm Ortloff, *DSWA: Grundsteinlegung zur Mole, Deutsches Kolonialblatt,* Vol.X Nr.18, 15.09.1899, 627.

118 Pool, *Eisenbahnen in Deutsch-Südwestafrika*, 46.

119 *'Die Grundsteinlegung der Mole in Swakopmund,' WA*, 28.09.1899, 1. Translation to English by W.B. Lyon.

120 Kalb, "Water, Sand, Molluscs," 188–92.

121 For information on the workforce numbers for the mole, see 'Die Mole,' DSWAZ, 12.12.1903, 5; Ortloff, *Die Landungsverhältnisse an der Küste Deutsch-Südwestafrikas*, 36–37.

those he brought from Germany were "an extraordinary team and held themselves well . . . ." His views were without doubt colored by his nationalist tendencies, as well as the fact that some of these workers had previous experience working under him. The engineer's views did not hold for the others. Of those from the Cape Colony, he claimed "there were many truly dubious characters among them. Going further in signaling his disdain, Ortloff wrote: "If I didn't like people, I couldn't chase them away."[122] Some of these white workers did not fit the bill, abandoned the work site, and were replaced over time.

During the three years of construction, those from the Cape region increasingly came as a result of the outbreak of the South African War in October of 1899. The conflict between the British empire, the Boer South African Republic and the allied Orange Free State led to economic destabilization as well as widespread violence and death.[123] In comparison, German South West Africa was stable, undergoing an economic boom, and demand for labor was high. By 1901, a larger influx (*grösserer Zuzug*) of white political and economic refugees came from South Africa, primarily the Cape Colony, to GSWA. They were mostly Boers but included Germans as well. Some were reported as looking to stay but the majority were only there to look for jobs, and some found it working for the mole and train-line construction. It was reported that: "These (men), will as soon as order returns to South Africa go back . . . . As a result of this influx, the worker shortage that was slowing progress has ended and work (on the train and mole) has made ample advances."[124] There were also attempts to recruit hundreds of black workers from Cape Town for the mole, but the Cape government blocked this, likely because of local wartime labor demands.[125] Those fleeing the war and looking for work would be the first wave of increasing numbers of South Africans seeking jobs in the German colony to the north. Following waves numbering thousands beginning in 1904, would include many Cape Coloureds, Zulu and workers from the Transkei.[126] This new South African to GSWA 'worker corridor' would become one of the primary suppliers of labor to the GSWA settler region by the middle of the first decade of the twentieth century. While the South Africans made a sizable contribution to the mole workforce, Africans from the Ger-

122 Ortloff, 37. Translation to English by W.B. Lyon.

123 Robert Ross, *A Concise History of South Africa.* (Cambridge: Cambridge University Press, 2011), 72.

124 *'Von südafrikanischen Kriegsschauplatz'*, *DSWAZ*, 01.01.1902, 1. Translation to English by W.B. Lyon.

125 *'Die Otavibahn,' DSWAZ*, 09.10.1902, 1.

126 See chapter 2 and chapter 4 of this book for a detailed analysis of migrant South Africans working in GSWA starting in 1904 until 1914.

man colony made up the majority. Ortloff's preference for local African workers was clear: "I put them above the whites I got from Cape Town; it sounds harsh, but I have to say it."[127]

The number of Ovambo and Herero workers averaged 185 men between late 1899 and the end of August 1902.[128] Some Nama were also laboring on the mole project, but numbers are unclear. The Ovambo in particular, who were regarded as doing the best work on the construction site, had travelled hundreds of kilometers, from the interior of the colony to the coast.[129] The hydraulic engineer's remarks on the black workforce mixed backhanded compliments with patronizing and racist language. Ortloff stated they were good at their work but "needing to be treated sternly," like children. He may be referencing the fact that communication between black workers and white overseers was often further complicated by lack of ability to speak each other's language. Similar to Otavi and other work sites, black workers were either simply expected to understand German or the number of translators was inadequate. Regardless, he added that in the context of the entire work force, "I can give our black man the best review."[130]

The work itself took place at primarily two locations. First, there was a rock quarry about 1km north of the mole, where large pieces of granite were excavated, lifted with cranes, and brought on rail with the help of locomotives to the construction site. When this quarry was operating, about 300 workers, almost all Africans were employed there (See Figure 6 below). Large, quarried stones were used as the mole foundation.[131] Additionally, concrete blocks were also poured, with the biggest reaching about 10 cubic meters (m^3). Much of the mole components were massive and the labor must have been grueling (See Figure 7 below). Weather played a primary role in dictating construction progress (or lack thereof). Between January and May of 1900, work was halted because of inclement seas.[132]

127 Ortloff, *Die Landungsverhältnisse an der Küste Deutsch-Südwestafrikas*, 37. Translation to English by W.B. Lyon.

128 *'Die Mole,' DSWAZ*, 12.12.1903, 5.

129 Ortloff, *Die Landungsverhältnisse an der Küste Deutsch-Südwestafrikas*, 36–37; On Ovambo workers in relation to Nama and Herero at the mole construction site, see 'Deutsch-Südwestafrika', DKZ, 43, 23.10.1902, 413.

130 Ortloff, 36–37. Translation to English by W.B. Lyon.

131 Ortloff, 36–37.

132 *'Die Mole,' DSWAZ*, 12.12.1903, 5.

Even after work resumed, a German worker, Redeleit, who was guiding the laying of stones at the end of the mole was swept off by a wave and drowned before he could be saved.[133] Facing continuing difficulties, weather in June of 1901 also caused severe damage to the mole.[134]

Figure 6: Workers at the rock quarry for the mole.[135]

The so-called 'old guard' of German workers on the site stayed the entire three-year length of their contracts.[136] This may have been connected to good wages for white workers at between 7/- and 8/- per day.[137] But high pay and a large influx of workers during construction also translated into inflated costs for things like food

133 *'Aus dem Schutzgebiet,' WA*, 20.06.1900, 2.
134 Hermann Friedrich Ortloff, 'Der Bau des Hafens in Swakopmund,' Zeitschrift für Bauwesen LIV (1904): 346–364, here 680, 683, and 692, quoted in Kalb, "Water, Sand, Molluscs," 190–191.
135 Bildarchiv der Deutschen Kolonialgesellschaft, Universitätsbibliothek Frankfurt am Main (BADKGUBFM), Photo: A_00I_1330.
136 *'Aus dem Schutzgebiet,' DSWAZ*, 20.11.1901, 2.
137 *'Südwestafrika,'* DKZ, 46, 17.11.1898, 417.

Figure 7: D.S.W.A. Swakopmund. View from the mole. 63328 Verlag der Swakopmunder Buchhandlung G.m.b.H.[138]

and sleeping quarters, as well as a strain on the water supply system. A water main was constructed from the interior to Swakopmund to provide the growing town with a better water supply in 1898 as water usage increased.[139] For most white workers, wages could cover the costs, but for locals, visitors and black workers, these prices were a strain on daily life. Reports include the cost of sleeping on a bare floor with an overcoat and a blanket at the end of the century costing up to 1/- per night.[140] This inflamed a tight real estate market. Housing demand had already instigated *DKGfSWA* in the years prior, to use its longshore workforce to construct housing when no ships were off the coast.[141] By 1898 they were joined by private contractors and tradesmen from the Cape.[142]

138 'Swakopmund' postcard with a photo taken from the mole toward the shore, BADKGUBFM, A_00I_1346.
139 Sander, *Geschichte der Deutschen Kolonial-Gesellschaft für Südwest-Afrika*, 1:130.
140 *'Südwestafrika,'* DKZ, 46, 17.11.1898, 417.
141 Sander, *Geschichte der Deutschen Kolonial-Gesellschaft für Südwest-Afrika*, 1:101–2.
142 *'Südwestafrika,' DKZ*, 46, 17.11.1898, 417.

For African workers at the mole in Swakopmund, racism and related segregation meant that they lived separated from whites in *pontoks* (huts) near the customs office for the port by the beach. Women and children were a common presence. Uth, in describing some of the women, used the term 'Omama' (*Oomama*), Otjiherero for 'mothers,' and mentioned they wore typical Herero florid dresses and were accompanied by unclothed children. Similar to the work site at Otavi, the men working on the mole were probably joined by family and tribal members. But in contrast to the early 1890s at Otavi, by the end of the decade the rinderpest had laid low much of the great Herero cattle herds, meaning that many Herero were suffering from food scarcity. Begging for food was commonplace at Swakopmund. Uth describes Sunday rations (likely provisions for the mole workers) as consisting of rice, very low-quality meat, tea, and cooking sugar. Women prepared food in large kettles and the men grilled the meat over ashes.[143]

All black people in Swakopmund were subject to a crude night curfew, which translated into punishment for transgressors, who 'were no longer in good standing', via corporal punishment. This could entail a brutal cane beating: five, 10 or 20 times depending on the severity of the offense. The act was carried out by a black police assistant.[144] This mirrors penalties that continued and further developed in the post-genocidal period of the colony as, highlighted in the work of Marie Muschalek.[145] For those who received such punishment it was a very painful and humiliating experience. But life for all workers on the mole was also interspersed with joy. Whereas the town's tennis court and sports field in the early 1900s was left unused, entertainment often centered on the consumption of 'spiritual' nourishment in liquid form.[146]

Drinking beer, frequently in large quantities, was a common practice in early twentieth-century Swakopmund. This was assuredly part of the white workforce's routine and likely, while not 'legal', of black worker's as well.[147] A 1901 *Cape Times* special correspondent visiting GSWA had a Swakopmund subsection enti-

143 Uth, *Im Sattel und Ochsenwagen*, 14–15.

144 Uth, *Im Sattel und Ochsenwagen*, 25.

145 Marie Muschalek, *Violence as Usual: Policing and the Colonial State in German Southwest Africa* (Ithaca: Cornell University Press, 2019), 77.

146 Uth, *Im Sattel und Ochsenwagen*, 12–13.

147 As referenced in the Otavi section of this chapter, both Walvis Bay and the German colony outlawed the sale of alcohol to Africans; see SWACO Expedition to the Otavi Mines, 1892–1894.

tled 'The Universal Beer Bottle,' which highlighted their omnipresence.[148] The local *Swakopmunder Zeitung*, citing the same correspondent, wrote the following:

> As you can imagine, the consumption of beer in such a dry country as here is quite considerable. One notices whole heaps and walls of beer bottles. Here and there, with the bottoms turned upwards, they are used to form a kind of sidewalk, and I have seen borders of flower beds made in the same way: but there were no flowers in the beds. Needless to say, in these cases the bottles were empty. On a mooring place on the coast, a whole boatload of beer bottles was taken on board; they were destined for Cape Town and give a favorable impression of the Teutonic tendencies.[149]

Tycho van der Hoog's work on beer in Namibia points out that the first formal brewery in Swakopmund had opened the previous year in 1900, but by 1901 it seems that beer consumption was already at a very high level.[150] Uth remarked that while imported beer was expensive, at up to 1/- to 2/- per bottle at the bar, the locally brewed wheat beer, 'mild blonde' (*laue Blonde*), although not particularly tasty, was less than half the price at 6d per bottle. For whites, beer drinking seemed to go hand in hand with parlor games, such as the card game skat or rounds of nine-pin bowling (*Kegelbahn*), likely with bets involved, costing up to an eyewatering price of £1 19/-. Where whites drank, what they drank and what activities accompanied the imbibing were often delineated along class lines in the settlement. Already by the end of the nineteenth century, the *Deutsche Kolonialzeitung* mentioned elites only mixing with each other in the *Kegelbahn* club, whereas the second class of employees, and a third class of tradesmen mingled among other places, in a military club, which the elites tended to avoid.[151] People drank to escape boredom, the challenges of living in the fledgling settlement, as well as out of fear for typhus, which could occasionally be found in the water supply.[152] Typhus was a reoccurring scourge in Swakopmund, in particular around Christmas in the founding years, and into the early 1900s. It even had the moniker, 'Swakop fever' (*Swakopfieber*) because of its prevalence.[153] The workforce,

148 'Swakop Mouth,' *Cape Times*, 29.10.1901, 5; The Swakopmund residents' proclivity for alcohol dated back to the 1890s; see NAN, NAUK CO 879/40: Resident Magistrate, Walvis Bay 'Memorandum on the State of Affairs in the German Protectorate,' 8.1.1897.

149 ‚*Was ein Engländer von Swakopmund sagt,*' *WA*, Beilage zu Nr. 11 des "Windhoeker Anzeiger," 23.05.1901, 5. Translation to English by W.B. Lyon.

150 Tycho van der Hoog, *Breweries, Politics and Identity: The History behind Namibian Beer* (Basel: Basler Afrika Bibliographien, 2019), 23.

151 *'Deutsch-Südwest-Afrikanisches,' DKZ*, 52, 29.12.1898, 473.

152 Uth, *Im Sattel und Ochsenwagen*, 13–14.

153 ‚*Aus Swakopmund,' DSWAZ*, 04.12.1901, 2.

often defined by overconsumption, gambling and occasional work accidents, eventually completed the mole construction in early 1903.

On the morning of February 12, with the ocean as smooth as a mirror and the air clear, *Woermann-Linie* steamer 'Gertrud Woermann', with guests on board from Cape Town and Walvis Bay, anchored off Swakopmund, which was decorated with flags and hosting a large crowd. The harbor pinnace went to collect people from the ship to bring them to the mole. In addition to naming the colonial officials present, the paper described the following scene:

> On the embankment at the foot of the pier squatted the native workers, well over a hundred, many in festive garb, that is, as the native here go, dressed in European clothes. Further up, on the quay, the whites had lined up. Here, the veterans' association had lined up with the flag, the garrison, the [white] pier workers.[154]

The construction of the mole, which spanned over three years and cost approximately £122,310, faced immediate setbacks.[155] By 1903, and decidedly by early 1904, the mole's harbor was compromised by sand from the Swakop River, severely restricting its utility to high-tide operations.[156] A South African report from June 1903 questioned the mole's viability, with observations made after storm damage suggesting it was "useless, save as a small and precarious boat shelter . . . ."[157] This assessment was largely borne out; with the onset of war in 1904, the military's urgent need for efficient unloading led to the construction of a pier, first in wood completed in 1905, then in steel begun in 1912, effectively superseding the mole. The necessity for skilled longshore labor, particularly the Kru workforce, remained high, and as the later conflict escalated, their numbers grew.[158] This need for Kru labor would persist throughout the German colonial period in Namibia, as will be discussed later.

Transitioning from the mole's story to that of railway construction, it is notable that contemporary observers already saw the two as intrinsically linked. In 1899, the *Windhuker Anzeiger* observed that, "[d]irectly related to the railroad construction is the construction of the mole at Swakopmund; the two complement each other. One is only half without the other."[159] This sentiment captures the es-

---

154 *'Die Molenfeier,' DSWAZ*, 19.02.1903, 2. Translation to English by W.B. Lyon.

155 *'Die Mole,' DSWAZ, Beilage No.* 7, 12.02.1903, 5.

156 Kalb, "Water, Sand, Molluscs," 193.

157 Cape Town Archive Depot in Cape Town (CA), NA 612, Harbour Works, Swakopmund, 1901–3, Swakop Mouth Harbour Works, Native Affairs Office, Cape Town, 24.6.1903, 1.

158 Lyon, "From Labour Elites to Garveyites," 42.

159 *'Rückblicke und Aussichten II. (Fortsetzung),' WA*, 19.01.1899, 4. Translation to English by W.B. Lyon.

sence of Swakopmund's role as an essential port at the turn of the twentieth century, intertwined with the rail line construction that had commenced in 1897. Thus, we cast our gaze back to six years before the mole's completion, to the nascent stages of GSWA's inaugural long-distance, steam-powered railway.

Constructing the Swakopmund-Windhoek Railway Line

The construction of the Swakopmund-Windhoek railway, commencing in 1897, was envisioned by the colonial government as a vital commercial lifeline, linking Swakopmund, the colonial port of German South West Africa, with its capital, Windhoek. This artery of commerce aimed to facilitate the distribution of supplies to new settler farmers and the transport of their goods, including cattle. However, the early years of the railway were marred by exorbitant costs and service interruptions due to track issues, indicating a disconnect between colonial ambitions and on-the-ground realities.[160]

This initial period saw the railway offering little advantage over the traditional ox-wagon routes, with its high costs deterring farmers from regular use.[161] The true potential of the railway would not be realized until the Namibian War began in 1904, when significant military investments led to major repairs and enhancements, rendering the railway a reliable means of transport. The construction site itself, much like those at Swakopmund and Otavi, was a dynamic 'contact zone' where various workers, local communities, and management intersected. However, the railway's labor force was unique in its mobility, regularly relocating as construction advanced.

The impetus for the railway's construction can be traced back to a devastating cattle epidemic: the great African rinderpest panzootic. The outbreak, which began in the 1870s/1880s, likely originated in East Africa, though the exact vector remains a subject of debate.[162] The disease's arrival in GSWA around late-1896 is thought to have been carried by wildlife migrating from the lush pastures created by heavy rainfall in the Okavango delta.[163]

---

160 Bley, *Namibia under German Rule*, 132.

161 Bley, 132; For more detail on the early road history of colonial Namibia including the Bay Road, see Klaus Dierks, *Namibian Roads in History: From the 13th Century till Today* (Frankfurt/Main: Selbstverlag des Institutes für Wirtschafts- und Sozialgeographie der Johann Wolfgang Goethe-Universität, 1992), 43–53.

162 Clive Spinage, *Cattle Plague: A History* (New York: Springer US, 2003), 500–506.

163 Marquardt, "Open Spaces and Closed Minds," 140.

Colonial administrations throughout Southern Africa cooperated to mitigate the disease's impact.[164] The eponymous Koch vaccine, developed by the German bacteriologist Robert Koch working in the Cape Colony, proved to be a controversial but ultimately successful intervention. Despite setbacks, including the transmission of other diseases through inoculation, it saved a significant proportion of livestock in the Cape.[165]

In May of 1897, Koch's assistant, Dr. Kohlstock, arrived in GSWA to spearhead a vaccination drive. This campaign, initially focusing on the vital freight oxen of the Baiweg, was supported by soldiers trained in veterinary assistance.[166] Alongside these efforts, the German government erected a veterinary cordon of military outposts to isolate settler cattle from the Ovambo herds, a measure that, despite its substantial cost and limited success, underscored the strategic importance of cattle in the colonial economy.[167]

For Africans, rinderpest decimated the cattle population, hitting the Herero particularly hard. The disease compounded difficulties they faced, following Governor Theodor Leutwein's policy, since the mid-1890s, of systematic confiscation and sale of Herero cattle when they strayed off of their territory.[168] Highlighting the suffering of the Herero resulting from the decimation of their herds, Thomas Mayr, a German soldier stationed at Otavi, wrote:

> In many Herero locations, which had a [sic] 1000 cattle standing earlier, all but a pair of miserable oxen were snuffed out. [This was] especially noticeable in the Omuramba Omatako, a riverbed east of Grootfontein to the north, where another Herero location lay. Beginning in July, one can say [that all Herero livestock had disappeared] . . . . Most were poor, poorer than the Bushmen. [By mid-July, many were suffering from hunger]. The former living areas of Herero were abandoned. They [cattle] layed across these hundreds of watering places, yes thousands of dead cattle and [they] polluted the air. At Grootfontein, we had the dead oxen burned, so we could stay in this place, then when a wind came after that, it even stank here, then the Herero oxen polluted the air for many miles . . . .[169]

While Herero herds were almost completely wiped out, settler cattle often fared better. For example, in the Windhoek district and along the *Baiweg*, cattle deaths

---

164 Klemens Wedekind, *Impfe und herrsche. Veterinärmedizinisches Wissen und Herrschaft im kolonialen Namibia 1887–1929* (Göttingen: Vandenhoeck & Ruprecht, 2020), 123–129.

165 Wedekind, *Impfe und herrsche*, 123–129.

166 Wedekind, *Impfe und herrsche*, 136.

167 Miescher, *Namibia's Red Line*, 23–28.

168 Drechsler, *Let Us Die Fighting*, 89–90.

169 Scientific Society Swakopmund (SSS). Private Accessions, Thomas Mayr, quoted in Marquardt, "Open Spaces and Closed Minds," 150.

seemed to have not surpassed 30 to 50 percent.[170] But the mortality differential between vaccinated and unvaccinated cattle was stark. Surveys taken at Waterberg indicated that 50 percent of the vaccinated, and 95 percent of the unvaccinated herds died.[171] As a result, many Herero lost faith in the inoculation program but were forced to follow through with vaccinations.[172] Food became scarce as cow's milk was a staple of the Herero diet. Additionally, most lost the economic ability to hire themselves out as wagon drivers using their oxen and wagons because of such high cattle mortality rates.[173] Some began to collect wood to trade for food, others asked missionaries for help, and begging became commonplace.

Many Herero in this desperate situation went to look for contract work in the colonial economy in various industries. The German administrator of the Grootfontein district between 1897 and 1900, Philalethes Kuhn, mentioned that in the period of the rinderpest, he hired almost exclusively Herero.[174] Looking further afield between 1902 and 1904, around 500 to 800 Herero men left the colony to work on the Gold Mines at Johannesburg.[175] But in 1897, and the following years, work for the railway construction attracted large numbers of Herero, offering a temporary lifeline for some.[176]

For settler herds and the colonial economy, the panzootic also caused problems. By July of 1897, the disease was infecting the draft oxen which labored along *Baiweg* transport corridor. This brought the colonial supply line between Swakopmund and the interior to a standstill.[177] Wagons required large numbers of oxen, 14 animals when unloaded and up to 20 when loaded.[178] Not only did *Baiweg* ox-wagon transport become greatly reduced, but as a result prices also increased for goods purchased by settlers in the interior of the colony.[179] Even as

170 A.D. Sander, *Die Rinderpest und ihr Einfluss auf die wirtschaftlichen Verhältnisse in Deutsch-Sudwestafrika* (Berlin: Hermann Paetel, 1897), 11.
171 Gewald, *Herero Heroes*, 117.
172 Gewald, *Herero Heroes*, 116–117, 144; Charles van Onselen, "Reactions to Rinderpest in Southern Africa 1896–97," *The Journal of African History* 13, no. 3 (1972): 483.
173 Gewald, *Herero Heroes*, 123.
174 Philalethes Kuhn, *Die Herero* (Berlin: Reimer, 1907), 11.
175 Jan-Bart Gewald, "The Road of the Man Called Love and the Sack of Sero: The Herero-German War and the Export of Herero Labour to the South African Rand," *The Journal of African History* 40, no. 1 (1999): 25; although the German government got a kick back of just under £ 1 / recruit, the settler community, in particular was wary of losing needed labor to South Africa; see 'Aus dem Schutzgebiet,' DSWAZ, 09.10.1902, 1.
176 Bley, *Namibia under German Rule*, 125–126.
177 Dierks, *Namibian Roads in History*, 51.
178 Dierks, *Namibian Roads in History*, 44.
179 *'Kleine Mitteilungen,' DKZ*, 49, 4.12.1897, 503.

late as November of 1898, flour and rice shortages existed in Windhoek and supply of provisions hung precariously in the balance.[180]

Following the growing crises, with an eye to bypassing the necessity of ox-wagons along the *Baiweg*, the Reichstag in Berlin approved construction of a 60 cm, small-gauge railway line between Windhoek and the coast at Swakopmund. Questions remained as to whether this small gauge could handle the demands of the colony with arguments made for and against. This debate would continue throughout construction. There was some consensus however, that given the difficult geography through which the train line would be built, as well as drastic changes in elevation along the path, narrow gauge was the only suitable option for both a speedy construction and maintaining low costs compared to standard or cape gauge.[181] The initial contract to build a railway along that corridor, had been given to SWACO in 1892, but the company had up until that point only conducted an engineering survey for a trainline, mentioned previously, and not begun any construction. As it seemed certain that SWACO would not move forward with the project any time soon, the colonial department negotiated with the company to bring the scheme under government control. In exchange for taking the monopoly rights to build the railway from SWACO, the government gave SWACO the Ovamboland Concession.[182] The train line would be built on land that had been secured through further government negotiations with the DKGfSWA, which acquired it from local African leaders.[183]

While the land had already made the 'legal' transition from African to European ownership, the physical transformation of the environment via railway construction likely had a more significant physiological effect on those who lived in the vicinity. Perhaps symbolic of the infrastructure's eventual penetration into traditional Herero strongholds, a station would be constructed in Okahandja, on land donated personally by Paramount Chief Maharero, whose primary residence was nearby. Furthermore, likely connected with Maharero's growing dependence on German military power and money during his struggles against other Herero and Nama leaders throughout the 1890s, the Paramount Chief donated a six-meter wide strip through Hereroland for the new train line.[184]

180 '*Aus dem Schutzgebiet*,' *WA*, 24.11.1898, 2.

181 von Kries, '*Genügt die 60 cm-Spur in Südwestafrika?*,' DKZ, 26, 30.06.1898, 234–236.

182 Theodor Leutwein, *Elf Jahre Gouverneur in Deutsch-Südwestafrika* (Berlin: E.S. Mittler & Sohn, 1908), 133; Moore, "Namibia Report on Concession Companies up to 1920," 90.

183 On the agreement between the colonial government and the DKGfSWA, see Pool, *Eisenbahnen in Deutsch-Südwestafrika*, 25.

184 Pool, *Eisenbahnen in Deutsch-Südwestafrika*, 39.

Commencing construction in August of 1897, a group of soldiers and accompanying officers from the *Eisenbahnregiment Nr. 3* (Train Regiment Nr. 3), were sent from Germany to the colony with supplies for the first 80 km of tracks as well as parallel construction of a telegraph line.[185] The work began in September under the leadership of lieutenant Kecker with an early workforce of approximately ten Germans and nineteen African laborers.[186] An expanded workforce was necessary and the local administrator Ziegler in Okahandja, was given the role of trying to recruit workers. The first contract was signed between Ziegler and Herero chief Kavezeri. For every one of Kavezeri's people that was recruited for a three-month contract, he would receive about 5/-. Each worker was to begin in October and paid just under 10/- per month with free provisions.[187]

Similar to all of the project's recruitment agreements between Germans and African leaders, the contract was designed to benefit Kavezeri for recruiting his people and ensuring they remained at the work site. In many ways the recruitment dynamic was similar to the mine at Otavi of the early 1890s, whereby African leaders played a deciding role not only in recruitment, but also retention at the worksite, and occasionally pushed back against colonial management when conditions were inhospitable.

By October, Herero chief Tjiseseta had joined Kavezeri in sending almost one hundred followers to work at the train line construction. Moreover, Damara chief Cornelius Goreseb sent around 19 of his people to the line for work from Okombohe.[188] The inclusion of Damara labor under Goreseb was connected to a contractual obligation to the German government. In 1894 Governor Leutwein and Herero chief Manasse Tjiseseta entered in an agreement that transformed Damara, Herero and German colonial relations. For a very large sum of money paid to Tjiseseta, the Germans took control of Okombahe, a traditional Damara stronghold that had been under Herero rule. After signing a further agreement with Damara chief Cornelius Goreseb, the Damara living there had an "obligation, to provide labourers for government services."[189]

185 'Der Eisenbahnbau in Südwestafrika,' DKZ, 33, 14.8.1897, 326; R. Boethke, *Die Verkehrstruppen in Südwestafrika* (Berlin: Mittler, 1906), 39.

186 NAN, EVE 205, F 1aBd. 1, Kecker- AAKA, 21.9.1897, 2 from Pool, *Eisenbahnen in Deutsch-Südwestafrika*, 39.

187 NAN, EVE 30, A 5a Bd. 1, Arbeitskontrakt, pg. not numbered, cited in Pool, *Eisenbahnen in Deutsch-Südwestafrika*, 39.

188 Bley, *Namibia under German Rule*, 23–24.

189 Dag Henrichsen, "'Damara' Labour Recruitment to the Cape Colony and Marginalisation and Hegemony in Late 19th Century Central Namibia," *Journal of Namibian Studies*, no. 3 (2008): 79–80.

These terms were conducted while the German campaign against Hendrik Witbooi was underway, serving to pressure traditional leaders in central Namibia who wished to avoid a similar situation. The large payments to traditional leaders, both Herero and Damara, had also greased the wheels to allow the German colonial state more direct access to Damara labor. By mid-1898, reports of the worksite listed Damara as the majority of African workers. Joining the Herero and Damara, were Nama as well as over two dozen whites, mainly Germans from Cape Town.[190]

Nevertheless, enough workers were not to be had and in dire need of more, as well as additional supplies, the month of October in 1897 saw the arrival of a group of 150 additional soldiers from Germany for work on the line. They were joined by steam engines for the railway, eight in total that formed four 'twin locomotives,' small but efficient machines that operated in pairs on the narrow tracks.[191] Up until this point, the prior SWACO contract, which was by then renegotiated with the government, gave sole rights to the company to operate steam trains in this region. This meant that prior, the segment of the line that had been constructed was serviced by animal drawn wagons, ironic since the rinderpest had been a major catalyst for construction.[192]

As the line progressed over the next years, the workforce would wax and wane between 1897 and 1902 depending on demand for labor and local and migrant desire and capacity to work. This combined with whether the metropole sent workers from Germany and larger external factors, such as temporary white migration into the colony due to the South African War and increasing numbers of Ovambo migration south in the first years of the twentieth century. Initially, 1897 to 1898 saw a few dozen, and then hundreds of workers, including two waves of German soldiers, arrive on the worksite. By 1900 numbers of workers had ballooned to 800 to 900 Africans and 200 to 300 whites, including about 20 administrators, officers, and bureaucrats. November 1901 saw the number of African workers on the train line increasing to around 2,900.[193] However, the halting but nevertheless increasing numbers of workers over the years of construction were in the initial phases inconceivable.

In 1897 to 1898, African workers in particular, most who had come from the interior to the coast, found the colder climate inhospitable and would try to keep

190 'Die Arbeiterfrage beim Bahnbau in Südwestafrika', DKZ, 23, 9.06.1898, 209; Pool, *Eisenbahnen in Deutsch-Südwestafrika*, 40.

191 *'Aus dem Schutzgebiet,' WA*, 24.11.1898, 2; *'Rückblicke und Aussichten II. (Fortsetzung)', WA*, 19.01.1899, 3.

192 Gerding, *'Die Bahn Swakopmund-Windhuk', DKZ*, 26, 6.12.1900, 587.

193 *'Aus dem Schutzgebiet,'* DSWAZ, 13.11.1901, 1.

warm in their *pontoks*, especially at night. Adverse climactic conditions may have also made workers more susceptible to an outbreak of typhus that occurred in early 1898 as a result of contaminated drinking water.[194] The disease led to the death of 18 Africans and six Europeans. Following the outbreak, some African workers deserted and perhaps most symbolic of their desire not to be forced back to the worksite, fled to British controlled Walvis Bay.

Word of the bad working conditions spread inland. Of Herero Chief Tjiseseta's 30 men on the work site, 28 left.[195] For such an abandonment of the work site to happen at a time of food scarcity and malaria outbreak among Herero communities, the difficulties for workers on the train line were obviously manifold. African leaders' approval of their followers' return home, points to recognition that supporting their own people was often more important than profits accrued by their followers' continued work.[196]

The 1898 typhus outbreak exacerbated the already critical shortage of labor, prompting the colonial administration to devise a meticulous construction schedule that broke tasks down to daily goals in an effort to minimize disruptions. A seemingly sensible solution, the recruitment of Ovambo laborers from the north, was relatively challenging at the end of the nineteenth century, as relations between the polities and the colonial government was tepid at best. Therefore, recruitment drives extended across Southern Africa, but met with limited success; efforts in Basutoland failed to attract workers, and while some individuals from the Cape Colony did join the ranks, issues such as alcoholism hampered their effectiveness. The *Koloniale Zeitung* even proposed that Chinese labor could be the solution, though this idea remained unrealized. In lieu of this, it was suggested that a contingent of 100 German railway troops might replace the need for 400 to 500 unskilled workers – a claim that was likely inflated.[197]

This perceived efficiency of German soldiers was put to the test when 125 workers, along with two medical staff, were dispatched from Germany, arriving in October of 1898.[198] These white workers, in line with the pattern observed at other colonial sites, commanded much higher wages than their black counterparts. There was variability in their salaries, with initial recruits earning a robust

194 *'Die Arbeiter Frage beim Bahnbau in Südwestafrika,' DKZ*, 23, 9.06.1898, 209.

195 Pool, *Eisenbahnen in Deutsch-Südwestafrika*, 42–43.

196 NAN, EVE 205, F 1a Bd. 1, pgs. not numbered (Bericht Nr. 6, 10.02.1898, 3) and (Bericht Nr. 9, 5.5.1898, S.3) from Pool, *Eisenbahnen in Deutsch-Südwestafrika*, 43.

197 *'Die Arbeiterfrage beim Bahnbau in Südwestafrika,' DKZ*, 23, 9.06.1898, 209.

198 'Deutsch-Südwest-Afrikanisches,' DKZ, 52, 29.12.1898, 473; Pool, *Eisenbahnen in Deutsch-Südwestafrika*, 43.

5/- to 6/- per day – marginally less than what would later be paid for work on the mole.[199] Those who arrived later in 1898 were also well-compensated, taking home nearly £4 a month, which equates to around 4/- per day. Reflecting on their conditions, the *Koloniale Zeitung* remarked, "80 marks a month, free station, two suits a year as well as footwear, with eight-hour work days, where would such provisions be offered in other parts of the world?"[200]

But for white workers, better pay and provisions did not automatically translate into a more satisfied workforce. The new arrivals mentioned above convinced the workers at the construction site upon their arrival to strike. They probably realized the difficulties of the work as well as the location, and those already employed seemed to agree.[201] After two days the strike ended, seemingly with no real changes on behalf of the workforce, but it is perhaps the first example of a strike led by white workers in GSWA.[202] Their push for better working conditions, followed five years after the first strike in the colony, which was led by black workers at the Tsumeb mine mentioned earlier in this chapter.

Although detailed sources on worker perspectives are limited, the work and daily life related to the construction was clearly challenging. Catalogued within the *Swakopmunder Zeitung*, is a reference of a train line worker, mentioned only as 'W.' (most likely white, as German newspapers at the time almost always prefaced mentions of black workers with the term *Eingeborene*), who in August of 1902, cut open the veins in his left arm to end his life at Swakopmund. He was described as being "tired of life" (*lebensmüde*).[203] While he survived, 'W' perhaps symbolizes the very strenuous realities of railway work in the colony, including for relatively better off whites.

Conditions for black workers were far worse than for the average white in terms of pay, housing and labor conditions. Moreover, relations between African workers and white managers seems to have been particularly caustic. The following report by a Swiss socialist train worker, writing to a publication back home in 1901, urging compatriots not to come to the German colonies, highlights what may have been a common occurrence. A fellow African laborer was mistreated after having objected to the gang rape of his wife by the supervisor of the Swakopmund labor encampment and his friends. The woman had first been given

199 *'Die Arbeiterfrage beim Bahnbau in Südwestafrika,' DKZ*, 23, 9.06.1898, 209.

200 'Deutsch-Südwest-Afrikanisches,' DKZ, 52, 29.12.1898, 473.

201 Unfortunately, no details are given as to whether only white workers joined the strike, or blacks as well; see 'Deutsch-Südwest-Afrikanisches,' DKZ, 52, 29.12.1898, 473.

202 The author has been unable to find information as to whether there may have been any black-white collaboration in the strike.

203 *'Aus Swakopmund,' DSWAZ*, 12.02.1903, 18.08.1902, 2.

alcohol and was according to the account pliant to the white man's intentions.[204] While it has hints of at least some emotional solidarity, nothing is mentioned of whites intervening on behalf of the African woman who was raped, or her husband.

Some black workers for the train line, had by the early-1900s been employed on the worksite for two years without stop. Perhaps the existential challenges facing many at home, especially the Herero, made the provisions and pay of the work site bearable for many. From the perspective of white management, by October of 1901 African laborers were excelling at their work. In particular, many were doing jobs that previously had been undertaken solely by whites, such as stake out work and preparatory labor for the line's foundations.[205] Sources also mention black laborers employed working on bridge construction for the railway, including iron ramming to drive piles into dry riverbeds and the subsequent construction of the bridge framework. Employed Africans could also be found in workshops, probably for locomotive repairs, and operations at the beach at Swakopmund, doubtless related to loading cargo onto train wagons.[206] Mirroring the patronizing and backhanded 'complementary' language of Ortloff regarding black workers on the mole, a *Swakopmunder Zeitung* article wrote about black train workers: "These people have not only learned to work, but like to work, a truth that previously one would think is not possible."[207] Not stated in the paper is that perhaps many had no choice but to work in order to survive.

From the perspective of the railway as colonial infrastructure, by 1898, once the first 80 km of track was completed, locomotives could transport goods from Swakopmund to the station at Jakkalswater, where pasture for cattle was located. This overcame the difficulties of the 'desert belt,' separating the coast from the interior, where oxen would occasionally succumb to thirst and die. Afterwards transport for the remaining segment inland was easier and quicker.[208] But while this meant obvious benefits for transport options, rail-line advances also had negative effects for certain segments of commerce and business in the colony. By November 1898, only Baster oxen-wagons were coming to Swakopmund as their German counterparts decided to spare their oxen the arduous trip through the 'desert belt' and rather have freight sent by train over the first segment of track to be picked up. Partially resulting from the new competition created by the railway, Baster

204 Berner Tagwacht, Organ der sozialdemokratischen Partei des Kantons Bern, 18.9.1901; clipping of article found in NAN, ZBU 204, A IV w 2 Vol. 1. Publications specialia. Publications about the Protectorates.

205 ‚*Aus dem Schutzgebiet*,' *DSWAZ*, 30.10.1901, 2.

206 ‚*Aus dem Schutzgebiet*,' DSWAZ, 13.11.1901, 1.

207 ‚*Aus dem Schutzgebiet*,' *DSWAZ*, 30.10.1901, 2.

208 '*An unsere Freunde daheim*,' *DSWAZ*, 14.08.1902, 1.

wagon drivers' home community at Rehoboth, south of Windhoek, felt the economic repercussions in the following years. A mission report from Rehoboth in 1901 noted that the town was in crisis: drought reigned, locusts destroyed pasture, and the community was suffering from cattle raids. This situation was compounded by decreased earnings of freight drivers' waning business. The missionaries noted that as a result of these factors, hunger was common among the population.[209]

There was also some local settler pushback to the rail line construction, in particular the route it took. A group of settlers from Otjimbingwe, a crossroads of ox-wagon road networks between Swakopmund and Windhoek, wrote the 'Otjimbingwe Petition' around 1899, arguing that the train line would lead to diminished commerce for them as it bypassed their town.[210] This assertion did indeed become reality as the previously mentioned 1901 Rhenish Missionary report noted, "Karibib and Otjimbingue have completely reversed their roles as a result of the railroad passing over Karibib. While Karibib is a fast-flourishing trade and traffic center, Otjimbingue is becoming more and more quiet . . . ."[211] In addition, Swakopmund lost some commerce because of the decrease in visiting wagon transport. However, that compared favorably to the nearby harbor of Walvis Bay, which had very little business because of the new train infrastructure to the interior which began at Swakopmund.[212]

The Swakopmund-Windhoek train line was completed in June of 1902, over five years after construction had begun. The protracted construction period was due to a myriad of challenges: labor shortages, frequent track repairs from flooding or poor craftsmanship, the absence of a proper harbor for unloading supplies, and often, water and food scarcities. Additionally, there was a general lack of comprehensive planning prior to the undertaking. Subsequent massive repairs and improvements to the train line necessitated the mobilization of hundreds of workers, predominantly sourced from the Ovambo polities to the north.

This construction period highlighted critical aspects of labor development in the colony, particularly for large industrial projects. It demonstrated that even amidst economic, food security, and health crises affecting local African communities, poor working conditions could lead to worker dissent and attrition. Efforts

209 BAB (*Basler Afrika Bibliographien)*, Annual Report of the Rhenish Mission Society 1901, Report from Rehoboth (Bastards) by Missionaries Heidmann and Blecher II, (Barmen: Westdeutsche Druckerei, 1902), 24.

210 *'Rückblickend Aussichten II. (Fortsetzung),' DSWAZ*, 19.01.1899, 3.

211 BAB, Annual Report of the Rhenish Mission Society 1901, Report from Otjimbingue by Missionaries Olpp and Elger, (Barmen: Westdeutsche Druckerei, 1902), 27–28. Translation to English by W.B. Lyon.

212 *'Südwestafrika,'* DKZ, 17.11.1898, 416.

to recruit black laborers from neighboring colonies were largely unsuccessful. The strategy of using pay to incentivize local chiefs and headmen for recruitment and retention bore fruit only when the conditions at the work sites were deemed fair. In its nascent stage, the railway's success as a piece of colonial infrastructure was limited, serving merely as a technical link between the capital and the coast.

A remark by an African, perhaps Baster or Nama because he spoke in Afrikaans, during the construction of the railway station at Rössing, was possibly the clearest critique of the project: "Now the whites have gone completely insane, they are building a house in the middle of the desert."[213]

Indeed, they were constructing a structure 39 km east of Swakopmund in the desert, where water supply was far and few in-between. The project proved that early colonial attempts at train infrastructure would face extreme challenges, similar to the first Swakopmund mole and harbor that was sanded in shortly after completion. But as a result of these projects, the sunken financial and psychological cost of these ventures pushed the state to invest even more to ensure they would be serviceable. These early infrastructure projects, along with the 1890s / early-1900s SWACO expeditions to Otavi that confirmed large copper reserves in the colony's interior, helped to solidify colonial presence on the ground.

Two years after the railway's construction, an imperial decision to respond to a large-scale uprising of the Herero with massive deployments of troops and materiel made the railway more than a symbolic step in the modernization of the colony's infrastructure beyond wagon roads. Early in the war against colonial rule, the Herero cut the railway and telegraph line between Swakopmund and Windhoek. Symbolically, this was a severing of the vein between the German metropole and the colonial capital. It was soon repaired and did indeed serve as an essential lifeline to the interior. But also telling, and central to the next chapter is that during the conflict, it was wagons with skilled drivers that served as the primary and most effective form of troop transport and supply throughout the theater of war.

213 Kecker, '*Die Feldbahn Swakopmund-Windhoek*,' Daheim 36, 1900, 16. Translation to English by W.B. Lyon.

2 The Human Infrastructure of the Namibian War: Origins of the 'Namibian Labor Corridors' in War and Genocide, 1904–1908

From the mid-1890s to 1904, a crescendo of tensions destabilized colonial Namibia. The Herero people, facing relentless erosion of their land, culture, and power, stood on a precipice. Land expropriation, suffocating debts, and a judicial system rigged against them were the realities for the Herero, while German settlers and military forces harbored a growing distrust and paranoia.[1] The colonial powder keg first ignited with the Bondelswarts uprising in the south in October 1903, compelling Governor Leutwein and a significant German military detachment to divert their attention from central Namibia – just as Herero leaders were contemplating a stand against their oppressors.

In mid-January, under the command of Paramount Chief Samuel Maherero, a strategic and targeted Herero offensive besieged German farms and strongholds. This campaign, marked by a measured clemency that spared women, children, non-Germans, and missionaries, belied a discriminating resistance strategy. Over the ensuing months, the Herero leveraged guerrilla tactics and intimate terrain knowledge to mount a formidable challenge. As pressure mounted from Germany for a decisive victory, the battle-hardened General Lothar von Trotha arrived in June 1904 to take command, signaling a harrowing shift in the war's tenor.

The climactic encounter unfolded at Waterberg in August, where Herero forces, encumbered by civilians and cattle, were outflanked. The aftermath saw them flee into the Omaheke desert, a march to oblivion orchestrated by German troops under Major Ludwig von Estorff.[2] This relentless pursuit, intended not to capture but to annihilate by the desolate desert, heralded the first genocide of the twentieth century.[3] It was in this dire context that von Trotha, with chilling finality, penned his intent in October:

---

1 The origins of the Namibian War are complex and not discussed in detail here. For more, see Matthias Häussler, *The Herero Genocide: War, Emotion, and Extreme Violence in Colonial Namibia* (New York: Berghahn Books, 2021), 51–58; Marion Wallace, *A History of Namibia from the Beginning to 1990* (Oxford: Oxford University Press, 2013), 155–162; Jan-Bart Gewald, "Ovita ovia Zürn – Zürn's Krieg," in *Namibia-Deutschland eine geteilte Geschichte: Widerstand, Gewalt, Erinnerung*, ed. Larissa Förster et al. (Munich: Edition Minerva, 2004), 78–91.

2 Wallace, *A History of Namibia from the Beginning to 1990*, 163–164.

3 Dominik J. Schaller, "'Every Herero Will Be Shot' Genocide, Concentration Camps, and Slave Labor in German South-West Africa," in *Forgotten Genocides: Oblivion, Denial, and Memory*, ed. René Lemarchand (Philadelphia, USA: University of Pennsylvania Press, 2011), 62–63.

https://doi.org/10.1515/9783111374918-003

> The only question for me now was how to end the war with the Herero. The views about it, with the governor and some 'old Africans' on one hand and me on the other hand, are completely different. The former had wanted to negotiate for a long time and described the Herero nation as necessary working material for the future use of the land. I am of a completely different opinion. I believe that the nation as such must be destroyed, or, if this is not possible by tactical strikes, they shall be expelled operationally and by further methods from the country.[4]

The above quote contains one of the central contradictions at the heart of von Trotha's strategy. As had been argued by former Governor Leutwein and many early German farmers in the colony, destruction of the Herero was tantamount to economic folly.[5] In the previous chapter, we examined how many Herero had for the last decade played an important role as contract laborers in the rapidly expanding German colonial economy. The war's outbreak had already resulted in a largely diminished labor pool as many Herero had left work sites to join their fellow brethren in the war effort. For the Germans, the conflict created a subsequent increased demand for workers needed to carry out the mammoth undertaking of first transporting materiel and thousands of troops to the colony and then supporting them in combat. The military largely hired migrants as contract laborers, who were later joined by prisoner of war (POW) Herero and Nama forced laborers to fill the unskilled labor gap. Private industry, including companies involved in railway construction and port administration in the colony, would also expand operations employing some of the largest numbers of both migrants and forced laborers.

During the war, the German army would send around 19,000 troops to the colony from the metropole.[6] Soldiers came by ship from German ports and would land along the central coast of the colony at Swakopmund, and with the Nama polities' uprising by late 1904, also at Lüderitzbucht in the South. The German military operated across the expansive colony of GSWA including in veld, desert, and mountain terrain. For transportation, troops not only utilized the train line from Swakopmund to the capital, Windhoek, but they also relied largely on horses,

4 BArch, R 1001/2089, fol. 5f., Letter from Lothar von Trotha *Kommando der Kaiserlichen Schutztruppe* to the *Chef des Generalstabes der Armee*, 04.10.1904, 05. Translation to English by W.B. Lyon.

5 Bley, *Namibia under German Rule*, 79–80; Leutwein was not opposed to a 'struggle of annihilation' against the Herero if other means of submitting them to colonial rule were unsuccessful; see Häussler, *The Herero Genocide: War, Emotion, and Extreme Violence in Colonial Namibia*, 80–84.

6 Isabel V. Hull, *Absolute Destruction: Military Culture and the Practices of War in Imperial Germany* (Ithaca: Cornell University Press, 2005), 34.

camels, and ox-wagons to travel and be supplied across hundreds of kilometers of difficult terrain making up much of the arid colony.[7]

I argue that the capacity for the German military to travel to, disembark, deploy, receive provision, and fight within the colony of German South West Africa was only feasible with a 'human infrastructure' consisting of thousands of migrant laborers, most of them African, carrying out auxiliary, construction and transport jobs.[8] By 1905, as the war dragged on, many starving and desperate groups of Herero surrendered, were taken into prisoner of war camps, and were subsequently forced to labor for the government, private companies and the military. They were later joined in the camps by Nama. While forced labor made up a significant segment of necessary labor in the wartime economy, their work was confined to local jobs, sometimes in chains, whereby they could be kept in concentration camps and taken to work sites during the day. Furthermore, high mortality rates meant these workers made up a diminishing percentage of the workforce.

Migrant labor in particular filled demands for more skilled roles and those requiring mobility beyond specific locations. When confronting the colonial conundrum of how to supply labor to the colonial economy as mentioned in von Trotha's quote, the war and brutal extermination of Herero and Nama in the colony left no feasible alternative in the long term other than migrant laborers, who would eventually largely supplant locals as the majority of workers. Migrant workers – particularly from West Africa and South Africa – would also lay the foundation for what I have termed a 'labor elite' in German South West Africa, lasting from 1904 until WWI. These higher-paid and often higher-skilled laborers were joined by more numerous migrant workers coming from the Ovambo polities. Ovambo workers' expanding role in the colonial economy largely started during the war, and then increased dramatically with the opening of copper mines in the North and diamond mines in the South. The following chapter will cover the specific case of the Ovambo workers.

This chapter investigates the indispensable roles of skilled migrant laborers who provided the work necessary for the German war and wartime economy. Focusing on the increased demand for longshoremen in colonial ports and on transport ships, along with freight wagon drivers for military logistics, I scrutinize

---

7 For details on the importance of animal use during the war, see Martin Kalb, *Environing Empire: Nature, Infrastructure, and the Making of German Southwest Africa* (New York: Berghahn, 2022), 161, 171–72, 189–191, 200–201, 206–208.

8 The term 'human infrastructure' is a concept deriving from 'People as Infrustructure' developed by AbdouMaliq Simone in his analysis of social networks amongst and across various communities in Johannesburg, see AbdouMaliq Simone, "People as Infrastructure: Intersecting Fragments in Johannesburg," *Public Culture* 16, no. 3 (2004): 407–429.

their contributions within the larger conflict narrative – how they perceived the war and their place in a transitioning post-war colony, influencing demographic, economic, and industrial shifts in the region. While railway construction labor was pivotal to the colonial economy, it was peripheral to direct military support, with the exception of the expedient 'Otavibahn' train line, and the majority will be explored in subsequent chapters.

The colonial workforce from 1904 to 1908 was characterized by a dualistic labor strategy that employed both free and unfree labor, persisting until the concentration camps closed in 1908. In this period, free labor – relatively well paid and provisioned, often hired from beyond the settler zone – coexisted with Herero and Nama laborers who were conscripted into service under oppressive conditions. For clarity, 'free' labor refers to workers contracted voluntarily, with agreed wages and conditions, while 'unfree' labor (*Zwangsarbeiter*) denotes those coerced into work without consent, under slave-like circumstances or institutionalized violence.

In the broader African context, as Andreas Eckert notes, colonial powers, striving to make their territories economically profitable, frequently resorted to coercive measures to secure unfree labor.[9] Yet, in German South West Africa (GSWA), the unique element was the state-sanctioned genocide that precipitated a rapid shift in labor relations. This chapter illuminates what Stefano Bellucci terms "the grey zone between free and unfree labour" where even free laborers could find themselves in constrained circumstances – bound by employer coercion, subjected to violence, or trapped by economic dependencies.[10]

As we delve deeper, we'll see that migrant labor during this era, operating within an atmosphere of pervasive violence, had varied responses. Some openly criticized the treatment of Herero laborers, appealing to their governments, while others expressed fear for their safety, having witnessed the injuries and fatalities of fellow workers – victims not only of Nama and Herero combatants but also of German soldiers and white colonial military auxiliaries.

---

9 Andreas Eckert, "Wage Labour," in *General Labour History of Africa: Workers, Employers and Governments, 20th–21st Centuries*, ed. Stefano Bellucci and Andreas Eckert (Woodbridge: James Currey, 2019), 31–32; Stefano Bellucci, "Transport," in *General Labour History of Africa: Workers, Employers and Governments, 20th–21st Centuries*, ed. Stefano Bellucci and Andreas Eckert (Woodbridge: James Currey, 2019), 200.

10 Bellucci, "Transport," 201; On the topic of "free" vs. "unfree" labor in colonial Africa, as well as the often- fuzzy and shifting division between the two, see Brown and van der Linden, "Shifting Boundaries between Free and Unfree Labor"; Eckert and van der Linden, "New Perspectives on Workers and the History of Work," 150–151.

In structuring the narrative and analysis, I introduce the concept of 'migrant labor corridors' to describe the influx of workers to GSWA during this era.[11] The decline of the European labor supply, which had predominantly consisted of Italian workers until 1906, gave rise to three principal corridors that had been emerging since before 1904. These corridors became more pronounced and were firmly established by the war's end: the West African Labor Corridor, stemming from Liberia and its coastal neighbors; the South African Labor Corridor, rooted in the Cape Colony, notably the Ciskei and Transkei regions; and the Ovambo Labor Corridor, originating from the northern GSWA and southern Angola. Notably, the Ovambo corridor became the most prolific source of labor for the settler region.

By framing GSWA's labor dynamics within the broader context of these trans-colonial and trans-national flows, we can draw parallels between the colony's labor recruitment practices and those of other colonial administrations on the continent. This comparative approach reveals a shared colonial strategy across various territories – from Cameroon to the Gold Coast, French Equatorial Africa, São Tomé and Príncipe, South Africa, and German East Africa. These territories alike channeled labor towards burgeoning industries critical to capitalist expansion, such as gold mining, rubber extraction, cacao cultivation, and infrastructure projects, attracting workers from both local and distant lands.

Chronologically, in the first phase of the Namibian War, migrant workers would consist largely of West Africans, South Africans, and Italians. As the situation in the northern settler region tipped in favor of the German military by 1905, Ovambo migrants who had previously left worksites as the war began, would return to fill gaps in train line construction work, among other sectors.[12]

The evolving migrant labor work force mirrored a larger transformation of the economy. A government report from 1904 / 1905 noted that the colonial economy had essentially ground to a halt except for the construction of the Otavi railway, which had been deemed a military necessity, as well as the supplying of the German *Schutztruppe* and the settler population.[13] In particular, sectors such as colonial agriculture all but disappeared during the conflict, with most settler farms in the central region of the colony destroyed and cattle taken as the result of Herero raids. The German war damages committee in operation between 1904

11 For a visualization of the 'Namibian Labor Corridors,' see Figure 1.

12 Gregor Dobler, *Traders and Trade in Colonial Ovamboland, 1925–1990: Elite Formation and the Politics of Consumption under Indirect Rule and Apartheid* (Basel: Basler Afrika Bibliographien, 2014), 15.

13 Staats- und Universitätsbibliothek Bremen, Jahresbericht über die Entwickelung der Schutzgebiete in Afrika und der Südsee (Berlin: Mittler, 1906), HA 10 Ea 1502/10–1904/05, Einleitung, 7.

and 1906 estimated that the settler agriculture sector experienced £636,013 worth of damages, with £489,241 the result of cattle loses.[14] Agriculture would return, though it was other sectors which would take a much more prominent role in the economy by the end of the war and subsequent years: most notably mining. The construction of railway lines throughout the colony during the conflict was important in setting the foundation for the later expansion of the mining sectors. That is in terms of both transporting workers to the diamond mines in the south, as well as transporting ore from the copper mines in the north to the coast. Additionally, the post-war mining industry was made feasible by migrant labor, which quickly became most of the workforce in this industry. The wartime economy had resulted in the expansion of the migrant labor sector, including both the diversity of skill and background of those recruited, as well as creating new and strengthening old recruiting channels. Labor pools tapped for the 1904 to 1908 wartime economy transitioned into employment beyond military work as the war ended and the private sector resumed and expanded.

The escalation of migrant worker employment and recruitment during the war marks the transformation of GSWA into a hub for labor migration. From approximately 1904 to 1914, GSWA emerged as a destination of choice for workers from the three aforementioned migrant labor corridors. This development was a consequence of several factors: the availability of job opportunities, a reduced local African population resulting from genocide, comparatively better pay rates, and well-established recruitment networks managed by the German colonial government and private enterprises.

Moreover, the homelands of these workers were experiencing – or on the cusp of – transformations that made the prospects in GSWA more attractive for potential migrants seeking employment. While there has been extensive research on the migrant labor systems in early twentieth-century Southern Africa, particularly concerning the gold mines of the Rand and Rhodesia, as well as the diamond mines of Kimberley, this chapter, and the ones to follow, aim to integrate the experiences within German Southwest Africa into the broader narrative of African and, more specifically, Southern African labor history. We will start by looking at the Italian laborers in Namibia and the ephemeral worker corridor that ceased in the war's second year.

14 Paul Rohrbach, *Deutsche Kolonialwirtschaft. 1, Südwest-Afrika* (Berlin: Buchverlag der "Hilfe," 1907), 314–315.

The Failure of the European Labor Corridor: An Italian Job?

Construction of the Otavibahn, 1904–1905

> An Italian named Simon Antonio asked me urgently to be assigned to the big Krupp in Khan as he was afraid of the Hereros. I complied with his request and let him board the train to Karibib. At KM 196,5 the man suddenly shot with a revolver and wounded Oberleutenant Hermann. As Antonio was already running, a soldier Keißeling shot through Hermann and a native brakeman through the head so that the Italian fled and escaped. The sudden outbreak of a pursuit guard was considered to be the cause. I have already reported the incident to Captain Witt . . . .
>
> Gollhoffer [Director of Operations and Railway Maintenance on the State railway Swakopmund-Windhoek in German South West Africa][15]

> The Italian Simon Antonio was found yesterday evening with the wall building worker unit [*Maurertrupp*] at km 187, where he was arrested and delivered to the police authority at Karibib.
>
> Gollhofer. Regarding the deceased Simon Antonio [note at the bottom written afterwards][16]

These telegrams give a concise description of a fatal event in May of 1904 in GSWA. Simon Antonio was one of many Italian workers who had been hired to construct the *Otavibahn*, or Otavi Railway, and his fear was related to the fact that the train line was being constructed in an active war zone. Further, the sources point to the likelihood that he and others in his cohort were hired without prior knowledge of the conflict in the colony. Simon's request to transfer to Khan, where a German military unit and Krupp cannon were based, was sensible. His reason for firing on a German officer may have been related to his fear, desperation, and confusion after arriving in such a dangerous environment and fearing for his life.

This story in some ways encapsulates relations that existed between the over 1,000 mainly Italian and some Serbo-Croatian speaking workers (they will be referred to as they often labelled themselves while in the colony, i.e., the 'Italians') – from the Italian Kingdom, Switzerland and the Austro-Hungarian empire, who came to GSWA for contract work on the *Otavibahn* in early 1904 – and their Ger-

15 NAN, EVE [26] A.4.o vol 1, K. *Eisenbahn Verwaltung* (Sw.-Wi.), *Akten betr. Italienische Arbeiter*, Telegram from director Gollhofer to director Henning, 22.05.1904, 4. Translation to English by W.B. Lyon.

16 NAN, EVE [26] A.4.o vol 1, K. *Eisenbahn Verwaltung* (Sw.-Wi.), *Akten betr. Italienische Arbeiter*, Telegram from director Gollhofer to Windhoek, 27.05.1904, 5. Translation to English by W.B. Lyon. Details as to how or why Simon Antonio died, as mentioned in the note on the telegram, have yet to be found.

man employers. Relations between the Italian workers and their employers were often tense, with misunderstanding, fear, and occasionally violence being common states of affairs. As we will explore, their identity as southern European Catholics, amongst a largely protestant German settler population, meant they were often perceived as unequal in relation to other whites. Simultaneously, because of their status as Europeans, even when they were mistreated, they often received preferable outcomes to other contracted laborers who were black or mixed race. The Italian migrants' unique status within the colony, and inability to fit into the pre-defined racial and class categories of GSWA that further solidified during the war, were important grounds for the eventual collapse of the European Labor Corridor.

During the Italians' tenure in the colony, they would work in spurts broken up by strikes for better accommodation, treatment, and provisions. These included things such as a clean and steady water supply, and accommodation to avoid sleeping directly on the desert sand. While these workers proved very difficult for their employer, they also completed large segments of the railway between Swakopmund and Omaruru. Arriving in multiple waves from both Europe and South Africa starting in mid-1904 to early 1905, these workers were startled to find that they had arrived during a colonial war that had erupted with the Herero people.

The Italian government would, following worker complaints, send a representative to the colony in a largely unsuccessful attempt to improve the workers' situation. The Italians in GSWA would also become a topic of debate in the German Reichstag as well as a theme in Italian newspapers, where the German colonial administration was criticized for its treatment of the workforce. But why did Italian workers come to far-away German Southwest Africa and through what channels did they arrive?

From Italy to South West Africa

Arthur Koppel AG (hereafter referred to as Koppel), which had extensive experience constructing train lines in South Africa, the German colonies, and throughout the world, was contracted to build the *Otavibahn* by OMEG, which was in the process of opening its copper mine at Tsumeb.[17] Work on the railway began in

17 Sebastian Beese, *Experten der Erschließung: Akteure der deutschen Kolonialtechnik in Afrika und Europa 1890–1943* (Leiden: Brill Schöningh, 2021), 107–233; Mira Wilkins, "Multinational Enterprise to 1930: Discontinuities and Continuities," in *Leviathans: Multinational Corporations and*

late 1903. The firm had initially recruited Herero and other African workers for the construction, however the war's outbreak led to the abandonment of the work site as Herero left to join their kinsman in the war effort.[18] As the war raged in 1904, General Lothar von Trotha would prioritize the *Otavibahn* as a *Schnellbau*, or fast construction, to be used for strategic military purposes between the coast and Omaruru. This in turn meant that additional government funds were set aside to incentivize the quick construction via bonuses to Koppel in the case that speedy timelines were met.[19] With the train line construction now imbued with new importance because of the war, as well as additional profits to be made, Koppel turned to Italian subcontractors, who with experience building train infrastructure abroad, including in African colonies like the Congo Free State, seemed like a quick fix to the company's labor shortage issue.[20] Later Koppel would also recruit Italians directly for the project in partnership with the Italian government. Ads went out in various Italian newspapers, with promised wages (assuming six-day work weeks) at between £9 and £10 13/- per month, which were seen as attractive. Travel as well as provisions were also to be included in contracts.[21]

The first group of Italians, around 280, arrived in late April of 1904 under Italian subcontractor Luigi Zarossi, based in Swakopmund, who was then responsible for their provisions and payment.[22] Zarossi was financially backed by a Hamburg firm Th. & C. Möller that was primarily in the cigar trade but decided to participate in construction by financing Zarossi.[23] The company was making a gamble to diver-

the New Global History, ed. Alfred D. Chandler and Bruce Mazlish (Cambridge: Cambridge University Press, 2005), 45–79.

18 Mokopakgosi, "German Colonialism in Microcosm," 475.

19 VdR, Bd.: 202. 1903/05, Berlin, 1905, 130. Sitzung, Dr. Arendt (Freikonservative Partei), 31.01.1905, 4133.

20 Manu Karuka, *Empire's Tracks: Indigenous Nations, Chinese Workers, and the Transcontinental Railroad* (Berkeley: University of California Press, 2019), 41; Judith Schueler, *Materialising Identity the Co-Construction of the Gotthard Railway and Swiss National Identity*, Technology and European History Series 1 (Amsterdam: Aksant, 2008), 39; Jean-Luc Vellut, "Les bassins miniers de l'ancien Congo belge : essai d'histoire économique et sociale (1900–1960)," *Les cahiers du CEDAF*, no. 7 (1981): 1–70; Rosario Giordano and Elisabeth Mudimbe-Boyi, *Belges et italiens du Congo-Kinshasa : récits de vie avant et après l'indépendance* (Paris: L'Harmattan, 2008), 11–13.

21 NAN, BSW [57] XXII, Band II, Otavibahn, Advertisement in Italian newspapers: "ALLEGATO: ALLA DOMANDA SULL' ARRUOLAMENTO DI OPERAI PER LAVORI FERROVIARI NEL SUD-OVEST DELL'AFRICA," Rome, 17.8.1904, 192–193.

22 NAN, EVE [26] A.4.o vol. 3, Acta Italiener, contract between the Imperial government, Arthur Koppel and subcontractor Zarossi, 04.05.1904, Swakopmund, 34.

23 NAN, BSW [57] XXII, Band II, Otavibahn, Strike Zarossi und seiner italienischer Arbeiter, Letter to the governor of GSWA from Swakopmund Bezirksamtmann Fuchs, 10.09.1904, 115.

sify with the intention to cash in on the big money incentives offered by the military in exchange for quick construction. They had likely found Zarossi through their company representative Foscolo, also Italian, who was based in Swakopmund. Th. & C. Möller would later realize their investment to be a grave error as Luigi Zarossi would prove to be not only a bad subcontractor but an untrustworthy business partner.

The future challenges were symbolized in the arrival of the steamer with the first Italian workers onboard. A German officer on another ship waiting to offload at Swakopmund made the following observation of the transporter "Helen Woermann" writing:

> The people [Italians] shouted hurrah with enviable endurance, probably out of joy that they were to come ashore. As we heard, the captain of the ship had had a lot of trouble on the way with the rebellious company, and finally all German passengers on board had been armed with rifles to be able to counter a revolt of the Italians.[24]

A second wave of about 40 workers, originally from today's Croatia in the Austro-Hungarian empire, but at the time in Cape Town in South Africa, were hired directly by Koppel shortly after in late-May.[25] By August, a group of 150 men from Piedmont in northern Italy, working for a subcontractor by the name of Audibert would arrive from Italy.[26] Then by September another wave, recruited directly by Koppel from Italy of about 670 men put the total number over 1,100.[27]

Work, Strikes and Italian Interactions with Herero Forced Labor

From the experiences of the first Italians beginning work on the *Otavibahn*, it became clear that two underlying challenges for the new workforce – likely not fully understood upon recruitment – would always be present: namely, the physically demanding environment, and the fear of potential attack by Herero insurgents along the train line construction. The region east of Swakopmund along the planned

---

24 Erich von Salzmann, *Im Kampfe gegen die Herero* (Berlin: Dietrich Reimer, 1905), 34–35. Translation to English by W.B. Lyon.

25 NAN, BSW [57] XXII, Band II, Otavibahnbau, contract between Koppel and 40 workers, 30.05.1904, Cape Town, 72–73

26 NAN, OGW [68] *Generalia* XVI.2, *Kaiserliches Obergericht, General Akten betreffend Schiedsgericht mit italienischen Arbeitern*, Telegramm from Bezirksmann Dr. Fuchs in Swakopmund to Kiaserliches Gouvernement in Windhuk, 15.11.1904, 8.

27 NAN, BSW [57] XXII, Band II, Otavibahnbau, Arthur Koppel *Otavi-Eisenbahnbau* letter to the *Kaiserliche Bezirksamt* at Swakopmund, 15.08.1904, 81.

route was a harsh desert landscape for dozens of kilometers with almost no vegetation and water. Although there was a low chance of a Herero attack occurring at the worksite, the atmosphere amongst the workers in the early months was defined by fear. This was certainly a factor in the event related to Simon Antonio mentioned earlier. While construction would be undertaken, waves of progress were interspersed by strikes. Additionally, many unhappy workers abandoned the *Otavibahn* construction and went to work for employers in colonial towns, including Swakopmund, Windhoek and the railway hub of Karibib. This was attractive for artisans such as tailors and accomplished craftsmen, some of whom took work directly with the military for higher wages.[28]

For most Italian workers who stayed on the railway construction, many would partake in an early strike centered around a desire for better provisions, housing, wages, and police protection. Uneven power relations within the worker community also played a complicating role in the strike. Manipulation by the subcontractor Zarossi meant that many under him joined in the work stoppage without fully understanding that his intentions varied from theirs. In late August, Zorossi told Koppel he was bankrupt and had debt of £5,875. This, however, may have been a lie, as it seems that he was likely pocketing much of the money he was paid which should have gone to cover the needs of his workers. Although almost never taking personal responsibility, Zarossi was the reason behind much of his workers' woes, including not having proper housing and not receiving consistent water on the job.[29] He wanted to utilize the strike to divert attention from himself, and potentially to bring in more money. Once the strike began, he abandoned his workers, and in response they wrote to the government at Windhoek, distraught by their situation:

> We Italian workers ask for justice according to the existing laws. We have come with contracts signed . . . and we do not know for what reason the subcontractor Zarossi and Foscolo do not want us to work and threaten that those who work, will be prevented from doing so by the police. We obeyed, left work and followed the words of the subcontractor Zarossi, we went with him to the station at km 43 and stayed there waiting for him to settle accounts and to compensate for the damages to the contract. We waited from 24.8 to the 27.8 and he told us: "He who does not follow me, will lose all rights." We have expected him there, but we waited and he never arrived. Now we do not know why this is happening, and we turn to you Mr. Governor. The subcontractor Zarossi and Mr. Foscolo made promises we

28 NAN, EVE [26] A.4.o vol 1, K. *Eisenbahn Verwaltung* (Sw.-Wi.), *Akten betr. Italienische Arbeiter*, To the field command of the trains at Karibib from Buschmann, Swakopmund, 11.01.1905, 72.

29 NAN, BSW [57] XXII, Band II, Otavibahnbau, Arthur Koppel *Otavi-Eisenbahnbau* letter to the *Kaiserliche Bezirksamt* at Swakopmund, 15.08.1904; NAN, BSW [57] XXII, Band II, Otavibahn, Strike Zarossi und seiner italienischer Arbeiter, Letter to the governor of GSWA from Swakopmund Bezirksamtmann Fuchs, 10.09.1904, 115–116.

> didn't like, also the contracts were not signed in the presence of the workers . . . we were released from our contracts until further orders . . . .[30]

This plea reveals workers' frustration and the administrative chaos resulting from Zarossi which they faced. Many of these workers, disillusioned, eventually secured passage back to Europe. Their claims of ignorance regarding the strike's rationale likely served to elicit sympathy from the colonial administration in Windhoek, given Zarossi's contentious dealings with both the workers and the German government.

In the wake of Zarossi's failed contract with Koppel, efforts were made to rectify past errors. The subsequent batch of workers, arriving in September, was officially recruited through Italian channels and accompanied by Dr. Labriola, an Italian government inspector fluent in German, to ensure improved working conditions.[31] However, fresh challenges emerged with the arrival of another group under subcontractor Audibert. These Piedmontese workers, skilled tracklayers commanding higher wages for expedited work, soon initiated a strike over slow progress by preceding foundational teams, and inadequate provisions. Their success in negotiating new terms, facilitated by Labriola's mediation, marked a significant milestone in the colony's labor history since 1884. This success was likely influenced by their white identity, Italian government representation and high skill level, contrasting starkly with the treatment of contracted African workers.

Despite their achievements, the Italian laborers were not immune to the racial prejudices of the German settler community, who often viewed Southern Europeans condescendingly – a sentiment echoed in the treatment of Italian workers in Rhodesia and Nyasaland during the 1950s.[32] Simultaneously, their white identity played a crucial role in sparing them from the violent suppressions directed at African-led strikes, as later events at Wilhelmstal would demonstrate.[33] As the war progressed, the Italians increasingly found themselves working alongside forced POW labor, raising questions about their interactions and relationships with these forced laborers within the colonial labor system.

---

30 NAN, BSW [57] XXII, Band II, Otavibahnbau, letter to the Government of German South West Africa from 'all workers' (contracted by Zarossi), 01.09.1904, 130. Translation to English by W.B. Lyon.

31 NAN, BSW [57] XXII, Band II, Otavibahnbau, Letter to the *Kaiserliche Gouvernement in Windhoek* from *Kaiserliche Bezirksamtmann* (Swakopmund) *Fuchs*, Betrifft: Otawibahn. Im Anschluss an meinen Bericht vom 10.09.1904, 162.

32 Julia Tischler, *Light and Power for a Multiracial Nation: The Kariba Dam Scheme in the Central African Federation* (Basingstoke: Palgrave Macmillan, 2013), 156–159.

33 See Chapter 4, "The Karibib to Windhoek Wide-Gauge Line, the Wilhelmstal Massacre, and its Repercussions, 1910–1911."

In the following letter from Italian-speaking Austro-Hungarians sent to their consul in South Africa, we find hints of their interactions with African laborers. After writing complaints about having to pay for various provisions and housing, the letter states the following:

> Here in Swakopmund, three men have been punished by the head of construction for the worst work, which is usually only done by the captured Herero women, for the simple reason: The three men were ordered to Km 71 to readjust the track, with about 72 natives; there was an order to move to Km 96; they worked all day; at 5:30 in the evening the train came to take them away . . . . All the provisions and equipment had to be put on (the train), at 2:00 in the morning they arrived at Km 96; until everything was unloaded, it might be about 3 o'clock in the morning. They had eaten nothing or only a little the whole day and night, other than cold corned beef there was no other food; they made a fire and remained until daylight, the tent was not yet pitched, an order came to work, but they decidedly refused to work because they labored all night . . . if you work at night you want to have rest during the day, especially if you do not get paid overtime. The Koppel company has us by the throat.[34]

In this letter we can see that some Italians were undertaking strenuous night shifts and work was conducted alongside Africans, who were likely Ovambo, or else Herero forced laborers. The reference to Herero woman POWs typically doing the most brutal work in Swakopmund is telling of the division of labor. A Herero Headman, Traugott Tjienda, was a forced laborer on the Otavi railway and gave the following account:

> I was made to work on the Otavi line which was being built. We were not paid for our work, we were regarded as prisoners. I worked for two years without pay . . . . As our people came in from the bush they were made to work at once, they were merely skin and bones, they were so thin that one could see through their bones they looked like broomsticks. Bad as they were, they were made to work; and whether they worked or were lazy they were repeatedly sjambokked by the German overseers. The soldiers guarded us at night in big compounds made of thorn bushes. I was a kind of foreman over the labourers. I had 528 people, all Hereros, in my work party. Of these 148 died while working on the line. The Herero women were compounded with the men. They were made to do manual labour as well. They did not carry the heavy rails, but they had to load and unload wagons and trucks and to work with picks and shovels. The totals above given include women and children . . . . When our women were prisoners on the railway work they were compelled to cohabit with soldiers and white railway labourers. The fact that a woman was married was no protection. Young girls were raped and very badly used. They were taken out of the compounds into the bush and there assaulted. I don't think any of them escaped this, except the older ones.[35]

---

34 NAN, BSW [57] XXII, Band II, Otavibahnbau, Letter from Albert Antonelli, Kolling P., Franz Dlauhy, Karl Fritz and Bader Josef to the Austro-Hungarian consulate at Cape Town, 02.02.1905, 222. Translation to English by W.B. Lyon.

35 Silvester and Gewald, *Words Cannot Be Found*, 178.

Traugott's account is in stark contrast to the Italian experiences of adversity. While the Herero were undergoing slave-like conditions as forced laborers on the *Otavibahn*, the Italians were comparatively free. However, they often considered their work conditions substandard and hence their willingness to go on strike. An inability to easily leave the colony, or to find other work in GSWA, meant that they were on the spectrum of free labor, but with restrictions making their situation less free than say for German engineers working on the project. Such extremes in treatment by the colonial state and experiences of work were common during the war. Beyond working hours, what was life like for the Italian workers in German South West Africa?

Macaroni and Cheap Wine: A Day in the Life

Figure 8: Italian workers on strike joined by black workers, likely Ovambo, to take a photo, circa 1904.[36]

36 BADKGUBFM, Photo: A_00T_3096.

The photograph above (Figure 8) captures a candid moment of leisure among striking railway construction workers, both Italians and likely Ovambos, highlighting common pastimes like beer drinking and music, evidenced by the presence of a guitar and mandolin. The individuals perched in the tree suggest a relaxed atmosphere during the strike. Ovambo workers, like those pictured, played a significant part of the Otavibahn workforce alongside the Italians. As of September 1904, the composition of the Otavibahn's non-forced labor workers included approximately 1,100 white managers and workers, of which 900 to 950 were Italian, with others hailing from Austria, Germany, Serbia, and Montenegro, alongside about 500 free black workers, mostly Ovambo.[37] The photo also depicts a telling detail of the era's racial dynamics, with white workers standing and black workers typically positioned kneeling or sitting. Although the historical records are silent on the extent of social interactions between Italian and Ovambo workers, this image may subtly hint at some level of solidarity, perhaps even during strikes, although there's no explicit mention of such in written accounts. Intriguingly, anecdotes like that of Batista Oldani, an Italian worker who remained in GSWA and integrated into local African society, suggest that social mingling, while uncommon, was not unheard of.[38]

Turning to dietary habits, Italian workers had distinct preferences, favoring staples like macaroni noodles, rice, cheese, bacon, bread, coffee, and inexpensive wine, alongside the already mentioned beer. Notably, they showed a disinterest in the wheat beer popular among the German population.[39] Beyond their culinary choices, socializing across different white ethnicities did occur in private settings. An incident involving such an intercultural gathering, which took an unexpected turn, is detailed in the following account.

On May 8, 1905, in Omaruru, three Italians, an American and two Germans were at a hotel room drinking. One of the Germans named Tenner was a salesman and the other, Rockenhäuser was a laborer for the *Otavibahn*. The Italians were most likely his co-workers. The American's profession is unclear, but he

37 NAN, BSW [57] XXII, Band II, *Otavibahnbau, letter to the Kaiserliche Gouvernement in Windhoek from Kaiserliche Bezirksamtmann (Swakopmund) Fuchs, Betrifft: Otawibahn. Im Anschluss an meinen Bericht vom 10.09.1904, 166.*

38 NAN, SPO [011] 2/0/0411, District-Commandant, Police District No. 53, Omaruru, War: Emergency Measures (Secret), page not numbered.

39 *NAN, BSW [57] XXII, Band II, Otavibahnbau, letter to the Kaiserliche Gouvernement in Windhuk from Kaiserliche Bezirksamtmann (Swakopmund) Fuchs, Betrifft: Otawibahn. Im Anschluss an meinen Bericht vom 10.09.1904, 162.*

may have also worked for the railway. These men, after some time imbibing became very tipsy and Rockenhäuser began to berate the Italians. Tensions ran high and a fight seemed inevitable. Tenner tried to get Rockenhäuser to stop his insults but in response, one of the Italians, brown haired, mustachioed, and wearing a gray suit, grabbed a beer bottle and threatened to throw it at his assailant. Tenner took Rockenhäuser outside, but he continued his verbal onslaught within hearing distance of his targets. The three Italians were told to leave and as they went, the man in the gray suit threw a bottle, hitting Rockenhäuser in the head and leaving him unconscious. Tenner ran to get water for the wound and in the meantime the culprit and his comrades left without being identified. After some time, Rockenhäuser was roused from his state and told to sit at a table where he later passed out. The next day, the injured man was taken to a hospital, but he would later die of an infection from the wound.[40]

This incident not only reflects the underlying tensions between Germans and Italians in the colony, but also illustrates the varied worker dynamics within the free Otavi workforce. This singular event, while extreme, sheds light on the potential animosities and social complexities among workers of different hierarchies and nationalities. However, it's important to note that such confrontations were exceptions rather than the norm, with more amicable interactions typically prevailing, as exemplified by the restaurant *Trattoria Internazionale* (Figure 9) in Swakopmund, a popular gathering spot among the Italian community. Perhaps it was visited by the worker whose life we will explore in detail below.

Stepping into the life story of Carlo Colla, we uncover a unique window into the experiences of the Italian migrant workers in GSWA. Born in 1867, Colla's journey from the Tyrolean town of Ronchi to the heart of German Southwest Africa offers a poignant example of the diverse backgrounds and destinies that intersected in this colonial setting. Standing at average height, with an oval face framed by chestnut hair and gray eyes, he carried with him an Austro-Hungarian passport, identifying him as a day laborer. Intriguingly, the passport also bears notes in the margins, indicating a history of military tax payments from 1887 to 1891, possibly a substitute for conscription. This aspect of his life draws parallels

40 NAN, GSW [372] D 245/05, *Akten des Kaiserlichen Bezirks-Gerichts zu Swakopmund, Strafsache gegen Unbekannt (Italiener), Beglaubigte Abschrift der Aussage von Wilhelm Tenner Omaruru, 16.09.1905*, 2–3; NAN, GSW [372] D 245/05, *Akten des Kaiserlichen Bezirks-Gerichts zu Swakopmund, Strafsache gegen Unbekannt (Italiener),* Letter from the *Kaiserliche Bezirksrichter* to the *Ortspolizeibehörde* in Jakalswater, 12.

Figure 9: Italian guesthouse in Swakopmund circa 1904–1905.[41]

with Oswald Natalini, another Italian on the Otavibahn, who not only served in the Italian military but also later expressed a willingness to fight in WWI.[42]

Carlo's documents show that he received his passport in 1901 to travel to Germany, Italy, France, and Switzerland. Further, stamps on his passport also hint that he visited Spain and Buenos Aires, Argentina.[43] It would not have been uncommon if Carlo had worked in these various countries doing labor similar to what he undertook in GSWA. Between 1876 and 1914, six million Italians worked in other European countries. Four million migrated beyond Europe, most cyclically to the USA and Canada. Three million travelled to Argentina, Brazil and other countries in South America. Others less in number worked in North and South Africa and in Asia. In total migrants of this period from Italy were about 1/3

41 BADKGUBFM, Photo: A_00T_3096, *Gasthause der Italiener*.

42 NAN, ADM [51] 675/5, Repatriation General, (1) Indigent Italians in SW Africa (2) Italians –employment of–, Secretary of the Protectorate Herbst to the Italian Consul in Johannesburg regarding Oswald Natalini 02.11.1917.

43 NAN, NLA [19] C.5, Kaiserl. Bezirksgericht Windhuk, Akten betreffen Nachlaß des am 4. Februar 1906 in Windhuk verstorben von Carlo Colla, Passport of Carlo Colla, 10–12.

of Italy's 1911 population.[44] It is therefore not surprising that highly mobile workers, like Carlo Colla, seem to have been common amongst the Italians in GSWA. A later report from the South African occupying forces in WWI notes that the Italian Victorio Di Centra, came to GSWA twice in the first decade of the twentieth century interspersed by time spent in the USA.[45] While it is uncertain what jobs Colla undertook between 1901 and 1904, he potentially had been working in mining, as a later document from the colony notes this as his profession.[46]

Whatever employment Carlo had found throughout Europe and South America, by early-1904 at the age of 36, he had a contract for construction of the *Otavibahn*, beginning in late April of that year. He arrived with the first tranche of Italian speakers to the colony at Swakopmund under the management of Zarossi. By May 6, Carlo was one of 111 workers still on the job that had taken up direct contracts with the train administration instead of continuing work under Zarossi. Twenty-six others continued to strike for higher pay. Likely to lessen the chance of strikes spreading to their new employment with the train administration, the workers were dispersed at different stations along the previously constructed Swakopmund-Windhoek rail line. Carlo himself was one of four placed at the materials depot in Swakopmund. There, it is probable that he and four other comrades labored to load ox- and train wagons to supply the construction site. According to records, he worked at the main magazine depot in Swakopmund until at least early June 1904.[47] While some, like Carlo continued to work for the government, others left worksites without permission to return to Zarossi, or they departed the colony altogether, leaving government officials in disarray.[48] Colla, however, continued to work for the military in GSWA and by November of 1905, he had transferred to the interior receiving permission to work in and around the colonial capital, Windhoek.[49]

Related to Carlo Colla's job transfer, his estate file contains registration with the Windhoek police including a work permit. Such requirements were typically

44 Donna R. Gabaccia, "Worker Internationalism and Italian Labor Migration, 1870–1914," *International Labor and Working-Class History* 45 (1994): 64.

45 NAN, ADM [51] 675/5, Repatriation General, (1) Indigent Italians in SW Africa (2) Italians –employment of–, To work permit officer regarding Mr. Victorio Di Centa, 12.04.1918.

46 NAN, EVE [26] A.4.0 vol 3, Acta Italiener, *Verzeichnis der beim Proviant Depot beschäftigten Arbeiter* 26.05.1904, 40.

47 NAN, EVE [26] A.4.0 vol 3, Acta Italiener, *Nachweisung* über die Verteilung der Italienischen Arbeiter 6.05.1904, 43c–44

48 NAN, EVE [26] A.4.0 vol 3, Acta Italiener, To the management of the field railway (Otavi) from Gollhofer and Lange, Swakopmund 10–11.09.1904, 51.

49 NAN, NLA [19] C.5, Handakten zum Nachlaß des verstorbenen Arbeiters Carlo Colla, Carlo Colla registration with the Windhuk Bezirksamt, 7.12.1905, unnumbered.

only required of non-white workers, highlighting the restrictions placed on Italians within the stratified colonial society. While not made formal through law, Colla's registration displays that Italian workers' capacity to move and find work was regulated in a similar manner to non-whites. Though their time in the colony was largely transitory, Italian presence also raised alarms amongst Germans in GSWA. Matthias Häussler notes that the Italian workers' arrival caused displeasure amongst the settler community, mirroring their feelings toward Coloured workers from the Cape Colony.[50] Colla's work permit requirements are an additional detail highlighting how Italians were not accepted in the settler society.

Despite the German community's disdain, during this period of war workers like Carlo were needed by the military. Carlo Colla's work transfer at the end of 1905 was to a stone quarry for the German military's construction branch. After this point details are relatively scarce, but he died on the February 4, 1906. His file mysteriously does not seem to list the cause of his death. While uncertain, this could point to a work incident. Carlo's possessions found on his person when he died ranged from an old weapon, to boots, a mirror and about £14 in cash.[51] Records also show that his estate included both backpay from the military as well as bank accounts in both Southern Africa and Europe totaling around £150.[52] This amount of money was exponentially more than, say, the average liquid assets of Ovambo migrant laborers in the colonial economy at the time, who typically had less than a pound to their name.[53]

As for the assets of other Italian workers in the colony, records beyond pay rates are rare. The few estate files on Italians in the colony which note total assets show at least one other that had assets over £100 in 1918, and another (who died in the late 1920s) had a kingly sum of around £1,800.[54] However, being both a

50 Häussler, *The Herero Genocide*, 38, fn. 59.

51 NAN, NLA [19] C.5, Handakten zum Nachlaß des verstorbenen Arbeiters Carlo Colla, Letter from the *Militär-Baukreis* to the *Kiaserliche Bezirksamt Windhuk* 24.03.1906, 2; NAN, NLA [19] C.5, Kaiserl. Bezirksgericht Windhuk, Handakten zum Nachlaß des verstorbenen Arbeiters Carlo Colla, Verzeichnis der in der Nachlaßsache Carlo Colla am 12. Mai 1906 erbschriftmäßig ersteigerten Gegenstände, 3.

52 NAN, NLA [19] C.5, Handakten zum Nachlaß des verstorbenen Arbeiters Carlo Colla, Nachlass-Konto (Credit) for Carlo Colla, 23.

53 Lyon, "From Labour Elites to Garveyites," 45.

54 NAN, ADM [51] 675/5, Repatriation General, (1) Indigent Italians in SW Africa (2) Italians –employment of–, Letter to Pretoria from the South African Occupational Government in SWA regarding Victorio di Centa's request to go to South Africa for work, 17.04.1918; NAN EST [788] 854 Estate of the Late Agide Giacomelli (Italian), Certificate No. 854 of Estate of the late Agide Giacomelli Transfer, 21.06.1929; NAN, EST [788] 854 Estate of the Late Agide Giacomelli (Italian), First Liquidation and Distribution Account in the Estate of the Late Agide Giacomelli (No. 854), 2.

very small sample size and a group that stayed in the colony beyond 1905, they were likely much wealthier than most of the other contract Italian laborers in the colony between 1904 and 1905. While individual experiences and stories such as Carlo Colla's give insight into this group of migrant laborers and their place within the wartime economy, the early challenges this work force faced had consequences beyond southern Africa.

Repercussions from Windhoek to Rome and Berlin

In 1904 and 1905, the often-turbulent situation of Italians in GSWA, especially in relation to Zarossi, sent shockwaves back to Europe. In early October 1904, the Rome newspaper *Il Giornale d'Italia* wrote an article highlighting the misdeeds against the Italians in the colony. It stressed their claims of being lured to Swakopmund and promised fine work but instead when they arrived, Zarossi broke his contract with them. Furthermore, their conditions, according to the article, had been horrendous. It went on to highlight that they were not paid their due wages, and that the *Woermann-Linie* would not offer them discounted return ticket rates which were promised, and the prices were unpayable. When, some who decided to return to Europe were able to get tickets, they were forced to return to Hamburg and then go by land back to Italy.[55]

By February 1905, the topic was brought to the floor of the Reichstag as the tenuous situation had resulted in waves of strikes by Italians in the colony. August Bebel of the SPD said the following:

> I am unable to assert that these complaints are justified; but the fact that they are being voiced prompts me to raise them here. When we consider social reform, I assume that we are also obligated to provide an existence that can be considered humane for foreign workers to whom entrepreneurs in German territories provide work, who are required to manage enterprises at the behest and in the interest of the German government.[56]

In response to Bebel, the colonial department would claim that Italian complaints were overblown and that the challenges came down to Zarossi and his failings. The situation had complex origins and blame certainly could be placed at the feet of many beyond Zarossi, including Koppel and the military administration in the colony. Over the following years, most Italians would leave GSWA, many with dashed expectations of conditions and pay while in the colony. While the Italian government attempted on multiple occasions to intervene on their behalf, in 1905

55 VdR, Bd.: 202. 1903/05, Berlin, 1905, 131. Sitzung, Bebel (SPD), 01.02.1905, 4180–4181.
56 VdR, Bd.: 202. 1903/05, Berlin, 1905, 131. Sitzung, Bebel (SPD), 01.02.1905, 4181.

their representative for the workers in the colony, Dr. Labriola, would leave for work elsewhere. Austro-Hungarian workers, as previously quoted, had launched complaints to their consulate in South Africa with little effect on changing conditions.[57] Luigi Zarossi would flee to Canada where he would set up a bank and swindle more unwitting Italian migrants out of their money. A clerk at his financial institution, who learned from Zarossi was Carlo Ponzi, the man who gave birth to the so-called Ponzi scheme.[58] Luigi's misdeeds had spread to the Western hemisphere.

But in German Southwest Africa, the decision by Koppel to recruit Italian labor largely ended by 1906 and the employment of other migrant workers in the settler region proved a more stable long-term solution for labor shortages in the wartime economy. Let us now turn our attention to those workers recruited primarily in Liberia.

The West African Labor Corridor: Supplying the German War Effort

Beginning in the 1890s, West African Kru workers became a significant presence along the coast of German Southwest Africa, notably at the burgeoning offloading site that would evolve into Swakopmund.[59] However, their involvement in what would later become German territories dates back even further. As early as the mid-nineteenth century, before the formation of the German empire in 1871, Kru labor was extensively utilized by companies from cities that would subsequently be incorporated into Germany. Among these, Hamburg-based firms, especially the prominent *Woermann-Linie*, were notable for their reliance on Kru workers.[60] By the mid-1880s, with the establishment of the German overseas African empire, the recruitment of laborers from Liberia, particularly the Kru and Vai peoples, had become a cornerstone of the empire's economic framework.

The Kru, alongside other migrant labor groups such as craftsmen from Accra and Hausa soldiers from Lagos, played a pivotal role in the colonial economies across West Africa. Their presence was not limited to German territories but ex-

57 NAN, BSW *[57] XXII, Band II, Otavibahnbau,* Letter to the Austro-Hungarian Consulate in Capetown from Albert Antonelli, Kolling P., Franz Dlauhy, Karl Fritz, Bader Josep, 02.02.1905, 220–223.

58 'Charged with Forgery,' The Gazette (Montreal, Quebec, Canada), 15.02.1908, 3.

59 See Chapter 1, "Between Ship and Shore: Early Swakopmund Longshore workers."

60 For a detailed look at the *Woermann-Linie* and their business relations as well as labor practice during the war, see Todzi, *Unternehmen Weltaneignung*, 356–381.

tended to other African colonies including the Gold Coast, Congo, Angola, and Fernando Po.[61] Tristan Oestermann posits that the very fabric of colonial rule in West Africa was interwoven with the contributions of these migrant workers.[62] Yet, the reliance on Kru labor varied across regions. For instance, in Cameroon, the Vai labor from Liberia was gradually supplanted by local workers in the early 1900s. However, in German Southwest Africa, the outbreak of war in 1904 intensified the colony's dependency on Kru labor. Max Dinklage asserts – and I concur in my research – that the effective operation of GSWA's ports and, by extension, the German war effort, hinged on the Kru workforce.[63]

In the following sections, we will delve into the daily realities of West African laborers, both en route to GSWA and within the colony, including their interactions with forced laborers. But first, it is crucial to understand how Kru labor became so integral to GSWA's wartime economy. While many Atlantic coast colonies in Africa relied on Liberian labor during the late nineteenth and early twentieth centuries, the specific dynamics of the German-Liberian economic relationship warrant closer examination. Additionally, we must consider the role GSWA played within this broader labor landscape.

An overview of Liberian-German economic relations in the early twentieth century mirrors in part the increasingly important role Germany played in West African trade.[64] By the early twentieth century, two in three steamships in Liberian ports were German, and Germany controlled most trade with the Republic.[65] This mirrored the situation in the nearby British colonies of Southern Nigeria and the Gold Coast. For example, the German share of the export trade from Lagos in

---

61 Mark-Thiesen, *Mediators, Contract Men, and Colonial Capital*, 52–54; Martin, "Krumen 'Down the Coast,'" 405; Ibrahim K. Sundiata, "The Rise and Decline of Kru Power: Fernando Po in the Nineteenth Century," *Liberian Studies Journal* 6, no. 1 (1975): 25–41; Ibrahim K. Sundiata, *From Slaving to Neoslavery: The Bight of Biafra and Fernando Po in the Era of Abolition, 1827–1930* (Madison: University of Wisconsin Press, 1996), 129; Enrique Martino, *Touts: Recruiting Indentured Labor in the Gulf of Guinea* (Berlin: De Gruyter Oldenbourg, 2022), 32–56; William J. Samarin, *The Black Man's Burden: African Colonial Labor On The Congo And Ubangi Rivers, 1880–1900* (Boulder: Westview Press, 1989), 30–34; Brooks, *The Kru Mariner in the Nineteenth Century*, 52–56.

62 Tristan Oestermann, *Kautschuk und Arbeit in Kamerun unter deutscher Kolonialherrschaft 1880–1913*, Industrielle Welt (Cologne: Böhlau Verlag, 2023), 155–157.

63 Max Dinklage, *Liberia in seiner Bedeutung für Deutschlands Handel und zukünftige Versorgung* (Hamburg: Hamburg Boysen, 1918), 10.

64 A. Olorunfemi, "West Africa and Anglo-German Trade Rivalry 1895–1914," *Journal of the Historical Society of Nigeria* 11, no. 1/2 (1981): 25–29.

65 E. Forbes, "The Land of the White Helmet," 230, in George William Brown, *The Economic History of Liberia* (Washington, DC: The Associated Publishers, Inc., 1941).

1905 was 65 percent.[66] In 1904, the year in which the war began in GSWA, Liberia's largest trading partner was Germany, with £103,365 worth of imports. For comparison, Liberia's second largest trading partner Holland, was responsible for £72,355 worth of imports.[67]

Regarding the presence of white Europeans in the country, Max Dinklage, a joint proprietor of Woermann in Liberia, noted that most were merchants and of the total white population two thirds were German.[68] Further the Woermann company in particular had deep local roots, with stores at all entry ports, branches throughout the interior and traders in the hinterland.[69] In 1905, the second year of the conflict in GSWA, Woermann and the other German firms operating in Liberia, made up between 83 and 90 percent of foreign trade.[70] By the early 1900s, Woermann's presence in the country dated back more than fifty years. According to company reports, this was a prominent reason as to why the company could successfully recruit so many Kru during the colonial war in GSWA.[71]

Many of the West Africans working for *Woermann-Linie* during the war came from coastal Kru communities facing increasing pressure from the Liberian central government in Monrovia to conform to their tax and labor laws. These aimed at bringing the Kru coast and indigenous Liberian communities under more direct regulation from the government in Monrovia.[72] Incentives to work and stay abroad were increasing by the late-nineteenth century in Liberia as migrants didn't wish to pay sizable sums to the government and elders in home communities upon returning.[73] German shipping and port work from 1904 to 1908 and into the post-war period offered a lifeline of continued economic independence and opportunities. Such labor was also often more lucrative and had preferable shorter contracts than labor on West African plantations and mines. As conditions in GSWA during the war were difficult, in particular at Swakopmund, *Woer-*

66 Olorunfemi, "West Africa and Anglo-German Trade Rivalry 1895–1914," 27.

67 Sir Harry Johnston, "Liberia," Annual Report of the Board of Regents of the Smithsonian Institution, 1905, 250, in Brown, *The Economic History of Liberia*, 159; Wolfe W. Schmokel, "Liberia, Germany, Britain and the United States, 1905–1918" (unpublished paper, Burlington, VT, 1976), Frederick Dean McEvoy Collection, 1956–1979, Box 1, Publications and Manuscripts, Liberian Collections, Indiana University.

68 Dinklage, *Liberia in seiner Bedeutung*, 2.

69 Brown, *The Economic History of Liberia*, 159.

70 Oestermann, *Kautschuk und Arbeit in Kamerun*, 167–168.

71 BArch, R 1001/1865a Hafenanlage in Swakopmund, Woermann-Linie während des Aufstandes, 10.

72 Martin, "Krumen 'Down the Coast,'" 416–418.

73 Gunn, *Outsourcing African Labor*, 215.

mann-Linie paid higher wages in comparison to other job opportunities.[74] From the employer perspective, the war and related labor needs, as well as profits accrued handling military shipping and transport, meant *Woermann-Linie* was more willing to pay "the substantial two dollar fee" to the Liberian government for each recruit.[75] Levies demanded by Monrovia had been rising since the 1880s when such recruitment fees had been one dollar.[76] Regardless, *Woermann-Linie* maintained close economic ties with Liberia, and in 1903 the government gave the firm near-monopolistic rights for migrant labor recruitment. This played a major role in their successful finding and hiring of so many Kru during this period.[77]

Woermann-Linie's early twentieth-century economic success in Liberia, long relations with Kru communities and recruitment of their young men, as well as the company's experience by the beginning of 1904 in servicing the GSWA ports, laid a clear path to their dominance in shipping to the colony between 1904 and 1908. A German Colonial Department memo remarked in 1906 that *Woermann-Linie* controlled almost all shipping traffic to German West African colonies and South West Africa.[78] Further, the fleeing of most local workers in the colony in January of 1904 from the German ports made the necessity to recruit a large migrant maritime workforce all the more clear.

The Kru at Sea

Let us briefly review the overall numbers of Kru workers who made up a human infrastructure of laborers at the heart of the German empire's maritime shipping during the colonial war in early twentieth century GSWA. Over the course of the conflict working for *Woermann-Linie*'s landing operations in German Southwest Africa, 12,000 Kru would be hired. At Swakopmund alone, 1,200 would work on the shore and on ships that were being offloaded. As the result of the constant shifts in the amount of goods offloaded based on the German military's demand,

74 BArch, R 1001/1865a Hafenanlage in Swakopmund, Woermann-Linie während des Aufstandes, 24; Kru contract lengths in West and Central Africa could often be two years; see Brooks, *The Kru Mariner in the Nineteenth Century*, 45.

75 Enrique Martino, "Touts and Despots: Recruiting Assemblages of Contract Labour in Fernando Pó and the Gulf of Guinea, 1858–1979" (PhD thesis, Berlin, Humboldt University, 2016), 53.

76 Samarin, *The Black Man's Burden*, 32.

77 Oestermann, *Kautschuk und Arbeit in Kamerun*, 183.

78 BArch, R 1001/1865a Hafenanlage in Swakopmund, Auftrag zur Untersuchung der Hafenverhältnisse in Swakopmund, Report by construction director Kummer, 3.10.1906, 72.

the numbers of Kru workers in the colony was constantly in flux and exact numbers cannot be given for each year during the war.[79] However, no less than 21,233 Kru worked for *Woermann-Linie* steamers between 1904 and 1906 or on average over 10,600 during the first years of the conflict.[80] This is an increase to the average from the previous years, where Kru recruits had been around 8,000 to 8,500 annually.[81] Such large numbers of hires were not guaranteed and Kru, similar to other workers in the 'Namibian Labor Corridors,' used the high demand for their labor to petition for better working conditions and pay. A Kru strike in 1900/1901 resulted in wages for workers aboard Woermann ships to increase from about 1/- per day to 1/5d or essentially a 50 percent increase. A later four-month strike in 1903 in Monrovia attempted to increase daily wages to between 4/- and 8/- but was unsuccessful. The workers involved in the strike were temporarily barred from hiring and the headmen permanently. Importantly, partial wage substitution and general support by Kru women in Monrovia was essential in allowing for the Kru strikes.[82]

On most *Woermann-Linie* ships, while the number of Kru men likely fluctuated based on the supply of willing contract takers during the war, each vessel normally had about 150 Kru working on board. This was not only important to run the ships while at sea, but it also could be essential when longshore hands at port were not sufficient. In fact, in negotiations between *Woermann-Linie*, the military and the port administration at Swakopmund, the 150 Kru workers aboard each ship were considered essential to offload them. Conversely, chartered vessels from other shipping lines, which did not have Kru workers aboard, were discouraged from offloading at Swakopmund port.[83] An event that exemplified their critical nature aboard the ships occurred in November of 1904 in Lüderitzbucht when the port first saw a jump in incoming cargo. The harbor was overwhelmed with ships, and the arriving steamer *Hans Woermann* found it was not able to dock. However, the ship was guided by a recently arrived *Woermann-Linie* representative onshore and bypassed the bottleneck. The *Hans Woermann* offloaded at Robertshafen where no harbor infrastructure yet existed utilizing its Kru workers, surf boats and equipment on-

79 *Landungsverhältnisse in Swakopmund*, in Neue Hamburgische Börsen-Halle, 26.9.1904.

80 Dinklage, *Liberia in seiner Bedeutung*, 10.

81 BArch, R 1001/3229, *Kaiserlich deutsches Konsulat*. Monrovia. 20.2.1903, 163.

82 Todzi, *Unternehmen Weltaneignung*, 317.

83 BArch, R 1001/1865a Hafenanlage in Swakopmund, Abschrift zu K.A. 13354/04 Anlage 1, Swakopmund, 22.08.1904, 4–5.

board.[84] Workers on ships, in particular at Swakopmund, were assisted by a large group of Liberians onshore.

In the first year of the war and throughout the rest of the conflict, the port of Swakopmund was contracted out to *Woermann-Linie* where the company employed its single largest Kru contingent. This group of workers would wax and wane but the 1,200 referenced above was likely employed between the mole sanding in by late 1904 and the completion of a wooden pier in April of 1905.[85] The number of longshore workers on the beach also referenced by *Woermann-Linie* in their report on the war that may have been more typical, was between 400 and 600 men.[86] A reason for such large discrepancies may have been the number of ships offloading with Kru workers on board in combination with how many Kru were based at the port. As explored in the previous chapter, working conditions at Swakopmund were harsh and recruitment in West Africa was not easy. But the work undertaken during the war was on a much larger scale compared to the port labor prior to the conflict. Further, because of their necessity as a wartime workforce, those who took the contracts to work on the beach at Swakopmund were paid higher wages in comparison to other jobs. As a result, despite constant fears by the administration, sufficient workers could often be hired.[87]

After the wood pier was constructed by the military, *Woermann-Linie* and the German command believed that perhaps Kru workers would not be necessary and could be replaced by Ovambo and forced Herero laborers. However, this was proven to be false and Kru workers were still needed as certain supplies such as cattle, hay and wood necessitated offloading via rafts beached on the shore.[88] Despite their higher cost of employment, challenges in hiring, and the need to return workers after contracts to various locations along the West African coast, Kru labor's irreplaceability as a skilled and efficient workforce at Swakopmund meant their continued employment throughout the war. But what was the wartime labor situation at the other colonial port of Lüderitzbucht, where a natural harbor existed?

84 BArch, R 1001/1865a Hafenanlage in Swakopmund, Woermann-Linie während des Aufstandes, 32.
85 BArch, R 1001/1865a Hafenanlage in Swakopmund, Woermann-Linie während des Aufstandes, 25.
86 BArch, R 1001/1865a Hafenanlage in Swakopmund, Woermann-Linie während des Aufstandes, *39, 23.*
87 BArch, R 1001/1865a Hafenanlage in Swakopmund, Woermann-Linie während des Aufstandes, 24.
88 BArch, R 1001/1865a Hafenanlage in Swakopmund, Auftrag zur Untersuchung der Hafenverhältnisse in Swakopmund, Kolonial Abteilung by Fischer, 10.1906, Das derzeitige Lade- und Löschgeschäft, 15.

In late September 1904, with the Witbooi and much of the Nama joining the Herero in the uprising against the colonizers, the German military increased its presence and operations in the South.[89] As the only colonial port in southern GSWA, Lüderitzbucht became a main artery whereby German troops and supplies entered the south of the colony. In 1904 the port was run by the *Lüderitzbucht-Gesellschaft L. Scholz & Co*, a subsidiary of DKGfSWA, but this company soon became unable to handle the increase in shipping.[90] The German military first looked to take over operations, but by early 1905 they turned to *Woermann-Linie* to run the port.[91] While sources on the workforce manning the harbor early in the war are not abundant, it seems to be clear that until at least May 1906, according to Woermann, only "expensive" white workers were able to be employed.[92] This is potentially related to their quasi-subcontractor relationship with *Lüderitzbucht-Gesellschaft L. Scholz & Co* brokered via the military. The employment situation likely eventually changed. A statistic from January 1910 references 60 Kru living at Lüderitzbucht.[93] While this number was taken after the conflict subsided, the continued presence of Woermann in the town and references to Kru there point to an evolution of the workforce. While the port during the war was less reliant on West African labor than Swakopmund, the prior reference to the *Hans Woermann* offloading portrayed Kru ship hands as likely a necessary workforce at Lüderitzbucht. To understand what reality was like for West African workers during the war, let us first explore ship life followed by experiences for those based on shore. We will glimpse aspects of work, daily life, relations with soldiers, fellow contract workers and forced laborers.

---

89 Some Nama *Kapteins*, such as Jacob Morenga and Abraham Morris, had already engaged in guerrilla warfare against the Germans starting in 1903; see Werner Hillebrecht, "The Nama and the War in the South," in *Genocide in German South-West Africa: The Colonial War of 1904–1908 and Its Aftermath*, ed. Jürgen Zimmerer and Joachim Zeller (Monmouth: Merlin Press, 2008), 143–158; Ludwig Helbig and Werner Hillebrecht, *The Witbooi* (Windhoek: Cass, Longman Namibia, 1992), 45.

90 Jäckel, *Die Landgesellschaften in den deutschen Schutzgebieten Denkschrift zur Kolonialen Landfrage*, 186.

91 BArch, R 1001/1865a Hafenanlage in Swakopmund, Woermann-Linie während des Aufstandes, 35–36.

92 BArch, R 1001/1865a Hafenanlage in Swakopmund, Woermann-Linie während des Aufstandes, 38–39.

93 Hermann Thomsen, *Deutsches Land in Africa* (Munich: Verlag der Deutschen Alpenzeitung, 1911), 112.

Ship Life

Figure 10: Two Kru workers hired at Monrovia, Liberia aboard the steamer Entre Rios of the Hamburg-Südamerikanische Dampfschiffsgesellschaft in route to Swakopmund, GSWA.[94]

The photograph above (Figure 10), taken aboard the *Entre Rios* of the Hamburg-Südamerikanische Dampfschiffsgesellschaft (contracted by the *Woermann-Linie*) in April 1904, captures a rare and candid moment in the lives of two Kru workers. This image stands apart from the conventional colonial propaganda photography of the era, which often depicted African individuals in artificially constructed 'natural habitats' as imagined by European perspectives. Unlike many such photographs that either showcased the state's power through images of captives and criminals or glorified the industriousness of African laborers, this photo eschews such narratives.

Brent Harris has argued that colonial photographs of the 'other,' particularly Africans, were usually staged in 'natural' settings, meticulously crafted to project the colonial gaze for acquiring knowledge, often with an undercurrent of exoticism.[95] However, in the maritime context, Kru workers were integral to the machinery of capitalist industrial labor, making them perhaps less appealing subjects

94 The photo was taken by the German soldier Erich von Salzmann in mid-April 1904; NAN, Photo 24732, 'Kru Boys' by von Salzmann.
95 Harris, "Photography in Colonial Discourse," 21.

for photographers seeking the perceived exotic allure often associated with colonial imagery. This makes the photograph in question particularly intriguing, as it centers on Kru men in a state of rest, a stark departure from the more common depictions of Kru laborers as minor figures within larger scenes, typically engaged in strenuous activities like manning surf boats or unloading cargo on shores.

In the image itself we see two individuals who are young and at rest on a ship deck. The man closest to the camera is wearing loose fitting pants, and both have on vests and caps.[96] The men's employment on a wartime transport steamer reflects the common trajectory of many in Kru communities at the time. Adolescent males left their communities in West Africa for contract work with a general understanding that they would return to West Africa and bring with them a share of their earnings to their headmen, family, and elders.[97] As we shall see in later chapters, some Kru working in GSWA would buck these trends and stay for long periods, others indefinitely.[98]

On April 12, 1904, the men in the photo above (Figure 10), along with about 98 other contracted Kru boarded the *Entre Rios* via surf boats while the ship was at anchor in Monrovia, Liberia. Adult men were accompanied by many young boys, in makeshift shirts, who assisted loading boxes and crates on the ship. They were constantly hiding while the ship was at anchor, likely because their presence was not wanted. Von Salzmann mentions that the Kru chatted, swore, and smoked while moving about the ship. In addition to those busy loading the vessel with new cargo, post card sellers were on deck hawking their wares to the German soldiers and ship's company. Having Kru selling goods on the ship deck while taking on new recruits seems to have not been an uncommon practice.[99] A few Liberians of African American descent, some of whom were themselves captains in the Liberian Navy also visited the ship, taking the opportunity to enjoy some German beer in the mess hall.[100] Von Salzmann, who was an officer in the German military and was in close contact with the captain and others in charge of the ship, noted that prior to leaving harbor in Hamburg, the *Entre Rios* put out a request to the *Woermann-Linie*'s office in Monrovia to hire 100 Kru workers.

96 According to a German account, one piece of attire most Kru aboard ship did not wear was shoes; see Salzmann, *Im Kampfe gegen die Herero*, 34.
97 D. Frost, *Work and Community among West African Migrant Workers since the Nineteenth Century* (Liverpool: Liverpool University Press, 1999), 67.
98 See Chapter 5, "The Fall of the Kru Labor Elite and Challenges Under South African Rule."
99 Brooks, *The Kru Mariner in the Nineteenth Century*, 28.
100 Salzmann, *Im Kampfe gegen die Herero*, 23.

Highlighting their scarcity, the ship only expected 50 to be available, however 100 indeed were secured to work on the ship.[101]

The arrival of workers on the *Entre Rios* was overseen by representatives from the Liberian government, who played a crucial role in the labor recruitment process. The Liberian government capitalized on this opportunity by charging a recruitment fee of 3/9d per worker, amounting to a total of £19 just for those recruited for this particular journey. The ship's success in fulfilling its labor quota of 100 workers can be partly attributed to Captain Ihrke, a representative of the *Woermann-Linie*, who was known to have established strong rapport with the Kru community. Upon boarding the ship at Monrovia with the Kru workers, Captain Ihrke was warmly welcomed as a familiar and trusted figure.

This incident is indicative of the longstanding and deep-seated relationships that many *Woermann-Linie* managers had fostered with the Kru community over the years. A poignant example from 1921, in the aftermath of WWI, further illustrates this bond. During this period, when Woermann's operations in much of West Africa had been disrupted, representative Kurt Woermann embarked on a journey to reestablish the company's presence in the region. On this trip, he encountered a Kru chief named 'Toby,' whose allegiance to the Woermann company was demonstrated by his men, who proudly displayed a Woermann flag on their surf boat. Toby, emphasizing the long-standing working relationship between his community and the company, was keen on ensuring continued employment opportunities for his people. This enduring connection was further symbolized by Toby's son, who was buried in a casket made of German oak and draped with the Woermann flag.[102]

The workers hired by the *Entre Rios* were led by headman 'teapot' (his alias), who was employed as an overseer. Perhaps a comment on his long experience on European ships, it was noted that his English was very good. The steamer raised its anchor in Monrovia to continue to its destination and none of the Kru workforce jumped overboard, which on occasion occurred, as they were very capable swimmers and could easily do so if a job did not suit them.[103] Among the contingent were the two men pictured below, described as 'washers' at work on the *Entre Rios*. But, unfortunately, we are not given any additional information as to who they are, including their names.

---

101 Salzmann, *Im Kampfe gegen die Herero*, 22.

102 Dirk Bavendamm and C. Woermann GmbH und Co, *150 Jahre C. Woermann. Wagnis Westafrika. Die Geschichte eines Hamburger Handelshauses 1837–1987* (Hamburg: Verl. Hanseat. Merkur, 1987), 119–120.

103 Frost, *Work and Community among West African Migrant Workers since the Nineteenth Century*, 71.

Figure 11: Kru men working on deck. They were hired in Monrovia, Liberia on contract for the steamer Entre Rios of the Hamburg-Südamerikanische Dampfschiffsgesellschaft in route to Swakopmund, GSWA.[104]

The nicknames of workers, at least in communication with their European counterparts, were an important marker of Kru aboard German ships and an adaptation in passing between their community and that of the soldiers and German crewmates. They, like many Kru men of the late nineteenth and early twentieth century would take aliases discussed in Chapter 1, such as 'teapot,' which were adapted from European languages spoken by their employers. Aboard the *Entre Rios*, Erich von Salzmann writes of men who call themselves 'Bismarck,' 'Kameruner,' and 'Schwein.' One can deduce that in the case of these ship hands, their names were decided upon via a mixture of German they had picked up through their work, and occasionally names bestowed upon them, often with a dose of derision, over the course of their work on ships. Their aliases, coming from a mixture of European languages, hint at many Kru men's linguistic skills. A later observation from 1911 in Lüderitzbucht about African residents of the town, which included Kru, described numerous of them conversing with white residents in German.[105] Those from Kru communities often spoke the Kru language, but because so many were recruited from Kru migrant communities in largely English-speaking West African towns, such as Monrovia, pidgin English was com-

104 The photo was taken by the German soldier Erich von Salzmann in mid-April 1904; NAN, Photo 24734, '*Wäscher an Bord des Entre Rios*' by von Salzmann.
105 Thomsen, *Deutsches Land in Africa*, 112.

mon.[106] In fact, on wartime transport ships, pidgin English may have been a *lingua franca* for the workforce as von Salzmann references the language being frequently heard.

Jobs aboard the steamer varied; including washing and ironing as can be seen in Figure 11, caring for animal cargo such as horses (1,200 were on the *Entre Rios*), working in the engine room, mess room, or kitchen. Transporting horses was very important for the war effort and not including sub-contracted ships like the *Entre Rios*, the *Woermann-Linie* imported 10,999 horses on 30 ships between 1904 and 1906.[107] Von Salzmann remarks that Kru ship hands particularly respected the horses as they were relatively rare in Liberia.[108] Upon arriving at anchor off of Swakopmund, the Kru spent a day cleaning and scrubbing.[109] Before we delve into the labor involved in offloading a ship, life on board wartime vessels also included leisure.

While steaming to German South West Africa, the soldiers aboard *Entre Rios* often listened to a gramophone during meals in the mess hall. It was in fact used so often that by the time the ship reached Tenerife, their first stop on their way south, the gramophone was already beginning to malfunction playing "painfully lamentable sounds." Soldiers on board also entertained themselves by playing card games such as skat.[110] While similar details for Kru onboard their ship are lacking, later records do exist for Kru, who were aboard the ship *Steiermark* of the Hamburg-Amerika-Linie, all of whom were forced to disembark by the German military at Lüderitzbucht at the beginning of World War One. One such man, Bob Brown was listed as having a gramophone among his possessions.[111] Other records of Kru in GSWA catalogue the possession of musical instruments among personal belongings, with harmonicas and guitars being commonplace.[112] Further, following WWI, South African officials would often complain that the Kru population in the colony were inveterate gamblers.[113] While these remarks

106 SSS, (with the permission of Mr. Adolf Brock), unpublished Manuscript, E. Brock, *Reiserinnerungen, Afrikareise* 10.11.1903–08.05.1904, 3.

107 BArch, R 1001/1865a Hafenanlage in Swakopmund, Die Woermann-Linie während des Aufstandes in Deutsch-Südwest-Afrika, Anlage 2.

108 Salzmann, *Im Kampfe gegen die Herero*, 25.

109 Salzmann, *Im Kampfe gegen die Herero*, 25. Translation to English by W.B. Lyon.

110 Salzmann, *Im Kampfe gegen die Herero*, 14.

111 NAN, ADM [238] SWAKOP 264/9 Claims of certain Krooboys and other Natives, Bob Brown Kroo Boy.

112 NAN, BLU [146] G.5.a., Estate items of Kru Pieter, 66–67.

113 NAN, SWAA A492/2, Magistrate, Luderity- Secretary. 26/4/20 in Emmett, *Popular Resistance and the Roots of Nationalism in Namibia*, 139.

and records come more than a decade after 1904, it is likely that both playing cards and listening to or playing music were entertainment for Kru deck hands.

Though interactions between Kru and German shipmates where only in passing or on the job, one event brought a few together, the ancient line-crossing ceremony. This occurs upon crossing the equator, whereby the uninitiated go through a ritual. Aboard the *Entre Rios* the induction was undertaken for uninitiated officers and non-commissioned officers. Von Salzmann recounts:

> At 3 o'clock Neptune and Thetis arrived with their entourage and greeted the baptized with a speech in verse, then they went to the baptismal pool, which was formed by a sailcloth full of sea water hung over trestles. In the basin stood . . . two colorfully painted negroes who probably thought the whole thing was a main and state action. Now we were called one by one, received our baptismal names, were soaped up, shaved with a giant wooden knife and then transported backwards into the cool waters. Under resounding laughter, one went after the other, Neptune was inexorable.[114]

Most Kru onboard and likely those involved in the ceremony had been on far many more ships crossing the equator than the German soldiers, therefore they may very well have known that the event was not serious. Nevertheless, the personal account shines a light onto what may have occurred on other military transports at the time.[115] Steaming south from the equator, those on board had a week before they reached their destination. Eight days after taking on supplies and deckhands in Monrovia, the *Entre Rios* was 'in the roads' (*auf Reede liegen*) off Swakopmund on April 20, 1904. Both ports in GSWA, but in particular Swakopmund, required ships to wait offshore using their steam power to remain in location and wait until they could be unloaded. During the busiest periods of the war when the mole was out of operation this could take weeks.

By April 22, the vessel could begin offloading. Although at this time the mole was still largely operational, transport ships had to remain offshore as lighters and smaller boats would move supplies between the ship and the mole. While a later August agreement between *Woermann-Linie*, the port authority and the military would require *Woermann-Linie* to have four tugboats, 12 lighters, five barges, four rafts and 24 surf boats at Swakopmund, the port infrastructure in April was not as robust.[116] In late April, Swakopmund harbor had only one functioning tugboat, the *Pioneer*, at its disposal and it pulled a lighter between *Entre Rios* and the

114 Salzmann, *Im Kampfe gegen die Herero*, 26.
115 The author also went through a very similar ceremony when crossing the equator on a ship in 2008. This ceremony is not only quite old but also continues in the modern era.
116 BArch, R 1001/1865a Hafenanlage in Swakopmund, Abschrift zu K.A. 13354/04, Anlage 1, Swakopmund, den 22.08.1904, 37.

mole. The ship cleared some of the horse stalls on deck to create space for the offloading process. The first of the 1,200 horses on board were fit with large belts that went under their chest and the animals were then lifted by steam winch from the ship deck onto the lighter, which could fit 20 at a time (See Figure 12 below). The Kru deck hands became quite efficient and by the end of the day offloaded over 320 horses. Throughout the process the workers were very cautious of the horses stepping on their bare feet as some animals understandably became frantic in the disembarkation process.[117] Within a few days the ship was offloaded of its cargo of horses, troops, and supplies. Other ships brought additional types of animals including cattle, oxen, mules, and donkeys.

Figure 12: Using the steam crane to transport military horses from smaller vessels onto the mole in 1904. This photo does not portray the offloading of the Entre Rios but gives an idea of how animals were brought onto shore.[118]

Work animals, as well as cattle for consumption in the colony were limited and therefore many had to be imported on ships like the *Entre Rios*. They came not only from Germany but also South Africa and as far afield as South America. For

117 Salzmann, *Im Kampfe gegen die Herero*, 34.
118 BADKGUBFM, Photo: A_00H_1147, 1904, Swakopmund: Landung von Pferden bei der Mole.

example, at the war's outset, the army purchased 500 horses and 500 mules from Argentina with the first 100 arriving in February of 1904.[119] Most horses were for mounted troops, while oxen, mules, and donkeys were used to transport military supplies, provisions and water.[120] Many oxen from South Africa were also shipped with wagons and accompanied by drivers and cattle hands.[121] Some cattle were imported to be slaughtered and eaten especially as herds maintained by settlers in the north of the colony were mostly taken by the Herero early in the war.[122]

Whether offloading animals, troops, or supplies, the process soon slowed down in Swakopmund by June 1904. It was at this point when an increase in ships with cattle and feed from South Africa in particular, coincided with the worsening sanding in of the mole. Subsequently, the landing beach had to be reopened and manned by Kru longshoremen. Two Woermann ships had extreme delays, with the *Emilie Woermann* having to wait eight weeks and the *Ascan Woermann* an astounding 11 weeks. Further, at that time of year the beach itself was not always usable because of unfavorable weather conditions. On board the *Emilie Woermann* a large percentage of its Kru deck hands became ill as a result of the weather and its inability to go ashore. The extreme delay eventually meant that the vessel, including its cargo for the *Otavibahn*, had to return to Europe without offloading.[123] For non-Woermann ships that had to wait, the *Woermann-Linie* in charge of the port had to pay demurrage, or the cost to cover the crew, coal and maintaining the ships at sea while off the coast. This took a toll on the company's profits with the worst period of 1904 seeing 16 ships simultaneously 'in the roads' waiting to unload at Swakopmund.[124]

119 BArch, R 1001/1865a Hafenanlage in Swakopmund, Die Woermann-Linie während des Aufstandes in Deutsch-Südwest-Afrika, 8; Preußen / Großer Generalstab, *Die Kämpfe der deutschen Truppen in Südwestafrika. 1, Der Feldzug gegen die Hereros / auf Grund amtlichen Materials bearb. von der Kriegsgeschichtlichen Abteilung I des Großen Generalstabes*, vol. 1 (Berlin: Mittler, 1906), 60.

120 Kurd Schwabe, *Der Krieg in Deutsch-Südwestafrika 1904–1906* (Berlin: Weller, 1907), 193; Paul Eckardt, *Zwei Kriegsjahre beim südwestafrikanischen Train* (Berlin: Deutscher Kolonial-Verl., 1909), 18–22; Preußen / Großer Generalstab, *Die Kämpfe der deutschen Truppen in Südwestafrika. 1*, 1:200.

121 CA, NA 556, Statement by Isaac Magadi regarding the death of Robert Honose, Kronstadt, 22.04.1905.

122 BArch, R 1001/1865a Hafenanlage in Swakopmund, Die Woermann-Linie während des Aufstandes in Deutsch-Südwest-Afrika, 9–13.

123 BArch, R 1001/1865a Hafenanlage in Swakopmund, Die Woermann-Linie während des Aufstandes in Deutsch-Südwest-Afrika, 21–23.

124 BArch, R 1001/1865a Hafenanlage in Swakopmund, Die Woermann-Linie während des Aufstandes in Deutsch-Südwest-Afrika, 46; For more on Woermann-line's issues with demurrage during the war, see Todzi, *Unternehmen Weltaneignung*, 381.

As we shift our focus from the maritime challenges to the onshore activities at the Port of Swakopmund, it becomes evident that the dynamics of labor there were even more complex. The next section delves into the intricate interplay of free and unfree labor that characterized the port's operations, providing a deeper understanding of the labor landscape during this tumultuous period.

On Shore: Port of Swakopmund's Free and Un-free Labor Force

Figure 13: Kru workers offloading hay at Swakopmund in 1905.[125]

Above we see a photo (Figure 13) of shore-based Kru laborers employed by the *Woermann-Linie* unloading a raft full of hay for livestock in 1905 at Swakopmund after the wooden pier was fully operational. It is easy to see how this form of work could lead to workers getting sick. Notice the diversity of clothes the workers were wearing, especially hats which range from top hats to military caps and skull caps. Between the

125 NAN, Photo 05040, *Kruneger ziehen tief im Wasser stehend ein Floss mit Pressheu heran*, Swakopmund 1905', Provenance: A.0109, Stuhlmann.

raft and the pier in the background we see a black line which is likely the cable connected to a steam winch on shore used to pull in and beach rafts loaded with cargo.

The Kru based at Swakopmund had some of the most difficult work conditions for contracted free laborers during the war. As highlighted in the previous chapter, manning surf boats was not only dangerous work, but also required a high level of boat knowledge, strength and quick decision making in difficult ocean conditions.[126] As of 1904, Kru workers also assisted in a diversity of other roles including unloading beached rafts as seen above (Figure 13), offloading cargo at the mole, moving and bringing materiel to the supply depot, and as of 1905, working on the pier. More complex work included operating winches and loading and maneuvering train wagons and steam engines. Their skill as winch operators was so highly valued that a later record from nearby South African controlled Walvis Bay in 1925 stated that the government recruited 25 Kru from West Africa instead of hiring whites for the job because they would need to learn how to do their work from the expert Kru.[127] As shipments increased in 1905 and the pier became operational, the *Woermann-Linie* was concerned that there was too much non-skilled work that the Kru workforce was having to undertake.

Unskilled labor had mainly been undertaken by Herero and Ovambo workers at Swakopmund's beach before January 1904.[128] With the outbreak of the war they had left, putting more demand on the Kru. The *Woermann-Linie* attempted to again recruit Ovambo labor but had little success and by mid-1905 instead turned to forced labor.[129] The company put out an early request during the conflict to the government and company documents stating the following: "It had therefore been the goal of the landing operation management from the very beginning to get captured natives (*gefangene Eingeborene)* transferred in order to free the Kru workers for only boat work at the old landing place."[130] The company was even willing to pay full wages (all of which would go to the government rather than forced laborers) but the wish could initially not be fulfilled because there were not enough POWs. Once there were enough, forced laborers were transferred for use by the *Woermann-Linie* at the port. The company paid out of

---

126 See Chapter 1, "Between Ship and Shore: Early Swakopmund Longshore workers."

127 NAN, SWAA A492/2. SA Railways, Windhoek-Secretary, 30/11/25. See also Native Commissioner-Secretary, 6/5/22 from Emmett, *Popular Resistance and the Roots of Nationalism in Namibia*, 139.

128 'Deutsch-Südwestafrika,' DKZ, 43, 23.10.1902, 413; Sander, *Geschichte der Deutschen Kolonial-Gesellschaft für Südwest-Afrika*, 138.

129 BArch, R 1001/1865a, Protocol of a discussion between Adolph Woermann, Major Lequis, lieutenant commander Connemann und Dr. Müller, Swakopmund 22.8.1904, 39.

130 BArch, R 1001/1865a Hafenanlage in Swakopmund, Die Woermann-Linie während des Aufstandes in Deutsch-Südwest-Afrika, 24. Translation to English by W.B. Lyon.

its own expenses to buy tracks from the *Otavibahn* to install on the beach to more "intensively use their forced labor."[131] Seemingly the tracks were to allow for more supplies to be transferred between the shore and the military depot.[132] The forced labor not only consisted of men but also many women and children. Below (Figure 14) we see Herero women forced laborers pushing a wagon on the tracks referenced above on the beach at Swakopmund.

Figure 14: Herero forced laborers on the beach at Swakopmund, 1905–1906, pushing a train car; to the right of the women notice the tracks that Woermann-Linie installed specifically to take advantage of unskilled forced laborers for beach work.[133]

131 *"Sobald aber der Woermann-Linie die Überweisung von Gefangenen in Aussicht gestellt wurde, liess sie, trotzdem dies nach ihrem Vertrage Sache Fiskus war, für ihre Rechnung Geleise, die sie von den Beständen der Otavibahn kaufte, nach dem Strande legen, um diesen intensiv ausnutzen zu können"* from BArch, R 1001/1865a Hafenanlage in Swakopmund, Die Woermann-Linie während des Aufstandes in Deutsch-Südwest-Afrika, 24.

132 The company also paid to install a second steam winch on shore to bring in rafts loaded with cattle likely as an attempt to increase efficiencies of work on the beach; see BArch, R 1001/1865a Hafenanlage in Swakopmund, Die Woermann-Linie während des Aufstandes in Deutsch-Südwest-Afrika, 24.

133 NAN, Photo 25522. Provenance: A.0109, Stuhlmann.

In the photo above (Figure 14) we can see around eight Herero forced laborer women, pushing a train wagon, perhaps filled with wood as can be seen to the right, likely for building housing. They are likely headed from the beach to one of the outdoor storage locations run by *Woermann-Linie*, or the military. The woman second from the right looks as if she is coughing or collapsing. In the distance many ships can be seen waiting to offload their goods, troops and animals. In the top left we can see a beached surf boat, often used by Kru employees, and behind that what may be a tugboat going between the weighting freighters and the mole or pier. From 1905 until 1908, they and thousands of other captured or surrendered Herero and Nama were used to fill unskilled labor gaps in the colonial economy. As highlighted in the work of Kim Todzi, *Woermann-Linie* was one of the largest users of forced laborers at Swakopmund. In January 1905, the German military transferred 200 forced laborers to the company and in April another 115. Almost one tenth of workers in Swakopmund were forced laborers by this time.[134] From 1905 until the end of the war, unskilled forced labor was the other side of the coin from skilled Kru and white labor in enabling *Woermann-Linie* to handle such large imports during the conflict.[135] Life for forced laborers, who were mainly housed in concentration camps (some owned and operated by companies like *Woermann-Linie*) was inhumane and for many simply unbearable. A church document from 1905 describes the horrors:

> [At the beginning of 1905] . . . there [in the Swakopmund camp] were only very few Herero there (rebellion!). Soon, however, large transports of prisoners of war arrived. These were accommodated in miserable spaces made only of sackcloth and laths and set up behind double barbed wire which enclosed the whole area of the port authority dockyard. They were forced to live 30 to 50 people to a room without distinction of age or sex. On Sundays and holidays as well as workdays, from the early morning until late in the evening, they had to work till they dropped under the cudgels of brutal overseers. Their food was worse than meagre: For bodies weakened by life in the field and used to the hot sun of the interior, rice with nothing added was not sufficient to stand the cold and the unceasing exertion of all their energies in Swakopmund captivity. Hundreds were driven to their deaths like cattle and like cattle they were buried.[136]

134 VEM, RMG, Bericht Heinrich Vedders über die Situation der Afrikaner*innen in Swakopmund, Swakopmund 27.3.1905, 63; Landungsverhältnisse in Swakopmund, in: Neue Hamburgische Börsen-Halle, 26.9.1904 in Todzi, *Unternehmen Weltaneignung*, 377.

135 Todzi, *Unternehmen Weltaneignung*, 378–379.

136 ELCRN, Windhoek, C.V.31, Gemeinde Chronik, Swakopmund, 6 on.

Such circumstances for POWs were common. Despite high death rates of forced laborers at *Woermann-Linie*'s concentration camp at about 5.2 percent in late April to May 1905, the rates were still lower than at the main government concentration camp over the same period, at about 14.1 percent.[137] This is likely closely tied to economic interests, in that *Woermann-Linie* wanted its workers, whether free or forced, to live to carry out their job. Similar conditions are mirrored in another large private company in the colony, OMEG, which employed over 2,000 forced laborers for the Otavi train line construction, including 700 women and 620 children.[138] Records for forced workers list no escapees as well as no work on Sundays.[139] For *Woermann-Linie*, the same cannot be said. Workers would occasionally flee to nearby British controlled Walvis Bay. On one occasion, the company blamed missionary Heinrich Vedder of the Rhenish Mission Society (RMG), claiming that his church service, given to its forced Herero labor workforce in December 1906, allowed the workers to plan and later carry out an escape. Vedder denied the charge, but the company asked that missionaries not return to its concentration camp, in practice banning church services.[140] Clearly as of mid-1905, forced labor in GSWA was a growing segment of the workforce, including for Woermann, but how might these workers have interacted with 'free labor' in Swakopmund? Below we see the two coming into direct contact.

Below (Figure 15) we see *Woermann-Linie* surf boats manned by Kru taking aboard Herero prisoners of war at Swakopmund. Due to increasing demand for labor in the south at Lüderitzbucht to expand the harbor, hundreds of Herero forced laborers were transported from Swakopmund's government concentration

137 Jonas Kreienbaum, *"Ein trauriges Fiasko": koloniale Konzentrationslager im südlichen Afrika, 1900–1908*, Studien zur Gewaltgeschichte des 20. Jahrhunderts (Hamburg: Hamburger Edition, 2015), 223–224.

138 H. Drechsler, *Südwestafrika unter deutscher Kolonialherrschaft: der Kampf der Herero und Nama gegen den deutschen Imperialismus, 1884–1915* (Berlin, DDR: Akademie-Verlag, 1966), 299.

139 Zeller, "'Ombepera i koza – the cold is killing me," 73–74.

140 Archive of the Vereinten Evangelischen Mission Wuppertal-Barmen (BRMG), C/h 45a, Missionar Vedder, Swakopmund, to the Rhenisch Missionary Society, Letter from 31.12.1906, in Andreas Heinrich Bühler, *Der Namaaufstand gegen die deutsche Kolonialherrschaft in Namibia von 1904 bis 1913* (Frankfurt am Main: IKO – Verl. für Interkulturelle Kommunikation, 2003), 343.

Figure 15: Photo of a what are likely Woermann-Linie surf boats manned by Kru workers loading Herero prisoners from around 1905/1906 (note the completed wooden pier).[141]

camp to the southern colonial port.[142] The Herero in this image are about to be brought to a transport ship, and then to the notorious Shark Island concentration camp at Lüderitzbucht. At the end of the surf boat closest to the camera we can see one Kru worker and on the opposite end around four assisting with the lowering of more Herero aboard via a steam crane. This must have been an incredibly tragic moment for these Herero, as prisoners knew well of the wretched conditions at Shark Island. Not all chose to go, as missionary Heinrich Vedder recalled one Herero man who decided to cut his own throat and bleed out on the beach at Swakopmund rather than leave for Shark Island.[143] Others toiled on, whether in Swakopmund or in Lüderitzbucht with many dying of fatigue rather than suicide.

141 BADKGUBFM, Photo: A_00H_1192.

142 Casper Wulff Erichsen, "Forced Labour in the Concentration Camp on Shark Island," in *Genocide in German South-West Africa*, ed. Jürgen Zimmerer and Joachim Zeller (Monmouth: Merlin Press, 2008), 86–87.

143 Heinrich Vedder, *Kurze Geschichten aus einem langen Leben* (Verlag d. Rhein. Missions-Gesellschaft, 1953), 139.

A document that gives us some otherwise lost details of both forced and migrant labor in Swakopmund is the so-called "death registry for natives." It theoretically includes all non-white men, women, and children, who passed away in Swakopmund between July 27, 1905, and February 27, 1906. Those catalogued in the Swakopmund native death registry include individuals who had been working for the *Woermann-Linie* but also for a variety of other companies, as well as the government, and military.

The list is littered with forced laborers who died of "exhaustion due to privation."[144] The death registry includes some early colonial pass markers in Swakopmund. This method of tracking and identifying is part of what Jürgen Zimmerer points out was the colonial state's evolution towards more surveillance and control over the non-white population, first locally starting as early as the 1890s, and then as of 1907 with the 'Master and Servant Ordinance' colony wide.[145] Further, the register brings the entire African community in and around Swakopmund under one lens. In doing so the colonial bureaucracy did not distinguish between forced and free labor in noting mortalities.

The registry is a snapshot in time, one that is certainly incomplete, but nevertheless gives us valuable details. It was a period of extreme depravity and horrors for POWs, but others also died during this period as well. Therefore, it is worth us taking a deeper look. The Swakopmund 'death registry for natives' lists around 434 fatalities (See Table 1), which comprise people who had been laborers, both forced and contracted.

For those 232 who died in the concentration camps, listed as Herero (*Hererolager*) and 'native' (*Eingeborenenlager*), around 97 percent listed the cause of death as exhaustion (*Entkräftung*). Perhaps most tragic, about one third were 12-years-old or younger, and over 60 percent were women. Names are also occasionally included, giving details of humanity to the many unknown (*unbekannt)* entries. Two who died in the camps are named, both Herero soldiers (*Kriegsgefangene*), the 24-year-old Leonhard Katjunde, and 25-year-old Kawissassa, both of whom died of scurvy.

The registry also includes many forced laborers who died on the job, mainly Herero but also some Nama, with most laboring at the Port Authority (23), the mili-

144 Gewald, "The Issue of Forced Labour in the Onjembo," 101; Joachim Zeller, "'Ombepera i Koza – the Cold Is Killing Me: A history of the concentration camp at Swakopmund (1904–1908)," in *Genocide in German South-West Africa: The Colonial War of 1904–1908 and Its Aftermath*, ed. Jürgen Zimmerer and Joachim Zeller (Monmouth: Merlin Press, 2008), 76; Gesine Krüger, *Kriegsbewältigung und Geschichtsbewusstsein: Realität, Deutung und Verarbeitung des deutschen Kolonialkriegs in Namibia 1904 bis 1907* (Göttingen: Vandenhoeck & Ruprecht, 1999), 130.

145 Jürgen Zimmerer, *German Rule, African Subjects: State Aspirations and the Reality of Power in Colonial Namibia*, trans. Anthony Mellor-Stapelberg (New York: Berghahn, 2021), 84–92.

Table 1: Death Registry statistics.[146]

Ethnicity / Background	Number who died	Percentage of total
Herero	340	78%
Ovambo	51	12%
Damara (Klippkaffer, Bergdamara, Kaffer)	18	4%
Cape Coloured (Kapboy, Capeboy)	10	2%
Nama (Hottentott)	10	2%
Kru (Bassa Junge, Kruneger)	3	<1%
Zulu (Zulu-Kaffer)	1	<1%
Hindu	1	<1%
Total	**434**	

tary camp (16), *Woermann-Linie* (13) and a variety of other private businesses and government entities.[147] Giving an overview of the Swakopmund industries that used forced labor who died at this time, a total of 36 people passed doing port labor, 22 working for train line construction and train maintenance, and 21 for the military including the train divisions.[148] These numbers highlight the deadliest fields of forced laborer at the time. Unfree labor seeped into all aspects of the Swakopmund economy with Herero prisoners even made to work at the Swakopmund Book store (*Swakopmunder Buchhandlung*), where both one 18-year-old woman, and one 20-year-old man died of pneumonia in late 1905/early 1906.[149]

The death registry for natives also contains a few Nama, labelled "*Hottentott*," who were likely also forced laborers at Swakopmund. Of the ten on the list, three named Salmon, Keibeb and Adam were laborers at the military camp. Another was the 25-year-old Cilla, who died of a heart attack while contracted to the *Woermann-Linie*.[150] In addition to Herero and Nama forced labor, the list also includes 84 individuals who were free contract laborers.

A few overarching conclusions can be made from the information on non-Herero and Nama workers. Fifty-one, or over half, were Ovambo, emphasizing that by July of 1905 the migrant corridor between the Ovambo Polities in the north and the German settler region was safe enough to be traversed by migrant

146 Compiled from the 'Death Registry statistics' gathered for those who died at the Herero and military concentration camps, NAN, BSW [107] UA 10/6, *Totenregister für Eingeborene*, 1905–1906, 27.07.1905–27.02.1906.

147 NAN, BSW [107] UA 10/6, *Totenregister für Eingeborene*, 1905–1906, 27.07.1905–27.02.1906.

148 NAN, BSW [107] UA 10/6, *Totenregister für Eingeborene*, 1905–1906, 27.07.1905–27.02.1906.

149 NAN, BSW [107] UA 10/6, *Totenregister für Eingeborene*, 1905–1906, Records 1709, 1736.

150 NAN, BSW [107] UA 10/6, *Totenregister für Eingeborene*, 1905–1906, 27.07.1905–27.02.1906, Records 1648, 1522, 1397, 1518, 1602, 1625, 1613, 1509, 1605.

laborers. This is reflected in the large number of Ovambo recruits (500) for the Otavibahn that were already secured by September 1904.[151]

Ovambo workers were in the process, especially as the war took its toll on the Herero and Nama populations, of becoming the dominant ethnic group amongst the non-forced labor workforce. Of note is that all but three were men, mirroring the developing male centric migrant work coming from Ovambo communities.[152] Damara, also from the interior of the colony, but not as far afield as the Ovambo, seem to be employed in sizable numbers in Swakopmund. The list records 18 among those who died. Six were women.

By far the most fatalities of non-forced laborers on the list, 34, worked for the Damara und Namaqua Handelsgesellschaft mbH.[153] This trading company, founded in the 1890s by C. Woermann and the South West Africa Company was making brisk business during the war. The store was a place where settlers, soldiers and any interested customers could buy goods such as provisions, water pumps and various pieces of equipment.[154] Likely these contract workers, along with the forced laborers for the company were busy transporting goods from the port depot to the store in Swakopmund. That so many died engaging for the company who were not Herero and Nama might point to the reality that labor for Damara und Namaqua Handelsgesellschaft mbH was especially grueling.

Other industries beyond the sale of goods and the import business, who employed free laborers that died on the job were construction (9), the harbor (10), and train line building and maintenance (6). Pointing to bad work conditions, many contract workers, similar to Herero and Nama forced laborers, died of exhaustion (13), and of heart failure (20). Many also succumbed to causes related to weather, such as pneumonia (15), or malnourishment leading to scurvy (21).[155] While there is no denying that conditions for forced laborers were horrendous and in general much worse than for free laborers, contract workers also faced a variety of difficult work conditions in Swakopmund across industries. The cold, damp climate combined with challenging jobs, indecent living conditions for

151 Brenda Bravenboer and Walter Rusch, *The First 100 Years of State Railways in Namibia* (Windhoek, Namibia: TransNamib Museum, 1999), 65.

152 NAN, BSW [107] UA 10/6, *Totenregister für Eingeborene,* 1905–1906, 27.07.1905–27.02.1906, Records 1621, 1759.

153 The company still exists today and is known as the Wecke und Voigts Group; see https://weckevoigts.com/.

154 *Deutscher Kolonial-Kalender und statistisches Handbuch* (Deutscher Kolonial-Verlag, 1909), 128.; "Damara Und Namaqua Handelsgesellschaft MbH Vorgestellt Im Namibiana Buchdepot," accessed October 27, 2021, https://www.namibiana.de/namibia-information/who-is-who/organisationen/infos-zur-organisation/damara-und-namaqua-handelsgesellschaft-mbh.html.

155 BSW [107] UA 10/6, *Totenregister für Eingeborene,* 1905–1906, 27.07.1905–27.02.1906.

much of the workforce, and almost universal improper provisions made Swakopmund a deadly worksite. That numerous contract laborers died of conditions not dissimilar to many forced laborers in Swakopmund emphasizes the imprecise and blurry boundary between free and unfree African laborers during the war.

Kru workers also suffered a few fatalities (3) during the period documented by the death registry for natives. Among those listed are two young Bassa Liberians employed by the *Woermann-Linie*: one of them, an 18-year-old named Tom, succumbed to pneumonia. Additionally, the registry includes a twenty-year-old Kru laborer working for a trader, who died from complications of a severe burn sustained on the job.[156]

It is clear that compared to other groups of unfree or free laborers, Kru deaths during this period are low, especially when bringing into focus the fact that thousands of West Africans were at the port during the war. This very well may have had to do with better conditions due to their position as skilled longshoremen and ship hands in the conflict. As we will explore later, I argue that their position during the war, and especially in its aftermath was that of a labor elite. This meant that due to their high skill and relative irreplaceability by other groups of workers, both their wages and conditions were better, often much more so, than other contract laborers. While part of a larger wartime labor regime, which eventually included thousands of forced laborers, the role of Kru was essential in supplying the German military. They were a key component of the contracted laborers which made up the 'human infrastructure' supporting the war machine, especially in the period before forced labor was utilized. While Kru were mainly on ships and at the ports, Cape Workers, making up one of the other major migrant labor corridors, largely supported the military on land.

Ten so-called *"Kapjunge"* (Cape Boys) were also on the Swakopmund death registry for natives. This term is a catch all that most often included South African men from a Transkei, Ciskei, Cape Coloured, or Zulu background. I will use the term Cape Workers and bring out the various details of individuals when deemed necessary. Six of the listed Cape Workers died at the horse and cattle collection points (*Sammlungstelle*). They were part of a much larger migration during the war, the second worker corridor from South Africa that developed during the conflict.

156 NAN, BSW [107] UA 10/6, *Totenregister für Eingeborene*, 1905–1906, 27.07.1905–27.02.1906, Records 1673, 1676, 1774.

The South African Labor Corridor: Wagon Drivers as Essential Workers of the Colonial Army in German South West Africa

> After we landed at Swakopmouth (Swakopmund) we inspanned the oxen that came off the ship and loaded up the wagons, and then tracked to the Waterberg. There were some German soldiers with us, about 50. We tracked about all over the country. We travelled two months before we reached the scene of the war, water was very scarce and we were often delayed four or five days at a time, resting the oxen, we were illtreated on the way up. I myself was thrashed three times, one of these times I caught hold of the sjambok. The Dutchman I call Dannie put his pistol and shot me just under the right eye. I do not know if the pistol had a bullet in or shot . . . I show three scars on my face . . . .[157]
>
> Isaac Magadi, Wagon driver for the German Schutztruppe in German South West Africa Uitvlugt, April 22, 1905.

> The difficulty of procuring suitable drivers, in which duties natives must mainly be employed, induces me to call attention to the importance of treating these men properly.
>
> The non-commissioned officers and men told off to guard the wagons are to be strictly forbidden to kick or strike these men. If one of them has been guilty of neglect of duty the officer in command of the company, battery or detachment alone is to decide as to his punishment.
>
> Punishments are to consist mainly of deductions from pay. On the other hand all drivers are to be informed that uninterrupted good conduct for three months will give them a prospect of a special monthly wage.[158]
>
> Headquarters, Okahandja, 25.06.1904, Lothar von Trotha, commander of the Schutztruppe in German South West Africa

The quotes above give us insight from two different perspectives into the complex realities for South Africans employed by the German military between 1904 and 1907. In Isaac Magadi's account of work in GSWA, we hear experiences of abuse suffered at the hands of German soldiers and a South African Afrikaner overseer/ wagon conductor. The letter that follows by Lothar von Trotha to his troops identifies "native" wagon drivers as important for the colonial military and attempts to lessen occurrences of abuse by making such activities punishable. He also announces that good conduct by drivers will be rewarded by increased pay. Despite directives from the top down, worker mistreatment by the military would continue, to varying degrees, throughout the war. Simultaneously, workers like Isaac, would continue to take contracts in the colony, often while actively avoiding less sought-after opportunities, like underground mining work in South Africa. The numbers of South African migrants coming to work in GSWA between 1904 and

157 CA, NA 556, Statement by Isaac Magadi regarding the death of Robert Honose, 22.04.1905.
158 CA, NA 556, Order from Commander and Chief von Trotha to German Schutztruppe commanders in GSWA, Okahandja, 25.06.1904, 6. Translation to English by W.B. Lyon.

1907 numbered around 20,000 or approximately the same number of West Africans that were part of the *Woermann-Linie*'s operations supplying the war on ships and stationed at the colonial ports.[159] To understand why so many South Africans would come on contract to German South West Africa starting in 1904, we must first look at the 'labor question' in relation to both colonies.

The 'Labor Question' in Southern Africa and the Outbreak of War in 1904

The labor question, or how to procure and maintain enough laborers for business enterprises and government operations, was central to late nineteenth- and early twentieth-century colonial policy throughout the African continent. Labor shortages and how to solve them was a chief concern.[160] However, a deeper understanding of what drove Africans to work and to migrate for work was rarely comprehended on a deep level.[161] The reasons we have examined thus far that motivated, compelled, or forced individuals to work in GSWA were complex and often varied from person to person. This does not diminish the fact that imperial policy did attempt to effect African work patterns, and did have some influence on workers in the context of German South West Africa.

Within the context of the German empire, the 'labor question' was central to how those shaping policy in the metropole conceptualized the development of the colonies. A 1902 presentation at the 'Colonial Congress' meeting of the *Deutsche Kolonialgesellschaft*, or the German Colonial Society, titled "The Worker Question in the German Colonies," painted an unrealistically rosy picture of 'a day in the life' in an African village where workers went off to do a 'good days labor' at a German African plantation. It includes a line whereby the plantation owner "always has a sufficient supply of workers. He can accept the necessary punishment, as the worst

159 Bill Nasson, *Abraham Esau's War: A Black South African War in the Cape; 1899 – 1902* (Cambridge: Cambridge University Press, 1991), 177.

160 Much of the policy evolved in tandem with the European drive to end slavery in Africa; see Frederick Cooper, *Decolonization and African Society: The Labor Question in French and British Africa* (Cambridge: University Press, 1996), 25–28; in the period after World War One until World War Two, academics became more concerned with examining African social patterns and movements with the aim of seeking to find keys to control African workers; see Stefano Bellucci and Andreas Eckert, "The 'Labour Question' in Africanist Historiography," in *General Labour History of Africa: Workers, Employers and Governments, 20th–21st Centuries*, ed. Stefano Bellucci and Andreas Eckert (Woodbridge: James Currey, 2019), 1–13; Bill Freund, "Labor and Labor History in Africa: A Review of the Literature," *African Studies Review* 27, no. 2 (1984): 2–3.

161 Frederick Cooper, *On the African Waterfront: Urban Disorder and the Transformation of Work in Colonial Mombasa* (New Haven: Yale University Press, 1987), 1–2.

one the people know, is being let go." The speaker admits that "Unfortunately, things are far from like this on all German plantations."[162] As one could guess, this story of everyday worker/employer relations in the German colonies was far from realistic. The author would go on to argue why many German plantations in the colonies had issues, one reason being bad treatment of workers. The 1902 congress highlighted that, the 'worker question' was central to German colonial policy by the early 1900s and furthermore, had gone largely unanswered.

In the larger context of Southern Africa, the theme had become integral to South African businesses and governance following the aftermath of the South African War, which had ended in mid 1902.[163] As reported in the *Swakopmunder Zeitung* from early 1903, thousands of Africans who had been contracted on the Rand gold mines prior to the war, working two to three years of hard labor, were not returning. This crisis of the 'worker question' for the Rand mines had become a regular heading in Cape Town newspapers. The reason for African workers not wishing to return was clear, wages had been cut in half, and many had earned decent if not comparably high wages during the war working primarily as auxiliaries.[164] Furthermore, it was not uncommon for African auxiliaries who were demobilized at the end of the war to leave with sizable bonuses in cash and goods. As Bill Nasson has argued, these "labor aristocrats" who had experienced expanded freedoms during the war, also created real hiring challenges for the mines and other South African employers such as farmers. The 1902 and 1903 Cape Colony parliament received many complaints by a variety of employers that seemingly none could pay the wages comparable to those given out by the government during the conflict.[165]

The problem was no less acute in the Transvaal. Part of the labor gap at the gold mines was initially filled by Mozambican migrant labor in 1902. When the mines re-opened following hostilities, over 65 percent of all unskilled mine labor

---

162 Vietor goes on to criticize bad treatment of African workers among other factors as the reason for issues on many plantations in the German colonies; see Johann Karl Vietor, "Die Arbeiterfrage in den deutschen Kolonien," in *Sonderabdruck aus den Verhandlungen des Deutschen Kolonialkongresses 1902* (Berlin: Verl. Kolonialkriegerdank, 1902), 521–26.

163 For more on the labor question, in particular in the border region of GSWA and South Africa in the late nineteenth century and early twentieth centuries, see Kai F. Herzog, "Violence and Work: Convict Labour and Settler Colonialism in the Cape–Namibia Border Region (c.1855–1903)," *Journal of Southern African Studies* 47, no. 1 (2021): 17–36.

164 Nasson, *Abraham Esau's War*, 26–29; Bill Nasson, "Moving Lord Kitchener: Black Military Transport and Supply Work in the South African War, 1899–1902, with Particular Reference to the Cape Colony," *Journal of Southern African Studies* 11, no. 1 (1984): 25–51.

165 Nasson, *Abraham Esau's War*, 174–175.

came from the Portuguese East African colony.[166] This was at severely reduced wages, 23 percent below pre-war pay for black miners. But this pay failed to bring in enough labor and in the first quarter of 1903 wages were increased and as a result Mozambican migration increased.[167] Wages on the Rand eventually started to hit pre-war levels and the Rand lords pushed for other alternatives to reduce pay. Experiments hiring white labor had already been attempted and failed, primarily because whites would not tolerate the low pay.[168] But the solution decided upon by the mines, at least for the years to come would lie in the importation of Chinese labor, which began in 1904.[169]

As for local African men, especially those from the Transkei and Western Cape who had worked as military auxiliaries up until 1902, a new alternative abroad arose, contract work in German South West Africa. It was in 1904 that 'the labor question,' which had been a topic of debate in GSWA, but one seemingly with solutions at hand in the form of a mixture of mainly local and some migrant labor boosted by refugees from the South African War, became acute.[170] From the perspective of many migrant laborers from South Africa choosing to work in the German colony, it was not simply because of a desire to avoid underground work in the mines of the Transvaal, but the most sought after contracts in Southern Africa, despite the trying labor conditions.

The work of William Beinart and Colin Bundy has highlighted the massive flow of workers, especially those from the Transkei region to GSWA between 1904 and 1910.[171] Beinart in particular, via worker accounts, emphasized the depravities some faced there, especially while working for the military.[172] The difficult chal-

---

166 Rachel K. Bright, *Chinese Labour in South Africa: 1902–10 ; Race, Violence, and Global Spectacle*, Cambridge Imperial and Post-Colonial Studies (Basingstoke: Palgrave Macmillan, 2013), 23.
167 Patrick Harries, *Work, Culture, and Identity: Migrant Laborers in Mozambique and South Africa, c. 1860–1910* (London: James Currey, 1994), 181–182.
168 Elaine N. Katz, "The Underground Route to Mining: Afrikaners and the Witwatersrand Gold Mining Industry from 1902 to the 1907 Miners' Strike*," *The Journal of African History* 36, no. 3 (November 1995): 475–476.
169 Bright, *Chinese Labour in South Africa*, 37; van Onselen, *New Babylon, New Nineveh*, 29.
170 A report on the Boer War and related migration to GSWA highlights that migrants largely filled local worker demands in the early 1900s. *Swakopmunder Zeitung* (published as *Windhoeker Anzeiger*.), 01.01.1902, *'Vom südafrikanischen Kriegsschauplatze'*, 1.
171 William Beinart and Colin Bundy, "Introduction: 'Away in the Locations,'" in *Hidden Struggles in Rural South Africa: Politics & Popular Movements in the Transkei & Eastern Cape, 1890–1930*, William Beinart and Colin Bundy (Berkeley: University of California Press, 1987), 20.
172 William Beinart, "'Jamani' Cape Workers in German South West Africa, 1904–12," in *Hidden Struggles in Rural South Africa: Politics & Popular Movements in the Transkei & Eastern Cape, 1890–1930*, William Beinart and Colin Bundy (Berkeley: University of California Press, 1987), 176–177.

lenges many workers in the colony faced were real, but the numbers continuing to come throughout the German colonial period are indisputable. South Africans persistently arrived in GSWA despite increasing migration restrictions created by the Cape Colony and then South African Union.[173] Some even travelled hundreds of kilometers on foot from the Western Cape to the border with the German colony. Before we focus on worker experiences, let us first examine recruitment and transport to the colony.

Auxiliary Labor Demand, Recruitment, and Experiences in German South West Africa

In the months that followed the eruption of war in 1904 GSWA, it became clear as the Germans were planning their war strategy, that without sufficient train lines, ox wagons and skilled drivers would be crucial for the German military effort.[174] Of those locally recruitable Africans who remained in or near the German settlements, relatively few had advanced ox wagon skills, with notable exceptions such as the Baster community.[175] This lies at the heart of why the military largely was forced to recruit outside of GSWA for wagon drivers, as well as caretakers for the various military beasts of burden. The South African military drivers served a key element comprising the 'human infrastructure' of the German army in the Namibian War. The official German military publication on the conflict wrote the following explaining the role of the ox wagons:

> The heavy African wagon drawn by 18 or more oxen is the only means of transport that can be used here. It is clear that these bulky vehicles, which with the draft animals are more than 50 meters long, make troop movements infinitely cumbersome. Due to the lack of modern roads, all warlike operations are very sluggish and methodical, reminiscent for Europeans of the slow warfare of past centuries.
>
> Given the lack of settlements in the country and need for subsistence for the troops, they are dependent on the supply of provisions, and on larger marches they are therefore bound to the speed of the ox cart, which on average cannot cover more than 15–20 km in a day. The troops have to be supplied with everything they need from the rear, and even

173 Ulrike Lindner, "Transnational Movements between Colonial Empires: Migrant Workers from the British Cape Colony in the German Diamond Town of Luderitzbucht," *European Review of History* 16, no. 5 (2009): 679–695.

174 Train lines in the south would, similarly to the *Otavibahn,* be built during the war to ostensibly help the German war effort. See Chapter 4, "The Construction of the Southern Line (*Südbahn),* 1905–1909."

175 Preußen / Großer Generalstab, *Die Kämpfe der deutschen Truppen in Südwestafrika. 1,* 1: 14–16.

> water often has to be carried for miles on wagons. The supply of rations, ammunition, equipment and clothing is carried out by ox teams. Since the transport columns, in addition to troops defending them, are also dependent on the contents of the vehicles for their own sustenance . . . . The consequence of this is that, as long as there are no railroads, only relatively weak soldier detachments can be maintained (in the field) . . .[176]

Figure 16: An ox-wagon and German troops passing through the dry bed of the black Nossob ephemeral river in the Eastern theater of war in GSWA in 1904.[177]

The photo above (Figure 16) emphasizes many details highlighted in the previous text by the Prussian General staff on the auxiliary forces needed for the war in GSWA, ranging from the approximate eighteen oxen needed to pull the wagons, to the massive length of the transport column, and the 'cumbersomeness' of this form of transport. As a matter of fact, the wagon in the photo seems to have been stuck. The back left wheel is sinking into the dry riverbed, likely due to the weight of the heavily loaded wagon within the loose river sand. We see a group of German soldiers on the left and right of the wagon pushing. Their rifles have been set down, in a conical formation in the left of the photo, to give them more freedom of movement. A group of officers, to the right of the wagon are commanding the troops, one can imagine them saying 'on the count of three, heave!' Meanwhile at least two Cape wagon drivers are seen on both sides of the oxen, whips

176 Preußen / Großer Generalstab, 1: 8. Translation to English by W.B. Lyon.

177 BADKGUBFM, Photo: 082-2990-195, *Durchzug durch den Schwarzen Nossob*, Sammlung Jean Bantz: Bahnfahrt von Swakopmund – Windhuk. Ostabteilung. D.S.W.Afr 1904.

in hand, thrashing the animals to pull the wagon out of the rut. Such an image leaves no doubts as to the many challenges associated with the use of ox-wagons in the field. Further, with thousands of troops deployed in the colony, hundreds of such wagons and thousands of oxen were required to support the combatants. It makes it all the clearer why the German army and their recruiters turned to nearby South Africa, where many unemployed former wagon drivers were looking for work.

William Beinart has shown that one of the primary locations for recruitment in South Africa was in Cape Town. It was there that between June of 1903 and June of 1904, around 10,000 workers from the Transkei alone received passes to work in GSWA. By the end of 1903, Cape Town and the entire region was in an economic recession and the new arrivals, in addition to many locals were without work.[178] This meant that the German military's recruitment operations in Cape Town found droves of willing conscripts. Just at the native 'location' of Uitvlugt (later re-named Ndabemi) nearby Cape Town, over 400 men would be recruited by March 1905.[179] Documents from this period show that the Cape Government was adamant that those looking to find work in GSWA were "contracting themselves . . . entirely on their own responsibility and without the concurrence of the Government."[180] The administration did not want to be held legally responsible for possible issues, injuries or deaths that could occur in the neighboring colony during the war. It also seems that the Cape did not wish to be portrayed as helping the German war effort indirectly via the contracted migrants. Going a step further, there were also ministers in the Cape government who attempted, without success, to ban recruitment altogether, for example in early February of 1905 writing, "the Imperial German Consul-General has been informed that it is not considered desirable to issue licenses for the recruitment of natives for German South West Africa."[181] But recruitment continued nonetheless with others in the government open to such labor flows.

Recruitment also took place beyond Cape Town and the surrounding region, including in the Eastern Cape, where the Transkei and Ciskei are located. German military representatives would spearhead recruitment, and then delegated agents would handle getting actual contracts signed. This recruitment process was not always transparent and at times conducted illegally.

178 Beinart, "'Jamani,'" 2.

179 CA, NA 557, Recruitment of Natives for German South West Africa, Resident Magistrate's Office, Uitvlugt, 30.03.1905.

180 CA, NA 557, Recruitment of Natives for German South West Africa, telephone message transcript from the Native affairs Department at Cape Town, 23.02.1905.

181 CA, NA 557, Cape of Good Hope Administrator meeting No. 77 minutes, 04.02.1905.

One recruiter skirting the law was Commandant Potgieter. On the February 8, 1905, he was caught in Queenstown in the Eastern Cape recruiting without a license. The German consul in the Cape, upon learning of the issue requested that he receive permission and shared the terms of service for the recruits with the government. This included a statement that those going to GSWA would not be sent to the front, something near to impossible for most transport drivers in a theater of war. But those in the recruiting networks seemed content to 'bend the truth' to tap into the South African labor base.

Working with the recruiters were a variety of locals. In Potgieter's network was a Cape Worker agent by the name of Jim Brown in charge of the Cape Town area, and according to the local Native Affairs office, he was "not very particular in his promises as long as he gets boys."[182] Recruiter J. Gerst was also not on the right side of the government in his use (without permission) of two houses in Cape Town, 100, Loop Street and 68 Bree street as 'native barracks.' This is where workers would stay a few days to wait for steamers and get medical checks before being shipped out. He belatedly applied for permission arguing that Maitland and other locations were too far away from the port and he "will engage to keep them under perfect control, and in such a way that they can in no way annoy or inconvenience . . . residents.[183] Competition was fierce between recruiters with a certain Mr. Fourie working to take recruits from a Mr. Benadie working at the Cape Town port. Fourie seems to also have been against Potgieter, telling possible recruits that others didn't have permission to recruit, and they should instead sign on with him. Regardless of ethical qualms or official recruiting licenses, recruitment out of the Eastern and Western Cape to the German colony continued. Contracts for wagon drivers and auxiliary workers ranged from £3 to £5 per month, free passage and provisions were included, and depending on the contract could also incorporate free clothing. However, details ranged based on the recruiter and even the German military was aware that recruiters often made 'false promises.'[184] Recruits would be sent out in waves on ships, for example in early February 1905 a steamer left for GSWA with around 150 Cape Workers. Recruiters and their networks cashed in, first receiving 1/9d and later 4/- per head.[185] Business for these agents was brisk.

Despite the Cape government's concern that Cape Workers were potentially not taking contracts on their own volition, evidence seems relatively clear that before leaving, transport workers, certainly by November 1905 knew of the real-

182 CA, NA 557, Report, A95D, Cape Town 22.02.1905.
183 CA, NA 557, Letter from J. Gerst to the Secretary for Native Affairs, 24.02.1905.
184 CA, NA 556, Memorandum from the British Ambassador to the German Empire, 21.04.1906.
185 CA, NA 557, Secret Report, 13.02.1905

ity of work in the nearby colony. An account from Plague Medical Officer Anderson in East London states:

> I . . . am informed by Mr. Turpin of the Plague Staff that while they were awaiting the (medical) examination in the yard of the Court House, the other natives standing by were chaffing them, saying they were going to fight for the Germans. They appear to have perfectly understood where they were going to . . . .[186]

By this time, workers had also been returning from their six-month contracts sharing stories of their experiences. Relative knowledge of the war and conditions did not mean that Cape Workers did not find unwanted challenges, surprises and even death during their tours on contract to the north.

A group of workers, John Mamba, Jan Tusi, and Isaac Magadi (potential aliases), recounted their own experiences working in GSWA in relation to the deaths of fellow Cape Workers, Robert and James Honose (potential aliases). Isaac (a segment of whose testimony began this subchapter) had been living in the Ndabeni location outside of Cape Town, but he was likely from the Orange Free State (OFS), similar to Jan who came from Kroonstadt in the OFS. John Mamba rather came from Ntsangeni's location outside of Kentani in the Transkei. Jan explained his contract followed by his journey to GSWA and early work experiences while there:

> I joined to go to German West Africa on 15th June last. Robert Honose was our Native foreman. The pay promised was £5 per month free rations and clothes. We did not get the clothes. I did not get blankets. I sailed on the 24th of June (1904). Our work was feeding oxen and giving them water. We were fairly well treated on board the ship . . . . I arrived at Swakopmund 7 days after we left Cape Town. I was a week at Swakopmouth (Swakopmund) before the oxen were offloaded. The oxen were very wild when we offloaded them and several of us Natives were thrashed, I amongst the number, by a Dutchman named Vellem I do not know his other name, with a sjambok. I did not complain to anyone. I do not know who to complain to.[187]

Isaac relayed the following:

> In June 1904 Robert Honose asked me to join, and go as a driver of wagons to German West Africa the pay promised me was £5 per month and rations we also got blankets, we were promised clothes but did not get them. I was put on board the ship on the 17th of June last (1904), and had to work at feeding cattle, the voyage took five days to Swakopmouth (Swa-

186 CA, NA 557, P/280/05, Native Labourers for German South West Africa, re, Government Health Offices, East London, 16.11.1905; At the time, South Africa was dealing with an outbreak of the plague and hence the plague doctors; see J. Alexander Mitchell, "Plague in South Africa: Perpetuation and Spread of Infection by Wild Rodents," *The Journal of Hygiene* 20, no. 4 (1921): 377–382.

187 CA, NA 557, Statement by Jan Tusi. Uitvlugt (Ndabemi), 20.04.1905.

> kopmund). We then offloaded the cattle there were 60 Natives and 17 Cape Boys. Robert Honose was our native foreman, and a Cape Boy named David was foreman of the Cape Boys. There were four Dutchmen in charge of the cattle, the senior in charge was a man named Maritz, another was called Darnnie . . . we were well treated on board ship . . . .[188]

Both Jan and Isaac's experiences indicate how workers were transported with foremen as well as overseers. Further we see in their cases that Robert Honose was not only a recruiting agent but also acted as an overseer. This put him in a role where he likely had made money from their recruitment but was also responsible for their proper treatment while on contract. Although their experiences differed, general themes of employment included lots of movement with wagon columns either being deployed supporting German military units or transporting material between military depots. When wagon columns were sent into the field without soldier escort, they were given arms.[189] Isaac was part of the operation moving troops and supplies from June to the first week of August 1904 to slowly encircle Waterberg in preparation for the battle of Ohamakari which would occur on August 11.[190] John Mamba first was employed in country to move a herd of oxen from Swakopmund to Windhoek on foot, which is a distance of about 350km. This task was not only difficult, but could also be deadly, as John Mamba's brother had been killed in GSWA looking after cattle when enemy combatants killed him. John however survived, and after moving the cattle, he was transferred to Okahandja and was deployed with German troops into the field. He recalled:

> We went under a Dutch Conductor named Vellem [Willem] de Wat, we were very badly treated on this journey, when the oxen got tired and lay down, the conductor de Wat and a German Corporal used to thrash us with sjamboks and give us as many as 25 lashes, and tie us up to the wheel and beat us. I was not beaten myself but I have seen many others beaten in this manner, the reason the oxen got tired was the oxen were often without food or water for five days . . . . I also report that a native named James, I do not know his other name, was shot on the road to Jobendu [unknown location], James got sick on the way and the Dutch conductor Fischer Mafasta (This man is well known on the parade Ground, Cape Town) said that he might be shot as he was delaying wagons, the conductor told him to go and turn the oxen, and when he was about 20 yards away from the wagons two German soldiers shot him . . . we natives did not make any noise about this, as we were afraid that we should be shot ourselves . . . .[191]

188 CA, NA 557, Statement by Isaac Magadi, Uitvlugt (Ndabemi), 22.04.1905

189 CA, NA 556, Sworn Statement by Isaac Magadi. Uitvlugt (Ndabemi), 2, 22.04.1905.

190 Isabel V. Hull, *Absolute Destruction*, 34.

191 CA, NA 556, Sworn Statement by John Mambra, Uitvlugt (Ndabemi), 22.04.1905

Treatment of wagon drivers, as this account highlights, could be dreadful and conflicts between them and their Afrikaner overseers, as referenced in John and Isaac's earlier account – where he was shot by Afrikaner Dannie Louw – was a particular issue. The Afrikaner-Cape Worker conflict likely reflected violence by the Afrikaner population against black Africans in South Africa.[192] Soldier violence against wagon drivers was also a clear issue, but according to Isaac Magadi he had a good experience with German Officers, saying "[t]hey treated us well," emphasizing that "[i]t was the Dutch conductors that ill-treated us."[193]

Contracts would normally last six months, with extensions not uncommon, but some drivers could be pressured to serve longer, though additional pay was not always received. This is another example highlighting how during the war in GSWA, free labor could often be constrained. One conductor, who, in contrast to the above accounts, went out of his way to protest on behalf of Cape Workers was A.J. Anderson. An interesting character, he was a conductor for the Intelligence Department for the British army during the South African War who had been involved in the relief of Mafeking among other jobs. When working at the border with GSWA during the war, he gave information to the Germans, who were sending guns and ammunition across the border with Africans for the Boers.[194] Regardless of his prior allegiances, as a conductor in GSWA he worked with a group of drivers who were trying to get discharged after being forced to stay on the job longer than they agreed. He wrote:

> I have had under me natives in military wagons, who cannot get their discharge . . . . On the 15th July I left Windhoek with others for Kub und Lt. von [undecipherable] 5th Kol . . . at Kub received orders to proceed to Gibeon. The natives refused to go through with me unless an understanding on wages came to, as some of the natives time had already expired and another question they wished settled was if natives served over 6 months all the time should be paid to them, as their brothers who had served 7 & 8 months had only received 6 months' pay.[195]

An agreement between the commander and the military was made whereby these drivers would proceed to Gibeon if Anderson accompanied them. From there they would return to Kub, and then to Windhoek where they were to be dis-

192 For some potent examples of white violence against various non-white communities in South Africa from the nineteenth century up to the modern day, see David B. Coplan, "Erasing History: The Destruction of the Beersheba and Platberg African Christian Communities in the Eastern Orange Free State, 1858–1983," *South African Historical Journal* 61, no. 3 (2009): 505–520.

193 CA, NA 557, Statement by Isaac Magadi. Uitvlugt (Ndabemi), 3, 22.04.1905.

194 CA, NA 556, Particulars regarding character and antecedents of A.J. Anderson, Native Affairs Office, 30.11.1905.

195 CA, NA 556, Letter from A.J. Anderson to the Native Commissioner at Cape Town, 25.09.1905.

charged and paid. Instead, when they returned to Kub they were ordered back to Gibeon and the wagon drivers refused. They were forced to the civilian transport camp and Anderson immediately resigned in protest. He went to Windhoek to complain, but the drivers were to be forcibly interned until they could be replaced with re-enforcements from Windhoek. While it is not clear whether these drivers were able to get justice, Anderson's letter gives us additional insight into driver experiences. He wrote:

> [T]he death rate has been high amongst the natives (African wagon drivers) their treatment having been neglected until too late. I myself whilst watching in Windhoek having seen some 10 to 12 deaths, a hospital tent was erected near the transport camp, the natives refuse to go to the hospital as their brothers never come out again . . . the natives have received very bad treatment under the German Government. The cause as far as I can see is the German does not understand their language.[196]

We hear in Anderson's observation about the inability of the Germans to communicate in languages understood by workers echoes back to Manasse's comment in the previous chapter about the Otavi expedition members in the 1890s.[197] German colonizers inability to communicate with workers would not only cause problems for Cape Workers employed by the military, but it also would continue in other industries, as will be further explored in the following chapters. Anderson's remark about workers fearing German field hospitals would also be a continuing theme for contract workers in the colony. With many wagon drivers experiencing abusive conditions at the hands of the military, trust in their medical facilities was understandably very low. Whether in accounts of wagon drivers, or observations from some conductors like Anderson, the brutal nature of work for many wagon drivers in GSWA is clear. Their freedoms as contracted workers were often highly curtailed in the name of 'military necessity.' They were also working in the context of genocide and war, which they themselves observed. This included their accounts of forced labor and the concentration camps.

---

196 CA, NA 556, Letter from A.J. Anderson to the Native Commissioner at Cape Town, 25.09.1905.
197 See Chapter 1, "SWACO Expedition to the Otavi Mines, 1892–1894."

Cape Wagon Drivers' Perspectives on Concentration Camps and Forced Labor in GSWA

Figure 17: Forced laborers loading train car in Swakopmund.[198]

Above (Figure 17) we see an image of Herero women forced laborers at Swakopmund loading a train with what is likely bags of feed for cattle and horses. To the right in the image is a man with a wide brimmed hat who very well may be a Cape Worker holding the reigns of a horse. He is probably in the process of hitching the horse onto the train car to then pull it to one of the large horse or cattle Kraals located in wartime-Swakopmund. To the left we see a group of Germans, perhaps the man in a uniform is a military officer, and the man in a suit with no hat a businessman or colonial official. While we do not have an account of the Cape Worker in the photo, we do have the account below from a South African wagon driver, Henrik Fraser. He experienced similar scenes and recounted the following:

198 NAN, Photo 25521. Provenance: A.0109, Stuhlmann.

> When I got to Swakopmund I saw very many Herero prisoners of war who had been captured in the rebellion which was still going on in the country. There must have been about 600 men, women and children prisoners. They were in an encloser on the beach, fenced in barbed wire. The women were made to do hard labour just like the men. The sand is very deep and heavy there. The women had to load and unload carts and trolleys, and also draw Scotch-cart loads of goods to Nonidas (9 10 kilos. Away) where there was a depot. The women were put in spans of eight to each Scotch-cart and were made to pull like draught animals. Many were half-starved and weak, and died of sheer exhaustion . . . They were poorly fed, and often begged me and other Cape boys for a little food. The soldiers used the young Herero girls to satisfy their passions . . . .
>
> After six months at Swakopmund I was sent to Karibib towards the end of September 1904. There I also saw an enclosure with Hereros waiting for transport to Swakopmund. Many were dying of starvation and exhaustion. They were thin and worn out. They were not made to work so hard at Karibib and appeared to be less harshly treated.[199]

Another account from Cape Worker James Golibadi, who had multiple contracts during the war, shared similar recollections of abusive treatment toward Herero forced laborers during his second tour based in Windhoek around 1905/1906. He recalled:

> I could not help noticing the bad treatment meted out to the women prisoners by the German soldiers and conductors. The conductors are for the most part Dutchman and Germans born in South Africa.
>
> These unfortunate women are daily compelled to carry heavy iron for construction work, also big stacks of compressed fodder. I have often noticed cases where women have fallen under the load and have been made to go on by being thrashed and kicked by the soldiers and conductors. The rations supplied to the women are insufficient and they are made to cook the food themselves. They are always hungry and we laborers from the Cape Colony, have frequently thrown food into their camp.
>
> The women in many cases are not properly clothed. It is a common thing to see women going about in public almost naked. I have also noticed that women who had been recently confined and were compelled to work and carry heavy articles for transport.
>
> Old women are also made to work and are constantly kicked and thrashed by the soldiers.
>
> This treatment is meted out in the presence of the German Officers and, I have never noticed any officers interfering.[200]

James would go on to highlight injustices meted out to Cape Workers by soldiers and conductors including being beaten and flogged for small mistakes, and an instance of some Cape Workers being thrown into jail in Swakopmund without

199 Silvester and Gewald, *Words Cannot Be Found*, 174–175.

200 CA, NA 662 Part II, Statement by James Golibadi on his experiences working in GSWA, Ndabeni Location, 11.8.1906.

trial. He highlighted that much of the abuse would occur while officers were not present and they therefore often had no one to complain to.[201] In the words of both Henrik and James, we can see that prisoner pleas for sustenance, and Cape Workers throwing food into the concentration camps meant there was a degree of solidarity between the victims of genocide and the contracted auxiliary workers from South Africa. Certainly, some of the drivers and conductors who had previous experience in the South African War had seen and experienced, or perhaps even been interned in the British concentration camps themselves.[202] In these camps, Afrikaner and African civilians had been forcibly held. At least 20,000 Africans and 25,000 to 30,000 Afrikaners, mainly children, died in the camps due to lack of food, clothing and other deprivations.[203] Cape Workers experiences in both wars likely made them some of the only people to experience two of the earliest examples of concentration camps in the twentieth century. In GSWA they saw the grisly transformation of concentration camps as bases for forced labor as well.[204]

Johann Nouthout, an Afrikaner from South Africa working as a conductor for the German military, gave an additional account of POWs in the south of the colony. In particular, he shares his recollections of the concentration camp Shark Island (In operation from 1905–1907). Johann recalled:

> I left Cape Town during the year 1906, and signed on with the Protectorate troops in South-West Africa. I arrived at Lüderitzbucht, and after staying there a few minutes I perceived nearly 500 native women lying on the beach, all bearing indications of being slowly starved to death. Every morning and towards evening four women carried a stretcher containing about four or five corpses, and they had also to dig the graves and bury them. I then started to trek to Kubub and Aus, and on the road I discovered bodies of native women lying between stones and devoured by birds of prey. Some bore signs of having been beaten to

201 CA, NA 662 Part II, Statement by James Golibadi on his experiences working in GSWA, Ndabeni Location, 11.8.1906.

202 John L Scott, "British Concentration Camps of the Second South African War (The Transvaal, 1900–1902)," (Master's thesis, Tallahassee, Florida State University, 2007), 82, fn. 244; also, see S.B Spies, *Methods of Barbarism?: Roberts and Kitchener and Civilians in the Boer Republics, January 1900-May 1902* (Cape Town: Human & Rousseau, 1977), 192–193.

203 Jonas Kreienbaum, "Friedrich von Lindequist, koloniale Konzentrationslager und transimperiales Lernen," *Revue d'Allemagne et des pays de langue allemande*, 2016, 77; Scott, "British Concentration Camps of the Second South African War," 100.

204 Jonas Kreienbaum, "'Wir sind keine Sklavenhalter' – Zur Rolle der Zwangsarbeit in den Konzentrationslagern in Deutsch-Südwestafrika (1904–1908)," in *Lager vor Auschwitz. Gewalt und Integration im 20. Jahrhundert*, ed. Christoph Jahr and Jens Thiel (Berlin: Metropol-Verl, 2013), 68–83; some British Camps in the South African War also used African prisoners as laborers but not on the same scale as in GSWA; see Scott, "British Concentration Camps of the Second South African War," 164.

> death . . . . If a prisoner were found outside the Herero prisoners camp, he would be brought before the Lieutenant and flogged with a sjambok. Fifty lashes were generally imposed. The manner in which the flogging was carried out was the most cruel imaginable . . . pieces of flesh would fly from the victim's body into the air.[205]

Johann's disturbing account has a particular emphasis on women at the concentration camp. It reflects both a high percentage of women POWs, as many men were slain on the battlefield or still active combatants, in addition to a reaction to the inhumanity meted out on non-combatants. Relatedly, prior referenced descriptions of brutal treatment by Afrikaner conductors, like Johann, of wagon drivers under their oversight may also reflect the psychological adaptation and mental numbing to near universal wartime ill treatment by Germans of Herero and Nama.

In reviewing both South African wagon driver's experiences in the war as well as their observations of forced labor and concentration camps we have expanded both our understandings of how the Namibian War was conducted, as well as brought the stories of auxiliary workers into a more central role within the larger conflict. They importantly convey varying perspectives of the war and the conflict's impact not only in the colony, but also in the lives of many Transkei, Ciskei, Cape Coloured, and Afrikaner contract laborers from South Africa.

In reference to Cape Workers experiences in the war, Beinart has argued that it was not the harsh conditions or the enemy, but the employer that posed the greatest threat to wagon drivers.[206] While conditions were, as we have seen, beyond harsh for many drivers, I would counter that of the thousands of recruits, abusive accounts are relatively limited. This could of course be due to the lack of an ability to voice concerns and the common perception that to share complaints would likely result in termination of contracts. But regardless of the brutality of work in GSWA as military auxiliaries, migrant flows north did not dampen throughout the war.

Demand to take contracts cannot be understated and despite the Cape Government's attempts to stem the flow, workers still wished to get contracts and found ways to get them long after early arrivals returned home and shared their experiences. This is to say that realities for these migrants were complex. Cape Workers contracts in GSWA were no doubt challenging, making many question their moral compasses. Simultaneously, the difficult economic realities of postwar South Africa pushed men to find money even if it meant working for the German army as it committed egregious crimes against humanity. While not respon-

205 Silvester and Gewald, *Words Cannot Be Found*, 174.
206 Beinart, "'Jamani,'" 52.

sible for the atrocities, they were part and parcel of the support structure that allowed for them to occur. They were, along with West African laborers on ships and at the colonial ports of GSWA crucial 'human infrastructure' for the war between 1904 and 1908.

War's End and the Colonial Workforce's Transformation

In 1908 the war would end in German South West Africa. The workforce of the colony was permanently transformed by genocide, economic development such as railway expansion and new mines, as well as large-scale migration. This chapter focused on three elements of that labor transformation during the war, the failure of the European Labor Corridor as an alternative to local labor, the success of the West African Labor Corridor in maritime transport for the war effort, as well as the expansion of the South African Labor Corridor, which primarily via ox wagon drivers supplied the German military with provisions in the field and supported the over 19,000 German troops in the colony.

These labor flows into GSWA related to larger labor movements across Africa in the early twentieth century. For West Africans the often dangerous, difficult, and low paid work on plantations and mines across West Africa, pushed Kru workers to seek contracts farther afield. This built on past experiences of long-distance labor for Kru, ranging from their history as ship hands to distant contracts to the Guianas or Panama in the nineteenth century.[207] However in the context of GSWA and the ships supporting the war effort there, the contracts were often better paid, and while conditions could be difficult, they were often preferable to alternatives. For South African Cape Workers, their expanding migratory route to GSWA gave skilled labor a lifeline from the drudgery and low pay of most alternatives in South Africa, such as underground work in the mines. The mines in South Africa were also in the process of attempting to bring worker costs down by importing Mozambican, Chinese and other laborers. Workers leaving to work in GSWA from South Africa would become an increasing concern in the years after 1908 as we will examine in Chapter 4. For Italians in GSWA, they were part of a large global labor flow of Italian migrant laborers to locations not only in colonial Africa but also across North and South America in the nineteenth

207 Gary. G. Kuhn, "Liberian Contract Labor in Panama, 1837–1897," *Liberian Studies Journal* 6, no. 1 (1974): 43–52; Monica Schuler, "Kru Emigration to British and French Guiana, 1841–1857," in *Africans in Bondage. Studies in Slavery and the Slave Trade. Essays in Honour of Philip D. Curtin on the Occasion of the Twenty-Fifth Anniversary of African Studies at the University of Wisconsin*, ed. Paul E. Lovejoy (Madison, Wisconsin, University of Wisconsin Press, 1986), 155–156.

and twentieth centuries. While GSWA was largely a failed opportunity for Italians looking for work abroad, in the global context, their total numbers as migrants were likely only second to Chinese migrant labor.

While South and West African migrant laborers had little to no direct role as combatants in the war, or in the military decision-making process, they were necessary auxiliaries in the larger conflict. Their essential nature as a workforce had landed them wages which far exceeded other Africans working in the colony, including migrants from the Ovambo polities. They would form a labor elite in the colony that would last until the end of German colonialism. This chapter did not discuss the Ovambo Labor Corridor coming from the Ovambo polities. Some Ovambo individuals had, as previously discussed in Chapter 1, already worked in the settler region before the war. During the conflict and especially after, Ovambo laborers would become the third and, in many ways, most important migrant labor corridor until the First World War and beyond. Their importance in understanding the labor history of colonial Namibia will therefore be the sole focus of the following chapter.

3 Workers from the North: The Ovambo Labor Corridor, 1905–1914

This chapter focuses on the most central pillar of the 'Namibian Labor Corridors': migrants from the Ovambo polities coming south into the colonial settler region of German South West Africa for work between 1905 and 1914.[1] The Ovambo Labor Corridor was central for the economy of GSWA to cope with the acute labor shortage resulting from the genocide of two groups, the Herero and Nama. Before the war, both groups of people had increasingly been taking up a more central role as contract laborers.[2] The war against the Herero in particular left uncertain who would make up the colonial labor force in the following years. While some local peoples, especially Damara, were increasingly pushed into contract work during the war in the colonial economy, their limited numbers and skill sets meant that more recruitment further afield was necessary. As discussed in the previous chapter, many thousand Kru and South Africans who worked as military auxiliaries and transport workers played a central role in the military buildup, war, and eventual victory of the German colonizers by 1908.

While both South Africans and Kru – joined from approximately 1905 to 1908 by thousands of forced Herero and Nama laborers – played a central role in keeping the colonial economy functioning, it was Ovambo migrants who by 1908 would increasingly be at the center of the labor force. The following pages will highlight the role of workers from the Ovambo polities in building the post-genocide economy and infrastructure of the German colony, continuing to do so after the First World War, when South West Africa came under South African rule. In particular, I will reflect on the importance of individual experiences of Ovambo workers from 1905 to 1914. This will encompass an exploration of why so many went on contract, what their daily lives entailed, the role shared stories played in expanding southbound recruitment, and how the difficulties of travel fit into the larger decision-making process. Central to this analysis is an examination of how workers in the settler region spent their time after shifts ended; what entailed relaxation and enjoyment? In this regard, throughout the chapter, I will expand on a few additional themes, including transformations in the role of gender and generational difference, masculinity, belonging, urban segregation, the social value of work, and local hierarchies during colonialism. These themes will

1 The Ovambo polities will also be referred to as the northern polities throughout this text.
2 See Chapter 1 of this book.

https://doi.org/10.1515/9783111374918-004

help to contextualize the multifaceted experiences of the Ovambo workers beyond labor itself.

I also make the case that Ovambo migrant labor during this period not only consisted of adult men, but large numbers of young boys, and – at least at the Tsumeb Copper mines – women. This supplements the scholarship on Ovambo migrant labor, which has focused primarily on adult men. I will also highlight the essential role which Ovambo laborers played in the colonial settler region as consumers. This was particularly important to the colonial economy as most German soldiers deployed to GSWA during the war returned to Europe, removing their role as consumers; Ovambos filled this gap to an extent. Although Ovambo migrants found jobs in settler towns, construction and repair works for the colonial railways, and farms, the large majority worked in the copper and diamond mines by the time war ended in 1908. Work at these mines will be the primary focus of this chapter.

As Patricia Hayes has highlighted, the historiography of Ovambo migrant labor forms a significant part of Namibian history research.[3] However, a detailed exploration of individual Ovambo experiences during the German colonial period remains scarce, often limited to instances of abuse, injury, sickness, and death. This chapter seeks to enrich this narrative by exploring workers as individuals with agency, building off of Lovisa Tegelela Nampala's and Job Shipululo Amupanda's approaches while focusing on an earlier period.[4] I agree with Gregor Dobler's perspective that young Ovambo men viewed labor migration as a crucial part of their life planning, often willingly accepting risks and hardships in pursuit of work.[5]

In contrast to the approach taken by scholars like Richard Moorsom and William Gervase Clarence-Smith, who primarily rely on secondary sources, missing the nuanced experiences of individual workers, this study foregrounds these aspects as central.[6] Their omission in not engaging with primary sources is a significant limitation in understanding the complexities of Ovambo migrant labor. In contrast, Regina Strasseger's work on GSWA diamond mine labor is groundbreak-

3 Patricia Hayes, "A History of the Ovambo of Namibia, c 1880–1935" (PhD thesis, Cambridge, University of Cambridge, 1992), 146.

4 Nampala, *Infrastructures of Migrant Labour in Colonial Ovamboland*; Job Shipululo Amupanda, *Diamond Warriors in Colonial Namibia: Diamond Smuggling, Migrant Workers and Development in Owamboland* (Basel, Switzerland: Basler Afrika Bibliographien, 2022).

5 Dobler, *Traders and Trade in Colonial Ovamboland, 1925–1990*, 12.

6 W.G. Clarence-Smith and R. Moorsom, "Underdevelopment and Class Formation in Ovamboland, 1845–1915," in *Namibia 1884–1984: Readings on Namibia's History and Society*, vol. 16, ed. Brian Wood (London: Namibia Support Committee, 1988), 175–189.

ing and thorough in using archives, however it largely portrays Ovambo workers as victims, a narrative that my research challenges.[7] This is a common thread in the field, as seen in Mokopakgosi's general overview of Ovambo labor, which, while offering useful details, does not delve into the individual lives of workers.[8] Lastly, Steven Press' innovative approach brings GSWA diamond mining into a global business and political perspective, but still primarily views Ovambo workers through this same lens.[9]

By examining micro-histories and integrating them into broader socio-economic trends, my aim is to provide a more nuanced understanding of Ovambo laborers. This chapter not only enriches our understanding of their roles and lives but also extends beyond a Namibian focus, positioning GSWA's diamond industry within a larger African context. I explore how Ovambo migrant labor compares with other regions where independent polities faced the encroachment of colonial capitalism.

While existing literature has extensively explored the internal changes within Ovambo polities due to migrant labor, such as Meredith McKittrick's study of its impact on young men's liberation from gerontocracy, and Kletus Likuwa's recent work on women's economic and social support for laborers at home, this chapter takes a different angle.[10] It introduces a focus on the understudied aspect of women who joined men as laborers at Tsumeb during the German colonial period.

This chapter, therefore, contributes to an expanded view of the Ovambo migrant labor experience during the German colonial period in Namibia. It seeks to balance the narrative, providing insights into not just the collective experiences of these laborers but also their individual stories and the broader implications of their migration.

To begin our exploration of Ovambo migrant labor in GSWA, we first need to understand who these migrants were and the Ovambo polities from which they originated. Following this, we will delve into their experiences of recruitment, travel, labor on the mines, life beyond labor in the south, and for most their eventual return home.

---

7 Strassegger, "Die Wanderarbeit der Ovambo während der deutschen Kolonialbesetzung Namibias," 111–165.

8 Mokopakgosi, "German Colonialism in Microcosm," 528–541.

9 Steven Press, *Blood and Diamonds: Germany's Imperial Ambitions in Africa* (Cambridge: Harvard University Press, 2021), 113–131.

10 McKittrick, "The 'Burden' of Young Men"; Meredith McKittrick, *To Dwell Secure: Generation, Christianity, and Colonialism in Ovamboland* (Portsmouth: Heinemann, 2002); Kletus Muhena Likuwa, "Continuity and Change in Gender Relations within the Contract Labour System in Kavango, Namibia, 1925–1972," *Journal of Southern African Studies* 47, no. 1 (2021): 79–92.

Ovambos in the Settler Region and the Northern Polities

In the graph below we see some statistics of Ovambo people in the Police Zone from 1908 to 1913, including a breakdown of men, women, and children.

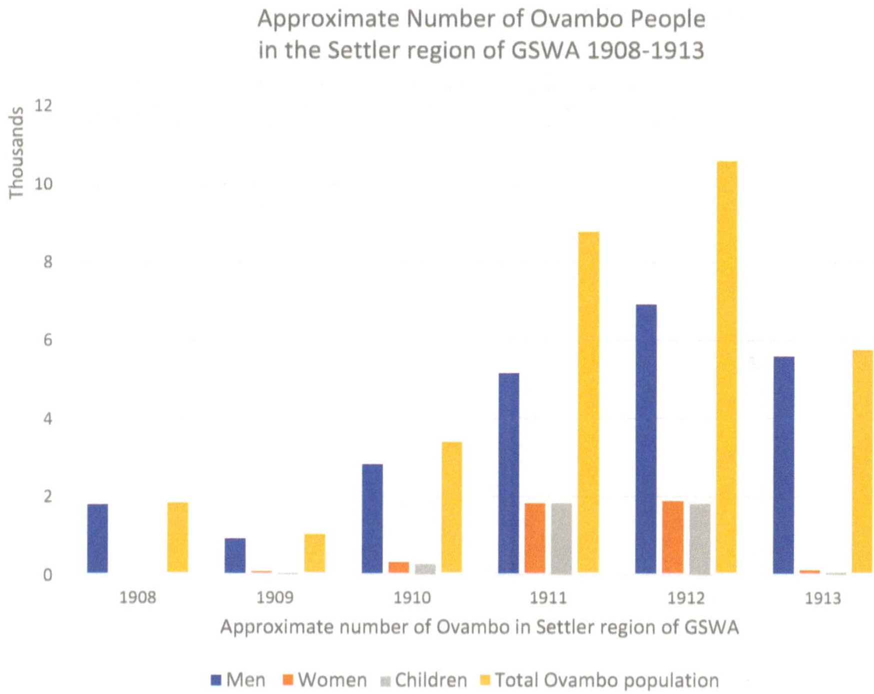

Figure 18: Approximate number of Ovambo Individuals in Settler region of GSWA 1908–1913. The graph begins in 1908 as comparable records from the previous years do not exist.[11]

The statistics above (Figure 18) come from the German colonial records, and while they are rough estimates, they give us a relatively good idea of the increase in Ovambo migrants to the Police Zone, including of women and children. The numbers balloon from the end of the colonial war in 1908 and the following rapid

---

11 Compiled from NAN, ZBU 172 A.VI.d Vol. 1, Population Statistics Natives and Coloreds Main Statistics, Population Statistics on the Natives and Coloreds Population at the Beginning of the Year 1908–1913.

economic growth in the colony until WWI.[12] We can see that in the data from 1911 and 1912 between 1,500 and 2,000 women and children were in the Police Zone. Most were to be found in the Grootfontein district (Figure 19), not very far south from the Ovambo polities themselves; and many likely took up work at the Tsumeb mines without a formal contract (at least in the earlier years).

During the entire 1908 to 1913 period, Ovambo migrants made up the largest share of migrants, except for 1909, in which there were approximately 1,275 Cape workers compared to 988 Ovambo workers in the Police Zone.[13] Let us briefly get an overview of where Ovambo migrants were living and working in the settler region.

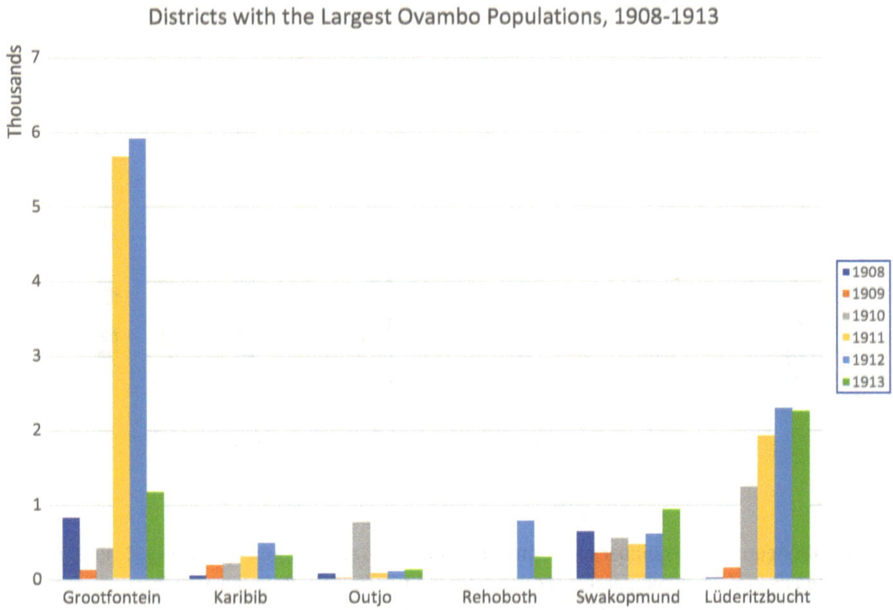

Figure 19: Districts in the Settler Zone with the Largest Ovambo Populations between 1908 and 1913. Statistics are from the first day of each year.[14]

12 Children, while not specified in the documents, are likely those under seven-years-old based on native pass laws, meaning that many who are classified as women and men are by modern standards also children.

13 NAN, ZBU 172 A.VI.d Vol. 1, Population statistics Natives and Coloreds Main statistics, the total colored population of GSWA (excluding Ovamboland and Caprivi) on January 1, 1909, 10.

14 Compiled from NAN, ZBU 172 A.VI.d Vol. 1, Population Statistics Indigenous and Colored Principal Statistics. The indigenous population of GSWA, so far as it is subject to administration, by administrative district, race, and sex, 1908–1913.

An important piece of data above (Figure 19) is that most Ovambo in the Police Zone were in the two primary mining districts: Grootfontein and Lüderitzbucht.[15] Swakopmund, as an important port and settler town, also had a consistently large Ovambo worker population as has been explored in the past two chapters. The populations at Karibib and Rehoboth were primarily employed for train construction. Outjo is perhaps the outlier for one year, in that Ovambo migrants there were likely working on farms, but after realizing the harsh and unpreferable conditions pursued future contracts in other districts. To summarize, the Ovambo migrant population in the Police Zone between 1908 and 1914 fluctuated between about 2,000 and 10,000 people, and the densest centers of population were in the two mining. Let's briefly review where these thousands of workers were coming from.

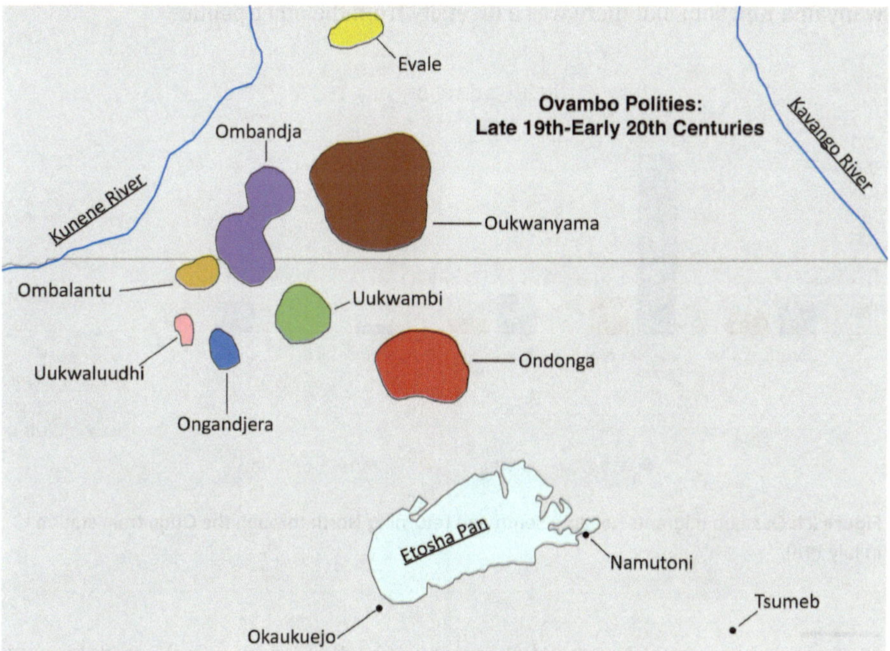

Figure 20: Map of the Ovambo polities, (Cartography by Bernard C. Moore).

15 The statistics for Lüderitzbucht are a slight undercount because of the ever-changing nature of the population due to migration inflows and outflows. For example, a monthly count of Ovambo workers at Lüderitzbucht's diamond went from 2,001 workers at the beginning of February 1912 to 3,615 workers the next month; see NAN, ZBU 0162 A.VI.a.8 Vol. 1, Annual report of the native commissioner 1913–1914, Annual Report of the Imperial Native Commission for Lüderitzbucht 1.4.1912–31.3.1913, Workforce, 53.

As we can see in the map above (Figure 20), there were many Ovambo polities in the German South West African and Angolan border region in the late nineteenth and early twentieth centuries. The German army Captain Viktor Franke made an estimate that the population stood at approximately 160,000 people around 1910. Of that population, the two largest polities, the Kingdoms of Oukwanyama at 100,000 and Ondonga at 25,000 people, were home to most Ovambo migrant laborers during the 1908 to 1914 period. However, smaller polities were not insignificant in size, and many laborers came from other homelands such as Uukwambi (population 20,000), Ongandjera (7,000), and Uukwaluudhi (7,000).[16] As to the proportion of individuals from the various polities working in the Police Zone, a 1910 colonial newspaper gives us numbers going through the important transit hub at Outjo Station in July. We can see below (Figure 21) that the largest number of migrants were coming from the Oukwanyama Kingdom, but there was a diversity from the other polities.

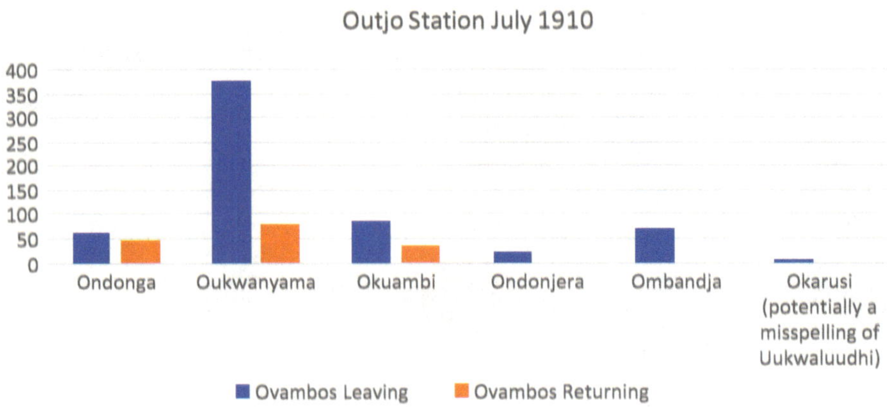

Figure 21: Ovambo migrants heading South and returning North through the Outjo train station in July 1910.[17]

16 Eirola, *The Ovambogefahr*, 243–244; Records from the diamond mines in the south from 1913 and 1914 indicate that most workers were from Okwanyama with but with sizeable numbers of workers from the Ombandja, Ongandjera, Oukwambi and Ondonga Kingdoms, see NAN, BLU [011] B.G.L Band 4–5, Diamond mine African worker estate Files.

17 The paper reports 62 Ondonga, 377 Oukwanyama, 86 Okuambi, 23 Ondonjera, 70 Ombandja, and seven Okarusi (potentially a misspelling of Uukwaluudhi) Ovambo people. Returning north through the station were 48 Ondonga, 80 Oukwanyama, and 36 Okuambi people. Compiled from *Windhuker Nachrichten* (WN), 'Verschiedenes,' 17.09.1910; a 1912 to 1913 report from the diamond mines also includes Ovambo workers from the Uukwaluudhi, and Ombalantu polities; see NAN, ZBU 0162 A.VI.a.8 Vol. 1, Annual report of the native commissioner 1913–1914, Annual Report of the Imperial Native Commission for Lüderitzbucht 1.4.1912–31.3.1913, 55.

By the early 1900s Ovambo rulers were in varying degrees of contact with the German colonial government and by 1911 some, such as King Iipumbu of Uukwambi had made deals to receive money from the German government in exchange for sending migrants south.[18] While pressure to go south was exerted by some polity rulers, many reasons existed for why individuals went on contract.

Why Go South? Going on Contract and the Process of Labor Recruitment

Central to understanding Ovambo contract labor is to ask why individuals would go south in the first place. The answer to the question 'why?' for Ovambo migrants is perhaps one of the more complex of the various groups of migrant workers we have examined thus far. Ovambo Migrants were coming from polities that were still largely independent from colonial rule, were not yet deeply dependent (beyond the wealthy royalty) on larger capitalist trade networks – especially in terms of crops and cattle – and the polities had very strong militaries to defend against colonial forces. However, since the mid-nineteenth century things had been slowly changing, especially as European long-distance trade had become more common in the polities.[19] That being said, Ovambo societies were still comparatively isolated for Southern Africa, especially compared to others that were also close to white settlement. Their integration into a wider economy was primarily through migrant labor. Hayes has argued that some of the only similar Southern African societies at the time, regarding their isolation, were perhaps the Venda or Mpondo.[20] This means that while on an individual level, workers' experiences in the settler zone could be very similar to others on contract, the larger context of their migration was quite different.

In exploring the multi-faceted answers to 'why go south?,' we will examine a few general themes related to migration such as ideas of 'modernity,' desiring various western goods, as well as social pressures.[21] Importantly, using a few individual estates including items and money of workers who died while on contract,

18 E.L.P Stals, *Duits-Suidwes-Afrika na die Groot Opstande: 'n studie in die verhouding tussen owerheid en inboorlinge* (Pretoria: Die Staatsdrukker, 1984), 50.

19 Siiskonen, *Trade and Socioeconomic Change in Ovamboland, 1850–1906*, 89–135.

20 Hayes, "A History of the Ovambo of Namibia, c 1880–1935," 10–11.

21 Philipp Prein has done insightful work on the wearing of western clothing, such as top hats, in the settler region by Damara, as a symbol of success and upward mobility; see Philipp Prein, "Guns and Top Hats: African Resistance in German South West Africa, 1907–1915," *Journal of Southern African Studies* 20, no. 1 (1994): 117–118.

we will examine what exactly workers were buying and planning on bringing back home.

In 1905 Rhenish missionary Wulfhorst, in referencing increasing Ovambo migration to the settler region wrote, "[n]ow Ovamboland is emerging more from its seclusion, & going to Hereroland has become in fashion."[22] By this year the German war against the Herero and Nama was raging, and relatedly demand for Ovambo labor, especially in building the Otavi railway, as well as for work in Swakopmund was increasing. From 1905 until late into the twentieth century, circular Ovambo migration became more and more engrained in the fabric of Ovambo societies.

In the missionary's description of the migration process as 'in fashion,' we get a glimpse of the power of word of mouth, and the influence of shared stories recalling work experiences in the settler region as a prime instigator of this early twentieth-century migration. The process whereby new workers were convinced to go south was often a social process. Wulfhorst went on to observe the following:

> They [returned migrant laborers] often stay together, especially on Sunday before and after church and tell their stories. The others, who have not yet been down south, listen intently and think that it must be a wonderful country, where one can eat rice to one's fill, drink coffee and brandy, always wear clothes, and even go to the store as a big man and buy things as desired. Why shouldn't the others also try their hand?
>
> Of course, most of them do not mention the dark side, that they often get beaten, that they get their 20 lashings with the whip, rightly or wrongly, only a few tell. Those who are in such a situation, do not feel like going back to Hereroland, but with time our people forget such things. The desire awakens anew and encouraged by others, they soon leave again, and so, unfortunately, their Christianity goes more and more downhill.[23]

From the mission perspective, as articulated by Wulfhorst, the contemporary form of migration was seen as having a deleterious effect on the Ovambo Christian community. He argued that this migration led to a decline in Christian religious practice and an increase in behaviors deemed 'sinful' by the missions.[24] This perspective

22 Archiv- und Museumsstiftung der Vereinte Evangelische Mission (VEM), RMG 2630 Mission conference in Ovamboland – Report from Wulfhorst, 2.10.05, Namakunde, „Was können wir tun für die zum Hereroland ziehenden Ovambojünglinge u. Männer, insbesondere für unsere Gemeindeglieder?," 1. Translation to English by W.B. Lyon.

23 VEM, RMG 2630 Mission conference in Ovamboland – Report from Wulfhorst, 2.10.05, Namakunde, „Was können wir tun für die zum Hereroland ziehenden Ovambojünglinge u. Männer, insbesondere für unsere Gemeindeglieder?," 13. Translation to English by W.B. Lyon.

24 Similar to Rhenish missionaries, Finnish missionaries in Ovamboland also saw migrant labor to the south as a negative influence on their Christian communities; see Eirola, *The Ovambogefahr*, 214.

highlights the tension between missionaries and changes wrought by capitalist influence and labor migration.

From the viewpoint of potential migrants, the importance of social interactions in promoting contract work becomes evident. Due to the relative independence of the Ovambo polities, recruitment was largely indirect, making these social dynamics crucial in individuals' decisions to work in the Police Zone. Wulfhorst noted that for men lacking livestock, such as cattle, migrating to the settler region presented an opportunity to earn money. This income was often used to purchase clothing and other goods, which were then brought back to the polities, sometimes being traded for cattle. This was significant as cash wages were scarce in the north, except for limited and lower-paying jobs at the missions.[25]

In the early twentieth century, Christian converts among the Ovambo people, though still a minority, began to influence broader community values with their shifting perceptions of success. Initially, these early converts often received Western clothing from missionaries as symbols of their new faith.[26] Over time, however, these garments came to represent prosperity and social standing, reflecting a broader societal change where traditional dress increasingly incorporated or was replaced by Western styles and materials.[27] This transformation was part of a global trend, particularly in regions influenced by Christian missions, and was seen in places as distant as the Hawaiian kingdom in the nineteenth century.[28]

Alongside traditional symbols of wealth like cattle and land, new indicators such as Western items started to gain prominence, becoming accessible beyond royal and elite circles. The allure of acquiring commodities like coffee and brandy, rare luxuries in the north, also fueled this migration. The scarcity of these goods

---

25 VEM, RMG 2630 Mission conference in Ovamboland – Report from Wulfhorst, 2.10.05, Namakunde, „Was können wir tun für die zum Hereroland ziehenden Ovambojünglinge u. Männer, insbesondere für unsere Gemeindeglieder?", 9–10.

26 VEM, RMG 2630, Report from Wulfhorst 1903: "Gibt es in unserer Ovambomission eine Frauenfrage? p. 85v f., quoted in, Dobler, *Traders and Trade in Colonial Ovamboland, 1925–1990*, 10; The National Archives of Finland (NAF), kotelo 986, Letter from Missionary Rautanen at Olukonda to Eduard Hälbich, 29.3.1917, 34.

27 Nampala and Shigwedha, *Aawambo Kingdoms, History and Cultural Change*, 127–128; Martha Ndakalako-Bannikov, "Changing Dresses: Owambo Traditional Dress and Discourses on Tradition, Ethnicity, and National Identity in Namibia," *Journal of Folklore Research* 57 (2020): 73–110.

28 Patrick Vinton Kirch and Marshall Sahlins, *Anahulu: The Anthropology of History in the Kingdom of Hawaii, Volume 1: Historical Ethnography* (Chicago: University of Chicago Press, 1994), 163–165; for a detailed look at the intersection of clothing and missions, see Robert Ross, *Clothing: A Global History* (Cambridge: Polity, 2008), 83–102.

intensified after the German imperial restriction in 1906, which limited outside access to the Ovambo polities and curtailed trading activities.[29]

The Ovambo aspiration for material improvement reflects a broader pattern observed across Africa. Young men from various groups were drawn to industrializing colonial areas in search of better economic opportunities. This trend is mirrored in the Shangaan laborers heading to Rhodesian gold mines in the early twentieth century, the Amatongas working in late nineteenth-century Natal, and the Kru engaging in maritime work aboard European ships in the mid nineteenth century.[30] Each of these groups, including the Ovambo, were motivated by the prospect of enhancing their economic status, despite the diverse challenges and contexts they encountered. Further, these opportunities could provide new pathways for increasing one's social status in ways that were previously impossible. Drilling down to the individual level, we have evidence of what drove Ovambo workers to go south in the estates of those who died while on contract during the 1905 to 1914 period.

One such worker, listed as 'Emmanuel' (likely an alias), given the pass number 1446, worked for the diamond mining firm Weiß, de Meillon & Co.[31] He died on June 17, 1910, of pneumonia and left behind the following: £1 4/- in cash, one pack of beads, a jacket, a mirror, and six slabs of tobacco. His estate was given to a fellow worker listed as 'Alanhina', pass number 1725 to take back to the Ovambo polities.[32] From his tobacco, regardless of whether he personally intended to use it, trade it, or gift it to others, we are reminded of the prevalence of smoking amongst much of the population in the settler region. Tobacco was part of provisions for all contract workers, at least on paper, and records show that among many Namibian people, since at least the mid nineteenth century, it was widely smoked.[33]

As the Ovambo region was only slowly integrating into colonial markets and trade networks by the early twentieth century, most Ovambo workers, such as Emmanuel, likely saw tobacco as a luxury good. This would not be dissimilar to parts of Africa, including western Central Africa, which initially viewed tobacco, upon introduction to markets in a similar fashion.[34] Emmanuel's pack of beads was a common possession amongst the Ovambo workers during this period.

29 Dobler, *Traders and Trade in Colonial Ovamboland, 1925–1990*, 16.

30 van Onselen, *Chibaro*, 88–89; Harries, *Work, Culture, and Identity*, 45–46; Mark-Thiesen, *Mediators, Contract Men, and Colonial Capital*, 75–76.

31 As almost all Ovambo names in the colonial record are likely aliases, I will no longer continue to point this out but it should be assumed unless otherwise stated.

32 NAN, BLU [168] Vol. 1, Death of natives in Diamond area, Estate of Ovambo Emanuel 1446, 6.

33 Chris S. Duvall, "Cannabis and Tobacco in Precolonial and Colonial Africa," *Oxford Research Encyclopedia of African History*, 2017, 18.

34 Duvall, "Cannabis and Tobacco in Precolonial and Colonial Africa," 19.

Beads had been used for trade in the Ovambo polities throughout the nineteenth and early twentieth centuries.[35] They were easily portable and took up little space. This was beneficial especially when many migrants would already be transporting bulky western clothing and textiles to the north. Beads as a form of currency had a long tradition on the African continent and beyond, including in the nineteenth century East African caravan trade, Tswana trade in nineteenth-century South Africa, and going back to the earliest contact between West Africans and the Portuguese.[36] Missionary observations from the Oukwanyama kingdom in 1906 note that beads, pieces of cloth, and Western clothing were all used as local forms of currency.[37]

Another Ovambo worker who died on the job with a detailed estate record was 'Maruru,' with pass number 944, who also worked for Weiß, de Meillon & Co. He died of Beriberi on June 21, 1910, and his estate included: 15/-, two pipes, two mirrors, a pair of scissors, four pieces of toilette soap, two packs of beads, one headscarf, three meters of cloth, one loin cloth, one shirt, one jacket, and one blanket.[38] As we shall later see when discussing worker health in the south, the soap could have played an important role in attempting to stay healthy in a work environment that could often be a hotbed for disease. Maybe most interesting is his three meters of cloth, which displayed how Maruru was converting his cash into tradable commodities beyond beads, for his return to the north.

Finally, let us look at the estate of Ovambo worker 'Gambisa,' pass number 7228. He had worked at diamond field number 809 and was taken to the Kolmanskop native hospital where he died on April 7, 1911. His cause of death is not listed but he left behind seven sacks of beads, one undershirt, one sweater, two women's blouses that were white, one blue shirt, one pot, three leather belts, a metal

---

35 Kalle Gustafsson, "The Trade in Slaves in Ovamboland, ca. 1850–1910," *African Economic History*, no. 33 (2005): 33–34, 42, 56.

36 Karin Pallaver, "A Recognized Currency in Beads. Glass Beads as Money in Nineteenth-Century East Africa: The Central Caravan Road," in *Money in Africa*, ed. Catherine Eagleton, Harcourt Fuller, and John Perkins (London: The British Museum Press, 2009), 21–24; A. W. Cardinall, "Aggrey Beads of the Gold Coast," *African Affairs* 24, no. 96 (1925): 290; Jean Comaroff and John L. Comaroff, "Cattle, Currencies & the Politics of Commensuration on a Colonial Frontier," in *The Political Economy of Everyday Life in Africa: Beyond the Margins*, ed. Wale Adebanwi (Woodbridge: James Currey, 2017), 44–45.

37 Martin Siefkes, "Einführung in das Tagebuch des Johannes Spiecker während des Herero-Nama-Aufstands in Deutsche Südwestafrika," in *Mein Tagebuch: Erfahrungen eines deutschen Missionars in Deutsch-Südwestafrika 1905–1907*, ed. Lisa Kopelmann and Martin Siefkes (Berlin: Simon Verl. für Bibliothekswissen, 2013), 22.

38 NAN, BLU [168] Vol. 1, Death of natives in Diamond area, Estate of Maruru 944, 8–9.

trunk, and £2 3/5d.[39] The women's clothing were particularly valuable in comparison to pieces of textile, and when one combines these with his other possessions we can see that Gambisa had a sizable estate before he died.

The items that 'Emmanuel, 'Maruru,' and 'Gambisa' left behind are diverse but also have a few general connecting threads such as tradable commodities for the north, like textiles and beads, as well as consumable items like tobacco, and liquid assets for use in the Police Zone in the form of German currency. All these workers likely intended to take these items back north in a metal trunk, common among most Ovambo estates, and then use them personally, give gifts, or to trade for cattle or other goods. One example of how trade functioned in the polities was from Missionary Spiecker, who noted during his trip to Oukwanyama in 1906 that a thimble of beads could buy him about a cup of millet.[40]

While these examples are informative as to what Ovambo workers would often buy with their earnings, most Ovambo estates from the German colonial period had little to no physical assets. This likely reflects that most individuals would have used their pay to buy goods on the way back home. Even more common than items in estates, were liquid assets and back pay. For example, in a group of ten Ovambo estates of men who died in October of 1910, six out of 10 workers were owed back pay. Three men had trunks left behind. Four are listed as having no possessions.[41] The amount of money that Ovambo workers who died on the job could vary from 3/- to £6 7/-. However, the large majority who passed away, died with estates of less than £1.[42] Looking at what the Ovambo men previously mentioned left behind gives us clear examples of what workers may have intended to use their earnings on.

In addition to the reasons listed above, more basic concerns also drove migration to work on contract. Food supply or lack thereof, especially during drought and subsequent famine, was a life-threatening reason for some to go on contract.[43]

---

39 NAN, BLU [168] Vol. 1, Death of natives in Diamond area, Police Report on dead Ovambo workers and their estates, Station Bismarksfeld, 29.4.1911.

40 Johannes Spiecker, *Mein Tagebuch: Erfahrungen eines deutschen Missionars in Deutsch-Südwestafrika 1905–1907*, ed. Lisa Kopelmann and Martin Siefkes (Berlin: Simon Verl. für Bibliothekswissen, 2013), 330.

41 NAN, BLU [168] Vol. 1, Death of natives in Diamond area, District Lüderitzbucht office's list of dead from the local hospital at Charlottental, 15.10.1910, 17; NAN, BLU [168] Vol. 1, Death of natives in Diamond area, District Lüderitzbucht office's list of dead from the local hospital at Charlottental, 2.2.1911.

42 Lyon, *Namibian Worker Database*; NAN, BLU [011] B.G.L. Band 4–5, 70 Ovambo worker estates containing relevant data.

43 Strassegger, "Die Wanderarbeit der Ovambo während der deutschen Kolonialbesetzung Namibias," 75.

Further, drought periods after 1897 were made more severe because of the rinderpest devastation of Ovambo cattle herds.[44] In the south, one could seemingly get regular meals and potentially be able to help family members back home with cash earnings. Conversely, regarding at least the Ondonga Kingdom, Finnish missionaries stated that at homesteads with sufficient food, it was much less likely that young men would go south.[45] Regardless of why Ovambo individuals went to work in the settler zone, the majority would first need to get a contract, especially those who planned to work south of Tsumeb.

With the outbreak of war in 1904, hiring workers became much more difficult for colonial actors in the Police Zone. Increased emphasis by employers was placed on recruiting Ovambo labor because of their vicinity to job sites, as well as lower wages compared to the alternative options such as the highly paid Italians, South and West African workers as discussed in the previous chapter. Construction of the Otavi Bahn – designated a military priority by General von Trotha – necessitated a large work force, and by the end of 1904, Italian labor was not a long-term solution. Two traders, Haag and Lenssen, were sent to the Ondonga Kingdom to recruit, and promising not to give alcohol to contracted workers, received the support of the Finnish missionaries based there. Additionally, they visited the Oukwanyama Kingdom and were able to secure, what they thought to be monopolistic recruitment treaties with both polities, although these were later said to be void by the colonial government.[46] Likely writing of this recruiting in 1905, missionary Wulfhorst stated:

> [T]he whites in Hereroland [the settler region] are also very fond of the Ovambo workers. Even at the beginning of this year, the district chief of Outjo wrote to Nande [Oukwanyama King] for workers. At the same time there were also two gentlemen here who wanted to make a contract with Nande so that he would give them the right to recruit in Oukwanyama. Now someone is here again to make contracts for the Otavi Railway. They go to great expense and hope for great things from the contracts, but in my opinion they have no value at all. The chiefs quickly say yes and everything else remains the same. [So there is no lack of recruiting workers, because natives are often sent from Hereroland to fetch workers.][47]

In the missionary's quote we garner a few recruitment realities in relation to Ovambo workers that not only were true for the war years, but for the rest of the

44 Mokopakgosi, "German Colonialism in Microcosm," 511.
45 Eirola, *The Ovambogefahr*, 214.
46 Eirola, *The Ovambogefahr*, 214–215; Mokopakgosi, "German Colonialism in Microcosm," 509.
47 VEM, RMG 2630 Mission conference in Ovamboland – Report from Wulfhorst, 2.10.05, Namakunde, „Was können wir tun für die zum Hereroland ziehenden Ovambojünglinge u. Männer, insbesondere für unsere Gemeindeglieder?,“ 5. Translation to English by W.B. Lyon.

German colonial period. Visiting colonial actors in the polities, be they military or civilian, often tried to secure recruitment arrangements, and Ovambo leaders frequently agreed. However, the independence, geographical separation, and general military strength of such leaders in contrast to the colonial state's lack of presence in the Ovambo region, meant that these agreements were only valid for as long as the polities' rulers wished to maintain them.

The reference above to workers from "Hereroland" fetching fellow countrymen to come south, was probably the more influential factor in additional men joining. This connects with the earlier quote regarding returned laborers convincing others to join. By August 1905, Finnish missionaries remarked that seemingly all young men from the Ondonga Kingdom were working on the Otavi railway, where approximately 2,000 Ovambo workers were employed.[48] Such a trend adds credence to the idea that by this time, going on contract was becoming an important signifier of identity amongst young men in the polities. But recruiting Ovambo workers piecemeal for specific projects could not support the labor supply needed by the colonial economy after the birth of the copper and diamond industrial mining sectors in 1907 to 1908.

Starting around 1908, hiring Ovambo labor transitioned to a formalized system based on recruitment centers just south of the polities, and related worker transport infrastructure. The use of rail for worker transport was not unlike the recruitment infrastructure built for the gold mines of the Rand in South Africa.[49] Connected to this imperial push for formalized Ovambo recruitment was also an increasing attempt by the colonial government to have more control over Africans in the settler region.

In 1907, pass laws were implemented that required all Africans in the settler region over the age of seven to carry government issued passes with them, or face penalties including arrest.[50] This law also applied to migrant laborers who were entering the region. The pass decrees coincided with new regulations that restricted all whites from entering the Ovambo polities without permission from the colonial government, making the north increasingly cut off from the settler region. To ensure migrant Ovambo individuals would be registered and given passes, they needed to go through one of two recruiting centers established at Fort Namutoni and Okaukweyo, both located near the "red line" to the south of the polities. On the return journey, migrants were supposed to again pass through either one of these locations to ensure they could be tracked.[51] Recruits were men

48 Eirola, *The Ovambogefahr*, 214.
49 Pirie, "Railways and Labour Migration to the Rand Mines," 715–716.
50 Zimmerer, *German Rule, African Subjects*, 84.
51 Zimmerer, *German Rule, African Subjects*, 260–261.

and boys above the age of seven. While this new system did greatly change the regulation of Ovambo labor, with the majority siphoned to Fort Namutoni or Okaukweyo before going south, many were able to bypass the recruitment centers and go directly to the copper mines at Tsumeb.[52] As the result of Tsumeb's relative closeness to the polities, workers did not need to utilize the colonial transport system, which required proper documentation, to get there. This is likely one reason that Tsumeb had such a large Ovambo population which included many women.

However, for the vast majority of Ovambo looking for work and arriving at the recruitment centers, they were not only able to get contracts, but also received additional provisions and clothing for the further journey. On a trip that for many had already been at least dozens of kilometers and would be hundreds before their arrival at work sites, this was essential.

At Namutoni or Okaukuejo, recruiters oversaw choosing potential recruits from arrivals. These recruiters were supposed to be individuals with knowledge of local languages like Oshiwambo, or economic independence (likely from the employers to avoid bribery). However, recruiters with such traits were seemingly rare. Strassegger describes them as particularly profit centric ruffians, many with backgrounds not relevant to their jobs ranging from questionable traders to former soldiers given work as payback for their service.[53] The potential high earning of recruiters also attracted German farmers, such as Mr. Kreft, who apparently gave up his farm in the Omaruru district and moved himself and his family to Okaukuejo to become a recruiter of Ovambo workers.[54] Examples like this point to how difficult life could be even for settlers to make a living in the colony, and how sectors generating incredible wealth, such as the mining and related recruitment attracted settlers and Africans alike. Most recruiters worked for firms, such as *Liebert & Beer* and *Carl Bödiker & Co.* Even *Woermann-Linie* had its hand in the business via one of its subsidiaries, *Woermann, Brock & Co.*, which as of 1909 was majority owned by the Woermann parent company.[55]

In negotiating and signing contracts, most workers had an idea of what was to be expected, from either a previous round working in the south or through

52 For more on how Ovambo society viewed the "red line" and their increasing separation from the settler region at this time, see Miescher, *Namibia's Red Line*, 69.

53 Strassegger, "Die Wanderarbeit der Ovambo während der deutschen Kolonialbesetzung Namibias," 64–65.

54 NAN, ZBU 2068 W.IV.i.8. Travel, food, and clothing for recruited Ovambo 1910–1913, Letter from Farmer Benningausen to the Omaruru District Office, Otjigondawirongo, 30.10.1910, 27.

55 Todzi, *Unternehmen Weltaneignung*, 365–366; Strassegger, "Die Wanderarbeit der Ovambo während der deutschen Kolonialbesetzung Namibias," 66.

stories from fellow countrymen. However, some recruiters did deceive recruits – especially first timers – about contract length and provisions. One clear case of deception was by recruiter Schulze, who in early 1914 signed a group of thirty-one Ovambo workers at Namutoni, to work in the diamond mines around Lüderitzbucht on six-month contracts. After the contracts were signed and before handing them to the police, who would then put them in a sealed envelope for the workers' foreman, Schulze secretly changed the contracts to nine months. On their way south at Conception Bay, the Ovambo men went to colonial police to change back their contracts to what had been agreed upon, which was done.[56] For Ovambo migrants, external factors like this often outside their control could and did at times interfere with their trip south and future work. Echoing the war period explored in the previous chapter, we will see other examples in the following pages, of how certain aspects of so-called contracted 'free labor' could and would continue to be constrained.

At the recruitment sites, Ovambo men and boys were given a medical examination and if deemed 'fit for work' (*arbeitsfähig*), received a contract (*Dienstvertrag*), an Ovambo passport (Ovambo Reise-Paß), and a metal pass token from recruiters and colonial police. As to what constituted fit for work by medical staff, this likely varied from examiner to examiner, and was seemingly lax resulting from almost constant work shortages in the south. Police Sergeant Schuster in the contract tempering case mentioned above reported a seven-year-old boy as part of the work group headed south. At seven years of age, he was considered too young, and his contract was revoked. But many young boys did head south and the age of seven was seemingly arbitrary, especially as boys could lie, or recruiters could let through individuals at their will.

Below (Figure 22) we see an example of how young some recruits could be. These young men and boys are on their way to the recruiting office at Tsumeb around 1913. The young man in the middle of the photo is wearing a pass token necklace indicating that he has already been through one of the recruiting centers.

An Ovambo Passport that was received at Namutoni provides an apt example of how the recruitment process went for individuals. We will briefly review the pass below and then return to it later to recall more of this migrant's journey, work, and eventually unfortunate death on the return trip.

56 NAN, ZBU 2071 W.IV.I.2 Vol. 1, Ovambo Worker contract and obligations of the employer under the same, specialia, 1911–1914, Polizeistation J.Nr. 57, Report on a work contract with Ovambos by Police Seargeant Schuster, Empfängnisbucht (modern Conception Bay), 24.02.1914.

Figure 22: Tsumeb 1913: Ovambos on the way to the mine's labor office.[57]

As we can see below (Figure 23) 'Kasino' was from Ondonga and was recruited in Namutoni on March 26, 1913, by the firm Rudolf Seibert. The contract was to begin when arriving at the diamond fields (*Diamantfelder*) in the south. His employer was listed as the Lüderitzbucht Chamber of Mines, which was a conglomeration of the large diamond mines of the south. We see on the top left page written by hand that he would later be assigned to work at the *Koloniale Bergbaugesellschaft* (KBG), which was one of the larger mines operating around Lüderitzbucht. Lastly, on the lower two pages we see that his pay would be 20 Marks, or slightly under £1 monthly, with the possibility that this could increase based on performance. Pay depending on the Ovambo worker at the mines would vary between 10 and 20 Marks.

Payment of £1 per month was essentially the highest initial wages paid by employers to adult Ovambo male workers in the settler zone. This rate, while often not offered to first time recruits, young boys, women (at Tsumeb), or indi-

57 BADKGUB, Photo PA02_013.

Figure 23: Kasino Ovambo's pass and work book.[58]

viduals who were not in prime health, was average for men working for larger, wealthier companies (especially at the diamond mines). They aimed to outcompete other potential employers with less resources, like farms, for Ovambo laborers. As described by Strassegger, farmers tended to pay as low as 3/- to 5/- monthly, drastically less than what workers could earn at the diamond mines.[59] Furthermore, cases of farmers not giving Ovambo workers proper clothing, in one case only 'short sacks' that could not protect individuals from the cold can be

58 NAN, ZBU 2068 W.IV. i.8. Travel, food, and clothing for recruited Ovambo 1910–1913, Ovambo-Reisepaß & Dienst Vertrag for Kasino, 30–33.

59 Ovambo workers for the Otavi railway were paid the same rate plus rations; see Friedrich Ammerman, "Wheels of Empire: The Otavi Railway and German Colonialism in South West Africa, 1882 – 1914" (Master's thesis, Berlin, Freie University, 2018), 45; while typical for the mines, Strassegger shows that for other work pay was on average lower; see Strassegger, "Die Wanderarbeit der Ovambo während der deutschen Kolonialbesetzung Namibias," 158.

found in the archives. Even more draconian, instances of farmers not paying workers seem not to have been uncommon.[60] Understandably, most Ovambo would avoid farm work if possible.

Comparatively high wages at diamond mines counter Mokopogasi's argument, that limiting Ovambo recruitment to Namutoni and Okaukuejo throttled Ovambo worker's capacity to search for the best wages.[61] Rather, the ability to sign a contract just south of the polities allowed workers to get some provisions and to receive partial free transit via train or in the early years by ship to the mines. High demand for Ovambo labor was something workers themselves could take advantage of via colonial infrastructure, which transported them hundreds of Kilometers, over terrain that would have been near to impossible on foot. Let us now transition to focus on worker's travel to work in the settler zone.

Journey South to the Settler Region

Ovambo migrants who went on contract between 1907 and 1914 could be recruited to a diversity of worksites, but as discussed previously, the lion's share went to either the copper mines at Tsumeb, the diamond mines around Lüderitzbucht, or train construction, which was underway throughout the colony depending on the year. To get an overview of those leaving to the south through Namutoni and Okaukuejo let us examine some government statistics.

As we can see in Figure 24 below, around 6,000 to almost 12,000 Ovambo workers were leaving annually from Namutoni and Okaukuejo combined between 1910 and 1914. Furthermore, we know that from 1911 to 1914, between one-third and one-half of those recruited were going to the diamond mines. The data for 1910, with only 13 percent going to the diamond mines, may have been the result of large numbers of South Africans still arriving for work in the south prior to the passing of more restrictive South African colonial migration policies, which will be explored in the following chapter, as well as particularly high demand for labor at the copper mine at Tsumeb.

The Tsumeb copper mine, operated by OMEG, had opened in 1906, two years before diamonds were discovered in the south. It drew approximately 30 percent

60 NAN, ZBU 2068 W.IV.i.8. Travel, food, and clothing for recruited Ovambo 1910–1913, Letter to the Kaiserliche Eingeborenen-Kommissariat Winduk from the Kaiserliche Gouvernement Windhuk, 18.07.1914; NAN, ZBU 0162 A.VI.a.8 Vol. 1, Annual report of the native commissioner 1913–1914, Annual Report of the Imperial Native Commission for Lüderitzbucht 1.4.1912–31.3.1913, 38.

61 Mokopakgosi, "German Colonialism in Microcosm," 517; This does not negate the fact that Ovambo workers were paid less than Kru and South African workers in the mines and in railway construction.

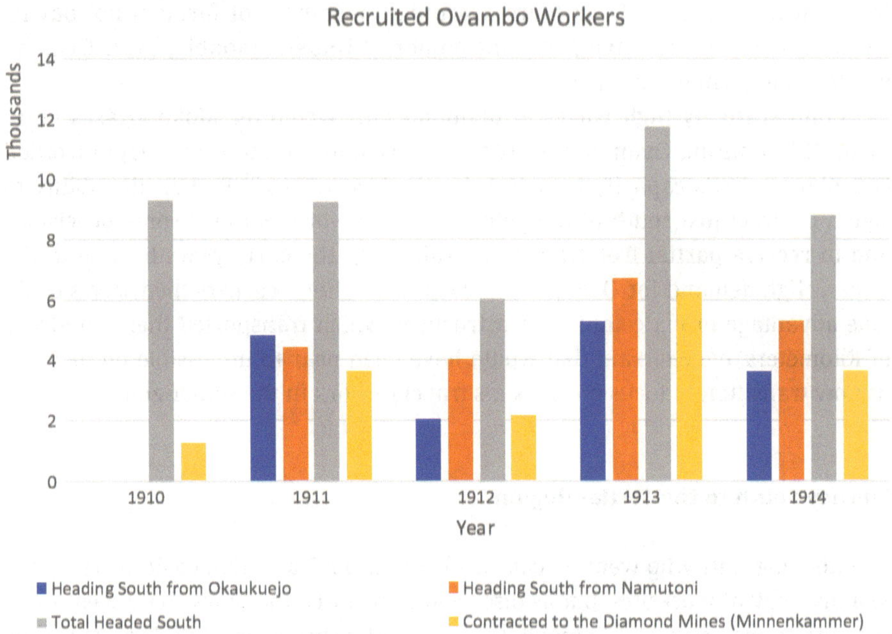

Figure 24: Ovambo Workers recruited at Okaukuejo and Namutoni for contracts in the settler region between 1910 and 1914.[62]

of all Ovambo recruits in the years from 1908 to 1914. Contracts for OMEG were particularly attractive because of the closeness to the north, a relatively large number of Ovambo and other African women living there, as well as the possibility to get three, two- or even one-month contracts compared to the more typical six-month contracts at the diamond mines.[63] Tsumeb's weather was also preferable to the extreme wind, cold temperatures, and dampness on the coast at the diamond mines. As to its popularity as a work site, Robert Gordon highlighted that by 1907, it was not uncommon during some months that over 1,000 Ovambo

62 Compiled from NAN, ZBU 2065, W.IV.h. 3 Vol. 2, Government Statistics, in Regina Strassegger, "Die Wanderarbeit der Ovambo während der deutschen Kolonialbesetzung Namibias. Unter besonderer Berücksichtigung der Wanderarbeiter auf den Diamantenfeldern in den Jahren 1908 bis 1914," (PhD thesis, Graz, Karl-Franzens-Universität Graz, 1988), 81–82; NAN, ABU 2065 Akten Nr. W. IV.h.3 Migration of Ovambo, 1910–1915, in E.L.P Stals, *Duits-Suidwes-Afrika na die Groot Opstande: 'n studie in die verhouding tussen owerheid en inboorlinge* (Pretoria: Die Staatsdrukker, 1984), 213.

63 Lüderitzbuchter Zeitung (LZ), 16.5.1913; NAN, ZBU 160, A.VI.a. 4 Vol. 3, M.K.-J.B. 1913/14, B.A. Lüderitzbucht-G., 17.6.1914, in Strassegger, "Die Wanderarbeit der Ovambo während der deutschen Kolonialbesetzung Namibias," 83.

workers were recruited by OMEG.[64] But the dangerousness of underground labor at Tsumeb also dissuaded many from seeking work there as we will later explore.

In the competition between OMEG and the Lüderitz Chamber of Mines (the organization representing most of the diamond mining industry around Lüderitzbucht), the latter was both larger and wealthier, held more sway over recruiters, the colonial government, and the governor. The diamond mining industry also used its heft, as the heart of the colonial economy, to get what it wanted. It even, in wishing to diminish OMEG recruits, threatened to lobby to legally change all contracts for Ovambo workers to nine months, including at Tsumeb, so that the copper mines no longer had this advantage.[65] Even without this maneuver, the diamond mines typically received the largest share of laborers from the recruiting centers. For migrants, the travel south varied greatly depending on whether they were to work at Tsumeb or farther south. Irrespective, Ovambo workers still had to undertake the initial arduous journey by foot.

Figure 25: Ovambo men and boys on their way south on contract. As they are leaving Namutoni they are likely headed to work either in the copper mines of Tsumeb or a train construction project.[66]

64 Robert J. Gordon, "Variations in Migration Rates: The Ovambo Case," *Journal of Southern African Affairs* 3, no. 3 (1978): 263.
65 NAN ZBU 2065, W.IV.h.5 Vol. 2, M.K.G., 8.7.1913, in Strassegger, "Die Wanderarbeit der Ovambo während der deutschen Kolonialbesetzung Namibias," 107 fn. 209.
66 BArch, Photo N 881 – Streitwolf, Kurt.- Bildbestand / Fotograf(in): o. Ang., Deutsch-Südwestafrika.- Wandernde Ovambo-Arbeiter, 1900/1914 ca.

In Figure 25 above we see Ovambo recruits heading south from the German military fort Namutoni which can be seen in the background. In the image we see men of varying ages, ranging from a middle-aged man at the center of the photo, to a boy to his right. Such a diversity of age was not uncommon. A 1912 annual report from the native commissioners based at Lüderitzbucht noted that most Ovambo diamond mine workers were between 20 to 30, a few around 40, and that some were, "hardly older than fourteen."[67] We not only have hints of who went south from photos, but also what people brought with them.

Details of what people are wearing and carrying in the image above can be cross referenced with oral history work, such as that by Lovisa Tegelela Nampala, who spoke with migrants who went on contract in the mid-twentieth century. Like the individuals in Figure 25, Nampala refers to men carrying sticks or palm stalks, called *omutenge/i*. They allow the men and boys to carry more items, more easily than simply with their hands.[68] Items being held include woven baskets for carrying things such as food, like bread made of *mahangu*. Also being transported are dried gourds, which were used to hold water for the long journey.

Some men, including the individual on the far left, and the man just to his right are wearing European pants and jackets. Depending on the year, their recruiter, or their employer, these could have been received at Namutoni. Cases of workers receiving low quality clothing and blankets, especially because of cost cutting recruiters, were not uncommon.[69] Worker clothes were particularly bad in the first few years of the diamond mines' opening. By April 1911, some improvements were made whereby the Lüderitzbucht Chamber of Mines agreed that it would pay for each recruit to receive a shirt, jacket, pants, suspenders, cap and two blankets.[70] However, problems with clothing and blankets provided to Ovambo workers would continue. The recruiting firm Bödiker itself said in April 1912 that blankets needed to be a higher quality and workers required three rather than two.[71]

In addition to challenges with clothing, some migrants also feared San attacks, which occasionally occurred.[72] Some migrants would sporadically be killed

67 NAN, ZBU 0162 A.VI.a.8 Vol. 1, Annual report of the native commissioner 1913–1914, Annual Report of the Imperial Native Commission for Lüderitzbucht 1.4.1912–31.3.1913, 55.

68 Nampala, *Infrastructures of Migrant Labour in Colonial Ovamboland*, 29–30.

69 Strassegger, "Die Wanderarbeit der Ovambo während der deutschen Kolonialbesetzung Namibias," 66.

70 NAN, ZBU 2068, W.IV.i.8. Travel, food, and clothing for recruited Ovambo 1910–1913, Letter to all members of the Lüderitz Chamber of Mines from chairman Pasel, 10.4.1911, 73.

71 NAN, ZBU 2068 W.IV.i.8. Travel, food, and clothing for recruited Ovambo 1910–1913, Bödiker to Herr Hauptmann, 25.04.1912, 105.

72 For an overview of the complex history that developed between the various San people in the northern region of GSWA, the Ovambo polities, German settlers, the German state, and Ovambo

and their goods taken. San raids were most common on the way home when migrants were burdened with goods purchased in the settler zone. The colonial records include instances where Ovambo fear of San kept some workers from travelling to locations such as Tsumeb.[73] For Ovambo headed south, the journey

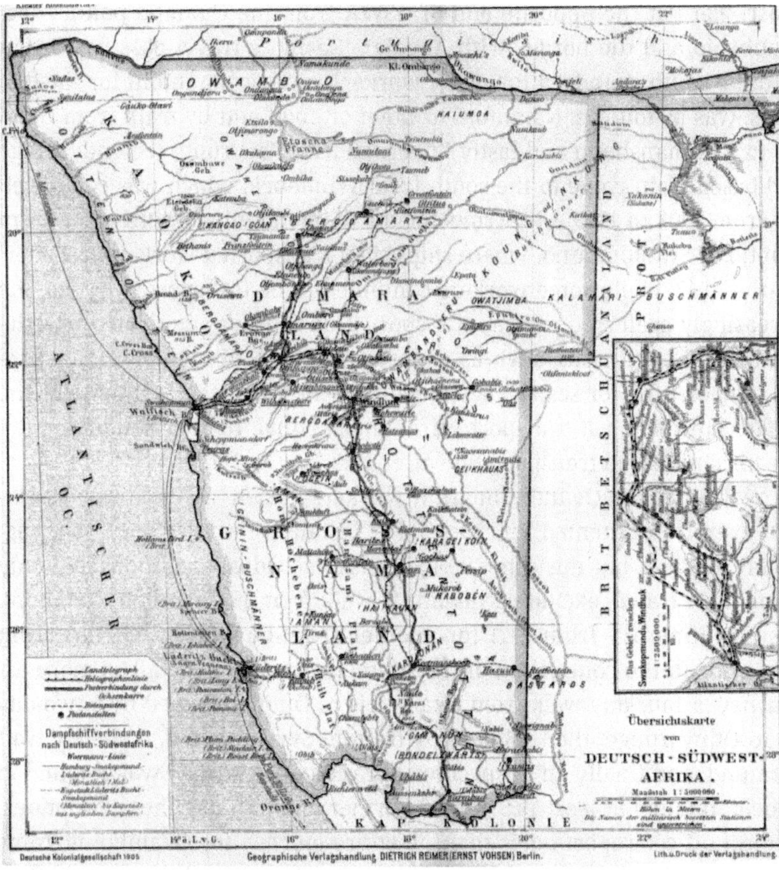

Figure 26: Map of GSWA circa 1905.[74]

migrants, see Robert J. Gordon and Stuart Sholto Douglas, *The Bushman Myth: The Making of a Namibian Underclass* (Boulder: Westview Press, 2000), 49–85.

73 Von Hirschberg, Bericht über die Expedition nach dem Okawango, Waterberg, 14. September 1910. NAN ZBU J.XIII.B.4 (vol. 3), Blatt 28 B. in Andreas E. Eckl, "Konfrontation und Kooperation am Kavango (Nord-Namibia) von 1891 bis 1921" (Diss., Universität zu Köln, 2004), 120–121.

74 Deutsche Kolonialgesellschaft, ed., *Deutscher Kolonial-Atlas: mit illustriertem Jahrbuch* (Berlin: Reimer, 1905), 11 on.

varied depending on their contract. Those headed to Tsumeb had a much shorter journey on foot, compared to the trip to Lüderitzbucht, which included travel by foot, train and for many also by sea. Let us return to 'Kasino' from the Ondonga kingdom to get an idea for one worker's individual journey.

The map above (Figure 26) shows us that the mines of Lüderitz (bottom left on the coast) were at the opposite end of GSWA from the Ovambo polities (between Okaukuejo and the border with Angola). 'Kasino''s travel pass noted that his route to the south, standard for many workers leaving Namutoni for the diamond mines, was as follows: Namutoni to Otavi on foot, and by train from Otavi to Karibib to Keetmanshoop and lastly Lüderitzbucht. This route took advantage of the land-based train route to the south from Windhoek, which was completed as of 1912. From 1908 to 1912, all recruits for the diamond mines were taken from Otavi or Outjo to Swakopmund, where ships then transported workers to Lüderitzbucht. After 1912, while some workers continued to be transported by sea, the mines increasingly preferred railway transport. This shift was motivated by a desire to minimize health risks, such as exposure to the cold climate of Swakopmund and the potential for sea sickness during ocean transport. Additionally, the costs for both land and sea transport were almost equal, further solidifying the preference for land-based transportation after 1912.[75]

The travel times for Ovambo migrant workers varied significantly, as evidenced by several documented itineraries. For instance, Kasino's document suggests a 14-day journey, but this estimate likely assumes ideal conditions and only accounts for train travel, excluding his initial walk from his home to Namutoni. In contrast, an itinerary from 1911 for another Ovambo worker starting from Okaukuejo, prior to the completion of the southern train line, details a more extended journey: a four-day walk from Okaukuejo to Outjo, followed by a two-day train ride to Otjiwarongo, then 1.5 days by train to Swakopmund, a six-day wait in Swakopmund, and finally an unspecified duration at sea from Swakopmund to Lüderitzbucht, totaling at least 13.5 days.[76] Further emphasizing these variations, a 1910 medical officer report notes that the entire journey for Ovambo migrants typically spanned about five or six weeks, indicating how travel times could fluctuate drastically depending on multiple factors.[77]

75 SSS, Woermann-Linie Jahresbericht 1913 (Swakopmund, 1913), 17.

76 Strassegger, "Die Wanderarbeit der Ovambo während der deutschen Kolonialbesetzung Namibias," 94–95.

77 NAN, ZBU 2071 W.IV.I.3, Medical treatment of workers, 1911–1912, Statement from the case report of the medical doctor Dr. Richter, regarding the Kolmanskop Diamond Mines Ltd., 8.

The individuals we saw earlier in Figure 25 were likely headed from Namutoni to Otavi (over 100 km away) by foot.[78] On this first leg of the journey after recruitment water was often scarce. The alternate journey from Okaukuejo to Outjo (120 km) is described as only having three locations along the way with water: Aimab, Otjiwasandu, and Ombika. Further, Aimab would not have water in the dry season. Adding to the challenges during the first segment of the trip, migrants often slept directly on the ground.[79] After this multi-day and difficult trek, migrants would wait at assembly points until they were boarded onto trains for either Swakopmund, or further south to Lüderitzbucht after 1912, like Kasino. Ticket costs were covered by their employers.

During the journey, most food provided was completely new to the migrants, and to make things more challenging, needed to be cooked. This meant that to prepare provided foods such as rice, beans, flour, or a wheat and flour mix called *boeremeal*, one needed to have the proper cooking utensils like pots, as well as enough firewood, water and importantly, enough time. Very often one or all these things were lacking. For those workers who were able to cook food long enough to eat, the often-new foods did not sit well with their digestion. Highlighting the issues, the recruiting firm Carl Bödiker, was scolded by the imperial government for not providing proper conditions for workers on the train journey south in October of 1912:

> I have instructed the local government offices to check the Ovambo Transports' accommodations and provisions . . . the provisioned food must be easy to prepare. Legumes (beans, peas) and corn, that are old, that need 8–10 hours to prepare, should be rejected . . . . Furthermore, pay attention enough water and wood are available for transports.[80]

There were occasions when provisions were provided that could be eaten without preparation, such as bread but this was rare. Irrespective of the quality of the provisions and when they were given out, colonial officials complained that the

78 According to Outjo Bezirkamt documents, the trek from Okaukuejo to Outjo was four days; see NAN, ZBU 2068 W.IV.i.8. Travel, food, and clothing for recruited Ovambo 1910–1913. Decree fom the Kaiserlichen Bezirksamtes Outjo regarding Ovambo recruitment matters, 24.1.1911, 39.

79 NAN, ZBU 2068 W.IV.i.8. Travel, food, and clothing for recruited Ovambo 1910–1913, Kaiserliches Bezirksamt Outjo to the Kaiserliche Gouvernement Winduk, Outjo, 4.10.1910, 11.

80 NAN, ZBU 2068 W.IV.i.8. Travel, food, and clothing for recruited Ovambo 1910–1913. Letter from the office of the *Kaiserlicher Gouverneur* to the firm Carl Bodiker, 15.10.1912, 139. Translation to English by W.B. Lyon.

migrants lacked proper planning to ration their provisions, despite many not eating for days prior.[81]

On the journey by train, sleep, rest and if possible, cooking happened at specially built accommodations located at some train stations along the route. These accommodations were often large, roofed edifices that could be drafty and cold, or too hot and stifling, depending on where they were located, the season, and what time of day it was. Ovambo migrants would gather at the shelters between stops on their way south to socialize, eat and rest.[82] In an attempt to lessen some of the various health and well-being challenges for travelling workers, some of these shelters, such as the one constructed at Mariental in 1913 intended to have fuel for making fires as well as cooking utensils. But it was complaints from German farmers, rather than workers themselves, that were often the impetus for such improvements. One came from a local Mariental farmer named Stumpfe. He wanted the planned shelter in Mariental to be built on his property and to receive payment in exchange for helping with the shelter's upkeep, such as providing workers with firewood and cooking utensils.[83]

Farmers like Stumpfe, whose property intersected with Ovambo migration routes, often tried their hand at cashing in on government infrastructure investments aimed at maintaining and facilitating Ovambo cyclical migration. Ironically many German farmers who complained about African incursions on their property and wishing to profit, had obtained their land through the colonial government or European concession companies. These often had gotten the land from Africans by various means, not uncommonly through economic or military pressure or outright stealing. This included land taken from Herero and Nama during the war and genocide. Later in the chapter focusing on the journey back north, we will see how colonial traders wished to make money from Ovambo migrants as consumers.

Beyond settler and government effects on the travel process for workers, mother nature was by far the most powerful actor. Weather, especially its extremes were defining factors of the journey south. The cold encountered by both Ovambo migrants who took the sea route via Swakopmund, as well as for those who travelled by train at night could be a real problem. The cold and dampness at Swakopmund contrasted dramatically to tropical weather in the Ovambo re-

81 NAN, ZBU 2068 W.IV.i.9. Travel, food, and clothing for recruited Ovambo 1910–1913, Lüderitzbuchter Minenkammer to the Kaiserliche Gouvernement regarding letter from 12.06.1913, Lüderitzbucht, 24.06.1913, 186.

82 NAN, ZBU 0162 A.VI.a.8 Vol. 1. Annual report of the native commissioner 1913–1914. Annual report for the Imperial native commission in Windhoek 1.4.1913–31.3.1914, II. health conditions, 87.

83 NAN, ZBU 2068 W.IV.i.8. Travel, food, and clothing for recruited Ovambo 1910–1913, Lüderitzbucht Chamber of Mines to the Kaiserliche Gouvernement, Lüderitzbucht, 2.7.1913, 187.

gion. This was exacerbated when layovers there could last up to six days. From Swakopmund, they were loaded onto transport ships where wind and cold continued and was compounded by seasickness. Few Ovambo passengers had prior experience at sea. Justifiably, those who were seasick could not eat the provisions offered on the transport ships.[84] Medical reports cite Ovambo workers who took the sea route coming down with colds, as well as more serious illnesses, such as pneumonia. For those on trains, seating was in third class wagons, which were open air.[85] The photo below, Figure 27, gives us an idea of what travel via train for many Ovambo migrants was like.

Figure 27: Africans, likely including Ovambos taking the train in wagons also intended for cargo. Notice the woman with a head scarf facing to the right closest to the camera as well as the brakeman on the far right. Based on the two twin steam engines, this is likely the Swakopmund-Windhoek train line operating between 1902 and 1910.[86]

84 NAN, ZBU 2071 W.IV.I.3. Medical treatment of workers, 1911–1912. Statement from the case report of the medical doctor Dr. Richter, regarding the Kolmanskop Diamond Mines Ltd., 9.
85 However, examples exist when 0°C temperatures led officials to install covering; see NAN, ZBU2071, W.IV.I.4. Vol. 1. Return trip and return trip costs 1905–1914. Chamber of Mines to Secretary Thomas, Windhoek, 12.08.1914, 75.
86 BADKGUB, Photo A_00S_2995; Gerhardus Pool, *Eisenbahnen in Deutsch-Südwestafrika, 1897–1915*, ed. Rolf-Reinhard Henke, trans. Kuno Budack (Namibia Wissenschaftliche Gesellschaft, 2009), 167–69"Zwilling – Henschel 5376/1900," accessed January 26, 2022, http://www.heeresfeldbahn.de/lokomotiven/deutschland/zwilling/168.html.

The locomotive seen above (Figure 27) is carrying various African passengers who were a mix of men and women, with Ovambo migrant workers likely included. The photo gives us an idea of how many black passengers used the railways in GSWA. Unlike train wagons for whites, those for black passengers, including Ovambo individuals, were otherwise used for cargo and had no protection from the elements. In 1912, the Lüderitzbucht Chamber of Mines attempted to have train wagons for their workforce going from the interior to the coast at Lüderitzbucht covered, or if they were not, pressure the railway administration to pay for sick workers who were arriving. The railway replied aggressively against any action:

> The legal provisions applicable to the protectorate railroads allow the accommodation of natives in open freight cars when they are transported by rail in larger groups. This procedure also corresponds to the practices of almost all German colonial railroads, just as the South African government railroads likewise transport uncivilized natives for the most part in open freight cars.[87]

The response and decision not to have wagons covered, citing prohibitive costs, South African policies, and racial tropes, makes instances where Ovambo workers had to sit on top of cargo unsurprising. The treatment of black workers as cargo and general disregard for their wellbeing was something mirrored in the South African WNLA train conductors transporting workers from Mozambique to the Rand.[88] Train transport cars for Ovambo workers were often dirty, did not have facilities for using the toilet, and added to the propensity for disease to spread amongst migrants.[89]

As the trains approached Lüderitzbucht, the desert impacted trains and travelers alike. The train line between Aus and Lüderitzbucht was where multiple natural factors collided. The climate becomes colder, shifting sands dominate the landscape, and harsh winds create both occasional sandstorms and constantly moving sand dunes. Sands would often cover up train tracks, necessitating crews

87 NAN, ZBU 2068 W.IV. i.8. Travel, food, and clothing for recruited Ovambo 1910–1913, German Colonial Train Company of Berlin to the Mining Chamber Management, Lüderitzbucht, 14.08.1912, 129. Translation to English by W.B. Lyon; NAN, ZBU 2068 W.IV. i.8. Travel, food, and clothing for recruited Ovambo 1910–1913, Lüderitzbucht Chamber of Mines letter to the Management of the Lüderitzbucht railway administration, Lüderitzbucht, 12.08.1912.

88 Charles van Onselen, *The Night Trains: Moving Mozambican Miners to and from the Witwatersrand Mines, 1902–1955* (Oxford: Oxford University Press, 2021), 11.

89 Strassegger, "Die Wanderarbeit der Ovambo während der deutschen Kolonialbesetzung Namibias," 99.

whose only purpose was to keep them clear. When migrants arrived in Lüderitzbucht, irrespective of their method of travel, a good number were suffering from general weakness.[90] This left them more susceptible to disease as they started their contracts.

A colonial doctor's note on a group of workers arriving at a Lüderitzbucht diamond mine gives an idea of the state of the workers when their journey was complete. On January 20, 1911, a group of 69 Ovambo workers arrived at Kolmanskop Diamond Mines Ltd. Within one week, a worker with severe pneumonia had to be taken directly to Charlottental hospital, three men had lung infections, and one had anemia.[91] This meant that around five percent of the recent arrivals were suffering from severe illness.

Statistics like these, while specific to one group of arrivals, align with general observations about new Ovambo workers' state of health, and they give us a picture of travel conditions that could be brutal. There were some actions beyond providing clothing, provisions, and occasional proposals to improve transit, taken by the mines to attempt to improve worker healthcare upon arrival. Most universal was vaccination against smallpox, which was given to all workers headed to the mines at either Swakopmund if they took the sea route, or at Lüderitzbucht if they arrived by train.[92] Smallpox vaccinations like these were not uncommon for workers and others under colonial rule including across the British, French, Spanish, Dutch, and German empires.[93]

Complications and pain related to such vaccinations, often using less refined technology than in the metropoles, could also increase distrust of colonial medicine.[94] Some examples of colonial vaccinations against smallpox started as early as in the

---

90 NAN, ZBU 2071 W.IV.I.3. Medical treatment of workers, 1911–1912. Statement from the case report of the medical doctor Dr. Richter, regarding the Kolmanskop Diamond Mines Ltd., 8.

91 NAN, ZBU 2071 W.IV.I.3, Medical treatment of workers, 1911–1912, Statement from the case report of the medical doctor Dr. Richter, regarding the Kolmanskop Diamond Mines Ltd., 9–10.

92 Swakopmunder Zeitung, ‚Ueber Eingeborenen – Hygiene', 01.06.1912, 1.

93 Christopher Ellis Hayden, "Of Medicine and Statecraft: Smallpox and Early Colonial Vaccination in French West Africa (Senegal -Guinea)," (PhD thesis, Evanston, Illinois, Northwestern University, 2008); Rajesh Kochhar, "Smallpox in the Modern Scientific and Colonial Contexts 1721–1840," *Journal of Biosciences* 36, no. 5 (2011): 766–767; Gabriel E Andrade, "A Great Inspiration for Today's Vaccination Efforts: Biographical Sketch of Francisco Xavier Balmis (1753–1819)," *Journal of Medical Biography*, 2021.

94 Wazi Apoh and Bea Lundt, *Germany and Its West African Colonies: "Excavations" of German Colonialism in Post-Colonial Times* (Münster: LIT Verlag, 2013), 107.

late eighteenth century, for example in Guatemala.[95] The history of mandatory vaccines against smallpox, also included those given to enslaved peoples transported from West Africa to the Dutch Caribbean in the early nineteenth century.[96] We will later return to worker health on the jobsite, but let us first take some time to review the diamond mines at Lüderitz and then what workers there undertook.

On Contract in the Settler Zone

The Diamond Mines

In April 1908, Zacharias Lewala, a Cape Worker employed on the Lüderitzbucht-Keetmanshoop train line construction from the coast to the interior, discovered what he thought to be a diamond.[97] Lewala had previously worked in the Kimberley diamond mines of South Africa and therefore knew what a raw diamond looked like. Zacharias reported the unidentified stone to the section line overseer, August Stauch, who would confirm it was indeed a diamond. Stauch and his soon to be business partner, engineer Sönke Nissen, would after buying land and mining rights eventually become wildly rich in the diamond boom that followed. By contrast, Zacharias Lewala would see none of the profits, but rather only benefit by being employed as a coach driver for Stauch.[98] After more than two decades of German occupation in the colony, including extensive explorations for valuable minerals, it took a migrant worker from South Africa with experience in the industry to find diamonds, right under their feet. Thereafter the region around Lüderitzbucht would become one of the most important diamond mining regions in the world. Colonial Germans and private firms would profit immeasurably.[99] At

95 Martha Few, "Epidemics, Indigenous Communities, and Public Health in the COVID-19 Era: Views from Smallpox Inoculation Campaigns in Colonial Guatemala," *Journal of Global History* 15, no. 3 (2020): 380–393.
96 Niklas Thode Jensen, "Safeguarding Slaves: Smallpox, Vaccination, and Governmental Health Policies among the Enslaved Population in the Danish West Indies, 1803–1848," *Bulletin of the History of Medicine* 83, no. 1 (2009): 96.
97 The construction of this train line will be covered in Chapter 4.
98 Ulrike Lindner, *Koloniale Begegnungen: Deutschland und Großbritannien als Imperialmächte in Afrika 1880–1914* (Frankfurt am Main: Campus Verlag, 2011), 385–386.
99 Press, *Blood and Diamonds*, 92–112.

the heart of this industry from 1908 to 1914 would be Ovambo and South African migrant labor.

To understand labor on the diamond mines near Lüderitz, we must first point out how and why they were unique in a regional context. GSWA's diamond mines differed greatly from their most prominent counterpart of the period, those of Kimberley in South Africa, as the diamonds in the German colony were alluvial, meaning that they were the result of an ancient river that had once coursed through the Namib desert. That river had run from deep inland all the way to the coast around Lüderitz, and had brought diamonds with it, depositing them along its path, as well as into the Atlantic Ocean. As climate and topography changed, the river dried up and transformed into a desert. This meant that diamond mines in the German colony were plots of land, where sand was searched through and sifted for the precious stones. Such mines differed greatly from the deep pit mine of Kimberley and its diamond rich veins of 'blue ground', or the aptly named kimberlite.

The recent work of Steven Press convincingly argues that the terrain that became the diamond fields in southern GSWA, was so different from 'blue ground' in South Africa or Brazil, that its perception as non-diamond terrain was one reason that it took until 1908 for the colony's diamond riches to be 'discovered.'[100] Following 1908, these unique diamond fields (See Figure 28 below) required distinctive forms of labor. Let us first take a bird's eye view of what diamond mining entailed in the area around Lüderitz from 1908 to 1914, and then home in on individual Ovambo experiences.

100 Press, *Blood and Diamonds*, 39–42.

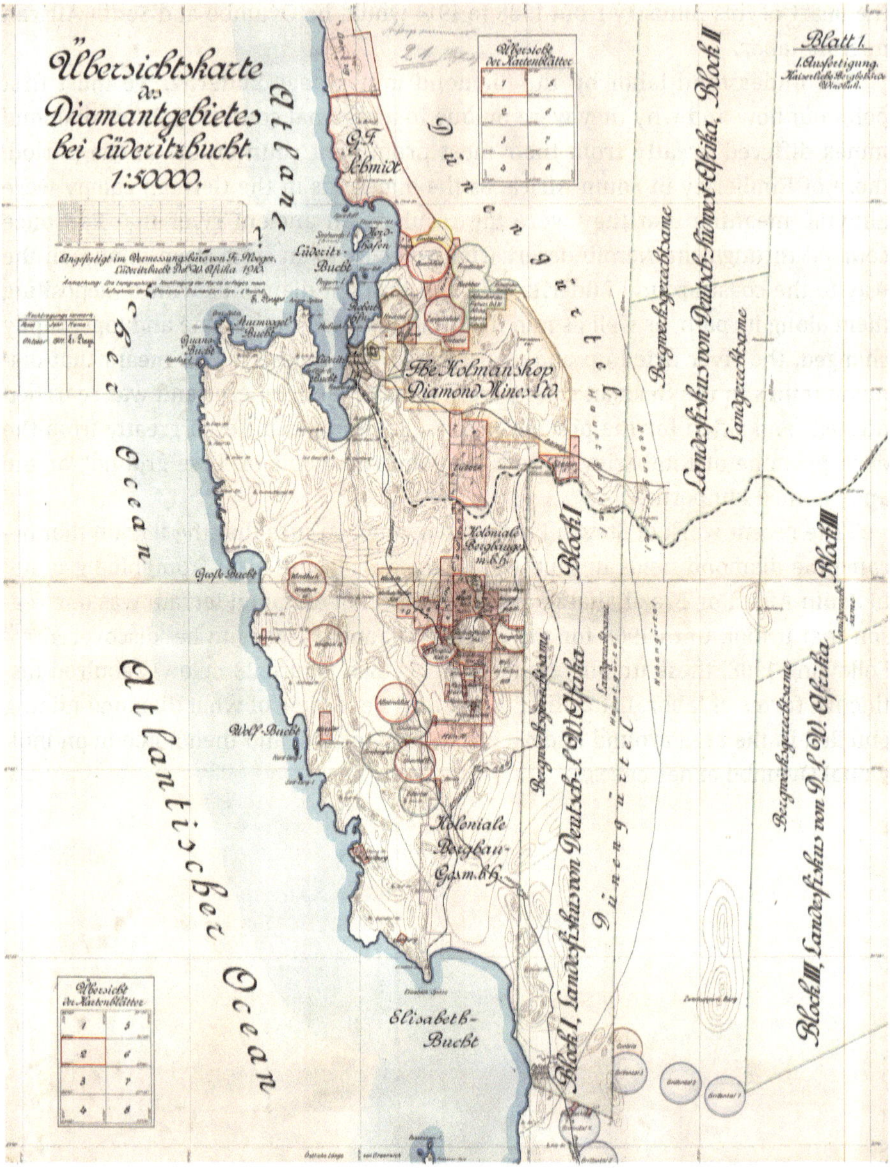

Figure 28: Map of the diamond fields around Lüderitzbucht in 1910.[101]

101 NAN, Übersichtskarte des Diamantgebietes bei Lüderitzbucht, Block III, 1910.

Some of the first mines in 1908 began operations with laborers crawling on all fours on the ground to search for diamonds, and when they were found, hand them over to Afrikaner or German overseers.[102] This of course was extremely intensive labor and must have also been mind-numbing. Below in Figure 29, we see an example of Ovambo workers doing just this form of work. They are wearing low quality, burlap like clothing, which was commonplace amongst Ovambo recruits who had received this apparel after signing. To the right a worker has given a possible diamond to a white overseer for confirmation. Patches of desert would first be checked in this manner to decide whether more intensive mining techniques should be undertaken. Although the photo may very well be staged, it gives an idea for how such work likely took place.

Figure 29: A troop of Ovambo workers searching for diamonds.[103]

As small plots were bought up by larger mines, more capital was injected into the companies allowing for further investment in equipment. The mining process evolved, becoming increasingly industrialized, and with it the work of Ovambo laborers changed as well. The more primitive mines soon had workers using basic sieves and basins for searching by hand. Others adapted large crank oper-

102 Press, *Blood and Diamonds*, 120–121.

103 BDKGUFM, Photo 019-2146-15, Photographed by von farmer von Zanthier 53, Das Untersuchen des Feldes auf Abbauwürdigkeit.

ated drum sieves that were developed specifically for the diamond mines of Lüderitz. The fields that were worked by hand would result in surreal sections of desert defined by pockmarks and piles of sand, not dissimilar to moguls on a ski hill before winds would again level out the landscape.

The most advanced diamond fields had by 1910/1911 begun utilizing steam and gas-powered trains for personnel, ore and equipment transport, along with electric shovels, washers, and cranes. Electric or gas-powered engines rather than steam powered ones were preferred because of a lack of water.[104] Some locations were not easily accessible for large equipment, but mining was still undertaken by hand.[105] Regardless of how technologically advanced the mines became, they all required considerable numbers of workers. Below, in Figure 30 we get an idea of the overall African workforce at the mines around Lüderitzbucht.

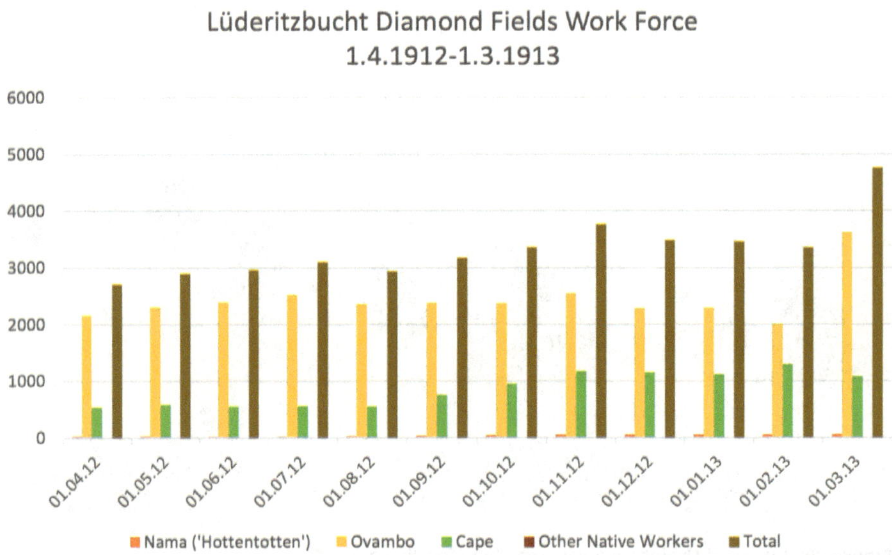

Figure 30: Lüderitzbucht Diamond Fields Work Force April 1, 1912 to March 1, 1913, broken down by various African workers.[106]

104 Emil Kreplin and Friedrich Knacke, *Die deutschen Diamanten und ihre Gewinnung* (Berlin: Reimer, 1914), 46–47.

105 Kreplin and Knacke, *Die deutschen Diamanten und ihre Gewinnung*, 52–54.

106 Graph created from data collected from NAN, ZBU 0162 A.VI.a.8 Vol. 1. Annual report of the native commissioner 1913–1914. Annual Report of the Imperial Native Commission for Lüderitzbucht 1.4.1912–31.3.1913, Workforce, 53.

In the above graph (Figure 30) we can see that the number of Ovambo workers on the mines from April 1912 to March 1913 varied from 2,000 to over 3,600 workers. Their percentage of the overall African work force in the Police Zone recorded in statistics during this period ranged by month from 65 to over 80 percent.

The big operations employed the largest work forces to support their increasing industrialization, while a dwindling number of smaller mines with little more than a handful of workers operated simple equipment. The smaller mines had under twenty workers, such as the *Bahnfelder Abbaugesellschaft m.b.h.* with a total of one white and fifteen black workers in July of 1913.[107] Contrastingly, one of the biggest mines, the *Koloniale Bergbaugesellschaft*, had 796 Ovambo workers in July of 1912.[108]

Figure 31: Photo of Ovambo young men and boys working at diamond field Bayer.[109]

In the photo above, Figure 31, we can see how young some of the Ovambo work force could be on the diamond mines. They were employed on the Bayer diamond

107 Kreplin and Knacke, *Die deutschen Diamanten und ihre Gewinnung*, 87.

108 Strassegger, "Die Wanderarbeit der Ovambo während der deutschen Kolonialbesetzung Namibias," 147.

109 BDKGUFM, Photo 019-2133-14. Photographer: Bayer, M., SWA 12 / Diamantenwüste Bayer, 57.

field. Workers such as those in the photo had workdays which varied based on the size of the mines. The two largest, which employed about two-thirds of the workforce, had nine and a half hour workdays with a 30-minute midday break. The other diamond mines had workdays of about 10 to 11 hours.[110] Pay for Ovambo workers on the diamond mines varied, with small boys (*ganz kleine Jungen)* paid around 9/7d monthly, and most adult men paid £1 per month. One mine paid all workers, regardless of age or size £1 monthly, and to create incentive for workers to take longer contracts, £1 4/4d for every month after six months.[111]

Figure 32: Labor on a larger diamond mine.[112]

While smaller mines had workers do a variety of jobs, the bigger mines like that above in Figure 32 had a more formalized division of labor. As in the photo, groups were given work at various stations, such as shoveling sand into sifters,

110 NAN, ZBU 0162 A.VI.a.8. Vol. 1, Annual report of the native commissioner 1913–1914, Annual Report of the Imperial Native Commission for Lüderitzbucht 1.4.1912–31.3.1913, 58.
111 NAN, ZBU 0162 A.VI.a.8. Vol. 1, Annual report of the native commissioner 1913–1914, Annual Report of the Imperial Native Commission for Lüderitzbucht 1.4.1912–31.3.1913, 59.
112 BDKGUFM, Photo 018-0212-09, K/R. Diamanten No 12 / No 9 / Bfu I 37 / Maschinelle Bearbeitung des Wüstensandes /lfd. No 170 / S.W.A.

who were operated by another group, and still others pushed carts on tracks or wheelbarrows of sand to be further processed. Ovambo workers also helped operate mechanized sieves, utilizing high pressure water and filter systems to separate diamonds from sand. Some machines were the size of homes and multiple stories high (see Figure 33 below). No matter what part of the process workers were involved in, overseers who were white Afrikaner or Germans, supervised, organized, and punished the African workforce. Under white overseers were headmen, typically Ovambo from the same polity and region as their fellow workers, who represented each group of Ovambo workers that had travelled together south. Later we shall examine their role on the worksite, especially when troubles with employers arose. The headmen system of Ovambo worker management on the mines was not dissimilar to the system we discussed in relation to South Africans in the previous chapter, although it is not certain what role – if any – they may have played in recruitment back in the polities. Utilization of headmen in the Police Zone by employers resembles colonial African labor practices in other parts of the continent, including in Ghanaian gold mining and the Cameroonian rubber industry at the turn of the twentieth century.[113]

By 1910/1911, the largest mines had more advanced industrial mining infrastructure, some of which was invented specifically for the unique nature of the diamond mines of GSWA as we can see below in Figure 33. This two-story so-called *Schiechelanlage* at the '*Unverhofft*' diamond field was operated by *Vereinigte Diamantminen*. They were first invented in 1910 and utilized both air and water to separate out diamonds from sand.[114]

As we can see in the photo below the machine was manned by no less than seven workers. At the top left of the *Schiechelanlage*, men with shovels would unload unprocessed sand. From their location the sand enters the filtering system. Running horizontal on the front of the building is piping with multiple gauges to let in water to chambers where the sand was filtered. In the diamond fields, water was very scarce and often had to be brought in from the coast. The construction and upkeep of such infrastructure, which by 1914 dwarfed even what we see in Figure 33, emphasized where much of mining capital investment flowed. Improvements for the Ovambo workforce came far behind.

---

113 Cassandra Mark-Thiesen, "The 'Bargain' of Collaboration: African Intermediaries, Indirect Recruitment, and Indigenous Institutions in the Ghanaian Gold Mining Industry, 1900–1906," *International Review of Social History* 57, no. S20 (2012): 17–38; Oestermann, *Kautschuk und Arbeit in Kamerun*, 177–184.

114 Schiechelanlage, named after an Engineer by the name of Schieche who invented them, would be patented and by 1914 produced in Lüderitzbucht; see Kreplin and Knacke, *Die deutschen Diamanten und ihre Gewinnung*, 52.

Figure 33: Diamond field 'Unverhofft' of the Vereinigte Diamant Minen.[115]

Ovambo workers did, however, push for improvements, using methods like work slows, and strikes to leverage their power. But within the context of the Lüderitzbucht area, the harsh environment, distance from the Ovambo polities, and constant cycle of new workers, created limits to labor organization. Let us examine the story of the death of Itere, an Ovambo worker who was employed with the *Bahnfelder-Diamantgesellschaft* in 1912. The events surrounding this incident provide valuable first-hand accounts of fellow Ovambo from the work site, including views of daily labor, overseer-worker relations, and group protest through strikes on the diamond fields.

The Itere affair: A Death in the Diamond Fields

On October 8, 1912, a group of 50 Ovambo workers from *Bahnfelder-Diamantgesellschaft* went on strike and marched from the mine to the regional administrative office (*Bezirksamt*) at Lüderitzbucht. The next morning German police 'escorted' (likely forced) the workers back to their worksite. Native Commissioner Tönjes had been notified and asked to investigate, also arriving at the mine on the 9th. The Ovambo workers engaged Tönjes, stating that an overseer at the mine, Stangenberg, had killed

115 BDKGUFM, Photo A_0MM_5619.

Itere, a fellow Ovambo laborer, and they asked Tönjes to investigate and deliver severe ("*streng*") justice. Mr. Roth, the mine manager, claimed they were lying, and urged the native commissioner to investigate the reason for the strike.[116] The lines were drawn and the words of the Ovambo workforce were pitched against the mine management and overseer.

At the diamond field, Stangenberg brought commissioner Tönjes an Ovambo worker, who had been busy using a hand operated machine, for questioning. The worker, according to the Native commissioner report stated:

> Itere was often reporting as sick and wanted a certificate stating his sickness from Stangenberg so that he could go to the hospital. He was however always put to work with the remark that he was lazy rather than sick. Shortly before his death, it must have been on the 5th of October, I first saw him turning a machine, and as he couldn't do it, he was made to carry boxes of sand. I also saw that Stangenberg hit Itere with a shovel. Itere went in his pontok (housing) that evening and did not come out again for work. Two days later he died in the pontok. They (the workers) were very frightened and walked to Lüderitzbucht to report the event.[117]

Another worker confirmed the story, although he did not see the actual blow by Stangenberg against Itere, but further explained that Stangenberg often hit workers. After hearing the result of interviews conducted by Tönjes, the mine manager Roth claimed, "[f]or me the thing is decided, the blokes are all liars!"[118] Tönjes continued to interview more workers, almost all who confirmed or supported the original claim. Stangenberg attempted to paint them as frauds. His case was weak, if not paper thin. As Tönjes left the work site, a smaller Ovambo worker (likely a young boy) with a shovel ran up to him to ask: "Are you going to let him continue to beat us?"[119]

The investigation into the death of Itere clearly pointed to Stangenberg as guilty of murder, and Tönjes believed that to be the case. However, the racist judicial system of the colony led to a complete debasement of justice. In a following trial, Stangenberg was not punished for his crime but rather told in the future to outsource any need for future punishment of workers to the local police depart-

116 NAN, ZBU 2063 W.IV.f.2. Native mine workers. Specialia 1912–1913, Letter from the Native Commissioner to the Imperial Government at Windhoek, 31.10.1912, 28–29.

117 NAN, ZBU 2063 W.IV.f.2. Native mine workers. Specialia 1912–1913, Letter from the Native Commissioner to the Imperial Government at Windhoek, 31.10.1912, 29–30. Translation to English by W.B. Lyon.

118 NAN, ZBU 2063 W.IV.f.2. Native mine workers. Specialia 1912–1913, Letter from the Native Commissioner to the Imperial Government at Windhoek, 31.10.1912, 31–32

119 NAN, ZBU 2063 W.IV.f.2. Native mine workers. Specialia 1912–1913, Letter from the Native Commissioner to the Imperial Government at Windhoek, 31.10.1912, 32.

ment. This mirrors Marie Muschalek's work that has brought this concept of police as the arbiter of 'proper violence' against Africans in GSWA to the fore. She also points out how utterly unclear colonial policy was as to when employers and when the police were allowed to punish workers.[120]

Stangenberg's employer only gave him a warning, saying they did not want to be known as an abusive company and warned that future complaints would be met with his firing.[121] Later, the Deputy Commissioner for Lüderitzbucht would claim that after Stangenberg's acquittal, he continued to beat Ovambo workers. The head of the *Bahnfelder-Diamantgesellschaft*, Roth, would publish in the local Lüderitzbucht newspaper that their Ovambo workers, at least the 'ringleader,' needed to be punished, "as fast as the deputy commissioner's complaint had been filed against Stangenberg."[122] Roth's wish to punish the Ovambo workforce was not undertaken. The reference to a 'ringleader' may be an indicator of the role of Ovambo headmen as key labor leaders in the south, especially when issues on the work site arose. It is likely that similar to the South African construction workers we will examine in the next chapter, headmen were key to organizing and in cases such as the murder of Itere and Stangenberg's abuse, leading the workforce to push for improved conditions. As for these workers, their efforts to receive justice fell on deaf ears and nothing was done to punish the overseer.

The 'Itere Affair' brought to the fore the extreme discrimination in cases of abuse by white overseers of Ovambo workers. It also echoed the words of Missionary Wulfhorst, who as mentioned previously, noted that Ovambo men back from contract did not typically speak of cases of abuse in the south, although they often happened.[123] I do not think, as Wulfhorst presupposed, that they forgot these experiences, rather they perceived both the benefits of contract in the south and the harsh world they had experienced there, often deciding that the reward was worth the risk. As Robert Gordon argued, it is not conditions that guided workers' reactions per se, but rather how they interpreted circumstances in their situation, and relatedly how they attempted to achieve their goals within the confines of a repressive labor system.[124]

---

120 Muschalek, *Violence as Usual*, 136.

121 NAN, ZBU2063 W.IV.f.2. Eingeborene Minenarbeiter. Specialia 1912–1913, Letter from the Native Commissioner to the Imperial Government at Windhoek, 31.10.1912, 42–43

122 LZ, 'Die Behandlung der Eingeborenen,' 19.10.1912. Translation to English by W.B. Lyon.

123 VEM, RMG 2630 Mission conference in Ovamboland – Report from Wulfhorst, 2.10.05, Namakunde, „Was können wir tun für die zum Hereroland ziehenden Ovambojünglinge u. Männer, insbesondere für unsere Gemeindeglieder?," 13.

124 Robert J. Gordon, "Some Organisational Aspects of Labour Protests Among Contract Workers in Namibia," *South African Labour Bulletin* 4 (February 1978): 117.

Itere's death and the related fallout also gives us insight into much of the German colonial and company rationale in the colony. The core concepts that drove their relations with migrant labor were the following: racial inequality was a given fact and should guide decision making regarding Africans, worker productivity was core to the colonial economy and should be guaranteed by any means necessary, including occasional violence, and lastly, ensuring a consistent and willing labor force was important, but secondary to the other presuppositions.

Therefore lashings, beatings, or worse for 'lazy' or 'unruly' workers – according to this logic – was necessary, and decisions by whites that fell into these categories, were largely above reproach. This logic was often echoed by various colonial and company officials. The Omaruru district officer wrote the following to the Imperial government in Windhoek regarding a report of abuse, submitted by a Ovambo headman in 1911, which included an Ovambo worker being punched in the face by a white worker at the Doll store in Otjiwarongo (central GSWA):

> Like most experienced colonial officials, I am generally imbued with the utmost goodwill for natives and, in particular, the great importance of Ovambo for our country, but after all, in my obedient view, the difference between white and black must be preserved to the extent that it does not immediately, merely on the unproven assertion of a native with criminal complaint against so far blameless whites and threatening arrest penalties against dutiful officials.[125]

This statement typifies much of the colonial government's thinking towards Ovambo migrants. They and employers knew the paramount importance of these workers to the economy, but in situations where they were asked to put the workers' needs or desire for justice above those of colonists, industry or the colonial government, workers were clearly of less concern. Nevertheless, within this ecosystem, Ovambo migrants pushed for the best employment opportunities possible, regarding pay, provisions, and importantly proximity to the Ovambo polities. As we mentioned earlier, the Tsumeb mines fulfilled many of those desires.

The Tsumeb Mine

In comparison to the surface mines of the pre-colonial period – and even the shafts dug in the 1890s and early 1900s – the mines of OMEG in and around Tsumeb by 1906 were a much bigger operation. The preparations to begin industrial mining started in January of 1904 when the recently arrived OMEG director, Theodor Gath-

---

125 NAN, ZBU2068 W.IV.i.8. Travel, food, and clothing for recruited Ovambo 1910–1913, Kaiserliches Bezirksamt Omaruru letter to the Kaiserliche Gourvernement Windhoek, Topic: Ovambo mistreatment in Otjiwarongo at the Doll company, 29.10.1911, 69.

mann, hired ninety Ovambo workers to get the site operational in advance of the planned construction of the *Otavibahn* train line. But the colonial war with the Herero began only a few days after the arrival of Ovambo recruits, thus delaying work. Still, by 1906 the mine and train line were operational. The railway, in addition to serving as a conduit for worker and colonist passenger transport, allowed copper ore to be exported from the interior of the colony to Swakopmund. This meant Tsumeb copper could be sold on the global market without the higher transport costs of ox wagons, which had negated revenues in the 1890s and early 1900s. Further, by 1907, Tsumeb had copper smelters and a pump that delivered water from the nearby lake Otjikoto.[126] The large OMEG investments in the railway, smelting operations, deep mines, and a large primarily African workforce, dropped costs for exporting copper and made the mine profitable within a few years.[127]

As an employer, OMEG's Tsumeb mine afforded Ovambo workers not only the ability to work relatively close to their homelands, but the weather was warm compared to the coast, soon had a diverse African community, and hired on relatively short contracts.[128] Those contracts in turn often-allowed Ovambo migrants to return home more easily for agricultural tasks like crop harvesting.[129] Additionally, the Tsumeb worker location, unlike most worker compounds around Lüderitzbucht, included a good number of Ovambo women, many who undertook manual surface labor for the mines. Missionary Lang wrote on the subject, "[h]ere there is enough money for all the people, also women and girls to work at the mine, when they also want work."[130] Child labor amongst the entire African community in Tsumeb was also very high. Resultingly, the Rhenish missionary school

126 Schatz, *Tsumeb zu O.M.E.G.'s Zeiten*, 11–15, 27.

127 BArch, R 8024/208. The South West Africa Company Limited, Report of the Proceedings at the Ordinary General Meeting, 22.04.1913, 153–157; Lyon, "The South West Africa Company and Anglo-German Relations, 1892–1914," 37.

128 I will refer to Tsumeb as a copper mine, but in reality it had a great diversity of minerals. Even more plentiful, although less profitable, than copper was lead that was mined by OMEG; for more on the environment of Tsumeb, see SWACO Expedition to the Otavi Mines, 1892–1894; on the contract lengths at the Tsumeb mines see, VEM, RMG 1.631 b, B/c II 58, Ferdinand Lang, Band 2 1899–1919; 1942; 1942, Letter from Missionary Lang to Olpp, 13.2.1912, Tsumeb, 91; BAB, Annual Report of the Rhenish Mission Society 1910, Tsumeb, (Barmen: Westdeutsche Druckerei, 1911), 36.

129 That being said, depending on the recruiter longer contracts of nine and even 12 months in certain cases, seem to have not been uncommon as some Cape Workers' complaints make clear; see NAN, BCL [12], British Consul, 29/11 Consul A, Letter from D. Jason and others to British Consul Muller at Lüderitzbucht, Otavi mines at Tsumeb, 02.1911.

130 VEM, RMG 1.631 b, B/c II 58, Ferdinand Lang, Band 2 1899–1919; 1942; 1942. Letter from Lang to the Inspector, Tsumeb, 14.3.1911, 75. Translation to English by W.B. Lyon; a report from 1908 at the Tsumeb mines, notes Ovambo women as the primary workers sorting ore; see 'Otavi-Minen- und Eisenbahn-Gesellschaft', DKZ, 18.1.1908, 39.

that worked with the local African community had low attendance during working hours, and by April of 1908 no students were attending school during the day because all the children were working in the mine. Rather missionary Lang, based at Tsumeb, found his night classes were well attended.[131] It was noted that students spoke fluent German, which perhaps was indicative of close work between the white and black workforces.[132]

Figure 34: Photograph of Ovambo (and likely Cape Workers) workers at the Tsumeb mine, around 1908.[133]

Above (Figure 34) we can see men, women and children working side by side sorting ore at the mine. Notice on top of the piles of ore are two African foremen. On

131 Missionary reports in particular often reference women and children working in the mines; see VEM, RMG 2.529 a C/h 46 a Tsumeb (mit Grootfontein, Gaup, Otavi), Vol. 1 1907–1939, Visitations-fragebogen Tsumeb, 12.8.1912, 331; VEM, RMG 2.529 a C/h 46 a Tsumeb (mit Grootfontein, Gaup, Otavi), Vol. 1 1907–1939, Conference report on the work of Missionary Lang from 1.10.1907–30.04.1909, 374.
132 BAB, Annual Report of the Rhenish Mission Society 1908, Tsumeb, (Barmen: Westdeutsche Druckerei, 1909), 33–34.
133 BDKGUFM, Photo 014-2183-08, Tsumeb Mine / Sortieren d. Erze.

the embankment to the far right is a white overseer. The worker with a hat, under and to the left of the white overseer, wearing what appears to be a blanket in a fashion like a poncho, has a pattern resembling a sample found in the archives given to recruits at Namutoni and Okaukweyo.[134]

Recounting a similar scene to Figure 34, a November 1906 *Deutsch-Südwestafrikanische Zeitung* article described female surface workers at the mine. Based on the year the article was written, the workers described below could very well have been forced laborers although the original piece makes no distinction between 'free' and 'unfree' mine workers.

> The working tools are sometimes still of the most original and simple kind. A large pile of ore, which is still stored here from the first exploration work, is removed in order to bring the usable rock to be reprocessed. In an uninterrupted double chain, native women carry small wooden basins on their heads, move back and forth between the ore pile and the sorting site, chattering and laughing.[135]

Women, like those mentioned above joining men and children in the workforce at Tsumeb, resulted in a blurring of differences in work undertaken between genders and generations. This likely had the effect of eroding, at least temporarily traditional delineations in Ovambo society. Further, there were no doubt instances, where headmen were under an overseer and receiving similar pay to other workers, broadening the breakdown between traditional class hierarchies. The power African leaders in this area projected in the 1890s, which we explored in Chapter 1, had by this period diminished substantially. At the same time, the diversity in the Ovambo community no doubt led to a stronger sense of social belonging at the northern worksite compared to the male only environment of the diamond mines. We will explore more of the non-work social dynamics in the following section.

The population of the African workforce at Tsumeb had grown rapidly following the mine and train line opening in August of 1906. As the copper mine was preparing to open, OMEG locally employed around 150 black workers in May of that year. This increased, as we can see below (Figure 35) in the graph to an average of 678 workers between 1907 and 1910, and eventually peaked at 1,300 by 1914.[136] Numbers of employed were highly seasonal, reflecting the short contracts, with the highest average number of workers between June and July.

---

134 NAN, ZBU2068 W.IV.i.8. Travel, food, and clothing for recruited Ovambo 1910–1913, Blanket sample from Carl Bödiker & Co. 'Bavaria', 110.

135 Tsumeb, DSWAZ, 21.11.1906, 1. Translation to English by W.B. Lyon.

136 Schnorbus, Heidi, and Otavi-Minen-Aktiengesellschaft, ed. *Die Geschichte der Otavi-Minen-AG: 1900–2000; ein ereignisreiches Jahrhundert* (Frankfurt am Main: Brönners Druckerei Breidenstein, 2000), 73.

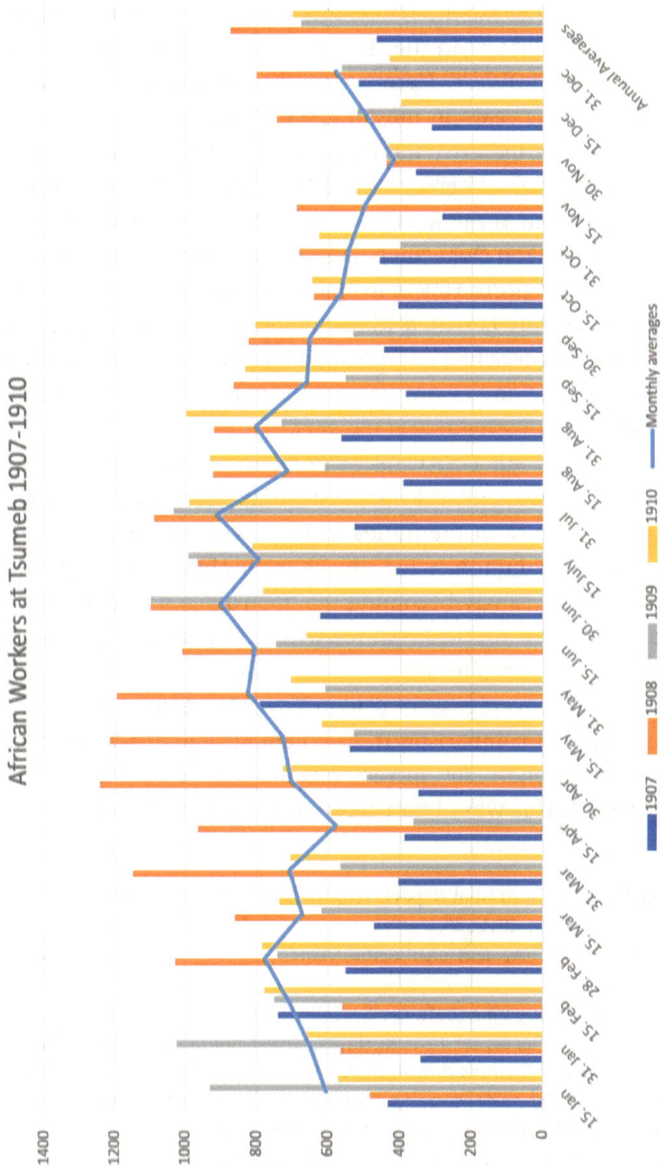

Figure 35: Graph of African Workers at Tsumeb 1907–1910.[137]

137 Compiled from NAN, ZBU 2071 W.IV.I.3, Medical treatment of workers, 1911–1912, Number of native workers 1907–1910 (inclusive Cape Boys), 2.

The location community grew alongside the workforce from around 700 to 800 people in May of 1906, to 3,000 by 1911.[138] In the first years of the mine's operation, workers included many Herero POWs.[139] Herero worker numbers however seem to have decreased in the following years, as most in the colonial economy were employed on white farms in the period after the war. Those who remained worked mainly at the smelting works, while others could be found processing ore, including women.[140] The largest segment of the workforce was Ovambo and came from a variety of polities with Ondonga and Oukwanyama most prominently represented. However, based on missionary reports, Oukwanyama workers seemed to have decreased in 1912 because of recently crowned King Mandume's policies. Adding to the trend, by this time the Portuguese had militarily subjugated some of the polities (Ombandja and Evale) in their colony of Angola and were increasing pressure on Oukwanyama to send laborers to Portuguese employers.[141]

Local missionaries highlight other Africans at the location and employed by the mine including Damara, Nama, and Zulu (From the Cape).[142] Lastly San, comprising some forcibly sent to work at the mines in 1908, were also working for OMEG.[143] The diversity of the community led the Rhenish Missionary report of 1910 to declare that it was increasingly becoming the 'metropole of the north.'[144] This was in stark contrast to the southern mines where only males, primarily Ovambo and Cape workers, were employed.

At Tsumeb black workers on average were paid just over 1/- per shift plus provisions, which was competitive in comparison to the diamond mines. White mine workers, who numbered seventeen in 1906, increased to an average around 120, and were paid about 14/- per shift. This was almost three times comparable pay to Eu-

138 Spiecker, *Mein Tagebuch*, 281; BAB, Annual Report of the Rhenish Mission Society 1910, Tsumeb, (Barmen: Westdeutsche Druckerei, 1911), 36.

139 Jäckel, *Die Landgesellschaften in den deutschen Schutzgebieten. Denkschrift zur Kolonialen Landfrage*, 236–237.

140 Schnorbus and Otavi-Minen-Aktiengesellschaft, *Die Geschichte der Otavi-Minen-AG*, 73.

141 On Mandume's reign and migrant labor, see Patricia Hayes, "Order out of Chaos: Mandume Ya Ndemufayo and Oral History," *Journal of Southern African Studies Journal of Southern African Studies* 19 (1993): 90, 104–105; missionary records however contrast with Haye's argument that migrant labor was supported by Mandume. Missionary Lang says that the numbers of Kwanyama migrants to Tsumeb dropped off compared to the past because of Mandume's reign; see, VEM, RMG 1.631 b, B/c II 58, Ferdinand Lang, Band 2 1899–1919; 1942; 1942. Letter from Missionary Lang to Olpp, 13.2.1912, Tsumeb, 91.

142 VEM, RMG 1.631 b, B/c II 58, Ferdinand Lang, Band 2 1899–1919; 1942; 1942. Letter from Lang to the Inspector, Tsumeb, 14.3.1911; Schnorbus and Otavi-Minen-Aktiengesellschaft, *Die Geschichte der Otavi-Minen-AG*, 73.

143 Gordon and Douglas, *The Bushman Myth*, 54.

144 BAB, Annual Report of the Rhenish Mission Society 1910, Tsumeb, (Barmen: Westdeutsche Druckerei, 1911), 36.

rope. Such pay attracted a diverse assortment of white workers, from former German soldiers following the war against the Herero and Nama, to Austrians, Italians, Russians, and Portuguese.[145] There were, however, reasons why individuals might not want to work for OMEG. Tsumeb, unlike the surface level mining of Lüderitzbucht, had shafts located deep underground, where heat and fumes made the work grueling. Ovambo workers, like many others, disliked underground work and would occasionally skip a few shifts a week. The heat from steam pumps could be so intense that workers would occasionally pass out while underground.[146]

Figure 36: Ovambo and white workers laboring underground in the Tsumeb copper mines. They are building wooden supports to keep the tunnels from collapsing. Picture likely dates between 1906 and 1914.[147]

145 Schnorbus and Otavi-Minen-Aktiengesellschaft, *Die Geschichte der Otavi-Minen-AG*, 73; Schatz, *Tsumeb zu O.M.E.G.'s Zeiten*, 14.

146 Paul Gerhard Söhnge, *Tsumeb, a Historical Sketch* (Windhoek: Committee of the S.W.A. Scientific Society, 1976), 39; looking to avoid gruelling underground mining work was not uncommon across various groups of Africans in Southern Africa, including the Ciskei men who did not wish to go in the deep level gold mines of the Rand; see William Beinart, "'Jamani' Cape Workers in German South West Africa, 1904–12," in *Hidden Struggles in Rural South Africa: Politics & Popular Movements in the Transkei & Eastern Cape, 1890–1930*, William Beinart and Colin Bundy (Berkeley: University of California Press, 1987), 167.

147 BDKGUFM, Photo A_0SS_7350. Tsumeb: Untertagebau, Abbau IV. Sohle, Lore auf Schienen.

Based on cramped, claustrophobic work conditions seen above in Figure 36, it is not surprising why workers may have opted not to go down if possible. Details on which black laborers went down in the shafts is not clear from the written record, but children and women normally worked above ground. However, some workers that went down were young, as the first reported fatal accident in the shafts in 1909 killed a fourteen-year-old Ovambo boy.[148]

The General Strike of 1910

One attribute of underground work was that black and white workers were in very close contact because of the tight confines. White workers underground primarily took on more technical specialist work, such as pump men, pipe fitters, plate layers and timberers, whereas black workers did less skilled labor, such as shoveling, working with pickaxes, and assisting skilled white workers. Racialized breakdown of labor in underground mining in GSWA shared similarities to how gold mining functioned on the Witwatersrand.[149] Such working conditions may have been a contributing factor as to why both white and black workers participated in the mine's first major strike of 1910. In that year, a large part of the mine collapsed resulting in three Ovambo laborers dead and three more badly injured. The incident led the entire workforce, including whites, to go on strike. All wanted better conditions and better pay before they went back into the 'mouse trap.' Ovambo workers were especially traumatized by the event and 300 left to return to the polities without their pay for the month.[150] Most however were forced back to the mines by the colonial police. Cape Workers also joined in the strike. Eventually the whites returned to work after concluding that wage increases were hopeless and they were joined by Herrero, Ovambo and then the rest of the workforce.[151] During the German colonial period this may have been one of the only events where black and white workers joined together in a strike. Unfortunately traces of the event in the historical record are limited, making deeper investigation into the strike, its aftermath, and individual experiences seemingly impossible. While we have touched on Ovambo work, strikes, and migration, much of their time spent in the south was not actually labor.

---

148 Söhnge, *Tsumeb, a Historical Sketch*, 39.

149 Katz, "The Underground Route to Mining," 468–469.

150 Schatz, *Tsumeb zu O.M.E.G.'s Zeiten*, 46.

151 VEM, RMG 2.529 a C/h 46 a Tsumeb (mit Grootfontein, Gaup, Otavi), Vol. 1 1907–1939, Conference Report on Tsumeb and the region from Missionary Lang, 1.10.1910, Tsumeb, 357.

Despite participating in labor systems that saw them as little more than a black proletariat to be utilized for the colonial economy, Ovambo contracted laborers found time and made space to continue their lives when not in the polities of the north. Echoing the observations of Dunbar Moodie and Vivienne Ndatsche on South African gold miners, these black miners managed to retain a sense of identity and integrity despite the controlling systems implemented by their employers and the colonial state.[152] This resilience raises the pivotal question posed in the introduction: how did these workers spend their time after shifts ended, and what did relaxation and enjoyment entail for them in the settler region?

Life Beyond Work

Addressing this question, Ovambo workers in the Police Zone engaged in a variety of social activities that provided relaxation and enjoyment beyond their work. These included making and listening to music, imbibing alcoholic beverages, engaging in sexual relations, practicing religious observance, and gambling. However, only restricted views into these activities are present in the historical record, often appearing as complaints in the letters and reports of missionaries, colonial administrators, or business operators. This is largely because leisure was seen as anathema to productivity in the colonial mindset. Nevertheless, there are notable exceptions, with some non-work activities promoted, such as attending church services encouraged by missionaries, and the purchasing of goods promoted by traders and stores in the Police Zone. Importantly, colonial photography provides unique insights into these aspects of their lives, offering details that are otherwise lost in the written record.

The allocation of Sundays as days off at places like Lüderitzbucht and Tsumeb became a significant factor in shaping the non-work activities of Ovambo laborers. By January 1912, a Sunday 'work pause' was officially recognized in the Grootfontein district, home to the Tsumeb mines. Many Ovambo workers, wary of the dangers of mine shafts, embraced this respite, in contrast to many German white miners who chose to work for extra pay.[153] In 1913, the Lüderitz district saw similar regulations, though adherence varied, with some diamond mines op-

152 T. Dunbar Moodie and Vivienne Ndatshe, *Going for Gold: Men, Mines, and Migration* (Berkeley: University of California Press, 1995), 1–2.
153 VEM, RMG 1.631 b, B/c II 58, Ferdinand Lang, Band 2 1899–1919; 1942; 1942, Letter from Missionary Lang to Olpp, 13.2.1912, Tsumeb, 91.

erating for up to three Sundays per month.[154] However, by 1912, the largest diamond mines had ceased Sunday work.[155] These intermittent rest days provided Ovambo laborers with more opportunities to engage in activities beyond their contractual obligations, including religious practices.

Religion

The historical record illuminates the religious practices and spiritual beliefs of the laborers, primarily through the lens of missionary efforts at work sites. In areas with substantial African communities, like Tsumeb, mission stations and permanent church presences were established. Other locations, such as railway construction sites, farms, or the diamond mines around Lüderitzbucht, received only occasional visits from missionaries and African assistant preachers, including some of Herero and Ovambo origin. For instance, the Kolmanskop diamond mine received visits approximately every three weeks by 1910, offering services to Ovambo and a few Bondelswart workers.[156] Farms, more isolated, were visited even less frequently, yet some farmers around Grootfontein actively encouraged such visits by both Rhenish Protestant and Catholic missionaries, promising free food for these events. While this might suggest a concern for the workers' spiritual well-being, it appears that many farmers were motivated by the belief that occasional church visits would reduce the likelihood of their African workers leaving the farms.[157]

Below in Figure 37 we see Ovambo preachers *(Prediger)* connected with the Finnish protestant missionaries in the Ondonga Kingdom. Christianity, while originally evangelized by white missionaries in the colony, was increasingly being led on the ground by black church leaders like these men. Multiple churches in the colony,

154 NAN, BLU [011], B6n. Mining matters. Sunday rest at the mines, Lüderitz Mining Chamber to the Imperial Government, 24.1.1914, 60; NAN, ZBU 0162 A.VI.a.8. Vol. 1, Annual report of the native commissioner 1913–1914, Annual Report of the Imperial Native Commission for Lüderitzbucht 1.4.1912–31.3.1913, 58.

155 NAN, ZBU 0162 A.VI.a.8. Vol. 1, Annual report of the native commissioner 1913–1914, Annual Report of the Imperial Native Commission for Lüderitzbucht 1.4.1912–31.3.1913, 58.

156 VEM, RMG 2.509 a Lüderitzbucht C/h 23 a, Vol. 1 1904–1945, 1910 Annual Report from Lüderitzbucht, 303.

157 Reports around Grootfontein note that visits to farms were also occasionally an activity where Catholic and Protestant missionaries competed for followers, VEM, RMG 2.503 a. Grootfontein (mit Otavi), C/h 15 a, Vol. 1 1910–1946, Grootfontein Second Quarter Report from Missionary Parday, Grootfontein, 28.06.1911, 355.

including the Finnish and Rhenish Missionary Societies, had African preachers engaged with various communities.

Figure 37: Ovambo preachers, likely Ondonga in the early twentieth century.[158]

One Ovambo Rhenish preacher, who has left a written record was Hendrik Djuella. Uniquely, he received education in Germany and afterwards returned to work at the mission station at Gaub, located between Windhoek and Swakopmund. While a letter from him dates from 1901, it still gives an idea of what type of religious work Ovambo, and other African preachers engaged in. Djuella wrote:

> I am doing very good. Here in Gaub, I now also help in the school and that also goes well. But now this Nama language is very difficult to learn, but progress is already much better.

158 BDKGUFM, Photo 068-2179-252, Geistliche schwarze Helfer im Ovamboland. Finnische Mission SWA, Fotograf: Neumeister, Otto.

> Now Herero also come to church and after lessons . . . . I also told the inspector that I married a Bergdamara woman and she sends her regards.[159]

Henrik Djuella was not only involved in church services but also taught at the mission school. His linguistic talents included at least Otjiherero, German, his mother tongue of Oshiwambo, and his recently acquired Khoekhoe (spoken by many Nama) as mentioned in the letter. As the work of Djuella highlights, church services were given, if possible, in the mother tongue of the followers. But not all preachers and missionaries were such talented polyglots like Hendrik. One missionary report from 1909 Lüderitzbucht mentions that Missionary Laaf, who headed the community, could not speak Oshiwambo and didn't have a translator, therefore services to Ovambo workers could not be given.[160] By 1910, however, the community at Lüderitzbucht had an Ovambo assistant preacher who gave services to the Ovambo attendees.[161] In Tsumeb, David jaHilonda, another Rhenish trained preacher from the Ovambo polities, had been working there with the Ovambo community at least since 1910.[162]

While missionaries between 1905 and 1914 exerted considerable effort to integrate worker communities into Christian practices, their success was limited. Regular churchgoers constituted only a small fraction of the worker population at most sites. For example, a 1910 missionary report from Lüderitz noted that out of an estimated African population of around 1,200, only 74 were members of the Rhenish community, including a mere three Ovambo individuals. This low engagement, particularly among Ovambos, was attributed by the Mission to the challenges posed by distant and isolated mines.[163] Similarly, a 1912 Rhenish report from Tsumeb indicated that while the community had 355 church members, the larger worker population of about 2,000 remained 'pagans.'[164] This non-Christian majority, typical among the migrant Ovambo workforce, adhered to traditional belief systems, al-

---

159 VEM, RMG 1630, Bl. 114f., Brief des Hendrik Djuella an Missionsinspektor Schreiber (1901) in Christel Adick and Wolfgang Mehnert, *Deutsche Missions- und Kolonialpädagogik in Dokumenten. Eine kommentierte Quellensammlung aus den Afrikabeständen deutschsprachiger Archive 1884 – 1914* (Frankfurt am Main: KO-Verl. für Interkulturelle Kommunikation, 2001), 401. Translation to English by W.B. Lyon.

160 VEM, RMG 2.509 a Lüderitzbucht C/h 23 a, Vol. 1 1904–1945, Report from Missionary Laaf, Lüderitzbucht, 21.8.09, 308.

161 VEM, RMG 2.509 a Lüderitzbucht C/h 23 a, Vol. 1 1904–1945, 1910 Annual report from Lüderitzbucht, 303.

162 VEM, RMG 2.529 a C/h 46 a Tsumeb (mit Grootfontein, Gaup, Otavi), Vol. 1 1907–1939, Report on the Mission work at station Tsumeb in the conference year 1911+1912, 328.

163 BAB, Annual Report of the Rhenish Mission Society 1910, Lüderitzbucht, (Barmen: Westdeutsche Druckerei, 1911), 22.

164 VEM, RMG 2.529 a C/h 46 a Tsumeb (mit Grootfontein, Gaup, Otavi), Vol. 1 1907–1939, Visitations-fragebogen Tsumeb, 12.8.1912, 330.

though details are sparse in the colonial archives. However, research such as that by Kletus Likuwa on the Kavango community suggests the implementation of communal rules and taboos as central coping mechanisms to deal with the stresses of migratory labor, practices that may have roots extending back to the German colonial period for both Kavango and Ovambo communities.[165]

Beyond these glimpses of religious practice at the work site, we can glean information about the broader social life of Ovambo workers in the Police Zone. During their time in the south, they often cultivated a rich social and personal life, characterized by a blend of traditional practices and adaptations to their new environments.

Social and Personal Life

Figure 38: Above to the left we see a group of workers socializing around housing at Tsumeb during the first decades of the twentieth century. The photo to the right is a close-up of an okasandji from the late nineteenth-century Ovambo polities.[166]

165 Likuwa, "Continuity and Change in Gender Relations within the Contract Labour System in Kavango, Namibia, 1925–1972," 2.

166 The photo to the left, BDKGUFM, Photo 009-2079-1, Bfs I 44 / Eingeborene Minenarbeiter vor ihren Wohnhütten / – Otavi Mine / S.W.A.; the photo on the right, Photo of Object VME00069, INSTRUMENT – Vänersborgs Museum, Sweden – CC BY. https://www.europeana.eu/de/item/916106/vbg_object_VME00069; For an Oukwanjama variant of the instrument from about the first decade of the twentieth century, see Hermann Tönjes, *Ovamboland; Land, Leute, Mission. Mit besonderer Berücksichtigung seines grössten Stammes Oukuanjama.* (Berlin: M. Warneck, 1911), 82.

The photo above to the left (Figure 38) focuses on a group of Ovambo men socializing near worker housing at Tsumeb. In the bottom right of the photograph, we see a man playing an *okasandji*, or lamellophone, which is a traditional Ovambo instrument that integrates both an iron plate with keys to play and the shell of a melon as a sounding board.[167] Similar instruments are widespread throughout southern Africa, and is perhaps most famous in Zimbabwe, where it is often called the *mbira*.[168] In colonial Zimbabwe, music played with the *mbira* as well as the guitar and drums were a common way for migrant laborers to relax, like the workers in the photo above.[169] Another typical instrument that accompanied many travelling Ovambo migrant laborers was the *okambulumbumbwa*, or musical bow.

In the photo below (Figure 39) we can see a group of Ovambo migrants in Swakopmund around 1904/1905. In addition to looking cold because of the coastal climate and therefore wearing an array of clothing and blankets in an attempt to get warm, we can see they brought instruments with them from home. The individuals, third from the right and second from the right, seem to be holding *okambulumbumbwa*.[170] This photo also displays the changing world in which Ovambo migrants lived, where western textiles and traditional musical instruments, along with other new and old belongings and goods were increasingly becoming part of everyday life.

Playing instruments such as *okambulumbumbwa* and *okasandji* certainly made the hardships of their life in the Police Zone more bearable and allowed migrants to enjoy time off. Further, playing music from home certainly served as a buffer in far off locales and a bonding agent in challenging circumstances. In addition to playing instruments, singing helped ease the daily tribulations of

167 Tönjes, *Ovamboland*, 82.

168 Andrew Tracey, "The System of the Mbira," *African Music* 10, no. 1 (2015): 127.

169 Mhoze Chikowero, *African Music, Power, and Being in Colonial Zimbabwe* (Bloomington: Indiana University Press, 2015), 112–115; Ernest D. Brown, "The Guitar and the 'Mbira': Resilience, Assimilation, and Pan-Africanism in Zimbabwean Music," *The World of Music* 36, no. 2 (1994): 73–117.

170 For more information on the various musical bows, their origins in Ovambo society, and how they are played, see Sakari Löytty, "People's Church – People's Music," (PhD thesis, Helsinki, Sibelius Academy, DocMus, 2012), 47–48.

Figure 39: Group of about 15 Ovambo migrants in Swakopmund. Some of the men are carrying calabashes, palm-leaf baskets, and what looks like okambulumbumbwa.[171]

travel and work.[172] As highlighted by Minette Mans, Ovambo migrants sang *ondundwiilandjimbo*, or travelling songs, which were often call and response, and specifically sung while travelling to and from work in the settler region. These songs served as a means to fight off feelings of loneliness during their long journeys away.[173] Recollections by former migrant workers in Tsumeb, recount singing songs in anticipation of their return and playing the *okambulumbumbwa*.[174] References to Ovambo laborers singing while travelling and working is not dissimilar to practices by train line workers in the United States in the nineteenth

171 NAN, Photo 27000, Ovambo migrant workers, probably in Swakopmund, 1904/1905, Photographer: Stuhlmann.

172 Tönjes, *Ovamboland; Land, Leute, Mission. Mit besonderer Berücksichtigung seines grössten Stammes Oukuanjama*, 82.

173 Minette Mans, *The Changing Faces of Aawambo Musical Arts*, Basel Southern Africa Studies 11 (Basel, Switzerland: Basler Afrika Bibliographien, 2017), 40.

174 Mans, *The Changing Faces of Aawambo Musical Arts*, 38.

and early twentieth centuries. There, so-called 'gandy dancers' or railway section hands, who laid and maintained railway tracks, used songs to coordinate their work and pass the time.[175]

Alcohol consumption was also a regular part of life for laborers. Tsumeb was particularly well known as a drinking town, and missionary Lang described celebrations on the German Emperor's Birthday in 1912 as follows: "In one of the most popular locals of Berlin, it could not have been any worse than it was that evening."[176] Black people at Tsumeb were able to get schnapps of European manufacture via whites, although this was illegal according to colonial laws. However, alcohol was never distributed by the copper or diamond mines, at least in a regular fashion to workers, as was done in the early 1900s at the gold mines of Johannesburg as a tool of control.[177] Most commonly drunken by Africans in GSWA was sugar beer, which was often made in the locations.[178] Brewing traditional beer, was a job often undertaken by women, and likely the Ovambo women in the Police Zone were engaged in brewing.[179]

Physical relations and the sex life of migrant workers on contract is a subject that is perhaps the most intimate and the hardest to find direct sources of in colonial records beyond methods of control over black bodies. This is not to diminish that for Ovambo migrants, as for most people, physical contact and sexuality is an important part of life. Examples of sex coming through the colonial records are limited and very much biased towards if and how it was affecting employers, white people, or concepts of Christian morality. What is often not discussed and was without doubt very common were events such as everyday sexual relations between Africans in the Police Zone.

Sexual relations both between African men and women, and between men and men, occurred among migrant workers.[180] Reports from Keetmanshoop in 1913, home to a diverse community including both migrant Ovambo and many

175 Vanita Oelschlager, *The Gandy Dancers: And Work Songs from the American Railroad* (Akron: VanitaBooks, 2015).

176 Ndeutala Selma Hishongwa, *Women of Namibia: The Changing Role of Namibian Women from Traditional Precolonial Times to the Present* (Stockholm, Sweden: Förlaget By & Bygd, 1983), 19.

177 van Onselen, *New Babylon, New Nineveh*, 33.

178 VEM, RMG 1.631 b, B/c II 58, Ferdinand Lang, Band 2 1899–1919; 1942; 1942, Letter from Lang to the Inspector, Tsumeb, 14.3.1911, 75.

179 Hishongwa, *Women of Namibia*, 19.

180 I have not found examples of other types of sexuality or sexual identity in the colonial records.

Cape laborers working on the railways, reference sexual relations among the African community.[181] Details however are lacking. From the colonial perspective, of most concern was the subject of sex between African women and white men, which also occurred at Keetmanshoop, and how German doctors were attempting to control the outbreak of sexually transmitted diseases (STDs). In this case – and many throughout the colonial record on the topic of STDs in GSWA – a primary method of control was to force African women who had relations with white men to be examined by colonial doctors.[182] This seems to have had little effect on stopping the spread of disease but reinforced the practice of objectifying black women's bodies.

Regarding physical relations among Ovambo men, it appears that such interactions were most common in the mines of the South, where many male laborers, living apart from larger communities, often found themselves in close quarters. Homosexuality also played a traditional role in Ovambo communities that was connected with playing a traditional instrument, the Ekola.[183] Wolfram Hartmann and the work of Kurt Falk have written on sexual relations between Ovambo men in Lüderitzbucht.[184] Records of similar homosexual male relations, throughout southern Africa in the twentieth century exist, especially in the mining compounds of colonial Zimbabwe and South Africa.[185] Zackie Achmat has convincingly argued that these relations between men at the mines were not only to survive emotionally when away from home, but also simply for pleasure.[186] There were most certainly instances where simple personal preference was at play, although details like these

181 NAN, ZBU 0162 A.VI.a.8. Vol. 1, Annual report of the native commissioner 1913–1914, Regarding the reports for the years 1912/1913 for native punishments, Native Commissioner letter to the Imperial Government at Windhoek, Keetmanshoop, 1.9.1913, 31.

182 NAN, ZBU 0162 A.VI.a.8 Vol. 1, Annual report of the native commissioner 1913–1914, Regarding the reports for the years 1912/1913 for native punishments, Native Commissioner letter to the Imperial Government at Windhoek, Keetmanshoop, 1.9.1913, 31.

183 P.R. Kirby, "A Secret Musical Instrument, the Ekola of the Ovakuanyama of Ovamiloland," *South African Journal of Science* 38, no. 01 (1942): 345–351.

184 Wolfram Hartmann, "Ondillimani! Ipumbu Ya Tshilongo & the Ambiguities of Resistance in Ovambo," in *Namibia under South African Rule: Mobility & Containment, 1915–46*, ed. Patricia Hayes et al. (Oxford: James Currey, 1998), 286; Kurt Falk, "Homosexualität bei den Eingeborenen in Südwestafrika," *Archiv für Menschenkunde* 1, no. 13 (1925/1926): 202–214.

185 van Onselen, *New Babylon, New Nineveh*, 378 fn. 43; Moodie, T. Dunbar, Vivienne Ndatshe, and British Sibuyi. "Migrancy and Male Sexuality on the South African Gold Mines." *Journal of Southern African Studies* 14, no. 2 (January 1988): 230–231; Patrick Harries, "Symbols and Sexuality. Culture and Identity on the Early Witwatersrand Gold Mines," *Gender and History* 2, no. No. 3 (1990): 318–336; van Onselen, *Chibaro*, 175–176, 307 fn. 91.

186 Zackie Achmat, "'Apostles of Civilised Vice': 'Immoral Practices' and 'Unnatural Vice' in South African Prisons and Compounds, 1890–1920," *Social Dynamics* 19, no. No. 2 (1993): 92–110.

are not to be found amongst the written source base for Ovambo migrant workers in the early twentieth century.[187] Missionary records include a few scattered details of colonial sexuality, especially when they combine the topics of Christian ideals, interracial sex, and sex work.

Missionary Lang in Tsumeb recounted that at the Mine Hotel, where most white workers lived, the beer from their mugs would occasionally 'miraculously disappear' without them drinking it, with the inference that it was given to black women. It was deduced that this was one way of leading to sex between black women and European men. The old trope of alcohol leading to sex does not mean that this was a reason for sexual relations, but they do seem to have occurred. Dr. Scherer, who worked for the mine, told missionary Vedder that 15 black women and girls had abortions not wishing to have children because of their relations with whites.[188] Rumors between Christian missionaries in a colonial mining town come with their own very specific biases but this does not discount the fact that such relations did likely occur.

In the context of Tsumeb, sexual relations often intersected with the domestic work performed by African women for white men. Records indicate that women, formally employed as washers or servants, frequently also engaged in sex work. The extent to which these relationships were consensual or stemmed from significant power imbalances remains unclear, underscoring the complexity and varied agency within these interactions. For instance, some Herero women, many of whom had suffered forced sexual violence during the war, might have turned to sex work as a survival strategy in the following years. On the other hand, some women, including those from the Ovambo community, might have viewed sex work, including with mine laborers, as a means to support themselves, their children, and their partners.[189] 'Taboo' relationships were not limited to interracial dynamics; they also occurred within the white community. A notable case involved Dr. Scherer, who impregnated his white house servant, a married woman, and subsequently paid her £244 for her silence.[190]

---

187 Heterosexism has been a problem in African studies. For a brief overview, see Marc Epprecht, "The 'Unsaying' of Indigenous Homosexualities in Zimbabwe: Mapping a Blindspot in an African Masculinity," *Journal of Southern African Studies* 24, no. 4 (1998): 648–651.

188 VEM, RMG 1.631 b, B/c II 58, Ferdinand Lang, Band 2 1899–1919; 1942; 1942, Letter from Missionary Lang to Olpp, 13.2.1912, Tsumeb, 91–92.

189 Chapter 5 will return to this theme and how Cameroonian women, part of a larger forced exile community in GSWA, engaged in sex work as a method of supporting their families; see Chapter 5, "The Cameroonian Exiles: Women as the Backbone of a Small but Tenacious West African Community in GSWA."

190 VEM, RMG 1.631 b, B/c II 58, Ferdinand Lang, Band 2 1899–1919; 1942, Letter from Missionary Lang to Olpp, 13.2.1912, Tsumeb, 91.

The work of Luise White has shed light on the complexities and multifaceted nature of sex work in the colonial context, illustrating that motivations can be as diverse as the individuals themselves.[191] While the topic of sex work and sexuality among migrant workers in GSWA warrants further research, this chapter has provided only a cursory overview due to this book's scope. Beyond these social and intimate dimensions, migrant workers also had to navigate the challenges of meeting other basic needs, which were often the responsibility, at least technically, of their employers.

Housing, Health, and Provisions

For Ovambo migrants, the quality and nature of housing at their places of work varied considerably, reflecting the broader racial dynamics and segregation policies of the colonial society. In larger diamond mining operations in the south, workers were typically housed in expansive compounds, while those employed on farms often resided in small shacks either individually or with small families. A common thread, regardless of location, was the stark segregation between black and white workers' housing.[192] This segregation was a manifestation of the dualistic racial laws that permeated colonial society, systematically categorizing individuals as either white or black. Ovambo workers, classified as black, were consequently relegated to specific areas near settler towns, compounds adjacent to mines, or temporary housing near construction sites, distinctly separate from white residences. The housing provided to them was generally substandard, often located in areas that exacerbated health risks, further highlighting the myriad challenges they faced in their daily lives.

Below in Figure 40, we see an example of a large compound near the Bogenfels diamond field. These were some of the largest examples of compound style housing in the colony for black workers. In the photo below there are at least 85 people, which surely meant cramped and unhygienic living conditions. These buildings

191 Luise White, *The Comforts of Home: Prostitution in Colonial Nairobi* (Chicago: University of Chicago Press, 1990), 7–10.

192 Kru were the exception for black workers up until WWI in GSWA; see Lyon, "From Labour Elites to Garveyites," 45.

Figure 40: Ovambo workers at the location at Bogenfels mine.[193]

were made of corrugated iron, with wooden or cement floors.[194] At the smaller spectrum of lodging for workers, were *pontoks*, or traditional dome-shaped housing, made of sticks and covered with animal hide.

Dr. Richter, a medical officer of the Kolmanskop Diamond Mines Ltd. submitted a report to his employer regarding an outbreak of Typhus at the mine in June 1910. He argued that workers' poor health was primarily due to the condition in which they arrive after transit, combined with workers perceived 'preference' for unhealthy living conditions.[195] Dr. Richter observed that workers were very dirty, sleep two to three workers to a bed, and in some cases defecate and urinate on one another.[196] The doctor highlights, unintentionally, not customs of uncleanliness,

193 BDKGUFM, Photo 11478845, *Ovambo-Werft Bogenfels.*

194 NAN, ZBU 0162 A.VI.a.8. Vol. 1, Annual report of the native commissioner 1913–1914, Annual Report of the Imperial Native Commission for Lüderitzbucht 1.4.1912–31.3.1913, 57.

195 NAN, ZBU 2071 W.IV.I.3. Medical treatment of workers, 1911–1912, Statement from the case report of the medical doctor Dr. Richter, regarding the Kolmanskop Diamond Mines Ltd., 7–8.

196 NAN, ZBU 2071 W.IV.I.3. Medical treatment of workers, 1911–1912, Statement from the case report of the medical doctor Dr. Richter, regarding the Kolmanskop Diamond Mines Ltd., 7.

which did not exist, but rather the failings of the mine's capacity to care for sick workers. What he describes is the result of overcrowding, and unwell workers not getting proper treatment, both because of lacking medical assistance, as well as a distrust of European medicine by laborers.

Many Ovambo workers saw field hospitals as a place Africans went never to return, which could, depending on the illness and severity, be the case. Such distrust of western medicine also occurred at other Southern African worksites including the Rhodesian gold mines.[197] A 1913 to 1914 report from the GSWA native commissioner, highlighted distrust of European medicine in general by all Africans in the colony. The commissioner argued that better personal relations between doctors and their African patients could be a real solution, but this rarely occurred.[198] In the early 1900s in Tsumeb, the Ovambo community was served by a traditional medicine man, who competed with the German doctor for patients.[199] While he was not trained in the latest western medicine, he was working with members from his own community who trusted him. Western doctors, like the previously mentioned Dr. Richter, not only were unfamiliar with Ovambo culture, but were also condescending, which likely came through in their patient interactions.[200] However, not all Ovambo distrusted European doctors. For example, in the previously mentioned case of the Ovambo worker Itere, he had initially asked to visit the native hospital, although his request was denied. For those Ovambo workers, and all African migrant laborers not from the settler region wishing to visit a native hospital, employers were legally obligated to pay for their medical treatment for up to six weeks.[201] But for local African laborers (non-Ovambos), the costs could be quite steep and were a disincentive not to go to the hospital. For example, in Keetmanshoop, Africans not covered by their employers needed to pay 1/5d per day to get medical attention at the hospital. As a result, few non-migrant Africans required to pay such overheads went to the hospital.[202] Out of the entire Ovambo migrant

197 van Onselen, *Chibaro*, 59.

198 NAN, ZBU 0162 A.VI.a.8 Vol. 1. Annual report of the native commissioner 1913–1914, 32.

199 Ilse Schatz, Interview, March 3, 2017. Windhoek, Namibia. Interview regarding her family, the history of Tsumeb, the copper mines, and labor. One-on-one interview (with her son present) in nursing home with notes taken by hand.

200 Schatz, *Tsumeb zu O.M.E.G.'s Zeiten*, 19.

201 NAN, BLU [027], E.1.A, Bezirksamt Lüderitzbucht, 1896–1915, 1525/11 Copy, On the laws regulating the payment of migrant labor health care; after six weeks the costs for medical care would be transferred to the colonial government. For an example, see NAN, ZBU 2071 W.IV.I.3, Medical treatment of workers, 1911–1912, 1909, Bachstein-Koppel Baudirektion Windhoek letter to the administration of the Imperial Native Hospital at Windhoek, 26.11.1912, 20.

202 NAN, ZBU 0162 A.VI.a.8 Vol. 1, Annual report of the native commissioner 1913–1914, Native Commissioner, Keetmanshoop, 9.1913, 44.

labor population, death as the result of disease fluctuated and the cause varied based on location and employer.

Table 2: Ovambo worker mortality at Tsumeb and Lüderitz for 1909, 1910, 1912.[203]

Year	Annual Ovambo worker mortality rate in Tsumeb	Annual Ovambo worker mortality rate in Lüderitzbucht
1909	3,04%	5,6%
1910	2,35%	5,73%
1912	–	4,1%

As seen in Table 2 above, from 1909 to 1910 the mortality rate in Tsumeb improved for Ovambo workers dropping from 3.04 to 2.35 percent. In both years pneumonia and dysentery were the primary causes of death. The same cannot be said for Lüderitz district over the same period. In 1909, 5.6 percent of the Ovambo migrant population died. Migrant workers in the first quarter of that year were plagued by scurvy as the primary cause of death, followed later by pneumonia. Scurvy was likely the result of the early diamond mine operations not providing proper nutrition to workers. In 1910 Lüderitzbucht, the mortality rate increased to 5.73 percent with deaths attributed primarily to pneumonia. This was one of the highest recorded mortality rates for workers in the colony.[204] A later Lüderitzbucht report from early 1912 to early 1913 signaled a decrease in mortality of workers at 4,1 percent, with conditions seemingly having improved for workers over this period.[205] Pneumonia remained the primary cause of death, followed by intestinal inflammation and weak heart (*Herzschwäche*). This was followed by scurvy, although numbers suffering from this ailment were decreasing, which likely meant that provisions were also improving.[206] Despite improvements over time, the numbers point to the mines, especially in the south, as potentially deadly work sites. The mortality rates in the mines of GSWA, while bad, were still

203 Compiled from NAN, ZBU 2071 W.IV.I.3. Medical treatment of workers, 1911–1912, 1909–1910 Ovambo worker mortality statistics for Tsumeb and Lüderitzbucht, 3, 5; NAN, ZBU 0162 A.VI.a.8 Vol. 1, Annual report of the native commissioner 1913–1914, Annual Report of the Imperial Native Commission for Lüderitzbucht 1.4.1912–31.3.1913, 53, 56.

204 NAN, ZBU 2071 W.IV.I.3, *Medical treatment of workers*, 1911–1912, 1909–1910 Ovambo worker mortality statistics for Tsumeb and Lüderitzbucht, 3, 5.

205 NAN, ZBU 0162 A.VI.a.8. Vol. 1, Annual report of the native commissioner 1913–1914, Annual Report of the Imperial Native Commission for Lüderitzbucht 1.4.1912–31.3.1913, 53, 56.

206 NAN, ZBU 0162 A.VI.a.8. Vol. 1, Annual report of the native commissioner 1913–1914, Annual Report of the Imperial Native Commission for Lüderitzbucht 1.4.1912–31.3.1913, 56.

better than the worst years of the early twentieth century Rand mines, where exceptionally bad living conditions and provisions led to a black worker mortality rate of about 11 percent during the winter of 1903.[207]

The diseases and ailments from which many Ovambo were suffering in GSWA in the early twentieth century echoed other colonial mining operations in Africa. For example, a combination of excessive heat, extreme cold, and bad living conditions caused workers at the Kimberley diamond mines in the nineteenth century – especially in the first years of operation – to often come down with pneumonia.[208] Workers at the Rhodesian gold mines of the early twentieth century, especially those who had come from the Mweru-Luapula region, often suffered from scurvy.[209] At these mining locations, and especially in arid GSWA, water availability, and quality had a major impact on worker health.

Early water provisioning for African workers at the diamond mines of GSWA was described as brackish in consistency and barely suitable for consumption. Two Ovambo workers, Nagambari and Jakob, spoke of their experience at the *Diamantengesellschaft Phönix* in 1910: "[W]e often had to drink saltwater and had stomach and lung sickness. The little fresh water that existed in a barrel went to the white workers once it was half empty."[210] Instances where Ovambo workers were forced to drink the same water as pack animals were not uncommon.[211] Food provisions during the first years of the diamond mines were also substandard. Daily rations were often given at the end of the day, and workers were left to prepare meals on their own. This often resulted in real problems as workers were too tired to cook and would in some cases eat the ingredients raw, leading to indigestion problems. Further, there was often not enough wood or material to cook with.[212]

After a few years, the living and provisioning conditions for Ovambo workers began to show signs of improvement. For instance, a young Ovambo worker named 'Petrus' recounted in 1910 how he received ample provisions while working for the Koloniale Bergbaugesellschaft. A 1912/1913 report detailed typical provisions at the diamond mines, including rice, flour, potatoes, onions, tea, beans,

207 Harries, *Work, Culture, and Identity*, 187.
208 Robert Vicat Turrell, *Capital and Labour on the Kimberley Diamond Fields, 1871–1890* (Cambridge: Cambridge University Press, 1987), 160–161.
209 van Onselen, *Chibaro*, 53.
210 NAN, ZBU 2068 W.IV.i.8. Travel, food, and clothing for recruited Ovambo 1910–1913, Regarding increasing deaths of returning Ovambos, Okuakweyo, 9.9.1910, 15.
211 Press, *Blood and Diamonds*, 121.
212 NAN, ZBU 0162 A.VI.a.8. Vol. 1, Annual report of the native commissioner 1913–1914, Annual Report of the Imperial Native Commission for Lüderitzbucht 1.4.1912–31.3.1913, 57.

meat, lard, jam, milk, tobacco, matches, bread, and salt.[213] Additionally, the mines had cooking utensils and usually designated cooks among the workers to prepare meals. These supplies were distributed in the morning and could be consumed during lunch breaks or after work.[214] Despite these gradual improvements in living conditions, the life of Ovambo workers at mining sites, whether in the diamond mines of the south or the copper mines of the north, was inherently temporary. At the end of their contracts, most were eager to return to their homes, carrying with them the experiences and goods they had acquired.

The Trip Back North

The journey back north was not only a return to familiar territory but also an opportunity for workers to bring back purchased goods and acquire more en route. However, this travel was often fraught with difficulties. Challenges included employers sometimes failing to fulfill their contractual obligation to pay for the return journey and settlers along the route denying access to essential resources like water. The migrant workers' role as consumers was also significant for colonial merchants who relied on Ovambo laborers to purchase their goods. The number of workers departing the mines each month varied, with Tsumeb seeing the most fluid movement due to its relatively short contract durations and the feasibility of returning on foot. In contrast, those leaving the diamond mines typically relied on colonial infrastructure such as railways for their return journey.

Below (Figure 41) we can see that for the period from April 1912 to March 1913, most Ovambo workers left the Lüderitzbucht mines in January, November, and July. Those leaving for the whole period numbered 2,374 compared to 3,866 who were arriving. Most leaving had completed their contracts and were therefore entitled to transport and provisions. Others attempted, sometimes successfully to leave before their contracts ended, looking to do agricultural work back in the polities. The large majority returned safely but some would become sick in transit, a few would have goods stolen by San, and the unluckiest would even die.

During the early years of the diamond mines, the return journey was the most perilous. Already in October 1910, the local government in Outjo had been

213 NAN, ZBU 2068 W.IV.i.8. Travel, food, and clothing for recruited Ovambo 1910–1913, Regarding increasing deaths of returning Ovambos, Testimony of 'Petrus' regarding the death of returning Ovambos, Okuakweyo, 9.9.1910, 14.

214 NAN, ZBU 0162 A.VI.a.8. Vol. 1, Annual report of the native commissioner 1913–1914, Annual Report of the Imperial Native Commission for Lüderitzbucht 1.4.1912–31.3.1913, 57–58.

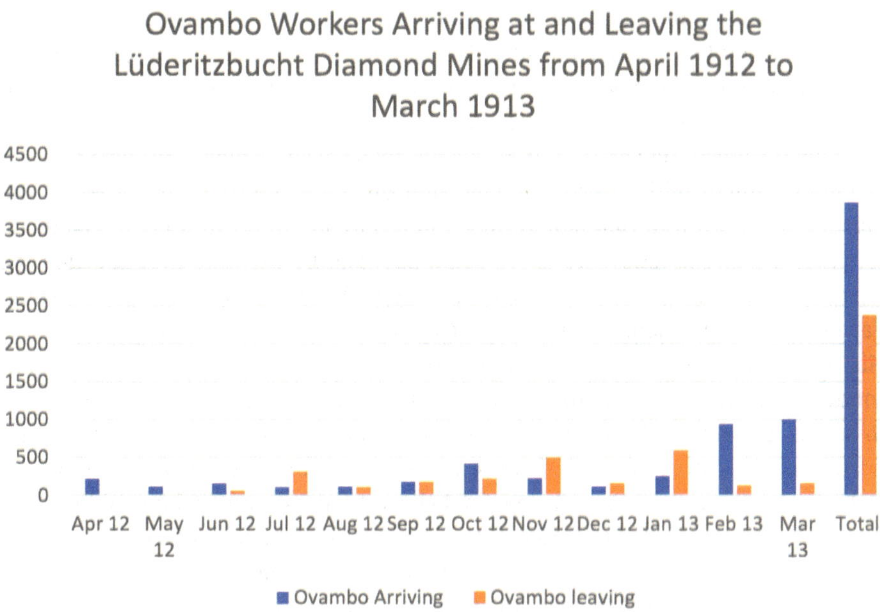

Figure 41: Graph of Ovambo Workers Arriving at and Leaving the Lüderitzbucht Diamond Mines.[215]

analyzing the problem and highlighted issues with workers not receiving enough food and water on the return journey.[216]

Exemplary of the challenges in the early years of the diamond mines was the story shared by an Ovambo man from Oukwanyama in his early twenties named 'Charly'. He had been working for 9/10d monthly and then later 14/7d per month in Lüderitzbucht for Langenmüller (likely an overseer at a diamond mine). While stating that his provisions at work were good, he was let go in mid-August 1910 without any food and had to care for himself and his troop of fellow workers (he did not share why they were fired). During the journey home he had to pay out of pocket for the leg from Swakopmund to Kalkfeld (he was transported on a ship from Lüderitzbucht to Swakopmund, for which the costs were covered). They only received provisions from the government when they arrived in Outjo in the north. On their journey by foot from Outjo to Okaukuejo, 15 of Charly's troop died

215 Compiled from NAN, ZBU 0162 A.VI.a.8. Vol. 1, Annual report of the native commissioner 1913–1914, Annual Report of the Imperial Native Commission for Lüderitzbucht 1.4.1912–31.3.1913, Graph II., 54.

216 NAN, ZBU 2068 W.IV.i.8. Travel, food, and clothing for recruited Ovambo 1910–1913. Letter from the District Office at Outjo to the Imperial Office at Windhoek, 4.10.1910, Outjo, 11.

because of lack of food and general weakness. He stated that because of such bad experiences by his fellow comrades, it was not unthinkable that King Nande ya Hedimbi of the Oukwanyama would possibly ban future workers from going to Lüderitzbucht upon hearing of this tragedy.[217]

Furthermore, the Ovambo man Petrus referenced earlier, who also worked at Lüderitzbucht with Charly, avowed that on the way home on the leg of the journey from Outjo to Okaukuejo they had to pay for water at a farm. Petrus infers that not all his fellow travelers could pay, and by the time they reached the next location with water, three migrants had died of dehydration.[218] The German Farmer Benninghausen, was likely the owner of the farm that Petrus mentioned. His property lay on the path of many travelling Ovambo workers going both south and north. He was notorious for forcing workers to pay or barter with him to access his water. Those travelling south would need to pay Benninghausen a portion of their provisions, and those travelling north would have to pay him a slab of tobacco or one blanket. He would chase away migrants who could not pay from his well, some of whom died of thirst.[219] In addition to bad farmer relations, from 1909 to 1912, San attacks on Ovambo returning home were particularly bad. Groups of three to five San armed with bows and arrows in addition to firearms, would hold up large groups of up to 60 Ovambo, taking many of the commodities they had brought with them.[220]

Such challenges and resulting complaints and requests for help led to improvements over time in the travel back north for workers, especially as their employers were forced by the imperial government to take responsibility for their work force on the return journey.[221] However, even by 1913 the journey still had its perils. The Ovambo worker alias 'Kasino' from the Ondonga Kingdom, as referenced earlier, was one of the workers who lost his life on the way home. In October 1913 he was returning from the diamond mines with a group of one hundred and four Ovambo workers. In Kalkfeld (about 66 km northeast of Omaruru on the way to Otjiwarongo), 'Kasino' came down with a sickness. At the Otjiwar-

217 NAN, ZBU 2068 W.IV.i.8. Travel, food, and clothing for recruited Ovambo 1910–1913, Testimony of 'Charly' regarding the death of returning Ovambos, 9.9.1910, Oukwakweyo, 14.

218 NAN, ZBU 2068 W.IV.i.8. Travel, food, and clothing for recruited Ovambo 1910–1913, Regarding increasing deaths of returning Ovambos, Testimony of 'Petrus' regarding the death of returning Ovambos Okuakweyo, 9.9.1910, 14.

219 NAN, ZBU 2068 W.IV.i.8. Travel, food, and clothing for recruited Ovambo 1910–1913, Letter from the District Office at Outjo to the Imperial Office at Windhoek, Outjo, 13.10.1910, 16.

220 Gordon and Douglas, *The Bushman Myth*, 57–58.

221 NAN, ZBU 2068 W.IV.i.8. Travel, food, and clothing for recruited Ovambo 1910–1913, Letter to the Imperial Office at Windhoek from the Imperial district judge Stintzing, Omaruru, 28.10.1910, 17.

ongo stop, he was kept with the rest of the group headed to Otavi rather than being sent to the native hospital. The blame for his death was placed on the recruitment firm, who on behalf of the mines, often handled the transportation coordination. Kasino's demise is an example where the priority of the recruiter, who would have to cover Kasino's medical costs, was on profit rather than on worker well-being.[222]

For the workers returning from Tsumeb, the path would often lead them first to Otavi where the further journey to northern polities was easier. It was also a place where sick workers, some returning home, would mingle with those who were healthy, and disease could easily spread. As a result, malaria outbreaks at Otavi amongst Ovambo migrants was not uncommon. But for workers looking to head home, Otavi was importantly where they could meet with local Africans, and purchase items.[223] This process whereby returning Ovambo bought goods, whether at Otavi, Swakopmund, Lüderitzbucht, or Windhoek was one of the central goals workers had since leaving home.

Below in Figure 42, we see Ovambo workers in the 1910s in front of Fort Namutoni carrying items they purchased to bring back home and preparing to continue their journey north. Most noticeable is the variety of western clothing items including hats, pants, jackets, and boots. The majority are also carrying trunks to transport smaller valuables, ranging from tobacco, to cloth, mirrors, scissors, and glass beads. The photo gives added visual testimony to the Ovambo estates we examined early in this chapter. It is a window into the material desires that lay the foundations as to why so many people went through all the trials and tribulations of travelling to, working in, and returning from the south. Their purchases were not only valuable to their new owners, but workers' role as consumers was important for the colonial economy.

While settlers often disliked having Ovambo migrants pass through settler towns or their farms, store owners lobbied the government to allow them to shop and barter at their locations. A statement to the publisher of the *Deutsch-Südwestafrikanische Zeitung* in 1912 written by local Windhoek businesses states:

> The undersigned has noticed that Ovambos, arriving here from Ovamboland and going from Lüderitz to Ovamboland, are given no opportunity to make purchases in Windhoek! Since the latter are by no means without money, but have a very well-filled sack, it would probably be in the interest of the local merchants, and the shopkeepers, that a method

---

222 NAN, ZBU 2068 W.IV.i.8. Travel, food, and clothing for recruited Ovambo 1910–1913, Letter regarding the dead Ovambo Kasino from the recruitment office of Rudolf Siebert to the Imperial Government at Windhoek, Otavi, 27.10.1913, 24.

223 NAN, ZBU 2068 W.IV.i.8. Travel, food, and clothing for recruited Ovambo 1910–1913, Letter from OMEG Company Doctor Scherer to the Imperial Government Windhoek, Tsumeb, 8.9.1913, 1.

> would be created not to deprive the natives of these purchases. Otherwise this (money) would flow to the Portuguese rather than the Windhoekers![224]

Figure 42: Ovambo migrant workers at the Namutoni checkpoint on their return from contract.[225]

The letter goes on to suggest that Ovambo workers be allowed, under police guard, to visit shops that are in the close vicinity of the station where workers would stop while in transit to and from work sites. Another store owner, Mr. Hoffmann, had a shop in Usakos and wished to sell goods to Ovambo migrants in transit at Swakopmund in 1911. His sentiments were like the Windhoek business owners in that he thought migrants had no opportunity to purchase goods (at least at his store). However, his application to sell to them was denied and the government claimed he aimed to taken advantage of the workers.[226] What examples like these make clear,

---

224 NAN, ZBU 2068 W.IV.i.8. Travel, food, and clothing for recruited Ovambo 1910–1913, Letter to the editor most likely in the *Deutsch-Südwestafrikanische Zeitung*, 1912, 124. Translation to English by W.B. Lyon.

225 NAN, Photo 28281, Ovambo migrant workers at the Namutoni checkpoint, probably on their return from contract, undated, probably 1910s.

226 NAN, ZBU 2068 W.IV.i.8. Travel, food, and clothing for recruited Ovambo 1910–1913, Letter from the Swakopmund county district to the Imperial Government, 13.2.1911, 32.

is that workers were important consumers who benefited colonial shop owners. Ovambo migrants would eventually bring most of these goods back north. The importation of diverse commodities from the settler region would continue to more closely link the Ovambo polities' economies with the colonial economy of GSWA. Circular migration played a role in not only economic, but also social, and by WWI political change to the northern polities. We will turn to this subject in the last chapter of the book.

Conclusion

Through this chapter, we've delved deep into the experiences of thousands of migrants from the Ovambo polities, who formed the backbone of the 'Namibian Labor Corridors' and became the predominant group of contract workers in the colony from 1908 to 1914. Their migration and labor, crucial in the aftermath of the 1904 to 1908 war and genocide, were transformative for the settler economy, with their impact most pronounced in the mining industry. This exploration has revealed the diverse composition of the Ovambo workforce, encompassing not only adult men but also a significant number of children and women, particularly at the Tsumeb mine.

We have brought to light the individual lives of these Ovambo workers, contributing to a richer understanding of early twentieth-century labor history in colonial Namibia. Despite the scarcity of written records by the Ovambo themselves, estate records and photographs have provided invaluable insights into their experiences.

This chapter also underscores the need to consider the broader labor dynamics in the colony, including the roles of South African and West African migrant laborers. These 'labor elites,' pivotal during the genocidal war against the Herero and Nama, continued to play a crucial role in the colonial economy, albeit in a precarious position. This sets the stage for the next chapter, where we will further explore these themes, delving into the complexities and nuances of labor relations in colonial Namibia.

4 Privileged but Precarious West and South African Migrants: Labor Elite and Entrepreneurs, 1908–1914

South and West Africans filled a unique role in the economy of German South West Africa after 1908 until the First World War. During this period, I argue they were an African migrant elite in the colony, consisting of both laborers and entrepreneurs, largely stemming from the high pay and often skilled jobs they filled that could not easily be replaced. Their relative 'elite' status meant a comparatively high level of assets and material possessions in comparison to local Africans, as well as Ovambo migrants. Further, contrary to these other groups, they often had a capacity for mobility within GSWA that was not afforded to other individuals categorized as 'black' by the colonial government. Their work ranged from port labor to train line construction, mining, and deck hands on ships between South Africa and GSWA. Some also took on more niche roles as assistants in banks, bookstores and pharmacies, clerks for the government, cooks, and servers at restaurants. Among this migrant elite a small community ran their own businesses, working as entrepreneurs in colonial towns. A few of these entrepreneurs competed successfully against white owned companies.

I posit that German South West Africa from 1908 to 1914, with its burgeoning diamond industry, expanding infrastructure projects, decimated local African population, and the challenging Namibian climate, presented a complex blend of opportunities and challenges for African migrants. Despite facing harsh policies under colonial rule, including explicit racial restrictions, these migrants perceived GSWA as offering relatively favorable conditions, thus making it a magnet for skilled labor and entrepreneurial ventures from Southern and West Africa. While individual agency was pivotal in driving these migrants to the colony, several enabling factors played a crucial role. These included a relatively weak and overstretched colonial administration, especially following the war, when the return of most German soldiers to the metropole weakened the colonial administration, and the escalating demand for skilled labor by employers.

However, the prominent presence of the migrant elite, markedly wealthier than the often destitute local African population, as well as Ovambo migrants, and in some cases attaining similar or even higher economic status than whites, stirred unease among certain settlers and soldiers. This white anxiety created a situation whereby the migrant elites' position was precarious. They were at times chastised, rebuked or worse for supposedly bringing their 'foreign concepts' of the role of Africans within the larger hierarchical order with them. In practice

https://doi.org/10.1515/9783111374918-005

this meant that the West and South Africans in the colony would at times push back and protest actions by employers that were seen as unjust or abusive. When colonial actors and employers believed that the colony's African migrant elite pushed too far against GSWA's racial and economic barriers, violence could and was at times used against them by company and mine overseers, the police, and the military. This ranged from lashings with the sjambok to at its most extreme, deadly violence. The most notable example of such an event was the Wilhelmstal massacre of South African railway construction workers, which will be examined in detail. Further, this precariousness also applied to those connected with port industry, especially the Kru, as WWI beginning in 1914 would result in the elimination of their sector.

The simmering tension between African labor elites and white settlers not only exacerbated existing conflicts but also significantly influenced local labor training policies. In response, settler society manifested its anxieties by deliberately obstructing the training of local Africans for skilled jobs. Migrant labor, being transient, was tolerated as they were expected to eventually leave the region. In contrast, settlers aimed to ensure that local Africans were largely restricted to low-paid, unskilled jobs. This strategy was epitomized by the Landesrat's (settler-run Territorial Council) actions in 1911. Echoing the ethos of keeping GSWA a 'Land of the White Man,' the council cancelled £732, previously allocated by Governor Seitz for training local Africans in skilled construction and trade work.[1] This decision was not only a reflection of the racial prejudices but also a deliberate move to keep local workers out of skilled labor roles.

However, as paying West and South Africans cost employers more money, their preference was over time to attempt to recruit other equally skilled migrant workers who would accept lower pay. The idea of replacing the African elite in the colony was however unattainable. Alternatives included contemplating recruiting Indian or Chinese migrant laborers in mass. Some attempts were made around 1910, with small groups of Indians eventually brought to the Tsumeb mine and for work in Lüderitzbucht trading stores. But hiring Indian migrants soon became impractical because of barriers put up by the British imperial administration.

Further, China pushed for equal protections to whites for their citizens if they were to come, which the colonial GSWA government would not accept.[2] Al-

1 'Schwarze Pläne,' DSWAZ, 4.7.1911, 1.

2 Stals, *Duits-Suidwes-Afrika na die Groot Opstande*, 56–58; the Chinese government had previous experience with labor recruiting to Southern Africa, in particular South Africa. Chinese migrants faced a myrad of issues there, including push back from white workers; see Peter Richardson, *Chinese Mine Labour in the Transvaal* (London: Palgrave Macmillan, 1982), 166–187; for a discussion of Indian and Chinese labor in German East Africa, see Minu Haschemi Yekani, "'Inder und Chinesen werden unsere Kolonie nicht in die Höhe bringen.' Arbeit, Klima, und der 'Rase' Dis-

though increasing numbers of Ovambo workers were hired, as reviewed in the previous chapter, the overall demand for labor could not be fully met. In addition, Ovambo workers could not fill certain roles where they lacked specific skills, like longshore work. As a result, thousands of South Africans, and hundreds of West Africans would continue to be employed. While still being unable to enjoy the full freedoms and economic benefits of being white, they were clearly in a unique societal class.[3]

Beyond GSWA, the West and South African labor flows to the colony have not been thoroughly contextualized within continental wide labor movements, which this chapter aims to do. German South West Africa was a location which combined what Tristan Oestermann has referred to as the West African Labor Market (*der westafrikanische Arbeitsmarkt*), with the skilled labor market of South Africa.[4] While 1904 marked the opening of GSWA as a hub combining these two labor markets, by 1908 the new labor flows, centered around German South West Africa were solidified.

The growth of the 'Namibian Labor Corridors,' including GSWA as a meeting point between the West African and South African labor networks, meant that the colony and its industries were competing, often successfully, for skilled labor within two markets beyond the boundaries of primarily German colonial control. Important in this process was the central role of private industry conducting business in GSWA, which will be discussed in this chapter. Competing employers of the Southern African labor market included the gold mines of Johannesburg and Rhodesia as well as the diamond mines of Kimberly. The West and central African labor market employers encompassed the rubber trade in Cameroon and the Congo Free State/Belgian Congo, the plantations on Fernando Po, and the gold mines of the Gold Coast.

As paying West and South Africans cost employers more money, their preference was over time to recruit equally skilled workers who would accept lower pay. The idea of replacing the African elite in the colony was however unattainable. Alternatives included contemplating recruiting Indian or Chinese migrant laborers in mass. Some attempts were made around 1910, with small groups of Indians eventually brought to the Tsumeb mine and for work in Lüderitzbucht

kurs in Tansania (1885–1914)," in *"Deutsche Arbeit": kritische Perspektiven auf ein ideologisches Selbstbild* (Göttingen: Wallstein Verlag, 2018).

3 The few mix-race Cape Workers who were eventually classified as white within the German colonial system fit into a unique small category of migrants although their experiences can, because of their very small numbers, be considered an exception rather than a rule. See Lindner, "Transnational Movements between Colonial Empires," 687–689.

4 Oestermann, *Kautschuk und Arbeit in Kamerun*, 162–165.

trading stores. But hiring Indian migrants soon became impractical because of barriers put up by the British imperial administration.

In developing the concept of an African migrant elite in GSWA, I expand on my argument from my 2021 article, "From Labour Elites to Garveyites: West African Migrant Labour in Namibia, 1892–1925."[5] I deepen my thesis of an African labor elite to a broader migrant elite in GSWA by integrating non-Kru West Africans in the colony, including a few dozen from German Togo. While a small number of individuals, they played unique roles in the economy, for example as laundromat owners in the ports. Importantly, the following includes South Africans as part and parcel of the colony's African labor elite.

This chapter builds upon and diverges from existing scholarship on South Africans in German South West Africa (GSWA), placing their experiences within the broader labor markets of Southern and West Africa.[6] While scholars like Beinart have focused on the Transkei and Ciskei as labor reserves for South Africa, this work centers on the experiences in GSWA, particularly in the context of the genocide's aftermath and its impact on labor dynamics in the region.

In contrast to scholars who have covered the Wilhelmstal massacre, this chapter examines this event as a critical point in the precarious status of Cape Workers in GSWA. It also delves into the broader context of railway construction in the colony, exploring management changes and the conditions that contributed to potential violence. Expanding the historiography of GSWA, this chapter underscores the continued significance of South African labor in the local economy beyond the implementation of restrictive Union migration laws as well as increased Ovambo migration to the settler region.

Defining African Migrant Elite in German South West Africa

Before we delve into the body of the chapter, I would like to clarify how and why I am using the term 'African migrant elite' to refer to the central actors in this chapter, i.e., African skilled laborers and entrepreneurs from West and South Africa. As Gregor Dobler argued in illuminating his use of the word 'elite' in relation to Ovambo traders in Namibia during the period of South African colonial-

5 Lyon, "From Labour Elites to Garveyites."

6 Beinart, "'Jamani'"; Zimmerer, *German Rule, African Subjects*, 278–294; Heinrich Loth, "Zu den Anfängen des Kampfes der Arbeiter Südwestafrikas gegen den deutschen Imperialismus," *Wissenschaftliche Zeitschrift der Karl-Marx-Universität Leipzig, Gesellschafts und Sprachwissenschaftliche Reihe*, no. 3 (1961): 351–356; Lindner, "Transnational Movements between Colonial Empires"; Lindner, *Koloniale Begegnungen*, 377–407.

ism, the word "provokes the question of perspective and power . . . ."[7] In regard to perspective, I am using that of the colonial work force as a whole, and those who are African in particular. That is to say, their status was 'elite' when seen from the perspective of Ovambo, Herero, Nama, Damara, and San workers in the police zone. This 'elite' status was certainly not true from the perspective of whites in the colony, although many and especially those whites low on the socioeconomic ladder saw them as a threat to the colonial racial hierarchy. Further, the term only denotates their status within GSWA, not in their home regions. This has to do with the very particular history and economy of German South West Africa between 1908 and 1914, i.e., acute labor scarcity, in particular of skilled labor resulting from genocide, combined with a powerful economic upswing from the diamond boom.

Shifting to Dobler's question regarding power in defining 'elite', in the context of this chapter, I interpret migrant elite's power most clearly with their capacity to partake in activities and enjoy material wealth that other Africans could not. This is not to say that other Africans didn't have certain levels of freedom or accrued assets, but it was simply put, less than those elites examined in this chapter. This revolves around a larger debate surrounding how 'free' was African 'free labor' in GSWA between 1908 and 1914. I argue that the 'migrant elite' South and West Africans of this period were by far, the freest of the diverse Africans in the settler zone during this period. So much so that certain freedoms which they enjoyed were not so different from those of the white population, however almost always with restrictions.

To give specific examples, which will be discussed in detail in this section, South and West Africans had their own unique and rich social circles, which included vibrant Christian communities, soccer and tennis clubs, as well as gambling, drinking and dancing locales. Their housing was also of a higher quality than for most other Africans in the colony. For those working at the shipping companies, they were able to continue to live in the white only districts of the port towns even following the end of the war in 1908. Many purchased a variety of expensive commodities, including wardrobes filled with fine suits and Panama hats, gramophone record collections, watches, and musical instruments like guitars and banjos. Some had their own wooden homes, rare for non-whites because wood was expensive in the coastal ports. Instances also exist where the African migrant elite made financial investments, such as life insurance, largely impossible for other Africans in the colony who lacked the financial means as well as access to such offerings. Their position was often in stark contrast to local Afri-

7 Dobler, *Traders and Trade in Colonial Ovamboland, 1925–1990*, xii.

cans increasingly constricted under expanding racial laws in the colony. The African elites remained to a certain extent unaffected by the increasing constrictions because of their necessary and largely irreplaceable role in the economy.

In summary, this chapter engages with the themes of migrant elite origins, experiences, and lives in GSWA, moving beyond a strict chronological approach to encompass the broader dynamics from 1908 to 1914.[8] We will look at how during the Namibian War and the following years, railway construction in the colony melded military and private management in attempts to continue train line expansion more efficiently, economically, and in some cases brutally.[9] Then we will turn our attention to the West African migrant elite in the colony from 1908 to 1914 and explore their work, businesses, and lives primarily in the colonial ports.

GSWA's 'Colonial logistics': The Role of the Military and Private Enterprise in Train Line Construction, 1905–1912

Below in Figure 43 we can see the GSWA railway construction projects from 1905 to 1912 in which South Africans made up a large segment or at times a majority of the workforce. Although earlier employment of South Africans on GSWA train line construction dated to the 1890s and the original Swakopmund-Windhoek line, their numbers were small.[10] It was only starting in 1906, that many hundreds and occasionally thousands were employed to build the colony's railways. They were employed by a few private construction companies which were contracted by the German Reichstag to build certain parts of the railway lines.

Cape Worker employment by private firms was part of a larger trend in the German imperial policy in GSWA by 1905 to move beyond projects solely undertaken by the military. The railway construction projects examined in this chapter would be built using a combination of strategies, leveraging lessons learned from past projects, with both the military and private corporations working in tandem, or with private corporations leading the projects supported by the military.

Giulia Scotto argues that such private enterprise/colonial administration or military joint ventures in Africa were increasing, especially in this period of high imperialism. She labels this 'colonial logistics,' which melded the martial and neoliberal

8 To examine this period, we will also look at railway projects that began in 1905 and would continue into 1909.

9 This chapter does not go into the detail of diamond mine work as that was covered thoroughly in Chapter 3, "The Diamond Mines."

10 See Chapter 1, "Constructing the Swakopmund-Windhoek Railway Line."

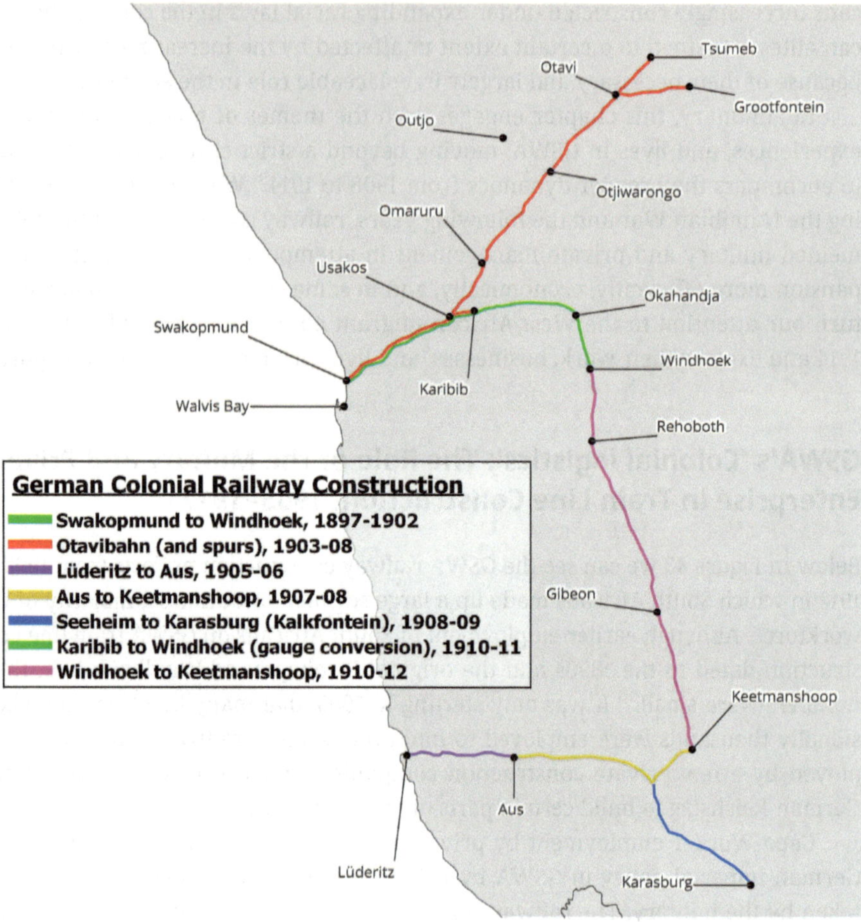

Figure 43: Map of the German colonial railways built between 1897 and 1912 (Cartography by Bernard C. Moore).

characteristics of logistics in the colonies at the time.[11] Companies like Arthur Koppel AG, which we will discuss in this chapter, played a pivotal role in colonial infrastructure projects, including railway construction. Their operations extended beyond working with the colonial government and military in GSWA and across the German empire. They were involved in a diverse range of projects worldwide, in countries

11 Giulia Scotto, "Colonial and Postcolonial Logistics," *Footprint: Delft Architecture Theory Journal* 23 (2018): 69.

and regions such as Bolivia, Denmark, Brazil, British India, Japan, Britain, the Netherlands, Austro-Hungary, Peru, Russia, and South Africa.[12]

Hybrid project management melding both colonial government, the military, and private firms in building colonial infrastructure had already existed by the late nineteenth century in places like early Rhodesia where the British South Africa Company governed, fought wars against local peoples, and built railway lines as it expanded its control northward.[13] In British and French West Africa at the end of the nineteenth and early twentieth centuries, colonial railway lines were often built by the colonial governments despite many private ventures often submitting proposals.[14] Contrastingly, in Dutch Java both the colonial government and private enterprise played a role in railway construction.[15] As for GSWA, the role of private companies in infrastructure construction and management grew and evolved over time.

Issues with solely German military management constellations for infrastructure construction had existed prior that shaped the evolution of outsourcing policy.[16] The first major railway project in the colony had been the Swakopmund-Windhoek railway line, begun in the late nineteenth century, which was led by military railway engineers.[17] While eventually completed, it was largely regarded as a failure with multiple sections needing early replacement because of shoddy construction, wash outs, and having some very sharp turns (which would eventually be replaced) that sometimes led to locomotives derailing.[18]

The next major railway line to be constructed, the *Otavibahn*, largely relied on outsourcing to the private firm Arthur Koppel & Co. by OMEG, which was building the line from its Tsumeb mine to the coast. Arthur Koppel & Co. further outsourced to smaller subcontractors, including Luigi Zarossi, which led to many

12 Bude Roland, Klaus Fricke, and Martin Murray, *O&K Dampflokomotiven. Lieferverzeichnis 1892–1945* (Buschhofen: Verlag Railroadiana, 1977), 16.

13 Scotto, "Colonial and Postcolonial Logistics," 70–72; Lunn, *Capital and Labour on the Rhodesian Railway System*, 17–25.

14 Olufẹmi Ọmọsini, "Railway Projects and British Attitude Towards the Development of West Africa, 1872–1903," *Journal of the Historical Society of Nigeria* 5, no. 4 (1971): 491–507.

15 Aloysius Gunadi Brata, "Exploring the Influence of Colonial Railways on Java's Economic Geography" (Munich Personal RePEc Archive, 2017), 6.

16 Examples also exist of successful military only infrastructure projects, such as the Jetty at Swakopmund. But this did not apply to train lines. Kalb, *Environing Empire*, 191–193.

17 Baltzer, *Die Kolonialbahnen*, 80.

18 The construction of Swakopmund-Windhoek railway line was discussed in detail earlier in this book; see Chapter 1, "Constructing the Swakopmund-Windhoek Railway Line."

complications and strikes with Italian workers.[19] Facing mounting labor issues and government pressure, Arthur Koppel & Co. took over from the subcontractors. The *Otavibahn* also relied on the military to supply forced laborers that made up a sizable portion of the construction workforce. In 1906 OMEG and Arthur Koppel & Co. were lauded by the colonial government for completing the project without their support or subsidies (of course no mention was made of the large numbers of mainly Herero forced labor POWs including men, women, and children, who played an essential role in making this possible).[20]

The southern train line in GSWA, or *Südbahn*, would also begin construction during the war. It was built in multiple sections: Lüderitzbucht to Aus, Aus to Keetmanshoop, and a branch line from Seeheim to Kalkfontein (see Figure 43 above). The Lüderitzbucht to Aus section would begin in December of 1905.[21] It would be built by the *Deutsche Kolonial- Eisenbahn-Bau- und Betriebsgesellschaft* (DKEBBG), with a provision for military assistance. DKEBBG was a subsidiary of Lenz and Co. founded by shareholders to build this project and other railway construction projects in German colonies, including in Cameroon. The DKEBBG would prepare the work sites and construct the embankment for the tracks, and the military would lay the tracks and finish the train line. The project was conducted by both the military and the DKEBBG until the end of 1907 when the military pulled out of the project.[22]

The last major railway construction projects in the colony were contracted out to private firms. One was the Windhoek-Keetmanshoop line, or *Nord-Südbahn*, which would connect the north and south of the colony. It was funded by the windfall gained from the sale of diamonds in GSWA as well as via a loan from the German parliament. The DKEBBG and the *Bau- und Betriebskonsortium Bachstein & Koppel* (Bachstein-Koppel) were both contracted to complete the line.[23] Bachstein-Koppel would build from Windhoek south and DKEBBG from Keetmanshoop north.

---

19 See Chapter 2, "The Failure of the European Labor Corridor: An Italian Job? Construction of the *Otavibahn* 1904–1905."

20 Bravenboer and Rusch, *The First 100 Years*, 74.

21 Quiring, Erich. "Die Eisenbahnen Deutsch-Südwestafrikas und ihre Bedeutung für die wirtschaftliche Entwicklung der Kolonie." (PhD thesis, Friedrich-Alexander-Universität, 1911), 22.

22 Bravenboer and Rusch, *The First 100 Years*, 111, 124; Nina Kleinöder, "Kolonialwirtschaft ohne Kolonien?: Deutscher Eisenbahnbau in Afrika im und nach dem Ersten Weltkrieg," in *1919 – Der Versailler Vertrag und die deutschen Unternehmen*, ed. Dieter Ziegler and Jan-Otmar Hesse (Berlin: De Gruyter Oldenbourg, 2022), 321; BArch R 1001/9649 Reichskolonialamt, Eisenbahnsachen und technische Angelegenheiten; In primary sources DKEBBG and Lenz are often used interchangably.

23 Bau- und Betrieb Konsortium Bachstein & Koppel was a consortium of three companies: Arthur Koppel AG, Zentralverwaltung für Secundärbahnen Herrmann Bachstein (CV), and the Handelsgesellschaft Briske und Prohl. See Bravenboer and Rusch, *The First 100 Years*, 150; this is not

The two lines would connect at Narib, approximately 210 km south of Windhoek and 295 km north of Keetmanshoop.[24] Both construction firms were supported by a company of soldiers each.[25]

Lastly, due to many issues with the first major railway line constructed in the colony, the Karibib to Windhoek section of the narrow-gauge Swakopmund-Windhoek line would be replaced with wide gauge. The section from Karibib to Swakopmund did not need to be replaced as the wide gauge *Otavibahn* (which included a segment from Karibib to Swakopmund) had already been constructed and the whole line was bought by the government from OMEG in 1910. The Karibib to Windhoek line was contracted out to Bachstein-Koppel and would begin in early 1910.[26] Although the later railway construction projects were largely outsourced to private firms, we will see that the military would still play a role, for example by allowing soldiers to be hired out for construction work. A group of soldiers contracted out for work on Bachstein-Koppel's Karibib-Windhoek project would be the instigators of the massacre at Wilhelmstal, which we shall examine in detail.

These private firms were also not viewed as equal in the eyes of those contracted. Of those Cape Workers hired in 1910 to 1911, the largest complaints and issues clearly lay with those employed by the firm Bachstein-Koppel. Conversely, the railway construction firm DKEBBG was viewed as an employer that responded to worker complaints or at least heard them out to an extent that was not mirrored by Bachstein-Koppel. According to the British consul representing South African workers at Lüderitzbucht, DKEBBG was largely the reason for the popularity of railway construction contracts in GSWA amongst Cape Workers.[27]

---

to be confused with Arther Koppel AG, which had been solely contracted to build the *Otavibahn*; see Bravenboer and Rusch, 59.

24 Quiring, "Die Eisenbahnen Deutsch-Südwestafrikas," 37; Baltzer, *Die Kolonialbahnen*, 89–93; Bruno Wägli, "Dampf in Südwest: Eisenbahnbau zur Kolonialzeit in Deutsch-Südwestafrika" (Bachelor Research Paper, Freiburg, Switzerland, Universität Freiburg, 2008), 61; Bravenboer and Rusch, *The First 100 Years*, 146.

25 "Etwas vom Bau der Nord-Südbahn in Südwest-Afrika," in *Süsserott's illustrierter Kolonial-Kalender* (Berlin: Wilhelm Süsserott, 1914), 83.

26 Bravenboer and Rusch, *The First 100 Years*, 143, 146–147; Pool, *Eisenbahnen in Deutsch-Südwestafrika*, 144–145.

27 National Archives of South Africa in Pretoria (NASA), GG 275 4/24 Report by the Consul at Luderitzbucht on the treatment of natives by the authorities in German South West Africa, Memorandum on the condition of Native and Coloured people in German South West Africa, Cape Town, 30.6.1910, 4–5; as we shall see, however, DKEBBG, would have no qualms using forced labor.

From Military Auxiliaries to Railway Construction Workers

South African Cape Workers, who initially came to the colony as wagon drivers and German military auxiliaries in 1904, were soon working in other sectors, primarily railway construction by 1906. They were actively recruited until 1912 and numbers employed in the colony were in the thousands until 1914. After the opening of the copper mines (1906) and later the diamond fields (1908), they also proved their versatility as laborers in the mining sectors. Ovambo migrants, as we explored in the last chapter, while drastically increasing in number starting in 1908, still could not satiate colonial labor demands. Cape Worker numbers continued to increase, and they remained the second largest group of African migrant laborers, after Ovambo, throughout the rest of the German colonial period.

In the years after 1904, recruiters of South African Cape Workers for contract in GSWA could utilize employment networks initially established by the German military and their subcontractors. Further, large numbers of Cape Workers remained willing to come on contract. One primary reason GSWA continued to be attractive for migrants beyond the high wages, was the continuing difficult economic situation in South Africa, which translated to trouble in finding jobs, and relatively low wages back home compared to the period prior and during the South African War (when many were working as wagon drivers).

Employers often found South African recruits preferable to Ovambo workers for several reasons. One key factor was the South Africans' willingness to commit to longer contracts, typically ranging from one to two years.[28] Despite their demands for higher wages compared to their northern counterparts, South Africans remained attractive due to the challenges associated with Ovambo workers. These included a high turnover rate due to shorter average contract lengths and the additional costs employers had to bear for their travel, either by train or boat.

Below in Figure 44 we can see that numbers of South Africans in the colony peaked with demand for railway construction employment in 1911 and overall numbers in GSWA remained above 1908 levels until the end of German colonialism. South African employment in large numbers within the railway construction industry would continue until projects were completed in 1912. In contrast to the claims of William Beinart, South Africans in GSWA were already employed in large numbers for railway construction in GSWA years before 1909, with hundreds on contract by 1906. His assumption may have been due to a focus primarily on recruitment numbers in South Africa rather than employment numbers

28 Lindner, "Transnational Movements between Colonial Empires," 685.

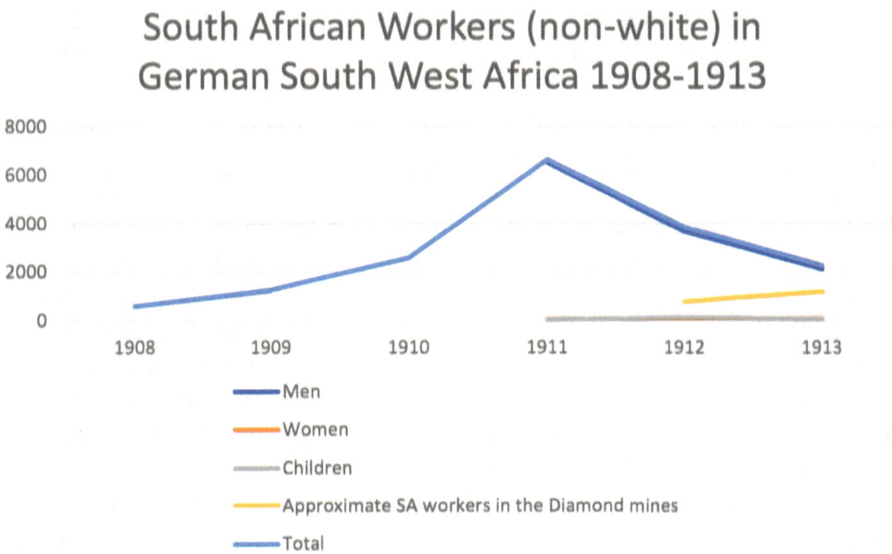

Figure 44: Approximate number of South African Individuals in the Settler region of GSWA from 1908–1913. The graph begins in 1908 as comparable records from the previous years do not exist.[29]

within GSWA, as well as primary analysis of South African files, with almost no use of documents from Namibian or German archives.[30]

Cape Worker Recruitment and Individual Organized Migration

Railway construction, because of its clear beginning and end date, promoted waves of recruitment for the private construction firms, and periods where recruitment demand ceased when projects were fully manned or completed. The first waves of recruitment of Cape Workers for the railway construction in GSWA began in 1905/1906 and subsided by 1908/1909. In 1910, with the rebuilding of the Karibib-Windhoek line and the beginning of the large north-south line construction, recruitment and employment in train line construction increased dramatically and the Cape Worker population in the colony peaked at over 6,600 in 1911.

29 Compiled from NAN, ZBU 172 A.VI.d Vol. 1, Population Statistics Natives and Coloreds Main Statistics, Population Statistics on the Natives and Coloreds Population at the Beginning of the Year 1908–1913.

30 Beinart, "'Jamani,'" 53.

Many South Africans' desire to travel to GSWA for work on their own accord, combined with railway companies wishing to reduce overheads, led to employers not paying for their travel to and from the colony.[31] Cape Worker transport via ship to and from GSWA was expensive and unlike Ovambo workers, companies hiring them were not legally obligated to cover such costs.[32] Already in 1907, many contracts for companies like DKEBBG and other employers of Cape Workers would not include the cost of travel to and from the colony and instead make workers cover these costs. Further, many South Africans desperate for work, even without contracts, would attempt to travel to GSWA by ship, train, and by foot on their own accord. Employers in the German colony could take advantage of this by hiring such workers once they crossed the border, skipping all the extra costs associated with recruitment and organizing travel. The self-organized journeys could be dangerous, costly, and migrants would often face barriers from both South African and German colonial governments.

One example of a Cape Worker, who undertook travel to GSWA without employer or government support was Peter Foster from Maitland near Cape Town. He crossed the border into the German colony in February of 1907. At Ariam in southeastern GSWA, 12 kilometers from the South African border he wrote the following words to his family: "Ma Mother I am still wandering as a spring bock . . . this is a very dry country." In later letters to his brother John he stated, "I am far, in a distance [distant] land here unworthy of doing my willing here. But I must do as the Germans bid me god strengthen you . . . . [I]s there any work in C. Town[?]"[33]

We can see in these quotes from Peter's letters above that his work in GSWA was difficult and that he was looking to see whether there were opportunities back in Cape Town. His letters give us some additional context that while many were coming to GSWA for work, their time in the German colony could be very challenging. He had been laboring in GSWA, likely for the railways, but by the end of 1907 his mother Rachel and brother John in Maitland no longer knew his fate. The German colonial government did not have records of him having died. His seeming disappearance highlights how worker organized transport to GSWA work sites could result in unpredictable and sometimes deadly outcomes.

31 Cape Workers were paid much more than other non-white workers for the railways.

32 See Chapter 3, Why Go South? Going on Contract and the Process of Labor Recruitment.

33 CA, NA 727, Wages due to Labourers who died in German South West Africa 1905–1909, Inquiry re: Peter Foster, 27.12.1907, 7.

Hundreds attempting to get railway contracts for work in GSWA in early 1908 South Africa were turned away.[34] By 1909 recruitment in South Africa continued but was limited. One recruiter for GSWA based in Cape Town, J.S. Rossouw, an officer for *Woermann-Linie* who had taken out a recruiting license, hired in small batches based on demand from employers in the German colony. He did not use sub-agents and his hires were drastically outpaced by desire for contracts. South African colonial officers believed Rossouw used extremely difficult health tests to limit the individuals who were recruited.[35] As we shall see later, this lull in recruiting through official channels would pick up in 1910/1911.

It was through the prolific numbers that had already been to GSWA or were writing letters home, that signaled to family, friends and their communities that work across the border was still to be had and could bring in substantial income. Even when South Africans had not been recruited and did not have permission from the South African or German government to travel there, many would find new routes to the neighboring colony. Exemplifying how networks and opportunities came together to allow Cape Workers to cross into GSWA is the story of a man called 'French.'

In early 1910, 'French' led a group of 13 Cape Workers that had left Cape Town, travelled through Upington, and eventually arrived at Rietfontein in the north-western Cape to cross through the desert at the border. 'French' had previously been a wagon driver for the German military and said that he was 'well known' in GSWA. Using his past work experience as credentials, he was able to convince South African magistrates to grant travel permits, and then German authorities for permission to enter the colony. His group, after a long and difficult trek, combined with a large investment of their time and money, appeared to have found work on the other side.[36] The group's feat shows us a distinct example of how some of the hundreds of Cape Workers who travelled to the border could have successfully arrived in GSWA and found work.

If individuals could make it across the border to the mines, towns or railway projects under construction, work could often be had, and typically with very good wages. The pay scale of Cape Workers in GSWA typically ranged from £3 to £4 p.m.,

---

34 CA, NA 719, F473(ii), Papers relating to Native Labour, 1908–1910, Letter No. D.3/245/08 to the Resident Magistrate of Uitvlugt, 31.03.1908.

35 CA, NA 719, F473(ii), Papers relating to Native Labour, 1908–1910, Letter from Cape Town Native Affairs to John Elliot of Lady Frere, 18.2.1909.

36 CA, NA 719, F473(ii), Papers relating to Native Labour, 1908–1910, Office of the Resident Magistrate, Rietfontein, Re: inspection of passes issued to natives, 21.1.1910.

but £5 p.m. was not unheard of.[37] Cape Workers made at least three times the average Ovambo worker pay. In the southern towns, such as Lüderitzbucht, work in guesthouses and restaurants could pay exorbitant sums because of the diamond boom. For example, in larger hotels, one settler stated that Cape Workers employed as clothing washers could make up to £7/16/5 p.m.[38] Jobs with such pay typically outcompeted opportunities back in South Africa. The resulting migration patterns and preference for work in GSWA caused tensions in South African government and industry.

Response of the South African Government to Cape Worker Migration

While strong demand for Cape Workers existed in GSWA, the Cape government (or post-1910 Union government) increasingly attempted to control migration in order to retain workers and fill labor shortages at home. One method of control was to restrict their capacity to purchase tickets directly to Lüderitzbucht or Swakopmund in the neighboring colony. As a workaround, many individuals in Cape Town looking to migrate to GSWA received permits from the local government to travel to Port Nolloth, in the northwestern Cape, with the secret intention of then crossing by land into GSWA. By early 1910, those arriving by ship to Port Nolloth had little to support themselves and found disappointment when they could not easily get permission by local authorities to go to the German colony.

An increasing group of impoverished would-be migrants built up at Port Nolloth. To lessen the pressure on local authorities, many were given permits to travel to the Okiep copper mines, around 130 km to the southeast, but whether work could be found was questionable.[39] Regardless of whether jobs were indeed there, they would certainly pay less than work across the border.

In 1910, many migrants from the Eastern Cape, including the Transkei, would first come to Cape Town before developing a plan to get to the German colony. But without permission to be in Cape Town some would be caught, as was a group of

37 Wages for Cape Workers on the diamond mines were often around £3. For an example of workers at KBG, see NAN, BCL [12], DKG to British Consulate in GSWA regarding Cape Worker Nedi Nr. 8734, 19.8.1911; for an example of wages for Cape Workers employed for the Südbahn, all over £3 p.m., see NAN, BCL [12], DKEBBG letter to the British Consulate in GSWA regarding Willie Williams Nr. 1434, 22.9.1911.

38 Clara Brockmann, *Briefe eines deutschen Mädchens aus Südwest* (Berlin: E.S. Mittler & Sohn, 1912), 80–81.

39 CA, NA 719, F473(ii), Papers relating to Native Labour, 1908–1910, Resident Magistrate's Office Port Nolloth, re: Native Labourers Proceeding to German South West Africa, 14.3.1910.

20 who had come by train and were eventually shipped back. Their initial train tickets, which they had paid for, were however reimbursed.[40] A March 1910 circular from *Native Affairs* in Cape Town made clear that the considerable numbers of migrants coming to the North-Western Districts were often not aware of entry restrictions into GSWA. It stated:

> [D]emand for unskilled labour in German South West Africa being fully met by the local supply and occasional batches recruited in the Cape Peninsula and proceeding under written contracts of service, Natives proceeding under written contracts of service, Natives proceeding independently, upon arrival at the border, are turned back by the German Police and distressing cases of hardship have occurred through failure of strength or food supply for the dreary return tramp. Natives eluding the Police at the Border and entering German Territory are liable to arrest and punishment . . . .[41]

The circular above clearly highlights the struggles for those trying to get to GSWA without a contract. But it does not explain why so many people were still coming to the border, which lay in the fact that despite official German policy, demand for labor was still very high. This was paired with low wages in South Africa and a continuing recession. As we shall see, around the end of the first decade of the twentieth century, demand for labor in South Africa was increasing, although wages were not.

One Upington Magistrate, because of his vicinity to the border with GSWA, knew the situation quite well. Already in August of 1909 he had been contacted by the Okiep Copper mines, which were short of labor, and were adamantly requesting that Cape authorities intervene with migrants and attempt to redirect them to the copper mines.[42] Local magistrates in the northeast were however relatively clear eyed in writing that migrants passing through to GSWA went on to

> obtain employment on the railway works at a very lucrative rate . . . one far in excess of that offering at the copper mine . . . . It is apparent from the number of natives proceeding to German territory that the restrictions upon natives entering the territory, by the German authorities have been withdrawn in practice, as I have not heard of a single occasion in which natives have been obliged to return to this colony owing to a lack of employment in German South West.[43]

40 CA, NA 719, F473(ii), Papers relating to Native Labour, 1908–1910, Resident Magistrate's Office Cape Town, Telegram, Regarding Circular from March 4th , 8.3.1910.
41 CA, NA 719, F473(ii), Papers relating to Native Labour, 1908–1910, Resident Magistrate's Office Port Nolloth, re: Native Labourers Proceeding to German South West Africa, 4.3.1910.
42 CA, NA 719, F473(ii), Papers relating to Native Labour, 1908–1910, Telegram from the Okiep Copper Mine Manager to the Colonial Government Native Affairs Department Cape Town, 17.8.1909.
43 CA, NA 719, F473(ii), Papers relating to Native Labour, 1908–1910, Telegram from the Okiep Copper Mine Manager to the Colonial Government Native Affairs Department Cape Town, 17.8.1909.

He ended by stating that the police of the Cape were doing everything they could to keep 'natives' in Upington in the colony.[44]

Beyond local South African issues and policy to deal with individuals attempting to migrate to the neighboring German colony for work, pressure around 1910 was building to do more to curtail migration. The founding of the Union in this year meant that the Rand Mines were no longer simply represented by the Transvaal colony, but the Union government. The Rand, needing a massive supply of labor, put increasing pressure on the new national administration to reduce the number of Transkei workers going to GSWA and rather divert them to Johannesburg. This as we have explored was against the wishes of most workers from the Eastern Cape, who by and large preferred and actively pursued contracts for above ground railway construction and mining work in the German colony compared to the below ground labor of the Rand mines.[45]

In the years preceding 1910, the Rand already had growing local labor demands and was becoming more vocal about not wanting to compete with the neighboring colony for recruitment. The numbers of Transkei recruits for the Rand had increased from 12,909 hired in 1907 to 27,859 by 1910.[46] Chinese migrant labor, which had made up a sizable number of workers on the Rand starting in 1904 was being phased out by 1907 when no new migrants were coming into the colony. By 1910, essentially all Chinese workers had been repatriated.[47] In that same year migrants from southern Mozambique followed by the Cape made up most of the work force in the Rand mines. About 60,000 men had come by train from the Eastern Cape alone.[48]

At the same time, the number of South African migrants in German South West Africa would peak at 6,652 in 1911.[49] South African future estimates from 1910 were that about 3,000 South African workers would be needed on average in the German colony.[50] Despite these numbers being small in comparison to the Rand's recruiting numbers, the mines of South Africa saw the GSWA worker corridor as a competitor, preferred by many would be workers from the Eastern Cape, which also put pressure on the Rand to increase wages and improve work-

44 CA, NA 719, F473(ii), Papers relating to Native Labour, 1908–1910, Resident Magistrate's Office, Upington, 17.08.1909, re: natives proceeding to German S.W. Africa; this counters Beinart's claims that pay rates in GSWA had by 1909 dropped on average to 2/- per day; see Beinart, "'Jamani,'" 55.
45 Zimmerer, *German Rule, African Subjects*, 279.
46 'Die Anwerbung eingeborener Arbeiter in Kaffraria,' LZ, 23.07.1910, 1.
47 Bright, *Chinese Labour in South Africa*, 183–184.
48 Pirie, "Railways and Labour Migration to the Rand Mines," 717.
49 NAN, ZBU 172 A.VI.d Vol. 1, Population Statistics Natives and Coloreds Main Statistics, Population Statistics on the Natives and Coloreds Population at the Beginning of the Year 1911.
50 'Die Anwerbung eingeborener Arbeiter in Kaffraria,' LZ, 23.07.1910, 1

ing conditions. The post-South African War era had been a period of wage cutting and related sky-high profits for the gold mines of South Africa.[51] They did not wish to give these gains up.

Contrasting with the views of the Rand lords, the ruling South African National Party (SAP), under the leadership of former Afrikaner general Louis Botha, first Prime minister of South Africa, saw German Southwest Africa as a way of increasing funds coming into the colony. The large majority of migrant worker pay checks from GSWA were sent as remittances to families in the Cape and were therefore seen as helping the South African economy. The "S.A. News," a party mouthpiece of the SAP, estimated that the prior mentioned 3,000 migrant South African workers in GSWA would on average be paid £3/10 per month. As almost all of this income was sent home as remittances, that meant approximately £400,000 of additional purchasing power for families of migrant workers, and £50,000 in recruitment fees going to the South African government.[52]

Such arguments were also confirmed by the history of the proceeding years and clearly highlighted the importance of GSWA for the South African economy. The Namibian War from 1904 to 1908 had already proven that remittances, combined with German purchases of cattle and products from South Africa (which continued until the end of German colonialism), had been significant in helping the Cape Colony get through the economic downturn in the years after the South African war.[53] This was a prominent reason that the new South African Union continued to support migrant work to GSWA, at least in the first years of the government. But support of free movement of workers to GSWA was already starting to wane by early 1910, as only one recruiter for the German colony was allowed to work in the Transkei. The whole system would be greatly challenged by the events at Wilhelmstal in October of that year. Shifting from government policy, let us now look at the actual experiences of work in GSWA by Cape Workers starting with the first major project in the south.

The Construction of the Southern Line (Südbahn), 1905–1909

The construction of the railway line between Lüderitzbucht and Kubub in late 1905 was a direct response to the escalating conflict in the southern region of German South West Africa (GSWA) between the Nama captaincies and German

51 See Chapter 2, "The 'Labor Question' in Southern Africa and the Outbreak of War in 1904."

52 'Die Anwerbung eingeborener Arbeiter in Kaffraria,' LZ, 23.07.1910, 1.

53 'Die Anwerbung eingeborener Arbeiter in Kaffraria,' LZ, 23.07.1910, 2.

forces. Lüderitzbucht, serving as the nucleus of German military operations in the south, was crucial for offloading troops and supplying the army. Kubub, chosen for its readily available grazing and water access, was a strategic inland point for the military. Similar to the Otavi railway construction in the north, the German military, under the leadership of General von Trotha, deemed this southern rail line a military necessity.

Consistent and reliable transport for the military in the south via ox-wagons and camels along the *Baiweg*, the dirt road from Lüderitzbucht to Kubub, was under threat because of an outbreak of rinderpest.[54] The military believed the *Baiweg* to be at capacity by the end of 1905, due to limited grazing and water. A train line would drastically increase their capacity to transport to the interior.[55] Further, reliable, and secure access to Kubub during the war was essential, as the site was used to graze up to 1,200 oxen and 2,000 small livestock used by the military and their auxiliaries. Such arguments secured funding from the Reichstag in Berlin by the beginning of 1906.[56]

The construction project was contracted out to the Lenz subsidiary DKEBBG with close military support. While the military would utilize soldiers for part of the labor, the firm would hire African contract workers.[57] As the result of the southern line's distance from the north, Ovambo labor could not be easily recruited, and the project instead turned to other potential laborers. Hundreds of South Africans, worked in the desert alongside Europeans, and around one thousand Herero and Nama men and women forced laborers. The POWs were malnourished and therefore had limited capacity for hard labor. Like the Otavi line, the early project through the sand dune belt along the coast was difficult to supply. Both donkey carts and camels were used for provisions and water.[58] But in contrast to the Otavi train line construction, where water was obtained from ground sources near Swakopmund, the water from condensers at Lüderitzbucht cost the *Südbahn* construction project an astounding 33 times more for water than for the *Otavibahn*.[59]

The challenging work conditions of the southern line also impacted Cape Workers, and their families back home, many who during the economic down-

54 'Reichstagssitzung von. 2. Dezember 1905', DSWAZ, 3.06.1906, 13.

55 Bundesarchiv-Militärarchiv (BArch-MA), MSG 105/9, Zur Geschichte der deutschen Eisenbahntruppen, Die Verpflegungsschwierigkeiten im Groß-Namalande und die Eisenbahn Lüderitzbucht-Kubub; Schwabe, *Der Krieg in Deutsch-Südwestafrika 1904–1906*, 403.

56 Baltzer, *Die Kolonialbahnen*, 86.

57 Bravenboer and Rusch, *The First 100 Years*, 113.

58 'Lüderitzbucht-Kubub,' DKZ, 15.9.1906, Nr. 37, 361.

59 '*Bahnbauten in Deutsch-Süd-Afrika*,' LZ, 4.9.1909, 1.

turn in South Africa were especially dependent on these wages. This made it all the more difficult for families of workers when for example, during the early phase of construction at least three Cape Workers died from typhus, dysentery, and heart disease between April and May 1906.[60] The workers all came from the Eastern Cape and one, 'Henry' (alias) Nxarana from the Alice District, was survived by his wife Elisa, who in receiving relatively little money from 'Henry''s estate wrote to a South African magistrate at Ndabeni Location near Cape Town:

> The diseased [sic] was my husband and I should like to know and obtain his wages according to the period of time which he stayed in German West Africa. The only money I received amounts to £1/5 which seems as if [it] was discovered in a purse round his arm as we are informed that they are paid on their arrival in Cape Town![61]

Unfortunately for Elisa it does not seem that she received any additional funds. With the difficult economic situation in the Eastern Cape in particular, such a loss of income could have been catastrophic for her family.

While the line to Kubub was completed in 1906, the extension to Keetmanshoop was already begun by the end of March of 1907 and the project alone employed 351 whites and 262 Cape Workers. On the previous rail section, a good number of the white workers had been Germans from upper Silesia, but many did not renew their contracts for further work. To bolster the workforce a group of 200 Croatians were employed on the railway. Soon the white contract laborers surpassed 500 and Cape Workers numbered 850. POWs, largely Herero, capable of hard labor for the project, had dropped to 507. This decrease from previous levels on the Lüderitz-Kubub segment likely had much to do with mounting sickness, malnourishment and deaths occurring over the previous year.[62]

In the various sources on railway work in GSWA for this period, we get an idea for the physical challenges of the labor, the technical details of what was constructed, the makeup of workforces, as well as mortality and illness statistics. Sources from Cape Workers or families as referenced above often are concerned with sickness, death, estates, and travel. What we rarely can perceive is an idea for what life was like on the transitory railway construction work sites as encampments moved along with the growing train lines. A glimpse can be garnered

---

60 CA, NA 727, Wages due to labourers who died in German South West Africa 1905–1909, Kolonial-Eisenbahn Betriebsgesellschaft, Bauleitung Lüderitzbucht-Kubub, Report of diseased native boys, Lüderitzbucht, 21.07.1906.

61 CA, NA 727, Wages due to labourers who died in German South West Africa 1905–1909, letter from Elisa Nxarana to the Resident Magistrate at Ndabeni Location, 29.09.1906.

62 'Bahnbau Lüderitzbucht-Kubub,' WN, 15.04.1908, 6.

from photography, as we explored in depth in the last chapter in relation to Ovambo workers.

The work of J.P. Daughton on the Congo-Océan railway points to photography as a starting point for highlighting the harsh contrasts between white colonial administrators and African laborers in French Equatorial Africa.[63] In GSWA we have seen how photographs of forced laborers (analyzed in Chapter 2) brought to life the extreme depravities of the Herero and Nama working at a variety of work sites. Photos of Cape Workers in GSWA are often in sharp contrast to those of African workers we have examined in the previous chapters, with at times blurry distinctions between Cape Workers and whites on the work site or at encampments. This is probably symbolic of their hazy categorization in the colony as migrant Africans from outside of GSWA and a labor elite. Below (Figure 45) we can see a group of workers at rest along the Lüderitzbucht-Keetmanshoop line accompanied by soldiers in the background.

Figure 45: Group of train workers along the Lüderitz to Keetmanshoop railway. Based on the existence of trees and a well they are likely on the segment between Kubub and Keetmanshoop.[64]

63 James Patrick Daughton, *In the Forest of No Joy: The Congo-Océan Railroad and the Tragedy of French Colonialism*, First edition (New York: W.W. Norton & Company, 2021), 2–10.

64 NAN, Photo 23467, Date: 190?, Between 1906–1909, Provenance: A.0898 *Erinnerung an den Bau der Lüderitzbucht-Eisenbahn*, Remarks: Probably Lüderitzbucht railway construction.

The image above (Figure 45) of workers along the *Südbahn* line dates from between 1906 and 1909 and may coincide with the completion of a segment of the railway along the southern line and hence the seeming postures of anticipation and observation. It may be just prior to an official ceremony of a new railway section opening. There seems to be a relatively relaxed atmosphere with black and white workers mixing. On the left-hand side we can see a mingling of black South African and white contract workers sitting on the edge of a well, many looking to the left, where we glimpse a railway train car.

We can see that the clothing of the workers, both white and black, did not greatly differ, reflecting the similar western clothing preferences, and pay rates between whites and Cape Workers. The Cape Workers constructing the *Südbahn* were often paid about 4/10- to 6/7- per day, with the high pay rates reflecting the difficulty in recruiting other contract workers.[65] Further, after the first 50 km of construction, forced laborers used on the project were simply incapable of conducting hard labor because of sickness and general weakness. These labor challenges meant that Cape Worker pay rates were up to three times higher than for Ovambo workers on the *Otavibahn*, and about 1/10- to 2/7- more per day than the first Italian workers recruited under sub-contractor Zarossi for the Otavibahn.[66]

In Figure 45 we can also see tents in the background which are reminiscent of the typical sleeping arrangements for train line workers in the field. At the center behind the group of workers are German soldiers, including a brass band, likely part of the free work force which as mentioned combined both soldiers and contracted workers.

As the photo includes trees it was taken past the coastal desert belt. It also does not highlight forced laborers and in some ways symbolizes the transition away from POWs forced to work on the *Südbahn*, as the DKEBBG concluded their inefficiency as a workforce. The *Windhuker Nachrichten* made a direct correlation between the failure of the forced labor regime in the south and the increasing employment of Cape workers stating:

> The hope that the construction could be carried out mainly with prisoners of war proved to be deceptive. The Herero were not able to cope with the unfamiliar maritime climate and the heavy work, so that Cape boys who had proven themselves as workers had to be taken on to an increasing extent.[67]

---

65 For early pay rates from the *Südbahn* construction, including rates paid to the government for the forced laborers, see Quiring, "Die Eisenbahnen Deutsch-Südwestafrikas," 22.

66 'Bahnbauten in Deutsch-Süd-Afrika,' LZ, 4.9.1909, 1; NAN, EVE [26] A.4.o vol. 3, K. *Eisenbahn Verwaltung* (Sw.-Wi.), *Akten betr. Italienische Arbeiter*, Contract between Zarossi and Koppel, 2a.

67 'Bahnbau Lüderitzbucht-Kubub,' WN, 15.04.1908, 6. Translation to English by W.B. Lyon.

The construction project of the southern train line from Lüderitzbucht to Keetmanshoop was eventually extended by 1909 with a branch line from Seeheim to Kalkfontein (todays Karasburg) in the southeast of the colony (see Figure 43 above). The high Cape Worker pay, restricted capacity to use forced labor, and high-water costs made the *Südbahn* much more expensive to build on average per kilometer, at about £3,418/km than the other major wartime railway project, the *Otavibahn*, at about £1,465/km.[68] Such high costs for the *Südbahn* made future projects seem like potential money sinks, although the growing diamond industry would change how projects could be funded.

The *Südbahn* as well as the *Otavibahn* had largely received military and imperial German support as well as immense funding because of the colonial war against the Herero in the north and Nama in the south. But as the war came to an end, these lines were increasingly becoming important for the economic growth of the colony. This was significant as most German troops left GSWA from 1907/1908 and the local economy faced the same prospects of recession that had riddled the South African colonies after the South African War ended in 1902.

GSWA's mineral deposits were seen as a key to the future economic stability of the colony. OMEG's copper mine at Tsumeb was central to this economic model, especially before the discovery of diamonds in the colony, and the mine benefited in November of 1906 from the completion of the *Otavibahn* to connect it with the coast at Swakopmund. This would facilitate the exporting of ore as well as transporting of goods and people.[69] The diamond fields of the south would also play a direct role in railway construction as we will see.

The Construction of the Windhoek-Keetmanshoop Line (Nord-Südbahn), 1910–1912

By 1910, the center of the colony had no train line in contrast to the north and south. This meant that the economic hubs of both the north and south were only connected via ship. A colonial newspaper article from February 1909 argued that such a north-south train line would allow the center of the colony to economically prosper giving sheep and cattle farmers in the central region the ability to cost effectively export meat and wool. In addition, it pointed to possible mineral deposits to be further explored and potential mining.[70] The military also supported

68 'Bahnbauten in Deutsch-Süd-Afrika,' LZ, 4.9.1909, 1.
69 Bravenboer and Rusch, *The First 100 Years*, 74.
70 'Nochmals von der Bahn Windhuk südwärts,' DSWAZ, Beilage, 13.2.1909, No. 13, 5.

the idea, arguing that a Windhoek to Keetmanshoop line would allow for quicker troop transport in the case of a hypothetical future uprising. According to the colonial government, this train corridor, in the long term, would enable a smaller contingent of soldiers stationed in the colony to effectively maintain German rule.[71]

However, it was the discovery of diamonds in southern GSWA in 1908, along with the resultant surge in labor demand, particularly for Ovambo migrants, and their transportation between the north and south, that heightened the economic appeal of such a north-south line. The capacity for Ovambo workers to be transported from the northern polities to the southern mines would, as we explored in the previous chapter, make the travel more efficient and often easier for Ovambo migrants in comparison to travel by ship between Swakopmund and Lüderitzbucht. The diamond finds also led to tax revenues to fund a large amount of the expensive rail projects of the post Namibian War period.

The building of the *Nord-Südbahn* starting in Windhoek was undertaken by Bachstein and Koppel and the project employed about 110 white laborers, 904 Cape Workers and 1,450 Africans from GSWA (including workers from the northern polities).[72] The section from Keetmanshoop north was contracted out to DKEBBG who employed about 120 white workers, 1,230 Cape Workers, and 1,840 Africans from GSWA.[73] One of the biggest feats of the construction was the building of the train line through the Auas mountains, the highest mountain range in the colony. Below (Figure 46) we can see two Cape Workers employed by Bachstein and Koppel likely taking a rest from work building the line south. Notice their clothing could just as well be worn by the Italian train workers mentioned in Chapter 2.[74]

71 'Eisenbahnprojekte II,' WN, 4.8.1909, No. 62, 1; 'Verhandlungen des Landesrats,' DSWAZ, 30.5.1911, 1.

72 Bravenboer and Rusch are not specific about which workers from GSWA were recruited for the project; see Bravenboer and Rusch, *The First 100 Years*, 153; photographic evidence confirms that Ovambo workers were contracted on at least the construction that started in Windhoek; see BAB, BPA.159 1 Karl Exler, Photo Album "Andenken an D.S.W. Afrika", 3, photo with label 'Ovambo Arbeiter.'

73 Bravenboer and Rusch are not specific about which workers from GSWA were recruited for the project; see Bravenboer and Rusch, 156.

74 See Chapter 2, Figure 8, "Italian Workers on strike joined by black workers, likely Ovambo, to take a photo, circa 1904."

Figure 46: Photo taken of two Cape Workers on the Nord-Südbahn construction in 1911. Based on the photo album chronology they are likely somewhere between 17 km and the construction of the line through the Auas Mountains.[75]

Cape Workers like the ones above (Figure 46) were engaged in some of the hardest work during construction of the *Nord-Südbahn* through the Auas mountains, just south of Windhoek. In Figure 47 below we can see a mix of workers, both white and black, including Cape Workers, as could be the man looking toward the camera on the right-hand side. While we do not know the names of the individuals in these photos, records especially from the British Consulate in Lüderitzbucht, which represented all South Africans in the colony regardless of race, give us some detailed insight into what life could be like for them and their families at home. Johannes Hendricks from Maitland was working for DKEBBG building the *Nord-Südbahn* northward from Keetmanshoop (the twin southern project to the one pictured in Figure 47). The firm Poppe, Schunhoff & Guttery recruited him

75 BAB, BPA.159 1 Karl Exler, Photo Album "Andenken an D.S.W. Afrika," 3, photo with label 'Ovambo Arbeiter,' 3, photo with label "Cape Boys"; according to Dag Henrichsen of the BAB, the photos in this album were taken by the German Karl Exler from Potsdam who was also employed on the *Nord-Südbahn*.

Figure 47: Photo of workers for Bachstein and Koppel laying the train line for the Nord-Südbahn through the Auas mountains.[76]

for DKEBBG in October of 1910.[77] His wife, Johanna Hendricks, wrote the following letter to the consulate in Lüderitzbucht after receiving news of his death:

> As I have received tidings from German West that my husband died June 22nd and he had his money on him: And my son came home on the fourth of July and he told me he went to the hospital as he heard that his father was dead but when he arrived there his father was dead already and some of the patients told him that the Head gentleman of the Hospital took the money and my son had to go and see him which he did and the gentlemen told him it is alright and took my address and he will send me the money but I have heard nothing yet. And also I have been to Cape Town 3 times already to the office but they can't help me . . . . I have a lot of children to keep and my rent has also run up lately as I was expecting my late husband by the first boat in August . . . .[78]

76 BAB, BPA.159 1 Karl Exler, Photo Album "Andenken an D.S.W. Afrika," 4, 'Am Auaspass.'
77 NAN, BCL [12], Death notice for Johannes Hendriks (No. 180).
78 NAN, BCL [12], Letter from Johanna Hendricks to the Consul Müller at Lüderitzbucht, 28.7.1911.

Slightly over one-week later Johanna would get a letter from Consul Müller letting her know that the money from the estate, £7/6/1, could be received from the Master of the supreme court at Cape Town.[79] However in her letter we can see the panic of not knowing if she indeed would be able to get the money owed to her. Through the mention of one of her sons having also been on contract, we can also understand that recruitment to GSWA could include multiple family members.

Johannes died of dysentery and estate records show that fellow workers on the north-south line who were Cape Workers and died in June also mainly suffered from dysentery (5).[80] His estate was slightly more than other South Africans on the project who died on contract at the time. A list from August 1911 of estates (11) to be given out, demonstrates most worth between £3 and £4 or likely around their monthly wages.[81] A later list from late August/early September catalogues estates (13) between £4 and £5, highlighting the likely typical range of wages.[82]

Johannes and his son were recruited and carried out their contracts during the period (1910–1911) which would see the highest number of Cape Workers employed in the colony. This period was also when the tragic event at Wilhelmstal occurred, where more than a dozen striking Cape Workers would be killed by German soldiers. Cape Workers pursuing good contracts in GSWA and pushing back against what they saw as employers' abuses would arrive at the limit of what the German colonial society would permit of its non-white work force. I argue that more than a misstep and overly aggressive response to a strike, the event was a symbol of what the German colony's post-1908 settlers, government, and employers demanded of its growing migrant labor workforce.

The Karibib to Windhoek Wide-Gauge Line, the Wilhelmstal Massacre, and its Repercussions, 1910–1911

Let us take some time to go into detail regarding the Wilhelmstal massacre and its aftermath. From this deep dive we will examine the mechanisms of disciplining

79 NAN, BCL [12], Letter from Consul Müller to Johanna Hendricks regarding the death of Johannes Hendricks, 8.8.1911.
80 NAN, BCL [12], DKEBBG construction management to Consul Müller regarding Cape Boys they employed who died in the Keepmanshoop native Hospital, 14.6.1911.
81 NAN, BCL [12], List of dead South African workers, including personal and estate information, Shared between the Consulate at Lüderitzbucht and the Inspector of Native Affairs at Ndabeni, 2–17.8.1911.
82 NAN, BCL [12], List of dead South African workers, including personal and estate information, Shared between the Consulate at Lüderitzbucht and the Inspector of Native Affairs at Ndabeni, 23.8.1911–5.9.1911.

both workers and employers as well as analyze ideas of justice and race in GSWA and South Africa. This case study is a partner piece to the 'Itere Affair' in the previous chapter regarding the killing of the Ovambo worker Itere on the diamond fields. In bringing these two events into dialogue, we can see the differences in how Ovambo and Cape Workers were treated, as well as certain similarities. While racism and colonial power structures played an important role in both events, perhaps it is the aftermath which is most telling. In one case the Ovambo workers seeking justice, were essentially ignored, whereas in the case of the Wilhelmstal Massacre a 'bi-colonial' investigation was undertaken with input from both metropoles. While one can posit that the difference had to do with the scale of the violence, and its appearance in the press across colonial and national borders, which is true, the status of these worker groups both on worksites, and in their home regions, also played an important role. To begin this analysis, we will first examine the buildup of railway construction labor prior to the event, relations in GSWA between employers, workers, and the government, and importantly how Africans from the Union travelling to GSWA after the debacle interpreted the massacre.

The diversity of sources for Wilhelmstal are unparalleled for a single event involving migrant workers in GSWA, with worker interviews, a report by an official Union investigative committee, company representatives ranging from overseers to the head of local operations, the British consulate in Lüderitzbucht, native affairs representatives from both colonies, the German military, the governor of German Southwest Africa, newspapers in the Union and GSWA, the Prime Minister of the Union of South Africa, and high-level administrators of the British empire sharing their views on the event. Observations from these varying sources do not always line up in the smaller details, blurring the line between interpretation and facts, but the overlapping aspects of stories give more credence to their probability. Emphasis will be given to the accounts of Transkei survivor testimonies to examine worker perspectives in detail.

As of 1907, travel and transport between Swakopmund and Karibib could largely be handled on the new *Otavibahn* cape-gauge line, but the Karibib to Windhoek section of the original railway desperately needed to be rebuilt, as its shoddy construction made its long-term viability questionable.[83] The state train line between Karibib and Swakopmund would be rebuilt by Bachstein-Koppel using cape gauge and a slightly different route than the original narrow-gauge line. In addition, the new construction would smooth out turns and reduce the

83 Further, it was one of the only major sections of the railway that was still using narrow gauge and had issues with carrying capacity; see Bravenboer and Rusch, *The First 100 Years*, 95–98.

steepness of inclines that had been problems with the previous construction. It was begun in April 1910 and completed by August 1911.[84]

The thousands of recruits from South Africa in 1910 included a group of 600 who were hired by Bachstein-Koppel from the area around Port Elizabeth (todays Gqeberha) in the Eastern Cape for the Karibib-Windhoek railway reconstruction. This project soon became defined by worker mistreatment, ranging from insufficient provisions to a payment system that was opaque at best and contract breaching at its worst. Therefore, it was no surprise that large numbers of Cape Workers on the project were dissatisfied, and both strikes and work slows for improvements were not uncommon. Bachstein-Koppel did not just have occasional worker issues, but their worker relation problems were systemic and often intentional. The situation became a powder keg as company overseers and management seemed unwilling to budge.

For one group of about 80 Transkei workers the situation would turn violent at the hands of German soldiers and management. This would be the embodiment of the worst excesses of colonial logistics in GSWA regarding the treatment of contracted workers in a private corporation / military joint venture construction project. The Wilhelmstal massacre occurred in October 1910 and would result in 12 Cape Workers being slaughtered, four dying subsequently, and 10 others injured.[85] Contrastingly, no military force was used against the Italian strikes of 1904–1905 during the war, or the cross-racial Tsumeb strike of 1910. The proto-Apartheid racial laws of GSWA were evolving in a way so that black individuals, and most mixed-race individuals, who in the German bi-racial categorization system would normally be considered black, could at any time be subject to extreme violence or even death.

The reports of Cape Workers Sizana Jafta and Bout Ompi give us some valuable firsthand perspective of laborers who were at Wilhelmstal. Both were from the Eastern Cape, around the area of King William's Town northwest of East London and were hired by the recruiter Kurz in February of 1910 for the Karibib to Windhoek reconstruction project.[86] One initial failure of the recruitment, that led to future issues, was that Bachstein-Koppel did not conduct proper medical exams on recruits prior to offering contracts. This meant that a sizable number of workers upon reaching GSWA were not in proper condition to work or could not perform

84 "Eisenbahnprojekte II," WN, 4.8.1909, No. 62, 1; Bravenboer and Rusch, 147–149.

85 NASA, GG 276 4/27, Collision between troops in German South West Africa and Cape Natives employed there, List of Labourers Killed and Wounded at Wilhelmstal.

86 NASA, GG 276 4/26 Collision between troops and Cape natives in German South West Africa. Forwards affidavits by two of the boys concerned, Affidavit of Sizana Jafta, King Williamstown, 25.11.1910, 1.

tasks at the same level as healthy laborers. This was a drastic change from the previous years when overly strict exams were conducted, indicating that the exams often had more to do with formal hiring demand than the health of the recruits. We will return to the repercussions of this for the work force later.

All new recruits for the Karibib-Windhoek line were transported by ship from East London to Swakopmund, where they were then taken on a twelve-hour train ride to Karibib. They had European (likely German or Cape-Dutch speaking) overseers, and the workers were divided up into groups of 100.[87] The workers also had, at least formally, a representative who had been hired by Bachstein-Koppel from South Africa, who was embedded in Windhoek with the company management, named Mr. Quandt.[88]

Once the laborers were at Karibib, they worked for 14 days until the end of the month. During this period they slept outside according to the affidavit of Bout Ompi. Worker contracts were supposed to include housing, along with rations and a salary of £3 per month, meaning that within the first days of work, laborers' agreements were already being broken.[89] As the new month began, the workers were told by Bachstein-Koppel that they would not be paid for the previous two weeks, but rather their pay would begin with the start of the new month. At the end of their contract, they could stay on to work an additional sixteen days, which when combined with the unpaid initial two weeks, they would receive pay for the additional month.[90]

According to the Transkei worker Sizana, at the end of the first full month, the workers were paid £3. At the end of the second month the workers received varying pay, between £1 and £2, as their employer claimed that they owed £2/10 each for their steamer tickets. Upon asking their overseer A. Hümpel when they would have their fares paid off, he replied that after the next month their fees would be paid. At the end of the second month, they all received £1 and were told that their fares were then paid. Another issue with wages was made clear by the British consul Müller at Lüderitzbucht, who wrote: "If for any reason such as sickness, leave etc, a labourer did not work, 2/6 a day was deducted from his wages.

---

87 NASA, GG 276 4/26 Collision between troops and Cape natives in German South West Africa. Forwards affidavits by two of the boys concerned, Affidavit of Bout Ompi, Cathcart, 30.12.1910, 1.

88 NASA GG 4/26 Collision between troops and Cape natives in German South West Africa. Forwards after from the British Consul covering a communication from a Mr. Quandt, Letter from Quandt to Müller, Swakopmund, 30.4.1911, 1.

89 NASA, GG 276 4/26 Collision between troops and Cape natives in German South West Africa. Forwards affidavits by two of the boys concerned, Affidavit of Bout Ompi, Cathcart, 30.12.1910, 1.

90 NASA, GG 276 4/26 Collision between troops and Cape natives in German South West Africa. Forwards affidavits by two of the boys concerned, Affidavit of Sizana Jafta, King Williamstown, 25.11.1910, 1.

This, worked out on any basis, is an excessive deduction, and I am given to understand was not universally applied."[91]

Bout Ompi in giving his recollections of early problems, highlighted that they were not well treated, and that by the fifth month, when wages were due, they were not paid. His group of workers complained to their overseer who claimed that he was the one blocking pay. We know from later analysis by consul Müller, that confusion was widespread amongst this workforce as to pay, and how it could be docked from monthly salaries. Further, overseers and managers seemed to have gone out of their way to reduce compensation when possible, whether it was justified or not. As for Bachstein-Koppel, the cases for deducting pay were tenuous at best and one of the main reasons for the protest and strike preceding Wilhelmstal.[92]

These building issues for Cape Workers combined with two reactants that would eventually lead to violence. One was, as we have discussed, that train projects (with the exception of the *Otavibahn*) starting with the southern line in late 1905, to the Karibib to Windhoek reconstruction project in 1910, combined private contractors and military support/work on construction.

Second, in this particular case Bachstein-Koppel had not given thorough medical checks to recruits before leaving South Africa. This meant that a sizable number of laborers were not in good health and subsequently overseers labelled the workforce at large as lazy or purposefully working slow. While some healthy laborers, increasingly angered by inadequate pay and provisions were actively working slow or inefficiently, others were simply incapable of performing the tasks at the required level. Complicating the situation even further, Bachstein-Koppel did not wish to give workers 'ideas' by sending unwell laborers home easily. They presumed that healthy workers would pretend to be unwell to go home with those who were suffering from medical conditions.[93]

The factors listed above created a combustible situation. Bout Ompi explained that he and fellow Transkei workers in his group went to their overseer

91 NASA, GG 275 4/24 Report by the Consul at Luderitzbucht on the treatment of natives by the authorities in German South West Africa, Memorandum on the condition of Native and Coloured people in German South West Africa, Cape Town, 30.6.1910, 4.

92 NASA, GG 275 4/21 Affray between troops and Cape boys in German South West Africa, Report Upon the Condition of cape Colonial Natives Employed by the Railway Construction Firm Bachstein-Koppel, and the occurrence at Wilhelmstal on October 4th Where Natives were Killed by Military, 4–5.

93 NASA, GG 275 4/21 Affray between troops and Cape boys in German South West Africa, Report Upon the Condition of cape Colonial Natives Employed by the Railway Construction Firm Bachstein-Koppel, and the Occurance at Wilhelmstal on October 4th Where Natives were Killed by Military, 8–9.

to complain about not getting wages, and as tensions rose, they went to an engineer on the train line with a translator to convey their complaints. According to the recollections of Sizana Jafta, overseer Hümpel responded to workers' continuing critiques and attempts to get full pay by telling them, "[y]ou are getting tiresome now and you will get lashes and be shot because this is not Englishmen's country." When they went to the engineer Hanssen in charge of their segment of rail he also replied aggressively and threatened that they were not in "English country" and could be shot.[94] The repeated use of such a claim infers that overseers and management for Bachstein-Koppel clearly thought of South Africa as a colony where black workers had better conditions, which according to them would not be emulated at their work site.

A prior June 1910 report from Consul Müller on the condition of Africans both local and migrant in GSWA already highlighted issues relating to excessive violence used against local African workers and those from the Cape, and a generally volatile situation for railway construction in the north. The memorandum from Müller stated, "I have felt rather nervous that the boys employed upon the northern railway would prove dissatisfied with their treatment . . . . If there is considerable trouble it may be necessary to discourage in every possible way the emigration of our colored people to German South West Africa."[95] Müller's worries were well placed. Four months later, the laborers for the Karibib-Windhoek line working their 12-month contracts would be on the verge of 'considerable trouble.'

With relations deteriorating between the workers and overseer Hümpel, they attempted to get engineer Hanssen to replace him, which eventually was denied. As issues were not able to be vented, and problems went unsolved, the workers who had wanted "an overseer who would treat us fairly" went on strike. A group of 76 Transkei workers under Hümpel left the worksite with the intention of speaking with the company management at Windhoek to ensure they got a new overseer.

They began to walk in the direction of Windhoek and eventually reached Okahandja, about seventy-two kilometers north of the capital. Three white policemen met them, asked where they were going, and after learning of their plan told them to stop.[96] Accounts differ at this point but in general it seems that the work-

94 NASA, GG 276 4/26 Collision between troops and Cape natives in German South West Africa. Forwards affidavits by two of the boys concerned, Affidavit of Sizana Jafta, King Williamstown, 25.11.1910, 1.

95 NASA, GG 275 4/24 Report by the Consul at Luderitzbucht on the treatment of natives by the authorities in German South West Africa, Memorandum on the condition of Native and Coloured people in German South West Africa, Cape Town, 30.6.1910, 1.

96 NASA, GG 276 4/26 Collision between troops and Cape natives in German South West Africa. Forwards affidavits by two of the boys concerned, Affidavit of Bout Ompi, Cathcart, 30.12.1910, 3.

ers were promised that they would get a new overseer and were sent back to the worksite, where they returned to work for a few days.

A later analysis of the event by Quandt, the 'representative' for the workers at Bachstein-Koppel, had a few different details. In 1911 he wrote a letter to Consul Müller after he was no longer employed by Bachstein-Koppel detailing his perspective of the massacre. The letter was seemingly an attempt to rid himself of blame but was also clearly a damning analysis of the company's handling of the event. His letter, contrary to the workers' affidavits claimed that they, upon not getting their demands met, refused to go back to work. As a result, he asserted the company decided to cut rations and water, to force the workers back to the job.[97] Regardless of whose details were correct, Bachstein-Koppel seemed set on utilizing aggressive and contract breaking tactics against its workers who were 'causing issues'.

As the Transkei workers near Wilhelmstal seemed likely to continue to protest, engineer Hanssen left to speak with German soldiers, who had been contracted to build the railway and were nearby. He convinced lieutenant Albrecht and around 120 of the soldiers under his command, initially unarmed, to confront the disgruntled workers.[98]

The intention was clear, intimidate the workers into accepting conditions as they were, or punish them through violence. The police were not notified, indicating that following 'proper channels' for worker unrest was very much not the intention. The soldiers contracted were railway workers, but in coming to Wilhelmstal to confront the Cape Workers without orders from higher commanders, they were taking on another role, one of vigilante colonial justice. This was in many ways the embodiment of colonial logistics whereby the barriers between the colonial state, the military, and private enterprise were completely broken down. The potential for violence as the language of power was all but certain.

The soldier-workers acted in a deputized fashion, and at the instigation of overseer Hümpel and engineer Hannsen attempted to arrest three to five of the workers' foremen, who also served as translators. According to Ompi's recollection the group was divided on whether the foremen should be given to the au-

97 NASA, GG 4/26 Collision between troops and Cape natives in German South West Africa. Forwards after from the British Consul covering a communication from a Mr. Quandt, Letter from Quandt to Müller 30.04.1911, 3.

98 NASA, GG 4/26 Collision between troops and Cape natives in German South West Africa. Forwards after from the British Consul covering a communication from a Mr. Quandt, Letter from Quandt to Müller 30.04.1911, 4.

thorities.[99] Then most of the soldiers and Hannsen left via train to collect guns. They returned armed, including engineer Hannsen who was riding in a draisine (a motorized rolling-stock vehicle for individual transport) and had a shotgun.[100]

There are varying interpretations as to whether the Transkei workers then grabbed sticks, clubs, or anything that they could arm themselves with, but there seems to be agreement from worker sources that they did not attack. They were surrounded by armed German soldiers with their bayonets fixed. In the words of Sizana Jafta's testimony,

> Hanssen said 'The time for talking has gone by' and fired, killing George Nako . . . saying he was cheeky. The officer in charge of the soldiers then gave the word of command 'fire'. A volley was fired into us. The men between us and the picks did not fire but bayonetted us. Fourteen Natives were killed outright and eighteen wounded. Two of the wounded men died in the morning. I was one of the wounded. A bullet knocked the bowl of my pipe off and as I was taking the stem which remained between my teeth out of my mouth another bullet took off the little finger on my right hand. I then lay down among the dead and wounded and covered myself up with the entrails of a man from Wartburg station who had been bayonetted. This man's name was Gqobisa . . . .[101]

This horrendous recollection was also confirmed in the words of Bout Ompi who highlighted that they did not fight back despite the impending slaughter stating, "I did not see any violence offered the soldiers by any of us, not one attempted any assault by using his stick or anything else. In my gang there were three of my relatives and none of them have returned."[102] The violence by the whites at the scene was almost a universal affair as Quandt noted that even Hannsen's draisine driver joined in the bloodbath and ".was quite proud . . . that he had POTTED

99 NASA, GG 276 4/26 Collision between troops and Cape natives in German South West Africa. Forwards affidavits by two of the boys concerned, Affidavit of Bout Ompi, Cathcart, 30.12.1910, 3.

100 Zimmerer uses a German government report to describe the events of the day, whereas this chapter focuses on worker testimony, and company representatives. Slight differences in the sources exist. For example, Zimmerer states that Lieutenant Albrecht would relay the situation to Captain Willeke, who would bring German mounted soldiers, with the intention of arresting the worker 'ringleaders.' Regardless of a few of the details, what is certain is that German soldiers, eventually armed, would confront the Cape Workers and violence ensued. See, Zimmerer, *German Rule, African Subjects*, 281.

101 NASA, GG 276 4/26 Collision between troops and Cape natives in German South West Africa. Forwards affidavits by two of the boys concerned, Affidavit of Sizana Jafta, King Williamstown, 25.11.1910, 3–4.

102 NASA, GG 276 4/26 Collision between troops and Cape natives in German South West Africa. Forwards affidavits by two of the boys concerned, Affidavit of Bout Ompi, Cathcart, 30.12.1910, 5.

three . . . ."[103] In the documentation provided by Quandt, can be seen the haunting words which were based on a doctor's analysis, "[a]ll shot or struck from the back; not one from the front."[104] The massacre was of men who were all trying to escape.

The response from the administration in GSWA communicated to the South African government blamed the event clearly on the workers and placed the soldiers and their actions in the right. The acting governor of GSWA at the time, Bruckner, even went so far as to state that after supposedly not-obeying orders from the military, the workers "charged the soldiers and commenced attacking them; thereupon the latter made use of their arms."[105]

The press in the German colony also stood on the side of the German soldiers, referring to the Cape Workers as mutineers (*Meuterer*) and inferring that some of them were difficult types (*schwierige Gesellen*), already in the sights of the police and that they should have already been arrested.[106] They also similar to the German government claimed that the workers, armed with sticks, attacked the soldiers, who then had to respond with deadly force.[107] As the event was discussed in the South African parliament and British press by November, the papers in GSWA howled at the claims of 'German barbarity' from the British and British South Africans, as they simultaneously lauded the South African Boers for their 'calm' and 'restrained' perspective on the event.[108]

By and large the GSWA government, which would conduct investigations along with the South Africans, would stand by their early claim that the soldiers were in the right, despite all evidence to the contrary. The press in GSWA as well as much of the populace seemed to agree.[109] However, the government in the German colony did not wish for such an event to occur in the future and pressured

---

103 NASA GG 4/26 Collision between troops and Cape natives in German South West Africa. Forwards after from the British Consul covering a communication from a Mr. Quandt, Letter from Quandt to Müller 30.04.1911, 5, (emphasis in original).

104 NASA, GG 4/26 Collision between troops and Cape natives in German South West Africa, Fforwards after from the British Consul covering a communication from a Mr. Quandt, Letter from Quandt to Müller 30.04.1911, 4.

105 NASA, GG 275 4/19 Affray between Cape boys and German troops in German South West Africa, Translation of a letter from Acting Governor Bruckner of GSWA to the Governor General of Pretoria, 12.10.1910, 2.

106 This article also cites the GSWA newspaper WN, see 'Die Unruhen unter den Bahnarbeitern im Norden des Schutzgebiets,' LZ, 15.10.1910, 1.

107 This article references the GSWA newspaper DSWAZ having a similar pro-soldier perspective; see 'Die Vorgänge in Wilhelmstal,' LZ, 29.10.1910, 5.

108 '*Wilhelmstal im Urteile der Union,*' WN, 30.11.1910, 1.

109 Settlers such as Carl Schlettwein supported the soldiers' actions; see Zimmerer, *German Rule, African Subjects*, 286.

both Bachstein-Koppel to improve conditions as well as send compensation to the families of the victims.[110] Eventually the company would give out a total of £750 in compensation to the families of victims.[111]

Internal German investigations of the event did find severe cases of worker abuse and much blame was placed on Bachstein-Koppel and its white overseers and local management. The company ordered that Hümpel should be dismissed, and Hanssen recalled to Germany and put on another job. The company however did not blame Hanssen for the event.[112]

We can see here a difference to the punishment meted out after the Wilhelmstal massacre compared to the 'Itere affair.' While in both cases there was severe injustice, Hümpel was at least dismissed and Hanssen relocated, while Stangenberg, the overseer in the 'Itere affair,' was allowed to keep his job and continue abuse his behavior. This exemplifies the power of international pressure, as well as the different status both groups had within the workforce.

As for the soldiers, a military court concluded that lieutenant Albrecht was in the wrong and had no right to intervene in the event. However, the court also stated the following of Albrecht:

> After the events already described that had gone before, he believed it to be his duty to intervene without further orders in the interests of the authority of the State and the standing of the white race, being confirmed in this error by something his superior, Captain Willeke, had said on the previous day.
>
> Lieutenant Albrecht's actions thus did not go beyond the limits of the authority that he believed himself to possess. Thus he lacked that awareness of the illegality of an action that is required to constitute a punishable offence.[113]

Captain Albrecht's superior Captain Willeke, who also had played a key role in the use of violence, again mirrored the racialized logic of shooting and bayonetting the Cape Workers at Wilhelmstal in stating after the fact:

> If I had allowed the threatening attitude of the kaffirs to cause me to withdraw the armed company without forcing them to lay down their weapons, I would have severely damaged the authority of the German Government and of the troops and the standing of the white race, and endangered the life and safety of the civil persons employed on constructing the railway.[114]

110 NASA, GG 277 4/83, Collisions between German troops and Cape Natives at Wilhelmstal, Letter from the British Consul for GSWA to Foreign Office, 20.3.1912, 1.

111 Beinart, "'Jamani,'" 59.

112 Zimmerer, *German Rule, African Subjects*, 283–284.

113 Court Order, Imperial Schutztruppe for South West Africa – Court of the Schutztruppe Central Command (transcript), 5 December 1910, BAL R 1001/1234, 95a–97b in Zimmerer, 284.

114 Willeke to CSW (transcript), 9 January 1911, BAL R 1001/1235, 25a–26b in Zimmerer, 285.

The event at Wilhelmstal, when compared with other GSWA colonial responses to white and mixed-race strikes discussed in this book, clearly highlighted the racialization of colonial violence. These views would also be mirrored in newspapers back in Germany. The *Cape Times* would reference a German newspaper, *Vossische Zeitung*, which stated that unlike the British denial of refuge for 'Hottentot' (Nama) rebels between 1907 and 1908 in the Cape, the Lüderitz British Consul's inquiry into Wilhelmstal weakened 'white prestige.'[115] In other words, the denial of sanctuary by the British (South African colonies) of those who had fled German genocide was interpreted as solidarity of the 'white race' in Southern Africa. Conversely, the negative South African reaction to the October 1910 massacre of Transkei workers was treacherous to the white race.

I argue the violent response at Wilhelmstal was, on a micro-scale, an action to ensure racial hierarchy, inclusive of these migrant labor elites, who often broke the increasingly tight economic and social norms of the colony, using deadly force. The German worker-soldiers through the taking up of arms against the Cape Workers were projecting more universal German colonial policies in GSWA, which embodied the end goal of subjugating all non-whites as a black proletariat.

However, Africans in the Cape were British subjects and were therefore entitled to certain rights, which the Cape government looked to protect in GSWA, mainly through its consulate in Lüderitzbucht. These rights often contrasted with colonial government and business practices in GSWA. As the Lüderitzbucht consulate wrote of the GSWA post genocidal period, "[n]ative administration had become considerably harsher as a result of the recent rebellions . . . ."[116]

On a very practical level, the Wilhelmstal massacre caused a crisis for the future of migrant labor recruitment in South Africa for work in GSWA. The repercussions resulted in a South African investigation and German promises of improvements in worker conditions. The Union investigation would not only examine the massacre at Wilhelmstal but also hear the perspectives of three thousand South African workers along the railway lines in the colony.[117] In the coming years, the Union government aimed to use the bloody event as a symbol of how Cape Workers could be treated in the colony to clamp down on worker out-migration, and perhaps most importantly to instead attempt to redirect migrants toward employers in the Union.

115 'Wilhelmstal Tragedy', Cape Times, 4.11.1910, 9.

116 NASA, GG 275 4/24, Report by the Consul at Luderitzbucht on the treatment of natives by the authorities in German South West Africa, 1.

117 NASA, GG 277 4/84, Collisions between German troops and Cape Natives at Wilhelmstal, Report on visit to German South West Africa by Dr. Phil. Rubusana, Enoch Mamba, Charles Wakefored and H. Jungheinrich, Windhuk, 13.1.1911, 1.

Increasing pressure from South African businesses ranging from fruit farmers to the Rand mines made such policies more likely. A confidential document from December 1910 on the fallout of the Wilhelmstal disaster written by South African Prime Minister Louis Botha embodied the changing tide of South African government sentiment. Botha stated:

> Up to the present recruiting to a certain extent by German Agents in the Cape Province has been sanctioned by the German Government prohibit all recruiting in their territory. There is reason to believe that a large number of natives from the northern parts of German South West Africa could be procured for the Transvaal Mines and Ministers feel that some measure of reciprocity should be afforded. They would suggest that representations be made to the German Government to this effect with an intimation that, if permission to recruit labourers in German South West Africa be unconditionally refused, this Government will feel bound to consider the withdrawal of the facilities now given to German Agents to recruit within the Union, and that in view of the scarcity of labour now prevailing in the Transvaal, it may be found necessary to discourage the entry into the country of voluntary labourers, though Ministers regards that as an extreme step which they would be very loath to take.[118]

Headwinds were clearly facing the future of formal recruiting channels from the Union to GSWA. Related to bad publicity following Wilhelmstal and growing internal business and public pressure in South Africa, by 1912 no new recruitment licenses were given out for the German colony.[119] As we described earlier however, many Cape Workers had for years been travelling to the colony without formal contracts and this continued. The underlying realities had not changed, both demand for labor from GSWA employers, and demand for decent above ground contracts by South Africans remained. Informal migration flows meant that the number of South Africans in GSWA still remained in the thousands up through 1914. Moreover, German assurances to ameliorate working conditions and prevent incidents like Wilhelmstal from recurring appeared sufficient to mitigate any significant deterrence among potential recruits.

Importantly, the South African Wilhelmstal investigative committee, while very critical of German treatment of Cape Workers in GSWA, concluded that after their visit and meetings, future employment would still be supported and provide South Africans with good opportunities. One member of the investigative committee, Reverend Dr. Rubusana was interviewed by the Cape Argus in early 1911. He was the only member who was a black South African and he did not hold back in his criticism. But he also had the following conclusion:

---

118 NASA, GG 275 4/22 Affray in German SW Africa between Cape natives and troops, Confidential Letter to Minister from Prime Minister Louis Botha, Cape Town, 14.12.1910, 3.

119 Beinart, "'Jamani,'" 59.

> You think, then, that Cape boys can engage themselves for German South West Africa without fear? Yes. It would be a great mistake to stop recruiting in this country for German territory. In the first place, it would be an unwarranted interference with the liberty of the subject. The boys like to go. They did not lodge a single complaint against the nature of their work, and so long as their grievances are attended to there is no reason why they should not be allowed to go.[120]

Rubusana's words were mirrored in Cape Workers response following the event as they continued to go to the colony for work. Despite mounting South African business and political pressure following Wilhelmstal, the number of Cape Workers employed in GSWA would continue to increase into 1911.[121] Afterwards numbers would then decline but remain above 1908 numbers until WWI. This fact points to the strength of South African migrants' desire to work in the colony, despite the potentially violent and at times deadly conditions in GSWA. But Cape Workers in the colony were more than a work force. They were also a diverse community which engaged in rich lives.

Religion, Social Life, and Sport amongst the South African Labor Elite of GSWA

South Africans working in GSWA encompassed a broad variety of communities. As we have mentioned, those from both the Eastern and Western Cape made up a majority. Most coming from the Transkei and Ciskei areas were Christian and there was a long presence of missions in the region, especially amongst the Xhosa.[122] Missions in the Eastern Cape, and Christian communities connected to them, dated back to the first decades of the nineteenth century.[123] Various migrants from the eastern Cape were also devout in their religious practice in the German colony, such as a group of Wesleyen Methodist Zulu laborers at the Tsu-

120 NASA, GG 276 4/45 Collision between German soldiers and Cape Natives at Wilhelmstal, The Cape Argus Weekly Edition, 25.1.1911, German S.W. Africa. Native Labourers. Treatment and Grievances.

121 NAN, ZBU 172 A.VI.d Vol. 1, Population Statistics Natives and Coloreds Main Statistics, Population Statistics on the Natives and Coloreds Population at the Beginning of the Year from 1910–1913; this data confirms the assumption by Ulrike Lindner, and disproves the conjecture regarding post-1912 labor flows from the Union to GSWA by William Beinart and Jürgen Zimmerer; see Lindner, "Transnational Movements between Colonial Empires," 687; Beinart, "'Jamani,'" 59; Zimmerer, *German Rule, African Subjects*, 293–294.

122 Beinart, "'Jamani,'" 49; William Beinart and Colin Bundy, *Hidden Struggles in Rural South Africa: Politics & Popular Movements in the Transkei & Eastern Cape, 1890–1930*, William Beinart and Colin Bundy (Berkeley: University of California Press, 1987), 9.

123 Joan Millard, "Grass-Roots Pioneers of Transvaal Methodism," *Missionalia* 17, no. 3 (1989): 188.

meb copper mines in 1910. Rhenish Missionary Lang wrote of them: "The Zulus there are praised for being very churchly and have even organized a church concert to raise money for their ecclesiastical needs."[124]

Looking through the correspondence between many South African migrant laborers, references to God and faith are often present, especially when someone was sick or injured and could die. One example was a worker, writing to the wife of a fellow contracted laborer, Charlie, who died in January 1907 in Aus, likely working for the railway line. Correspondence by Charlie before he died was in Dutch, signifying he was most probably Cape Coloured. His surviving friend wrote to Charlie's wife, Mrs. M. Solomons, in Cape Town from Aus:

> I must also tell you that [the] doctor has been to see him several times in Hospital his [doctor's] words were always that he would never rise again. So he [Charlie] had trusted in God to relieve him and he said no more for he said his throat is so sore. He was taken and sewed up in his blankets and buried the same day . . . . I want you to send his age to us then I will make a head board and have his name written there on . . . . He said he trusted in god whether he was sick in town with you or here in Aus his time was due. He asked me to break the news to you that god will take care of you and your loving children and that you may meet again some day. That was his last words on his dying bed . . . .[125]

Clearly Charlie seemed to be a man of faith and his friend shared his enduring belief in God on his death bed. Unfortunately for Charlie he passed away and was quickly buried.

While the German colonial government and employer viewpoint on migrants' faith was often indifferent, there were religions and churches which they disliked. Independent African churches, or so-called Ethiopian churches, were chief among them. The Ethiopian churches in South Africa had their origins in late nineteenth century Eastern Cape and their independence was not only religiously minded, but anti-colonial ideology also circled amongst their leaders and membership.[126] William Beinart has argued that it is likely that Ethiopian ministers were amongst the Cape Workers who replaced the Karibib to Windhoek line and probably supported the work slows and strikes that preceded the Wilhelmstal massacre.[127] German newspapers from November of 1910 support the claim of the Ethiopian church as supporters of the workforce.[128] This meant that the

124 BAB, Annual Report of the Rhenish Mission Society 1910, Tsumeb, (Barmen: Westdeutsche Druckerei, 1911), 36. Translation to English by W.B. Lyon.

125 CA, NA 727, Wages due to Labourers who died in German South West Africa 1905–1909, Letter to Mrs. M. Solomons from Aus, 30.1.1907.

126 Beinart and Bundy, *Hidden Struggles in Rural South Africa*, 114–118.

127 Beinart, "'Jamani,'" 57–58.

128 ‚Zur Arbeiter-Beschaffung in Südwest. II', DSWAZ, 30.11.1910, 1–2.

Ethiopian movement was not only giving solace to some of the South African workforce in GSWA, but also playing a role in attempting to create better work conditions as well as fairer pay for their followers.

Some of the migrant labor elites were also joining the Rhenish missionary congregations, although numbers seemed to be few. Missionary Laaf writing about the African community in 1907 Lüderitzbucht stated that in addition to various local African peoples, "Kru, Cape Boys etc., at this time have little religious needs."[129] By 1908, according to Laaf, some had joined the mission's community in Lüderitz as he wrote, "[i]n addition to the Nama and Herero, other tribes such as Ovambos, Kru from Lome [Togolese migrants], Cape Bastards [Cape Coloured] and others are to a certain extent coming to church services."[130] As we shall see however, service attendance in Rhenish missionary congregations by the migrant elite was often fleeting.

While most of the African migrant elite in GSWA who were religious tended to be protestant Christians, that was not true for all. Another small segment of the African elite were Muslim. The Rhenish Mission data of the African population in Tsumeb included four likely Cape Malay Muslims. While few, they were more numerous than Catholics in the Tsumeb African community, which at the time according to Rhenish statistics were zero.[131] Further, a small number of South Africans in GSWA were potentially Hindu and coming from the Indian South African community.[132] One Indian South African who was contracted in GSWA was Mungal Pursod, who worked building the Lüderitz to Keetmanshoop train line and died of typhus in November of 1908. In Mungal's estate is what the German authorities listed as a 'skirt' (*Rock*), which was likely a *lungi* worn by many Indian men.[133] While religious diversity beyond protestant Christianity obviously did exist (we will mention Catholicism when discussing West Africans) and included other belief systems, what was perhaps common was not actively engaging in

129 VEM, RMG 2.509 a Lüderitzbucht C/h 23 a, Band 1 1904–1945, Letter from Missionary Laaf, Lüderitzbucht, 16.11.1907, 338. Translation to English by W.B. Lyon.

130 VEM, RMG 2.509 a Lüderitzbucht C/h 23 a, Band 1 1904–1945, Letter from Missionary Laaf, Lüderitzbucht, 4.11.1908, 323. Translation to English by W.B. Lyon.

131 VEM, RMG 2.529 a C/h 46 a Tsumeb (mit Grootfontein, Gaup, Otavi), Band 1 1907–1939, Visitations-Fragebogen Tsumeb, 12.8.1912, 330.

132 Although a majority of the Indian South African community were Hindu, others were Muslim or Christian. A later 1951 census estimated that amongst the South African Indian community about 67 percent were Hindu, 21 percent Muslim and six percent Christian; see S.D. Mistry, "Ethnic Groups of Indians in South Africa," *South African Medical Journal = Suid-Afrikaanse Tydskrif Vir Geneeskunde* 39, no. 31 (1965): 693.

133 NAN, BLU [146] G.5.a.: *Nachlass und Erbschaft. Farbige,* Nachlassverzeichnis des am 8.10.1908 an Typhus verstorbenen Indier-Boy Mungal Pursod No. 5603 – Keetmanshoop, v. Schacht Black, 48.

public religious life while in the colony, but instead participating in recreational activities.

The Rhenish Missionary Laaf highlighted a few of these activities in 1911 Lüderitzbucht amongst the Cape Worker community, saying: "They hold daily games: tennis, football, races, dance, suits, but they don't have time for church if I admonish them . . . these people are all from Cape Town themselves as they have experienced big city life, and they are by no means the best elements that come here . . . ."[134]

In the annual Rhenish Missionary Report Laaf submitted for Lüderitzbucht the year before, he also mentioned Cape Workers' drinking locales, as well as game clubs (*Spielklubs)*, where cards and gambling were seemingly the thing to do.[135] The observations by Laaf state a great deal about the Cape Workers he encountered, from their sporting, drinking, and gambling past times. Of course, not all were coming from Cape Town. As we have discussed many were coming from the Eastern Cape, but it is sensible to think that much of these pastimes were brought with them from South Africa.

The references to sports by Laaf are supported in various other sources. Soccer seems to have been the most universal sport (including among West Africans as we will later see), and some South African estates include soccer kit.[136] One such soccer player was the Cape Coloured man George Davis (alias George Grootkey), who worked at the Felsenkeller beer brewery in Windhoek.

George had lived for years in GSWA as of 1914 after having come from Cape Town. In Windhoek he was in a relationship with Anna Martin, who was Baster. Anna lived together with George in the Windhoek location in a house as of July 1914 and they had children together. In late October 1918, George died of the Spanish influenza which was sweeping the colony. Anna then inherited his estate worth £4/16/6.[137] Part of the estate was a soccer jersey that was sold at auction.[138] It would not be sur-

134 VEM, RMG 2.509 a Lüderitzbucht C/h 23 a, Band 1 1904–1945, Letter from Missionary Laaf, Lüderitzbucht, 1.5.1911, 283–284. Translation to English by W.B. Lyon.

135 BAB, Annual Report of the Rhenish Mission Society 1910, Lüderitzbucht, (Barmen: Westdeutsche Druckerei, 1911), 22.

136 For examples, see NAN, NES [006] 5753/818, Estate of Fred Neethling, Detailed Account of Sale of assets, Estate of Cape Boy "Fred Neethling"; NAN, BCL [12], Estate of Christian Beerwinkel.

137 NAN, NES [004], Estate of George Davis alias George Grootkey, Letter from Clerk in Charge of Locations to Officer in Charge of Native Affairs, Windhoek & District, Deceased Estate: Cape Boy: George Grootkey alias George Davis Cont. 24/7795. Your Est. 123 refers, 17.1.1919; NAN, NES [004], Estate of George Davis alias George Grootkey, Acquittance of Inheritance Received, 15.11.1919.

138 NAN, NES [004], Estate of George Davis alias George Grootkey, Detailed Account of Sale of Assets, Estate of Cape Boy "George Davis" alias George Grootkey.

prising, and perhaps even been likely, that soccer, and other sports, brought together various migrant workers from South and West Africa.[139]

Another South African migrant worker's estate, that of Fred Neethling also tells us of the popularity of music amongst the migrant elite, as his estate included a banjo. Fred had been working, according to a letter from his father for the head locomotive foreman Baxter in Windhoek in the years before 1918. However, before his death from Spanish influenza in October of that year, he had been jailed for an unspecified reason.[140] Fred's Banjo was just one of many instruments to have been found in various South African and West African estates. For example, the South African Jack Feck in Windhoek had a guitar, the Togolese man Joseph W.K. Mensah who worked at the Pomona Mine had a mandolin, and the South African Job also had a banjo.[141] One can assume that instruments were used not just in private, but also to make music for social gatherings where dancing, cards and gambling may have taken place. Whereas much of the labor elite seemed to enjoy playing music, and had instruments, a small subset could even afford the most expensive music entertainment, gramophones, and records. These were often members of the West African community in GSWA.[142] While this group of workers was numerically smaller than the South Africans in the colony, they played an outsized economic and societal role within the migrant labor community.

Wealthy West African Entrepreneurs and Skilled Workers

For West Africans, mainly working at GSWA's wartime ports, the end of the active conflict against the Herero and Nama in 1907/1908 led to a drastic decrease of their numbers in the colony. After having peaked at over 10,000, their numbers shrank to about 137 people by 1908, although numbers began to increase until an average of between 300–400 were working mostly in the ports.

As we can see above, mainly Liberian Kru were joined by individuals from the German colonies of Togo and Cameroon (includes at least one individual from Brit-

139 Evidence of other soccer players amongst the African community in the early twentieth century, such as Ovambo, has yet to be found.

140 NAN, NES [006] 5753/818, Estate of Fred Neethling, Death Notice for Native Hospitals, 30.4.1919; Letter from Adolf Neethling to Superintendent of Native Affairs, Windhuk, 20.1.1919.

141 NAN, NES [004] 5753/451 Estate of Job; NAN, ADM [211], Natives Lüderitz. German Subjects, Mesah Togoland 237 (8); NAN, NES [004] 5753/451 Estate of Job; NAN, NES [006] 5753/817, Estate of Jack Feck.

142 Examples of Grammaphone owners in the native estates include, NAN, NES [004] 5753/453, Estate of William Motha; NAN, NES [001] 135/147, Estate of Henry Lawson; NAN, ADM [211], Natives Lüderitz. 238 /13 Victor Bassajung Kroo Boy.

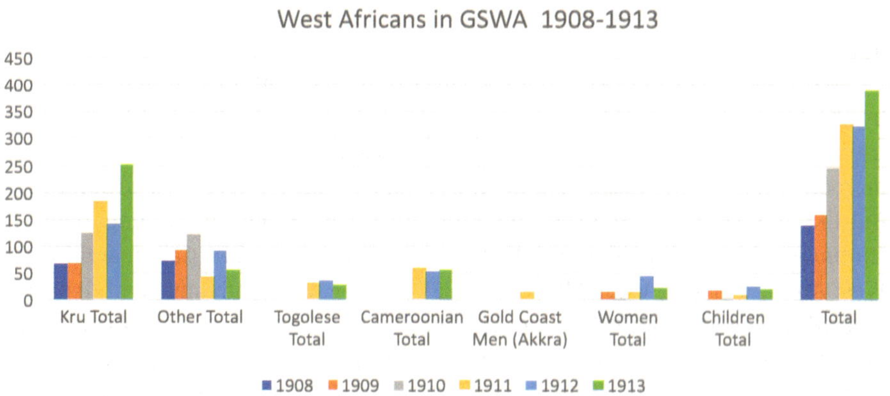

Figure 48: West Africans in GSWA 1908–1913.[143]

ish Lagos), as well as the British Gold Coast in GSWA. While most West Africans in the colony were men, those from Cameroon in particular included women and children who were accompanying their husbands and fathers. The Cameroonian men were former colonial soldiers in Cameroon who had been part of a failed mutiny and were afterwards exiled with their families to GSWA. Their experiences in the colony, including in World War One, will be explored in detail in the following chapter. Those referenced above in Figure 48 are to say nothing of the thousands of West Africans working on German merchant or military vessels, who continued to visit the ports working as ship hands. Many West Africans on land, however, would continue to be highly skilled, essential port workers. Others would go into diverse industries, from banking to bookstores and restaurants. West Africans would have the most privileged economic status of Africans in the colony, having on average over £30 in assets per person during the period from 1908 to 1914.[144]

Individual portraits allow us to see that from 1908 to 1914, not only were many West Africans diversifying the work they were doing, as well as locations they were employed in, but their unique status was bending the racial boundaries of the German colonial society. Unlike for the South African workforce, the number of West Africans in the colony was in the hundreds rather than thousands. Simultaneously, many of the economic roles they were filling were highly specialized cementing their place in the colonial society. As a result, we will examine

143 Compiled from NAN, ZBU 172 A.VI.d Vol. 1, Population Statistics Natives and Coloreds Main Statistics, Population Statistics on the Natives and Coloreds Population at the Beginning of the Year from 1908–1913.

144 Lyon, "From Labour Elites to Garveyites," 44.

how some West Africans were living in areas designated for whites only and others were running their own businesses.

West Africans were using their various skill sets to fill in economic holes left by the genocide, whereby the number of local Africans who could have been trained in skilled roles was limited. This contrasted with, for example German Cameroon, where many locals had been trained as skilled workers by around 1910. But like in GSWA, in Cameroon demand outpaced supply forcing employers to continue to hire well paid and skilled workers from places like Gabon and British West Africa. Further, West Africans in GSWA were taking advantage of demands created by the growing economy. At the same time, some were even competing against white businesses. Instances even exist of West Africans who were rather economically successful lending money to whites. This created tensions that came out in the press, although they were allowed by and large to continue in their various economic endeavors. Let us start with Kru individuals and then examine a few other West African experiences.

Pieter Dares and Kru in the Post-war GSWA Colonial Economy

Pieter Dares was a Kru man from Monrovia working in GSWA in the early twentieth century. He had been employed by the Swakopmunder Buchhandlung, a bookstore in Swakopmund, when he died on May 12, 1909, in Lüderitzbucht.[145] He probably came to the colony working for the *Woermann-Linie* as a longshoreman and eventually made a change, going to work at the bookstore. Pieter's affairs at his death were complex. Financially, according to a fellow Kru colleague, Edward, Dares had £55 to his name. Around £24 of this was held in Afrika-Bank's Lüderitzbucht branch.[146]

Pieter was in difficult circumstances when he died. He was in jail for reasons that cannot be deciphered, and he owed a good sum of his money to his soccer club. Fellow team-mates Pieter, Eduard, Toby, Tuies and Keins claimed that around £20 of Pieter's estate was owed to the club.[147] Furthermore, the government would charge almost £6 to cover his expenses in jail, which lasted 130 days, as well as translation and burial fees. Beyond his finances, Pieter had entrusted his last em-

145 NAN, BLU [146] G.5.a., 12 May 1909, Notice of death by the police sergeant of the Lüderitzbucht Colonial Office, 61.

146 NAN, BLU [146] G.5.a., 16/5/1909, Letter from Herrn Fläschendräger of the Afrika-Bank regarding the estate of Kru Pieter, 65.

147 NAN, BLU [146] G.5.a., 30/6/1909, Statement from the Fußballklub der Kruneger, 72.

ployer with a trunk full of personal possessions, which were to be given to his brother Hannes, who was working for the German settler Louis Worms.

Hannes' employment gives us some added detail as to what segments of society Kru were working for. Louis Worms was a prominent businessman who ran a store in Lüderitz that had opened in 1905 right about when the conflict between the Nama captaincies and the German colonial forces escalated. He benefited greatly from the wartime economy and by 1911 had become quite wealthy. His store sold everything from fine men's, women's and children's clothing, to fresh produce and quality furniture from South Africa.[148] Worms was also involved in the early Lüderitz diamond industry as an investor in the mine 'Germania,' although it is questionable how successful this venture was.[149] We also know that he was a member of the sport's commission, along with other high society Lüderitzbucht residents, that ran the local horse races.[150] These were a very popular pastime among the settler community.[151] In the years after 1907, more Kru in GSWA like Pieter and Hannes were working for establishments like Worm's store. Their skill in languages, and high level of adaptability from years doing a multitude of tasks on ships and at ports made them sought after in a variety of industries. Their wealth and prominence also often translated to many physical belongings. Pieter's estate was no exception.

His trunk was filled with a long list of possessions including a gramophone and records, a harmonica, a white suit, ties, Eau de Cologne, photographs, and caviar, among many other items.[152] His possessions and his liquid assets displayed that his work and resulting wealth allowed him to participate actively in the consumer culture of GSWA. Hannes, Pieter's surviving brother in the colony, received the estate, including Pieter's remaining £24. Then, on 28 May, little more than two weeks after his brother had died, Hannes left GSWA with the estate in his possession to return to their 'homeland' of Monrovia.[153] His steamer, *Swakopmund*, operated by the Hamburg-Amerika-Linie, left the port of Lüderitzbucht for the 'Northern Republic' (Liberia). Other records of Kru in GSWA from 1908 to 1914

148 'Saison-Ausstellung (advertisement for Louis Worms' Lüderitz store),' LZ, 27.2.1909.

149 ‚Bekanntmachung', DSWAZ, 20.3.1909, 3.

150 ‚Pferde-Rennen zu Lüderitzbucht am 11.4.1909 (Advertisement),' LZ, 13.3.1909, 1.

151 Lindner, *Koloniale Begegnungen*, 389; Olga Levinson, *Diamanten im Sand: das wechselvolle Leben von August Stauch* (Windhoek: Kuiseb-Verl, 2007), 103–115.

152 NAN, BLU [146] G.5.a., Estate items of Kru Pieter, 66–67.

153 NAN, BLU [146] G.5.a., Estate items of Kru Pieter, 68.

echo similar types of personal possessions. The most commonly held were multiple pairs of suits in various fabrics and colors, Panama hats, musical instruments, gramophones, soccer kit and photographs.[154]

The Kru community however did not only consist of adult men and was not isolated from other Africans. Government statistics show that by 1909 the first 'Kru' children were being counted in Lüderitz.[155] These children likely were with local women. While data from these years does not exist on African marriages in the ports of GSWA, we know that by 1920 Swakopmund included about four married Kru.[156] Kru men were not only partnering with local African women, but by 1913 at the latest two Kru women, one in Swakopmund and one in Lüderitz, were also included in statistics.[157]

Kru women, not traditionally employed on ships and without direct economic incentives from employers in GSWA, likely migrated through their own means or with the support of their partners. This suggests a level of mobility and financial capability unusual for most African women in the colony, as it implies they possessed sufficient resources to fund the costly journey from West Africa to GSWA. Such movement also indicates the Kru community's view of the colony as a potential long-term home. This trend mirrors the broader historical pattern of Kru settlement throughout West Africa and the Atlantic world during the nineteenth and twentieth centuries, with communities establishing roots in locations as diverse as Freetown, Fernando Po, and even Liverpool in Great Britain.[158]

One of the Kru women that was likely in GSWA by 1913/1914 was Helaria, who lived in the colony until at least 1919.[159] Her name can be found in an estate record of fellow Kru John Tappie who died in 1919 Lüderitzbucht of the Spanish influenza. Helaria bought a coffin for Tappie, for which she was later compen-

---

154 Lyon, *Namibian Worker Database*; NAN, ADM [211], Natives Lüderitz 237 (1), 237–238.

155 NAN, ZBU 172 A.VI.d Vol. 1, Population Statistics Natives and Coloreds Main Statistics, Population Statistics on the Natives and Coloreds Population at the Beginning of the Year 1909.

156 Lyon, "From Labour Elites to Garveyites," 52.

157 NAN, ZBU 172 A.VI.d Vol. 1, Population Statistics Natives and Coloreds Main Statistics, Population Statistics on the Natives and Coloreds Population at the Beginning of the Year 1913.

158 Oestermann, *Kautschuk und Arbeit in Kamerun*, 201; Frost, *Work and Community among West African Migrant Workers since the Nineteenth Century*; Sundiata, "The Rise and Decline of Kru Power: Fernando Po in the Nineteenth Century."

159 It is almost certain that Helaria arrived in the colony at the latest by 1914. That is because starting with the South African occupation of GSWA in 1915, West African migration to the colony all but ended. Further, a Kru revolt against the Liberation government of the same period further curtailed Kru outmigration. See Lyon, "From Labour Elites to Garveyites," 49–50.

sated via the sale of his estate.[160] The coffin cost £3/10, not a small sum, indicating that Helaria was relatively wealthy, or at least had access to a partner's or friend's sizable assets. While we cannot be certain, perhaps Helaria was married to one of the 114 Kru men in 1913 Lüderitz, and/or potentially mother to the one Kru child referenced in the government statistics for that year. In the 1908 to 1914 period, other West Africans were increasingly calling German South West Africa home.

Alfred Kulivo and Togolese Entrepreneurs in the Colonial Ports

Alfred Kulivo was a member of the wealthiest African elite in the colony, business owners in the port towns. The records that describe his life and death in Swakopmund during German and into early South African colonialism give us a great deal of perspective into the West African population in the colony beyond the Kru. His experience, as well as other Togolese and West African business owners exemplify that many companies run by the West African migrant elite in GSWA not only succeeded economically, but also competed effectively with other Africans and whites. They were in many ways a group straddling the divided worlds of whites and non-whites (black, Cape Coloured, etc.). That is to say in an increasingly racially divided colonial society these entrepreneurs could for example, operate businesses in the center of white settler towns while being married to local African women. We will trace Alfred Kulivo's life in Swakopmund, while interweaving the stories of fellow Togolese and other West African business owners in German South West Africa.

Alfred Kulivo's success was embodied not only in his accrued wealth, but also his business, '*Alfred aus Togo Wäscherei*' (Alfred from Togo's laundromat) in Swakopmund. The company name, however, likely did not designate his place of birth. Records indicate that his uncle Samuel Amenaur, and potentially Alfred as well, were not born in Togo, but rather Porto Novo in Dahomey, West Africa.[161] But both Alfred and his uncle Samuel, who had previously been employed in GSWA, were referred to in government documents, both German and after 1915 South African, as Togolese. Perhaps if they chose their own labelling this was

---

160 NAN, NES [003] 5753/ 431, Estate of John Tappie Kroo Boy, Memorandum from Native Affairs Luderitzbucht to Secretary for the Protectorate Windhuk, 14.04.1919.

161 NAN, NES [004], Estate of Alfred Kulivo 5753/455, Letter from British Consul-General in Monrovia, Liberia to Secretary of the SWA Protectorate.

rather clever, as people from Togo were favored as skilled laborers at the time and it may have further benefitted their business marketing.[162] The reference to the German colony of Togo seems to have been a trans-imperial marketing strategy by African entrepreneurs, selling both the idea of the German empire and the business owner as part of this larger empire. One could imagine this as a preferred business to frequent for patron settlers wanting to economically support the empire, in contrast to a laundromat run by someone from South Africa for example.

A 1911 Swakopmund newspaper article includes a segment on West Africans in the port, refences Alfred J. Mdingi, Alfred Kulivo's business partner, and says that many West Africans were primarily English speakers.[163] This was relatively normal for those who grew up in coastal Togo or other parts of West Africa, as pidgin English was in many ways a lingua franca in the region during the early twentieth century. This included the German colonies of Togo and Cameroon, where English was used and part of the colonial education system and military.[164] In German Togo, it was only in 1904 that English was largely removed from teaching in state and missionary schools, and German was taught instead.[165] But not all non-Kru West Africans in the colony were from Togo or as we will explore later, Cameroon. The colonial ports of GSWA were also home to people who came from British colonies, where English was the primary language of communication amongst disparate groups. Statistics from 1911 include among others a population of '*Akkraleute*,' or Akkra people, in Swakopmund.[166] They were likely from Britain's Gold Coast Colony.

Regardless of Alfred Kulivo's origin, we do know that other West Africans in GSWA who ran laundromats were indeed from Togo, including 'Benjamin Dark'

162 W. Hagens, "Der Togoneger als kaufmännischer Angestellter," *Koloniale Rundschau* 9 (1911): 570–571.

163 'Schwarze Pläne,' DSWAZ, 4.7.1911, 1–2; we do however have evidence that some, if not many Togolese in GSWA were also fluent in German; see NAN, NES [004], Estate of Alfred Kulivo 5753/455, Letter in German from Alfred Kulivo to G. Grützner regarding late payment for bread, 29.7.1918.

164 Oestermann, *Kautschuk und Arbeit in Kamerun*, 316; Gunter Tronje Hagen, *Kurzes Handbuch für Neger-Englisch an der Westküste Afrikas unter besonderer Berücksichtigung von Kamerun* (Berlin: Dingeldey & Werres, 1908).

165 Benjamin Nicholas Lawrance, "Most Obedient Servants," *Cahiers d'études Africaines* 40, no. 159 (January 1, 2000): 489.

166 NAN, ZBU 172 A.VI.d Vol. 1, Population Statistics Natives and Coloreds Main Statistics, Population Statistics on the Natives and Coloreds Population at the Beginning of the Year 1911.

(an alias), Robert Kanyi, and W. Lawson.[167] Togolese laundromat owners capacity to come to and work in GSWA and occasionally return home was made more feasible by the *Woermann-Linie* opening a monthly steamer between GSWA and Togo starting in 1909.[168] In addition to Togolese migrants running businesses in the ports, records show that a few were working for the colonial government and post offices as clerks, as well as in the diamond mines.[169]

Figure 49: Portraits in South African government documents of the former GSWA clerks, Paul Ayeboari (left) and Emmanuel Kwasi (right).[170]

While often referenced in the estates of the African migrant elites in GSWA, we rarely find photographs in the colonial records not from the collections of the colonizers. Above (Figure 49) we see two portraits from the personal identification documents of Togolese clerks who worked for the government of GSWA. They are Paul Ayeboari on the left, and Emmanuel Kwasi on the right. While we don't know how old they were in the photos, when Paul left SWA in 1924 following the wake of WWI and the German defeat, he was 36. According to his travel documents he was Ewe, 178 cm tall, and was originally from Djankasse near Aného, Togo.[171] Emmanuel was slightly younger at the time of his leaving, 31, but also

167 'Advertisement for 'Togo-Dampf-Wäscherei,' LZ, 4.2.1911, 3; NAN, NES [001], Estate of Robert Kanyi 135/141; NAN, NES [001], Estate of Henry Lawson Togo Boy No. 300 135/147.

168 *‚Deutsch-Südwestafrika,'* WN, 16.6.1909, 2.

169 NAN, ADM [211], Natives Lüderitz 237 (1). German Subjects, Rudolf A. Grann Togo Boy; NAN, ADM [211], Natives Lüderitz. German Subjects, Mesah Togoland 237 (8); NAN, NES [001], Estate of Henry Lawson Togo Boy No. 300 135/147.

170 NAN, SWAA [2233] A.494/2, Emergency certificate of Nationality for Paul Ayeboari; NAN, SWAA [2233] A.494/2, Emergency certificate of Nationality for Emmanuel Kwasi.

171 NAN, SWAA [2233] A.494/2, Identification document for Paul Ayeboari; his height was converted by the author to the metric system from 5' 10" to centimeters.

Ewe and from Kpandu in today's Ghana.[172] Notice that in both photos the clerks were wearing white suits. While we do not have many details about either Paul or Emmanuel's lives in GSWA, they highlight that West Africans filled a variety of jobs and positions in the colony, including in the colonial administration.

Figure 50: Advertisement for laundromat run by 'Alfred aus Togo und Alf. J. Mdingi'.[173]

As we can see from the advertisements above, multiple laundromats used 'Togo' in their advertising for GSWA newspapers. Figure 50, from 1909, is an ad for the business that eventually became solely run by Alfred Kulivo. The fact that he started the company with Alfred J. Mdingi was possibly to share the initial startup costs, as well as the risk. As to why laundromats were the industry they chose to set up businesses in, it was likely due to demand in the colony, as well as the profits to be made. Additionally, parallel examples exist of migrants in the nineteenth and early twentieth century taking advantage of economic booms in the colonial

Figure 51: Advertisement for 'Togo-Dampfwäscherei' (Togo Steamwasher).[174]

172 NAN, SWAA [2233] A.494/2, Identification document for Emmanuel Kwasi.
173 "Advertisement for Laundromat run by 'Alfred aus Togo und Alf. J. Mdingi,'" DSWAZ, 3.2.1909, 4.
174 "Advertisement for 'Togo-Dampfwäscherei' (Togo Steamwasher)," LZ, 12.9.1913, 3.

Figure 52: Advertisements for various West African laundromats in GSWA.[175]

world by opening laundry businesses. These include Chinese migrants in California following the discovery of gold in the mid-nineteenth century, and Zulu migrants in Johannesburg following the discovery of gold there as well.[176]

The ad from 1913, *Togo-Dampfwäscherei* (Figure 51) in Lüderitzbucht gives us another example of West African entrepreneurs in the ports within the laundry business. The advertisement states that it is the “first, biggest, cleanest and cheapest laundromat in the port.” While this was obviously marketing, based on the owners’ estate we will soon examine, there is no doubt that *Togo-Dampfwäscherei* was successful and brought in good profits. The success of Togolese laundromats came in direct competition with white owned businesses, including those run by women. Laundromats were one of the few industries where economically independent settler women were able to make inroads.[177]

One was operated by the Lüderitzbucht *Heimathaus* (homeland house) part of the *Frauenbund der Deutschen Kolonialgesellschaft* (Women’s Association of the German Colonial Society). The *Heimathaus* was a temporary home to support newly arrived white German women until they were able to meet white German settler men, with the intention of marrying, starting families and thereby expanding the settler population.[178] The *Frauenbund der Deutschen Kolonialgesellschaft* was an association that through its stated goals in many ways represented German colonial racialized policy.

---

175 “Advertisement for ‘Wäscherei,’” DSWAZ, 8.12.1920, 3.

176 John Jung, *Chinese Laundries: Tickets to Survival on Gold Mountain* (Yin & Yang Press, 2007), 2–3; van Onselen, *New Babylon, New Nineveh*, 275–308.

177 Golf Dornseif, “Waisen-Import und Dienstmädchen-Anwerbung für Südwest” (no date), 7–11, accessed January 23, 2023, http://www.golf-dornseif.de.

178 Sophie Burchard, “Die Konstruktion eines rassifizierten weißen Weiblichkeitsideals in der Zeitschrift des Frauenbundes der Deutschen Kolonialgesellschaft: Kolonie und Heimat: Deutsche Kolonialgeschichte in ‘Deutsch-Südwestafrika’ im Kontext von Geschlecht, ‘Rasse’ und Sexualität” (Master’s thesis, Vienna, Universität Wien, 2014), 123–24.

However, the *Heimathaus*' laundry side business in Lüderitz was confronted with the economic realities, in that many people seemed to prefer the price and quality of the Togolese competition. Running one of *Heimathaus*' main Togolese competitors in Lüderitzbucht, *Togo-Dampfwäscherei* were the proprietors, W. Lawson and R. Kanji, the successors of 'Benjamin' as referenced in Figure 51. 'Benjamin Dark' had started the business three years prior in 1908. By 1913, *Togo-Dampfwäscherei* had been in business at least five years despite new ownership and temporarily closing at least once.[179] It was an example of the West African community in Lüderitz taking advantage of the rapidly growing diamond-based economy which had started in 1908. The evidence of change in ownership around 1913 also indicated that West African companies in GSWA were adaptable. We have detailed information via an estate file on one of the new owners as of 1913, Robert Kanyi.

Robert Kanyi died in 1917 of pneumonia, and what he left behind clearly denotes that the *Togo-Dampfwäscherei*, similar to *Alfred aus Togo*, was a very successful business. Robert's estate comprised not only a variety of clothing, including suits and a white jacket (potentially similar to those worn by the Togolese Paul and Emmanuel in Figure 49 above), but also a bicycle, photos, a dozen books, a 34m^2 wooden house in the Lüderitzbucht location and of course, as one would expect in his line of work, unclaimed laundry.[180] He also had £23 in the bank and was owed a sizable £17 by one M. Wasserstein, who was most likely Max Wasserstein, the proprietor of a clothing store in Lüderitz.[181] In December 1918, the entire estate was valued at £74/2/10 according to government officials.[182] As Robert did not have family in South West Africa, most of his estate was divided among his uncle, Kueni Asiaku, and Robert's sister, both who were living in Porto Seguro, or today's Agbodrafo, in southern Togo.[183]

179 "Advertisement for 'Togo-Dampf-Wäscherei,'" LZ, 4.2.1911, 3.

180 NAN, NES [001], Estate of Robert Kanyi 135/141, Personal Effects of Robert Kanyi, Lüderitzbucht Location.

181 NAN, NES [001], Estate of Robert Kanyi 135/141, Letter from Native Affairs to Lüderitzbucht SWA regarding Estate of Robert Kanyi, 20.7.1917; Kolonial-Wirtschaftlichen Komitee, ed., *Koloniales Hand- und Adreßbuch 1926–1927* (Berlin: Süsseroth, 1926).

182 NAN, NES [001], Estate of Robert Kanyi 135/141, Native Affairs Department regarding the Estate of Robert Kanyi, Togo, Lüderitz, 10.12.1918; When compared to all estates in the *Namibian Worker Database* which is a compilation of over 1,154 estates from 1908–1917, only 7 estates have a higher estimated value.

183 NAN, NES [001], Estate of Robert Kanyi 135/141, Letter from the Secretary of SWA to the Secretary to the Administration, Lomo, Togoland, Windhuk, 10.8.1917.

His records also show us the interconnectedness of the Togolese community in the colony, as during the war Robert held £10 for a fellow Togolese resident of Lüderitzbucht, Alfred K. Adotevi, when he had to leave to the north of the colony during WWI.[184] Some connections in the GSWA Togolese community were cemented by family that had come to the colony together.

William Lawson may have been Robert Kanyi's business partner 'W. Lawson,' in *Togo-Dampfwäscherei*, but by 1918 (following the South African takeover of the colony) he was working at the Pomona Diamond mine. He outlived his uncle, Henry Lawson, who had lived and worked in Lüderitzbucht.[185] The South African government had to decide if they would auction off Henry's large estate, which like many other West Africans' in the colony included possessions that ranged from a variety of fine suits, a gramophone with records, over 20 books, photos, and a house in the Lüderitzbucht location. His nephew, William, told the government that Henry's parents, John Coloby Cook and Accoccco Coloby Cook in Boagie, Togo would first need to be contacted before the estate could be sold. This shows that not only were family ties tight in the colony for Togolese migrants, but relatively good communication was maintained with their home communities.

After the death of Robert Kanyi and Henry Lawson it is unclear what happened with *Togo-Dampfwäscherei*. Contrastingly, we know that in Swakopmund Alfred Kulivo took sole ownership from Alfred J. Mdingi in June of 1912 and the business was renamed *Alfred aus Togo Wäscherei*.[186] When Alfred Kulivo later passed away in November of 1918, the laundry service may have outlived his death. The advertisement for "Max und Wilhelm aus Togo" in Swakopmund from December 1920 (Figure 52) may point to them inheriting or buying the company after Alfred Kulivo's death. But let us now return to the life of Alfred to gain more insight into the community.

Alfred's economic success in Swakopmund was perhaps best embodied in his 1911 application for a £250 South African life insurance policy, which meant that his business was doing well enough that he could afford the regular payments required. Those payments were made up until Alfred's death in 1918, from which

184 NAN, NES [001], Estate of Robert Kanyi 135/141, Letter to the Native Affairs Department Lüderitzbucht from Alfred K. Adotevi, regarding claims of cash towards the late Togo-boy "Robert Kanyi", Lüderitzbucht, 18.11.1917.

185 NAN, NES [001], Estate of Henry Lawson Togo Boy No. 300 135/147, Native Affairs to the Secretary for the Protectorate regarding Estate Togo Boy Henry Lawson, deceased, Lüderitzbucht, 26.3.1918.

186 "Ad and announcement by Alfred aus Togo Wäscherei," DSWAZ, 18.6.1912, 4.

we can infer that the business successfully rode out most of the economic challenges of WWI.[187]

We do not know the exact year Alfred Kulivo came to GSWA, but it must have been prior to February 1909, when he published what was likely the first ad for his laundry business in the local Swakopmunder newspaper.[188] Documents show that prior to coming to the colony, his uncle Samuel had been working in Monrovia, Liberia. It is probable that Alfred and Samuel came to the colony together, perhaps through the German shipping industry's strong presence in Liberia.[189] We also know that following Alfred's death, Samuel returned to Liberia to work for F.A. Swanzy, a prominent trading firm that had been operating in West Africa, initially the Gold Coast, since the eighteenth century.[190] Such mobility and capacity to get good work in very diverse locations, was another indicator of the adaptability of the West African community that had come to GSWA for work.

Like other West Africans in GSWA, such as the Kru men Pieter and Hannes discussed previously, Alfred started out as a servant (*Diener*) to whites in GSWA. After making enough money, he then set off to pursue his own business using his previous earnings to cover necessary startup costs. Alfred Kulivo's business success eventually allowed him to give South African migrants and white settlers credit.[191] Like Robert Kanyi, Alfred's capacity to give out credit exemplified how the West African migrant elite of the colony were crossing into economic positions that no other Africans in the post-genocidal period of the colony could or did. On the topic, Alfred Kulivo's business partner, Aldred J. Mdingi, wrote the following in the *Swakopmunder Zeitung*:

> Some of us have as great a sense of rightness as the whites, and perhaps in some cases a greater one.
>
> Many natives (Africans) get into debts with shopkeepers, which they cannot pay, although they have continuous daily work. If this were dealt with more closely by law, not so many righteous people, including myself, would have to suffer. However, if a white man

187 NAN, NES [004], Estate of Alfred Kulivo 5753/455, The African Life Insurance Society, Limited, Application for Assurance, 23.10.1911.

188 "Advertisement for *Laundromat* run by 'Alfred aus Togo und Alf. J. Mdingi,'" DSWAZ, 3.2.1909, 4.

189 NAN, NES [004], Estate of Alfred Kulivo 5753/455, Letter from the South African Military Administrative office in Swakopmund to the Secretary of the Protectorate in Windhuk, 17.2.1919.

190 David Dorward, "Arthur London, Chief Agent of Swanzy and Co: A Biography of Imperial Commerce on the Gold Coast," *African Economic History*, no. 29 (2001): 63; Henry Swanzy, "A Trading Family in the Nineteenth Century Gold Coast," *Transactions of the Gold Coast & Togoland Historical Society* 2, no. 2 (1956): 1.

191 "Schwarze Pläne,“ DSWAZ, 4.7.1911, 2.

owes money to one of us, we always receive our right. What is the reason that wise men do not have the right to sue the natives in court?[192]

Alfred J. Mdingi and Alfred Kulivo had been giving out credit to customers, including South Africans who had a penchant to burn through their sizable earnings. Mdingi and Kulivo wanted the capacity to sue those Cape Workers who had not paid them back. It is clear evidence of African shopkeepers wanting, and being allowed by the publishers, to write their opinions in the white settler mouthpiece of Swakopmund. Although the newspaper commentary later points out how having Africans in such an economic position within the colony is unwanted, it also highlighted that they were a small minority, that they are migrants, and it is these factors that 'allow' them in contrast to local Africans, to be in such a position. Further, the commentary made clear that conflicts existed between various migrants, including between South African workers and Togolese laundromat owners. Insights such as these give us concrete evidence of the complexity of GSWA society whereby both race, class, and societal stature all played varying roles.

As a member of the African migrant elite, a West African, and a business owner, Alfred Kulivo straddled racial and economic categories that defied easy colonial categorization that existed at the time. Perhaps the complexities of individuals such as Alfred are one reason that he and others like him are essentially non-existent in large amounts of Namibian historiography. Exemplifying his complex identity, examples exist that his diet, or at least part of it, was very similar to white settlers.

In Alfred's estate, we can see that payments were owed at Alfred's death to the Swakopmund baker Grützner. We know from the receipts that Alfred's family was purchasing bread in February 1918 every two to three days.[193] This was expensive and their bill for the month was about £1/8/7, or more than the average monthly wage of £1 for most Ovambo workers. Buying fresh bread from the bakery on a regular basis was also a very colonial German custom, and the Kulivo family was part of this culinary culture.[194] His family's consumption patterns are not dissimilar from Gold Coast migrants, trained by protestant missionaries, liv-

192 "Schwarze Pläne," 4.7.1911, DSWAZ, 2. Translation to English by W.B. Lyon.

193 NAN, NES [004], Estate of Alfred Kulivo 5753/455, Receipt for Bread from Baker Grützner, 28.2.1919.

194 Germany in the twentieth century consumed more bread than any other country in Europe. William Rubel, *Bread: A Global History* (London: Reaktion Books, 2011), 150; the GSWA "Address book" of white settlers and businesses from 1914 shows that essentially every colonial settlement of size had at least one bakery; see *Deutsch-Südwestafrikanisches Adreßbuch: 1914* (Swakopmund: A. Schulze, 1914).

ing in French colonial Gabon at the end of the nineteenth century, who also enjoyed European style bread.[195] For Alfred's family it signified both their place in society and their status as privileged consumers in the colonial economy. At the same time Alfred was part of the local African community.

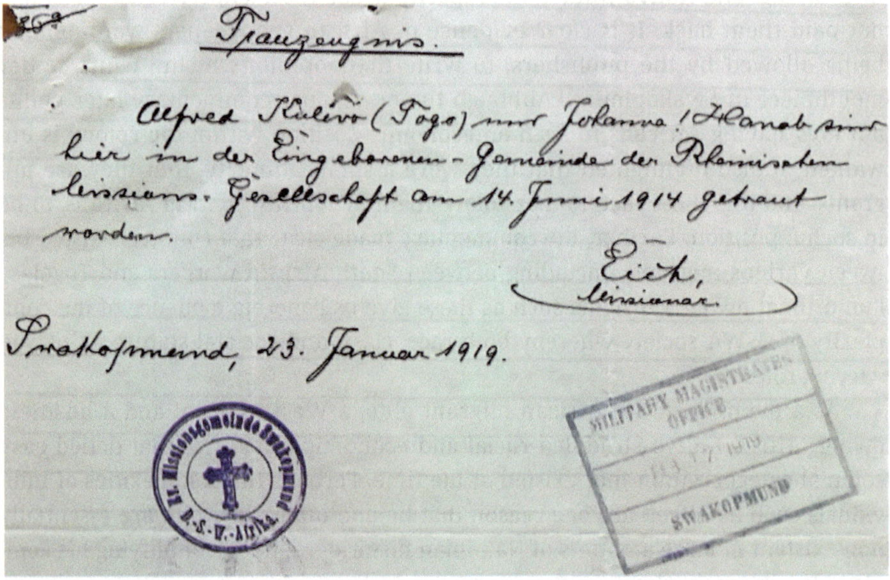
Trauzeugnis.

Alfred Kulivo (Togo) und Johanna !Hanab sind hier in der Eingeborenen-Gemeinde der Rheinischen Missions-Gesellschaft am 14. Juni 1914 getraut worden.

Eich, Missionar.

Swakopmund, 23. Januar 1919.

Ev. Missionsgemeinde Swakopmund D.-S.-W.-Afrika

MILITARY MAGISTRATES OFFICE SWAKOPMUND

Figure 53: A 'Wedding Certificate' by Missionary Eich of the Rhenish Missionary Society who led the Swakopmund community.[196]

Above (Figure 53) we have Alfred's wedding certificate which states that Alfred Kulivo was married to Johanna !Hanab, likely Damara, on 14 June, 1914.[197] The certificate tells us that Alfred was a member of the Lutheran Christian community run by the Rhenish Missionary society in Swakopmund. We also have hints that some in the GSWA Togolese community were likely Catholics. The Togolese man Rudolf A. Grann worked for the Lüderitzbucht German post office and at the outbreak of WWI left his possessions with a Catholic priest in Lüderitz. Unfortunately for Rudolf, the priest was forced to temporarily go to Cape Town during

195 Jeremy Rich, *A Workman Is Worthy of His Meat: Food and Colonialism in the Gabon Estuary* (Lincoln: University of Nebraska Press, 2009), 58.

196 NAN, NES [004], Estate of Alfred Kulivo 5753/455, Trauzeugnis, Swakopmund, 17.2.1919.

197 Namhila, *Native Estates: Records of Mobility across Colonial Boundaries*, 33.

the South African occupation and when he returned to the Catholic mission, Rudolf's possessions were gone.[198]

Alfred Kulivo clearly saw prospects for his future, and his experience in GSWA supported such an outlook. He purchased a new washing machine the month after his marriage for £8/12/10 indicating that Alfred had enough assets to reinvest in his business and stay competitive against other laundromats.[199] The First World War broke out in late July, which eventually would bring the German forces in the colony into conflict with neighboring South Africa.[200] The war brought an economic toll to most businesses in the colony. However, the surrender of the German military in GSWA and occupation by South African forces in 1915, led to local peace and the capacity to continue washing laundry. Alfred Kulivo would remain in business until his death of Spanish influenza in 1918. Despite Alfred's hard work, successful business, new wife, Togolese community connections in the colony, and survival through the First World War, he like thousands of others did not survive the global pandemic that followed the war.

After his funeral, with burial costs and outstanding bills paid, Johanna would receive 328 Marks from his estate, which in 1919 was only worth about £4/8/5.[201] The devaluation of the Mark throughout the war had proven punishing for his assets. Clearly Alfred had not had time to rebuild his former wealth in the wake of the slow economic years of the war. However in contrast, his uncle would, following years of tracking his whereabouts, receive Alfred's life insurance, totaling about £250.[202] Alfred had insured that at least part of his family would receive a sizable fortune, despite what the war and pandemic had wrought.

It is clear through the experiences of West and South Africans in German South West Africa between 1908 and 1914 that their place was often privileged compared to other Africans in the colony. Their wealth made them an African migrant elite, and although normally kept apart from white colonial society, the wealthiest such as business owners from West Africa were in many ways straddling both worlds. South Africans were the largest in number of the African elite during this period, making up a sizable portion of the mining and railway construction workforces. The many who worked for the railways experienced how

198 NAN, ADM [211], 237 (1), Natives Lüderitz, German Subjects, Rudolf A. Grann Togo Boy.

199 NAN, NES [004], Estate of Alfred Kulivo 5753/455, Receipt from Otto Günther, Swakopmund, 19.2.1919.

200 We will explore the effect of the war on the economy and migrant labor more in depth in Chapter 5.

201 NAN, NES [004], Estate of Alfred Kulivo 5753/455, Deceased Estate Voucher for Alfred Kulivo.

202 NAN, NES [004], Estate of Alfred Kulivo 5753/455, Letter from the African Life Assurance Society, Ltd. to the Miliary Magistrate Swakopmund, Protectorate of South West Africa, 7.2.1919.

the changing of railway management to private-military ventures could result, as it did at Wilhelmstal, in deadly violence. But in general, many profited from the high wages and diverse work possibilities in the colony. Taken as a whole, their numbers in the main industries, were only second to the Ovambo workforce. But for many in the migrant elite, the First World War would bring great economic and social change. Some migrant laborers would become involved in anti-colonial Garveyism in the Aftermath of the conflict. For Ovambo society, the First World War would be the beginning of the end of independent governance of their polities. Migrants from the north would become increasingly important to financially support the once independent region and migrants from other regions in colonial South West Africa would decrease in overall numbers. Let us now examine the end of the 'Namibian Labor Corridors' and the transition to Namibia as a South African colony.

5 The End of the ‘Namibian Labor Corridors’: War, Pandemic, Unions, and Garveyism, 1914–1925

By mid-1914, the ‘Namibian Labor Corridors’ – the system of extractive colonial capitalism in German South West Africa built on the foundations of genocide and migrant labor – had reached its zenith within the economic spheres of both Southern and Western Africa, as well as within the German empire. As mineral extraction of primarily diamonds and copper had become largely profitable, train and ship infrastructure allowed ore, workers, and products to course throughout the colonial nodes of industry and settlement. Consumerism, another engine of the colonial economy, both by settlers and the work force was increasing. By this late German colonial period, migrants in GSWA labored in mining, railway maintenance, and longshore work at the harbors. Some migrants also filled in niches that tended to be higher paying, including skilled servants for the colonial population or companies, government clerks, and occasional small business ownership.

Simultaneous with the rise in prominence of migrants within the settler zone of German South West Africa, survivors of the violence of colonial genocide began to rebuild. Herero and Nama communities largely found work on settler farms, and women, many having survived their slain menfolk, went to find work in colonial towns. Young boys, especially Hereros orphaned by war, had in large number been forced into servant roles within the colonial population and German military to survive. Other African communities that called the region home, from Damara to Baster and San, were attempting with varying degrees of success to survive within the new colonial order. GSWA’s economy and society in 1914 was largely stable thanks to economic prosperity brought about by diamonds and the use of violence to keep the peace. African laborers were caught in between the carrot of prospects of wealth, as well as the stick of the ever-present possibility of being on the receiving end of a rifle butt or bullet.

Most migrants were not integrated into local communities because they were seen as too transient. Some of course bucked this trend through intermarriage and establishing families in the settler zone, as discussed in previous chapters. Migrants by-and-large had been benefitting, at least to a certain extent, from the violence wrought upon the Herero and Nama. But by the second half of 1914, large changes would come to South West Africa, bringing together communities

https://doi.org/10.1515/9783111374918-006

that had long been in the region with those who had only entered GSWA en masse starting during the earlier war from 1904 to 1907.[1]

This last chapter will examine World War One and its aftermath in South West Africa, in particular the effect of the war on laborers, colonial capitalism, and African communities. The post-war analysis will encompass the impact of Spanish Influenza, which decimated communities starting around 1918, and it will also examine how the early 1920s witnessed glimpses of unionization, as well as a large proto-nationalist, anti-colonial, and pan-Africanist Garveyite movement. I argue that a worsening of the financial standing of many Africans and the horrors of the influenza, combined with a slow tightening of colonial control in the early 1920s, were instrumental in the rise and popularity of the Industrial and Commercial Workers' Union and the United Negro Improvement Association and African Communities League in Namibia.

In particular the UNIA, founded in 1914 by Marcus Garvey in Jamaica, soon spread to the United States and by the 1920s was growing in popularity throughout colonial Africa. Their slogan defined their goals, "Africa for the Africans, at home and abroad!" The Garveyite movement in SWA brought together local and migrant Africans in SWA in the early 1920s before it was snubbed out by the South African authorities around 1925. The focus of the chapter and book ends in this year, as it was about this date that South Africa, solidified and strengthened its hold over South West Africa. By the mid 1920's not only was SWA a Class C League of Nations Mandate under South African control, but Garveyism had also largely subsided, the Bondelswarts rebellion had been quelled, and the independence of the Ovambo polities ended with the region put under direct South African and Portuguese Angolan rule.[2]

Lastly, this period of transition to South African rule marked the shift of SWA from a colony at the center of German empire, to the periphery of the South African empire.[3] This was reflected in changes to the labor regime in the colony. As

1 This chapter encompasses the last years of German colonialism, the martial law period and early South African colonialism in Namibia. The martial law period in SWA is from the beginning of the South African military occupation of the colony in 1915 until the declaration of SWA as a Class C Mandate in 1920. The use of German South West Africa (GSWA) will apply to the period up until the South African occupation. For the period of the occupation and afterwards, South West Africa (SWA) will primarily be used. A few cases will exist whereby the region is described by its modern name Namibia as we engage with the period after this book's chronology ends.

2 Emmett, *Popular Resistance and the Roots of Nationalism in Namibia*, 122–125.

3 Although SWA was technically a mandate under South African oversight, many authors have argued that South African rule in SWA was imperial in all but name. For an analysis of the place of SWA within the larger South African empire, see Henrichsen et al., "Rethinking Empire in Southern Africa."

we shall see, Ovambo migrant labor would shift from part of a multi-pronged migrant labor system, to the overwhelming majority of migrant labor for the colony. This was solidified by both formal colonial rule established in the former Ovambo polities and the abandonment of the West and South African worker corridors (with a short-lived exception of Bechuana, Xhosa, and Basuto workers in the early to mid-1920s). Most Cape Workers had been forced out of GSWA as WWI began, ending by and large their wide participation in the economy as workers.

Under the South African government, much effort was placed on expelling West Africans remaining in the colony by the South African military occupation, although with little success. The new colonial government would focus more effort on assisting those from the Ovambo region, as well as crushing their political dissent through attempting to increase employment opportunities, food aid, and, when deemed necessary, direct military intervention.

The First World War and South African Rule in South West Africa

The First World War broke out in August of 1914 following a growing crisis that had begun in June with the assassination of Archduke Franz Ferdinand of the Austro-Hungarian empire. The war would rage for the next four years in Europe and spill over to the colonial possessions of the European powers in Africa, Asia and beyond. Although the lion's share of scholarship has focused on the war in the metropoles, growing scholarship has been written on the war in Africa.[4] Work on colonial soldiers has seen some excellent research, with Michelle Moyd's *Violent Intermediaries* as a recent keystone examining the lives of Askari soldiers in German East Africa, including during the war.[5] While the First World War in GSWA has received less attention, a few works have delved into a conflict that is often seen as a relative backwater to the European stage.[6] At the same time, World War One had a large impact on the future of the colony as rule passed from Germany to South Africa. While we will not be exploring the war in depth

4 For a general overview, see Robert Gerwarth and Erez Manela, ed., *Empires at War: 1911 – 1923* (Oxford: Oxford University Press, 2014).

5 Michelle R. Moyd, *Violent Intermediaries: African Soldiers, Conquest, and Everyday Colonialism in German East Africa*, New African Histories (Athens: Ohio University Press, 2014).

6 Gerald L'Ange, *Urgent Imperial Service: South African Forces in German South West Africa, 1914–1915* (Rivonia: Ashanti Publishers, 1991); James Stejskal, *The Horns of the Beast: The Swakop River Campaign and World War I in South-West Africa, 1914–15* (Warwick: Helion Limited, 2014).

as a military engagement, the following pages will build on scholarship that highlights individual African experiences, such as the work by Jan-Bart Gewald that explored the individual history of Mdamassi of Lagos prior to, during, and after the war.[7] However beyond the military, imperial and political significance of the war, it also played a large factor in destabilizing and then decapitating the former German colonial power base, creating ripple effects for Africans in SWA, including laborers.

The defeat of Germany in World War One led to an eventual loss of former German African colonies including GSWA but also Cameroon, Togo, and German East Africa.[8] By the early 1920s, all former German possessions in Africa were technically mandates within the recently created League of Nations.[9] However, they were colonies in all but name, split up between the British, French and for SWA: the South Africans. All of the German armies fighting on the continent had been defeated by the time of the armistice, with the exception of General Lettow-Vorbeck and 1,200 Askari troops in German East Africa, who waged a brutal but effective guerilla campaign until the end.[10] The conflict in South West Africa in contrast was far briefer. German South West Africa was invaded in August of 1914 by a primarily South African force of around 75,000 troops, which far outnumbered the *Schutztruppe*, or German protection force, of around 4,000 soldiers.[11] But what did the conflict and following colonial regime change mean for migrant workers in the colony?

As the 'guns of August' signaled bloody conflict for Europe in 1914, the German South West African administration quickly transformed the economy to a war footing. Windhoek took full control of the colony's industries including the mines, ports, and train lines to redirect their resources to the war effort. This resulted in a decision to completely stop labor recruitment in the Ovambo polities following a shutdown of the mines. Ovambo migrant laborers throughout the colony were sent back home, and most South African migrants were transported on

7 Jan-Bart Gewald, "Mbadamassi of Lagos: A Soldier for King and Kaiser, and a Deportee to German South West Africa," *African Diaspora* 2, no. 1 (May 1, 2009): 103–124.

8 These former colonies are the modern African nations of Namibia, Cameroon, Togo, part of Ghana, Tanzania, Burundi and Ruanda.

9 Mandates were former colonies of defeated powers in World War One, in which the League of Nations deemed that while they should no longer be colonies, those living in these mandates were not yet ready for self-rule. They were given signifiers A, B, C to designate how 'developed' they were on the path to self-rule. SWA was considered a C Mandate or the least ready for self-rule; see Leonard V. Smith, "Empires at the Paris Peace Conference," in *Empires at War: 1911 – 1923*, ed. Robert Gerwarth and Erez Manela (Oxford: Oxford University Press, 2014), 261–263.

10 Michelle R. Moyd, *Violent Intermediaries*, 3–4.

11 Stejskal, *The Horns of the Beast*, 2.

ship to Cape Town, and West Africans were largely forced into the service of the German military and colonial government.

The war's outbreak left most migrant labor in the colony without work or pay. The 'Namibian Labor Corridors' which had been the engine of economic growth during the period of German colonialism was over. We will first concentrate on the experience of West Africans during the conflict, as they were the one remaining group that was working in large numbers in the settler zone, albeit largely via force and coercion. We will then return to how migrant labor at large was reconstituted during the period of South African martial law.

The Cameroonian Exiles: Women as the Backbone of a Small but Tenacious West African Community in GSWA

In GSWA, those from the other German colonies were brought into the war effort. While many Togolese in the conflict do not seem to have been forcibly recruited into the military in GSWA, the experience of Cameroonians was by and large different.[12] The group from Cameroon consisted of about 50 soldiers who had served in the German imperial army in Cameroon and then revolted in July of 1909 in the town of Banyo. This uprising was put down and they and their family members, consisting of twenty-one women and seven children, were sent into exile in German South West Africa. In the GSWA statistics from January 1911, the first in which Cameroonians were counted, some in the community seemed to have potentially passed away with a total of thirty-nine men, thirteen women and six children counted in Lüderitzbucht.[13]

A few accounts exist from various Cameroonians of their experience in GSWA. According to one named Sabama, the group was initially imprisoned in Lüderitzbucht and then partially freed for supervised contract work in 1910. They were allowed to work for 15/- per month, or approximately 5/- less than most Ovambo migrant laborers. Only 3/- per month was actually given to the Cameroo-

12 This chapter will refer to all individuals that had been taken from German Cameroon to GSWA as Cameroonian although at least two were originally from Nigeria. This is not to assert that they were the same, but rather that they shared similar experiences in GSWA and formed a small community. For evidence that at least one more Nigerian in addition to Mbadamassi was part of the group in GSWA, see NAN, NES [001] 135/139, Estate of 'Ballamassy' alias Mdadamassi Lagos native, Letter from the Office of the Commandant Prisoner of War Camp at Aus to the Native Commissioner at Windhuk, 20.9.1915.

13 NAN, ZBU 172 A.VI.d Vol. 1, Population Statistics Natives and Coloreds Main Statistics, Population Statistics on the Natives and Coloreds Population at the Beginning of the Year 1911.

nian laborers in cash and the rest was kept by the government for 'safe keeping' pending their repatriation.[14] The writing of Jan-Bart Gewald highlights the experience of one individual in the group in particular, Mbadamassi, who was originally from Lagos, but through force was recruited into the German Cameroonian colonial forces.[15]

The type of work that Mbadamassi and the Cameroonian exiles did in GSWA was diverse, with some engaging in hard labor shoveling coal in the ports for tugboats, while other individuals like Mbadamassi took on more skilled roles. Likely due to his literacy and skill in the German language, he was sent to work at the supply depot at Swakopmund and then the quartermaster's office at Kolmanskop.[16] Sabama, on the other hand, was part of a small group that was sent to work at the German military outpost in the far north of the colony in the Kavango region at Kuring Kuru.[17] The approximately 3/- per month they were getting in cash was essentially starvation wages. The very small amount of pay the men received in GSWA did not account for the estates they eventually claimed to have lost during the war.

The reality was that a large amount of income claimed in the lost estates was coming from the women of the group, mainly wives of the former soldiers. While the occupation forces of South Africa initially thought the Cameroonian exiles were lying about their lost assets, the secretary of the German Magistrate confirmed that they were indeed telling the truth. Further, it was explained that much of the money the women were earning was through sex work.[18] The records include only limited amounts of information on these women, but for a few we have their names and some basic information. They included Yoki, the widow of Andreas, Kelu Nyongo, the wife of Ateba Nyongo, Menge, who was Fullah and likely had lost her husband, and Titie who was the partner of fellow Cameroonian Alexander

14 NAN, ADM [211], Natives Lüderitz 237. German Subjects. 237/13 Sabama Cameroon Native.

15 NAN, NES [003], 5753/442, Letter regarding Estate of Alexandre Jungu Cameroon Native from Native Affairs, Lüderitzbucht to the Secretary of the Protectorate, Windhuk, 31.7.1920; Gewald, "Mbadamassi of Lagos," 112.

16 Gewald, "Mbadamassi of Lagos," 114–115.

17 NAN, ADM [211], Natives Lüderitz 237. German Subjects. 237/13 Sabama Cameroon Native. Letter from the Secretary of the War Losses Commission S.W.A. to the Secretary for the Protectorate, Windhuk.

18 NAN, ADM [211], Natives Lüderitz 237. German Subjects. 237/13 Sabama Cameroon Native. Letter from the Native Affairs Department at Lüderitzbucht to the Secretary to the Protectorate, Windhuk, 17.4.1919.

Jungu.[19] The assets that these and other Cameroonian women built up during the period from 1910 to World War One were in some cases quite substantial.

One example is in the war compensation claim of the Cameroonian Ateba Nyongo, whose wife Kelu had passed by 1916.[20] However, due to Cameroonian men's low wages before the war, the size of their estate was likely because of her assets. It included four suits, two pants, one pair of riding pants, three pairs of men's shoes, two overshirts, two pocket watches, 300 marks in cash and six pairs of women's shoes, which were marked as belonging to his late wife.[21] Interestingly, in Ateba's claim he listed the costs of all the assets except Kelu's shoes. Regardless, even without the cost of those shoes included, the estate was about £32 using 1914 conversion rates. This was rather substantial and similar to the average assets of Kru laborers of the period. Another claim exists from the Cameroonian woman Menge, who was widowed. The items Menge claimed to have lost during the war were the following: two skirts, two dresses, a blouse, an apron, and a long cloth. The total estimated cost in 1914 was approximately £5 10/-. This amount, while far smaller than what Ateba claimed in his war reimbursement application, was still about five times the average estate size for Ovambo workers of the time. As with most West Africans, the Cameroonians lost their assets at the outset of the war. For Menge, she was made to work by the Germans at the hospital in

19 NAN, ADM [211], Natives Lüderitz 237. German Subjects. 237(6) Menge Woman Cameroon; NAN, NES [003], Estate of Alexander Jungen (Cameroon), Letter regarding Estate of Alexander Jungu, Cameroon Boy: Deceased from Native Affairs Department Lüderitzbucht letter to the Secretary for the Protectorate, Windhuk, 15.1.1919; NAN, ADM [211] 238, 237(4) Ateba Kamerun, List of damages from WWI to the property of Ateba, 26.2.1916; NAN, ADM [211] 237 German Subjects. 237/13 Sabama Cameroon Native. Particulars concerning 9 Cameroon Natives for Repatriation; Kelu Nyongo and a few of the Cameroonians are labelled as 'Sanaga' likely meaning they were from somewhere on the Sanaga river system in Cameroon. Others like Menge are 'Fullah' or Fulani, one of the largest ethnic groups in Cameroon; see Mark Dike DeLancey, Rebecca Neh Mbuh, and Mark W. Delancey, *Historical Dictionary of the Republic of Cameroon* (Lanham, Md.: Scarecrow Press, 2010), 186–187.

20 For all the compensation applications reviewed for this book, there is no case where the South African government awarded full reparation. The outcomes could be the result of bureaucratic bias against non-South African migrant workers. With no other records found for African migrant laborers for comparison and no bureaucratic notes arguing that the claims are exaggerated, the applications and the information regarding possessions and capital before the war will be taken at face value.

21 NAN, ADM [211] 238, 237(4) Ateba Kamerun, List of damages from World War One to the property of Ateba, 26.2.1916

Lüderitzbucht and forced to leave her things at the ordinance depot, where similar to other West Africans, her things were by the time hostilities had ended, stolen.[22]

For the Cameroonian men in GSWA at the outbreak of war in 1914, they were pushed into the service of the German military. However, unlike the Kru or Togolese, who already enjoyed many liberties in the colony, the Cameroonians were promised freedom in exchange for service with the military.[23] Given their years long forced exile, they probably saw the opportunity as potentially life changing in that they could at least hypothetically return home afterwards (if the Germans won and promises were kept). During the war they served in multiple capacities, ranging from mounted troops on oxen, to guards of both South African POWs, and local Africans interned later in the conflict.[24]

According to South African military reports, the Cameroonian soldiers were armed during the war but were not given ammunition.[25] Perhaps their German overlords feared another rebellion, especially as the war in the colony seemed more and more likely to be a losing proposition. By July 1915, when the conflict came to an end in the colony, the Cameroonian troops were captured at Grootfontein. They were sent to Aus in the south, interned with the German troops and tasked with the camp cleaning detail. It was stated by the South African military that the captured Cameroonian troops were "unfriendly to local natives," which perhaps denoted their frustration at having been forced to live in the colony for over five years.[26]

Cameroonian women, at least eleven, were on the other hand sent to Usakos where a POW and repatriation camp was established by the South Africans. According to a government document, the Cameroonian men argued their wives in Usakos were sick and starving and should therefore be transferred to join them at Aus. Three of these women were eventually released and convinced local officials to allow them to travel the 700 kilometers to Aus in order to attempt to free their menfolk.[27] Irrespective of whether their situation was as dire as argued in Usakos, their history of economically supporting the men, as well as a few being

22 NAN, ADM [211], Natives Lüderitz 237. German Subjects. 237(6) Menge Woman Cameroon, Personal Effects lost in the war, 10.3.1916.

23 NAN, NES [001] 135/139, Estate of 'Ballamassy' alias Mdadamassi Lagos native, Telegram No. I from Major Leisk Otavifontein to Major Pritchard, Windhuk, 21.7.1915.

24 Gewald, "Mbadamassi of Lagos," 115.

25 NAN, NES [001] 135/139, Estate of 'Ballamassy' alias Mdadamassi Lagos native, Telegram No. I from Major Leisk Otavifontein to Major Pritchard, Windhuk, 21.7.1915

26 NAN, NES [003] 135/139, Estate of 'Ballamassy' alias Mdadamassi Lagos native, Telegram No. II from Major Pritchard, Windhuk to Major Leisk Provost Marshall, Otavifontein, 23.7.1915

27 Gewald, "Mbadamassi of Lagos," 118–119.

able to get all the way from the north to the south of the colony to join their husbands, clearly demonstrates their strength as individuals.

The Cameroonian women in the colony, while small in number, seemed to play a large role in the economic stability of the Cameroonian exiles in GSWA, at least until the beginning of the First World War. For the community at large, they lost all or most of their assets and were pushed into increasingly challenging situations, from internment camps to economic precarity. Many of the men during the martial law period were made to work for the South African Railways (SAR), and some in the community asked for both compensation of war loses as well as repatriation to West Africa. For some, like Mbadamassi who died in September of 1917, the process of waiting for repatriation took too long, and his forced stay in GSWA became his permanent resting place.[28] By the early mandate years of formal South African rule over SWA, the remaining Cameroonians' situation seems to have not improved. A 1921 letter written by Petrus Auma and Ateba Nyongo on behalf of the Cameroonian community at Lüderitzbucht stated:

> [W]e have been deported from Cameroon to South West Africa for a time of seven years . . . there is at present, and also in the near future no chance to get any employment . . . . Soon after occupation of South West Africa by the Union Forces we have been informed by the former German Government, that from the new Administration free passages will be granted to us.[29]

For Ateba, Petrus, and others who wished to return home to the portion of Cameroon that had been under French rule since the early 1920s, their repatriation was denied by the French administration. Commissioner Hardy of the French Republic based in Yaounde wrote, "[t] he natives in question were deported to S.W. Africa for breach of discipline or offences against common law and their return to Camerun appears undesirable to me."[30] Such refusals were devastating and point to some remaining in SWA. By 1922, 10 Cameroonian men, nine women

28 He unfortunately never made it back to Nigeria and died while awaiting repatriation in Lüderitzbucht on 7.9.1917; see NAN, NES [001] 135/139, Estate of 'Ballamassy' alias Mdadamassi Lagos native, Letter from the Secretary for the Protectorate Herbst to the Government Secretary in Lagos, Nigeria 9.10.1917.

29 NAN, SWAA [2233] A.494/2, Native Affairs, Repatriation of Kroo Boys, Letter from Petrus Auma and Ateba Nyongo at Lüderitzbucht, to the Administrator of the Protectorate at Windhuk, 27.6.1921.

30 NAN, SWAA [2233] A.494/2, Native Affairs, Repatriation of Kroo Boys, Translation of Letter from Commissioner Hardy of the French Republic at Yaounde to the Secretary for Southwest Africa at Windhoek, 30.5.1922.

and five children remained, all in or around Lüderitzbucht.[31] Records have not yet been found about whether Cameroonian women returned to sex work in the South African colonial period, but the letter by Ateba and Petrus pointed to continued work challenges for the men. Unfortunately, the Cameroonian men were not the only ones forced into the service of the German military during the war.

The Fall of the Kru Labor Elite and Challenges Under South African Rule

At the beginning of World War One, Kru workers were labelled as 'alien natives', arrested by the German authorities, and forced into different positions to serve the government and army. One such West African was Hocky, a Kru man from Liberia who filed a personal effect claim for items lost in the war in September of 1920. He wrote:

> I came here in 1911. I worked for Woermann-Linie at outbreak of war. When I left Swakop I went to Nonidas by orders of Woermann-Linie then to Omaruru then to Aub then to Otjiwarongo and Khorab. I was cutting grass and looking after oxen. I got no money. I left my things with Woermann-Linie and when I came back everything was gone . . . . In time of war we were forced to be sent into country so I asked my master if I can take my things along with me so my master said no he is going to look after my things, when I came back I asked my master. He said I have to wait till the war is over.[32]

Hocky's possessions before the war included black suit trousers, two pairs of boots, a table lamp, multiple shirts, a cap, a Panama hat, and cash worth around £7. In his application for reimbursement, he listed his total assets before the war at just over £24, or slightly under the Kru average for the late German period.[33] As a result of his application for reimbursement, Hocky received £10, or less than half of his estate's previous worth.

The above recollection of eight months of unpaid forced work for the Germans was common for almost all Kru in the colony. They were required to work without pause while shadowing the military until the German surrender in July 1915. Their tasks included grazing horses, cutting grass, assisting troops, guarding POW camps, and mail delivery.[34] Simultaneous with their forced labor, Kru like Hocky were or-

31 NAN, SWAA [2233] A.494/2, Native Affairs, Repatriation of Kroo Boys, Prime Minister's Office, Minute No. 230, 28.3.1922, 1–2.

32 NAN, ADM [238] SWAKOP264/24, hocky Kroo Boy, 2–3.

33 NAN, ADM [238] SWAKOP264/24, hocky Kroo Boy, 3–4.

34 NAN, ADM [238] SWAKOP264/ 1–42; NAN, ADM [211] 238 1–23.

dered to leave their possessions and assets on the coast at their places of employment, in Swakopmund and Lüderitzbucht. As Hocky's account makes clear, after hostilities ended and they received permission from the South African military administration to return, they found their belongings were gone. The West Africans' possessions were likely stolen by either South African forces, German settlers or possibly even their former employers.

Following the South African military occupation, the economy slowly restarted. However, the 1918 arrival of the Spanish influenza laid waste to the workforce and threatened the colony's economic stability. Many had thought that the coming of the South African military in 1915 would mean more freedom for Africans and some even dreamt of self-rule.[35] But by the 1920s, as the South African colonial regime formalized its control, it became clear that these dreams would not be realized.

For Kru during the Union occupation from 1915 to 1920, their economic status changed dramatically. Records show that the average Kru who applied for war damage reimbursements, received only half of his lost estate.[36] Compounding this economic thrashing, in the years during the military occupation between 1917 and 1920, records for Kru workers who died show that average estate sizes were between £5 and £6. This is under half of their pre-war average.[37] The occupation period saw West Africans finding work for the South African Railways, repairing lines destroyed by the Germans in retreat. In 1916, railway lines were also built connecting Swakopmund to the South African controlled port to its south at Walvis Bay, which had a natural harbor. A 1916 South African report from the military occupation government stated:

> There is naturally a great deal of speculation amongst the German merchants and other property owners at Swakopmund regarding the future of that town . . . . The advantages of Walvis Bay as a port are however, so immeasurably superior to those possessed by Swakopmund that from the trading point of view, the fate of the latter place is sealed, and it will develop into a seaside resort for the Northern districts of the Protectorate . . . .[38]

As for longshore work which had been dominated by the Kru before the war:

---

35 Emmett, *Popular Resistance and the Roots of Nationalism in Namibia*, 148.

36 NAN, ADM [238] SWAKOP264/ 1–42, ADM [211] 238 1–23.

37 Lyon, *Namibian Worker Database*; 30 Kru files in the database of workers who died between 1917–1920.

38 NASA, GG 606 File D.B. 30/1723/9199: 'Report of the Administrator of the Protectorate of South West Africa, 1916', 27–28.

> A number of men previously engaged on the large re-inforced concrete jetty which the German authorities were constructing when the war broke out, are of course now idle, and the same may be said of the men formerly occupied on harbor and landing work. Under these circumstances it is surprising that the indigent list is not far larger.[39]

As for why the unemployment lists were not greater for the port town, increased demand for temporary railway labor most likely provided per-diem work. Furthermore, Walvis Bay's harbor likely absorbed others. However, the neighboring South African port, having already been a functioning harbor before the conflicts' outbreak, probably filled most of its labor demand with prior staff. *Woermann-Linie*'s operations at Swakopmund were in stasis as the occupational government kept them in forced shutdown. During the period since the beginning of the war the company increasingly relied on a credit line from Deutsche Afrika Bank, which put a limit on the salary and pay they could give to their remaining workers.[40]

From the beginning of November 1916, all Africans living in Swakopmund, including the Kru, were ordered by the military occupation to move to the 'location' (township): one and half kilometers north of town. While ostensibly the move was for health reasons, it was opposed by the local town government. In actuality, the likelihood of becoming sick for Africans who had lived in town and were forced to the 'location' increased. The substandard housing and living conditions there were exacerbated by the damp and cold climate. The 1916 *Woermann-Linie* report states that tumult erupted in the 'location' and the South African police opened fire and killed two Africans.[41] For the Kru living in formerly booming pre-war Swakopmund, 1916 brought an increasing likelihood of unemployment and deteriorating living conditions.

The other former Kru hub of employment, Lüderitzbucht, was also suffering economically. According to a 1916 report by the occupational government, the town "was largely dependent upon the forwarding of trade with the interior, but the linking up of the Protectorate railways with the Union Systems has caused a considerable decrease in the volume of this business, as storekeepers inland for the most part now import direct by rail from the Union."[42] Later it mentions that in Keetmanshoop, east of Lüderitzbucht, "quantities of beers, wines, spirits, food stuff, clothing and other articles of merchandise have been imported into the District from the Cape Province. Before the outbreak of the present war practically

39 NASA, GG 606 File D.B. 30/1723/9199: 'Report of the Administrator of the Protectorate of South West Africa, 1916', 42.

40 SSS, Woermann-Linie Jahresbericht (Swakopmund, 1916), 4.

41 SSS, Woermann-Linie Jahresbericht (Swakopmund, 1916), 18–19.

42 SSS, Woermann-Linie Jahresbericht (Swakopmund, 1916), 34.

the whole of the articles imported into the Protectorate were from Germany."[43] While it would go on to mention almost full employment in the Lüderitzbucht district, the long-term implications for its harbor were clear. The town's recent connection with South Africa's railway infrastructure decreased its importance as a port, and with it its need for the same number of skilled West African longshoremen as before. But what did the economic, political, and societal upheavals in the protectorate between 1915 and 1920 mean for the long-term prospects of the Kru?

As for work, the most easily accessible opportunities were repairing and extending the lines of the South African Railways. The SAR absorbed many laborers who otherwise had lost their former jobs.[44] This translated into high levels of employment even if much of it would only last through 1916. But for the military government, local Africans were a priority, especially as the Union of South Africa made its case for the colony to come under its oversight following the end of the First World War.

The Early SWA Labor Regime and 'Native Affairs' Under South African Rule

The South African goal to separate themselves from prior German mistreatment of the local African population, especially concerning the German 1904 to 1908 genocide of the Herero and Nama, was made clear in their publication of the "Blue Book" report in January of 1918.[45] The report highlighted German atrocities primarily through interviews of African survivors. In contrast to what the book argued was the German mistreatment of the local population, the Union sought to better manage local African affairs. Their goal was not made easier as famine affected the largest group of migrant laborers in the protectorate from the northern Ovambo polities. The so-called "famine that swept" in 1915 occurred simultaneously with an onslaught of Portuguese colonial rule in Angola to the north, which "created a famine of such devastating proportions that henceforth Ovambo would have to move elsewhere to make a living."[46] The catastrophe led thousands of Ovambo to move to the settler region in order to survive. For the government

43 NASA, GG 606 File D.B. 30/1723/9199: "Report of the Administrator of the Protectorate of South West Africa for the Year 1916," 31.

44 NASA, GG 606 File D.B. 30/1723/9199: "Report of the Administrator of the Protectorate of South West Africa for the Year 1916," 46.

45 Silvester and Gewald, *Words Cannot Be Found*, xix.

46 Jan-Bart Gewald, "Near Death in the Streets of Karibib: Famine, Migrant Labour and the Coming of Ovambo to Central Namibia," *Journal Of African History* 44, no. 2 (2003): 212–213.

coping with the crises, work and provisions for Ovambo migrants were the priority. By comparison, West Africans in the colony were essentially given no assistance because of their non-local status. That being said, Ovambos, including the high numbers fleeing the famine, could not match demand. The secretary of the Protectorate wrote in October 1916 that "the Railway Department is about 1100 short of their complement of Natives, and that the Mines require at least another 1000 . . . ."[47] Data taken from the 1915 to 1920 period, in particular estate files, clearly denote the new post-war migrant labor force, which had become overwhelmingly dominated by Ovambo workers.

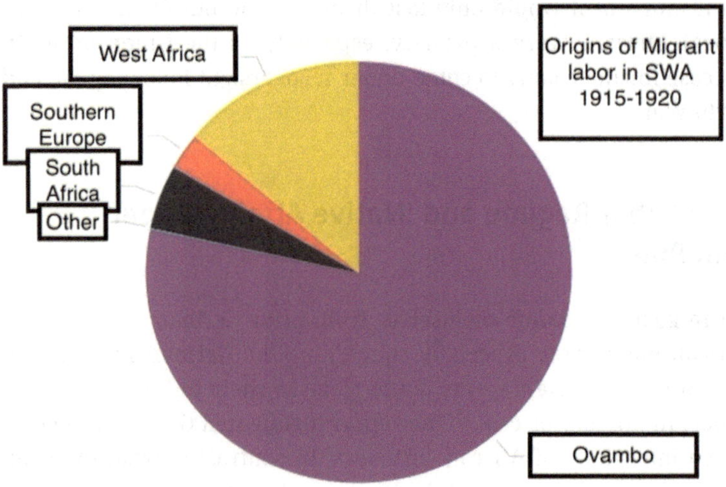

Figure 54: Approximate breakdown of migrant labor in SWA between 1915–1920.[48]

The above pie chart (Figure 54) clearly shows us that in the martial law period about 80 percent of all migrant labor now consisted of those coming from the Ovambo region, where the population was largely suffering from famine. The overall migrant labor composition of the post-war period varied distinctly from the 1908 to 1914 German period, where about one third of migrant labor was coming from the other, for-

47 NAN, ADM [77], Herbst in Windhuk, 14 Nov. 1916, to Gage, Karibib. From Gewald, "Near Death in the Streets of Karibib," 234.
48 Compiled from the *Namibian Worker Database* and the following files, NAN, NES [001]; NAN, NES [002]; NAN, NES [003]; NAN, NES [004]; NAN, NES [005]; NAN, NES [006]; NAN, NES [007]; NAN, ADM [51] 675: 5. Repatriation General; NAN, ADM [211] 237, Natives Lüderitz, German Subjects; NAN, ADM [238] SWAKOP264.

mer recruitment labor corridors of South and West Africa. One reason Ovambo workers were again headed south, after the German defeat was not only the result of famine, but changes in the politics of the region. Most dramatic was the 1917 killing of King Mandume of the Oukwanyama Kingdom by South African forces.

By the last years of German rule, and after years of reforms and attempts at lessening the Kingdom of Oukwanyama's economic reliance on migrant labor, Mandume increasingly viewed his policies as anticolonial.[49] By 1914, the Portuguese wished to crush the increasingly rebellious Oukwanyama Kingdom, which encompassed the border region of both Angola and SWA. With some victories but facing long term setbacks, Mandume had received a treaty of protection from the newly arrived South African forces in SWA by September of 1915. Oukwanyama had lost their territory in Angola, and Mandume moved his capital and government from Angola to SWA in the still-contested border region. In the following year, Mandume conducted raids into the newly Portuguese territory within Angola that was formerly under his rule. As a result of these anti-colonial policies, as well as Mandume's policy of increasingly concentrating power around his Kingship, he was progressively seen as troublesome not only to the Portuguese, but to the South Africans as well. Eventually, both Portugal and South Africa wished to have him removed from power. A December 1916 ultimatum to surrender to the South Africans was sent to Mandume, which he refused. By early 1917, it was decided that a South African expedition would be sent to Oukwanyama to defeat Mandume with Portuguese assistance if necessary. A large expeditionary force of over 800 troops entered Mandume's territory, and in a battle near Ehole, the South African forces – which greatly outnumbered their foe – killed Mandume in battle.[50]

No King was to replace him, and in the years following his death the independence of all the Ovambo polities deteriorated both north and south of the border. By the mid-1920s all the former Ovambo polities, including the region referred to as Ovamboland in SWA would come under formal colonial rule. From the perspective of the new South African colonizers, the primary purpose of the region was clear, as a labor supply pool for the colonial economy of the settler region.[51] This meant that by the mid-1920s, the occasional push back from various Ovambo leaders, against colonial migrant labor policies was now all but a thing of the past. Remaining leaders, such as King Martin ka Dikwa of the Ondonga, and prominent headmen were in power only with South African consent.

49 Hayes, "Order out of Chaos," 97–103.

50 Hayes, "A History of the Ovambo of Namibia, c 1880–1935," 233–235; for a detailed overview of the last year's of King Mandume's reign and his downfall, see Jeremy Silvester, *My Heart Tells Me That I Have Done Nothing Wrong: The Fall of Mandume.* (Windhoek: Discourse, 1995).

51 Hayes, "A History of the Ovambo of Namibia, c 1880–1935," 237–240.

The Ovambo migrants who were coming south for contract labor in the early years of South African rule consisted of a similar demographic to the late German colonial period.[52] Also coming from the north of the colony, were a very small number of workers, about one percent from the Kavango region. This mirrors the late German colonial period in which workers from the Kavango were never more than approximately 100 per year.[53] Only later in Namibian history, in the 1930s, did Kavango labor increase to non-trivial numbers.[54]

As can be seen below (Figure 55), most workers were coming from Oukwanyama, followed by Ondonga. Both kingdoms had been essential in supplying workers during German colonialism and continued to be during this transition period. The two largest polities accounted for around 75 percent of all transition period labor, but the dataset also includes information on workers from the polities of Uukwaluudhi, Ombandja, Ongandjera, Evale and Uukwambi, which together made up approximately 25 percent of the Ovambo workforce. Laborers from these smaller and primarily western political entities joined the migrant labor system in larger numbers during this period most likely because of the worsening drought and the formalization of South African colonialism. These workers from outside the dominant Oukwanyama and Ondonga Kingdoms had larger estates at about £1 10/- compared to the total Ovambo average at just under £1. While cause for this cannot be stated with certainty, there is reason to believe that because polities from the west began to send workers in larger numbers to the south only after World War One, laborers who did go may have on average been more fit for work. They therefore may have garnered slightly higher wages than those from Oukwanyama and Ondonga.

Included in the colonial categorization of workers from the north are just under 5 percent labelled as 'Portuguese natives', or put in other terms, those who came from Angola. While the border between colonial Namibia and Angola was undecided at the time and would indeed change in the 1920s, this designation of who were considered 'Portuguese natives,' between 1916 and 1920 is an insight into the administration's labelling of who was within their relative sphere of control. The term 'Portuguese native' most often is connected to the worker either being from Evale, which was deep within decided Angolan territory, or their being from Oukwanyama and Ombandja, which both straddled this yet undecided border zone.

52 Hayes, "A History of the Ovambo of Namibia, c 1880–1935," 243.
53 Eckl, "Konfrontation und Kooperation am Kavango (Nord-Namibia) von 1891 bis 1921," 120.
54 Kletus Muhena Likuwa, "Colonialism and the Development of the Contract Labour System in Kavango," in *Re-Viewing Resistance in Namibian History*, ed. Jeremy Silvester (Windhoek, Namibia: University of Namibia Press, 2015), 105–126.

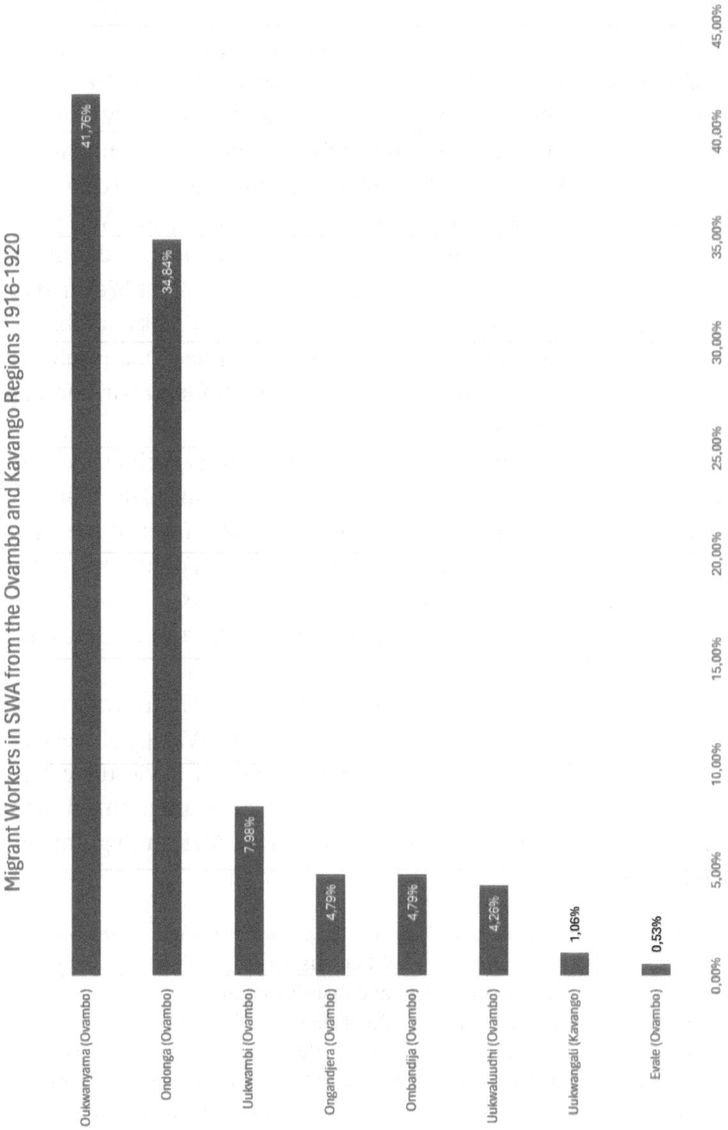

Figure 55: Breakdown of Ovambo workers in the police zone from 1916–1920 during the martial law period.[55]

55 Compiled from the *Namibian Worker Database* and the following files, NAN, NES [001]; NAN, NES [002]; NAN, NES [003]; NAN, NES [004]; NAN, NES [005]; NAN, NES [006]; NAN, NES [007].

Irrespective of where Ovambo workers came from, all who were labelled 'Portuguese native' during the 1915 to 1920 period had smaller estates than those considered 'local natives.' This may be coincidence or due to less previous contract work in SWA. As time progressed, numbers of recruits from Angola would only increase. The work of Bernard C. Moore on labor recruits to SWA in the mid twentieth century shows that by the late 1940s until 1970 between 20 to over 55 percent were coming from Angola.[56] Much of this would be due to preferable pay in SWA as well as the economic instability of Angola during its War of Independence that made contract work to the south increasingly attractive. In short, the First World War, Portuguese colonial policy, and the occupation of SWA by South Africa all formed the foundation for the dissolution of independent Ovambo polities. One result was that formal colonial rule in the north of SWA led to the Ovambo Labor Corridor providing a plurality of workers in the settler region.

For the African migrant elite who remained in the colony, primarily West Africans, the martial law period made their lives increasingly difficult. Work existed for the Kru in the early years of the occupation but often not of the same pay grade or in the same industry as their pre-war positions. For West Africans who did secure long-term work, it was mainly with the railways. As many goods were now shipped by rail from South Africa, the ports required much less longshoreman labor.

Kru workers' waning status, difficulties in the occupied colony with work, and an inability to easily leave for home because of World War One, were all compounded by growing desires by the occupying government to rid the colony of West African 'undesirables.' The South African government often linked them to social disorder and voiced open disdain toward the West African migrants exemplified in the following letter from 1916:

> [I]t would be very greatly [sic] to the benefit of the Protectorate if some means could be found of returning the Kroo boys to Liberia . . . . While it is true they are handy at harbours etc . . . they are such born and inveterate thieves and rascals that they are a constant source of worry . . . . I have convicted at the very least 30 of them . . . for theft . . . . [T]hey have also been convicted for being in possession of liquor . . . the railways naturally refuse to re-engage them and I have great difficulty in getting rid of them. I believe most of them are desirous of returning home and several have already spoken to me on the subject.[57]

---

56 Bernard C. Moore, "Smuggled Sheep, Smuggled Shepherds: Farm Labour Transformations in Namibia and the Question of Southern Angola, 1933–1975," *Journal of Southern African Studies* 47, no. 1 (January 2, 2021): 93–125.

57 NAN, SWAA [2233] A. 494/2, Liberians in S.W.A. Protectorate, 10.08.1916 Letter from the Military Magistrate to the Secretary of the Protectorate.

While some indeed wished to return home and others wished to stay, government representatives had a crueler suggestion for the West Africans in the colony. The Secretary of the Magistrate of Swakopmund and Walvis Bay recommended in 1917 that the Kru be sent to the Native Labour Contingent in France serving in the First World War.[58] Regardless of Kru difficulties, it is apparent that with or without consent, the government was intent on trying to repatriate or send them elsewhere, even if that meant into a war zone.

While the landscape had changed for Kru in the colony, opportunities back in West Africa did not offer a promising alternative. The First World War brought economic collapse to Liberia as its former trading partners, including Germany, no longer called at its ports. From 1915 to 1916 the powerful coastal Kru towns of Liberia staged an uprising against the central government. They cited an inability to pay taxes to Monrovia because of decreased economic activity as a central reason for the revolt.[59] Though the Kru were wealthy, skilled, and well-armed, they were no match for a Liberian government that was backed by the United States' military might. The intervention of the American cruiser *Chester* as well as US officers to assist the Liberian Frontier Force led to the eventual defeat of the Kru uprising.[60] The resulting victory by Monrovia "led to reprisals, devastation of the coast, and exile for many, with the effects lasting well into the twentieth century."[61]

A Pandemic Arrives: Spanish Influenza

In South West Africa, the last two years of the occupation, 1918 and 1919, were plagued by Spanish Influenza. This disease ravaged the population and perhaps made clear that there would be no return to the pre-war status quo for the Kru. As M.C. Musambachime has written, "[t]he Herero called it 'Kapitohanga' because it killed people fast[er] than the bullet."[62] This disease came on the heels of the end of the First World War and resulted in a massive number of deaths in colonial SWA. Statistics vary, but mortality rates in sub-Saharan Africa were between

58 NAN, SWAA [2233] A. 494/2, Liberians in the Protectorate, 04.08.1917 Letter from the Secretary of Native Affairs to the Secretary of the Protectorate.

59 Jo Mary Sullivan, "The Kru Coast Revolt of 1915–1916," *Liberian Studies Journal* 14, no. 1 (1989): 59.

60 Sullivan, "The Kru Coast Revolt of 1915–1916," 61.

61 Sullivan, "The Kru Coast Revolt of 1915–1916," 51.

62 M. Chambikabalenshi Musambachime, "'Kapitohanga: The Disease That Killed Faster than Bullets': The Impact of the Influenza Pandemic in the South West Africa Protectorate (Namibia) from October 1918 to December 1919" (Basel: Basler Afrika Bibliographien, 2000), 2.

five and 10 percent of the population.[63] It arrived in October 1918 via a train on its way from De Aar in the Northern Cape to Windhoek. The train staff and crew had the first symptoms followed by cases breaking out simultaneously in Keetmanshoop, Windhoek, and Karibib.[64] From there it spread throughout the colony and resulted in the death of a large number of migrant workers in both 1918 and the following year. Highlighting the point, of all the estate records for non-white workers in SWA between 1917 and 1920, just under half cite "Spanish influenza" as the cause of death.[65] The outbreak amongst the Ovambo population compounded the already difficult famine in the North. The effect on the Kru population over those years was also significant. Among the records of Kru deaths in the Protectorate between 1917 and 1920, approximately 40 percent were due to the Spanish influenza.[66] One such victim was Teeplalty alias 'Tom Glasgow' who died in October 1918.

Teeplalty was a Kru man from Monrovia who worked in Lüderitzbucht for the South Africa Railway Department. When he died, he possessed a modest number of things, especially in comparison to West Africans before the war. In contrast to colleagues prior to the conflict, he had no suits, no Panama hats, and no luxury items such as a record player. His most expensive possession was a watch, worth 15/-. Tom's total estate was £5 5/- after the sale of his personal effects, which is just about average for Kru who died during that period.[67] Within his file is also a letter from his brother, Teeplah Teah written from Freetown, Sierra Leone.

The letter was written before Teeplalty's death and relayed news of loss from home. Both Teeplah Teah's daughter and the two brothers' sister had died.[68] The influenza, while not referred to directly, was affecting both sides of the family, in West Africa and, unbeknownst to the sender, in SWA. The letter, typical of many sent to migrant laborers in SWA in the early twentieth century, combined news of births and deaths with a request for money. Teeplah states:

---

63 Musambachime, "'Kapitohanga: The Disease That Killed Faster than Bullets,'" 3.

64 NASA, GG 606 File a. 33/3370/3: "South West Protectorate Report of the Administrator for the Year, 1918," 53.

65 Lyon, *Namibian Worker Database*; NAN, NES [001]; NAN, NES [002]; NAN, NES [003]; NAN, NES [004]; NAN, NES [005]; NAN, NES [006]; NAN, NES [007].

66 Lyon, *Namibian Worker Database.*

67 NAN, NES [003], 5753-435 Estate Tom Glasglow, Deceased Estate; Kru decreases in estate sizes contrast quite clearly with Ovambo workers, whose average estate at around £1 remained essentially the same as before the war.

68 NAN, NES [003], 5753-435 Estate Tom Glasglow, 01.06.1918 Letter to Teeplalty from Teeplay Teah, 2.

> I am now in Freetown Sierra Leone and am hard up in every way. It is proper for you to send money to me here . . . . I will keep it save [sic] until you come . . . . Please reply me at once and please don't sent it empty [sic]. Our brother Kpameh Dae who had the headman job had refused to give me a chance . . . .[69]

Additionally, Teeplah Teah used social pressure in an attempt to influence his brother to act by mentioning that 'friends' had been sending '40 pounds or more so' back home.[70] If he was writing about South West Africa, this is most likely an exaggeration or untrue. Whether Teeplah was attempting to trigger feelings of sadness and guilt to get money, or his grievances were heartfelt, he would not succeed, at least not as intended, because of his brother's death. Teeplalty's file mentions his wife, but there is no detailed information on her whereabouts. It is not certain where the estate of around £5 was sent. The family difficulties both in West and South West Africa were without doubt. The account, while limited, gives a family's perspective on the Kru community's increasing challenges related to work, money and disease that had been compounding since late 1914. The estate of Teeplalty and other Kru whose data exists in the archival record show that in comparison to the years before the First World War, their average assets had shrunk dramatically.

With the end of the Spanish Influenza outbreak by 1920 and the creation of a South African civil administration in South West Africa, relative stability for the colony seemed on the horizon. But for local Africans, the defeat of the Germans and transition to South African control had not led to widespread change in the colony as many had thought possible. In the early years of the South African occupation, those who in particular had suffered under the genocide saw the new situation as an opportunity to regain lands lost. One Herero man, Fridoline Kazombiaze who spoke in the 1940s on the matter explained:

> What we don't understand is that when two nations have been at war, such as Britain or Germany or Italy, and when one or another of those nations is defeated the lands belonging to that nation are not taken away from them. The nation remains a nation, and their lands belong to them. The African people although they have always been on the side of the British people and their allies, yet have their lands taken away from them and we are treated as though they had been conquered.[71]

69 NAN, NES [003], 5753-435 Estate Tom Glasglow, 01.06.1918 Letter to Teeplalty from Teeplay Teah, 4–5.

70 NAN, NES [003], 5753-435 Estate Tom Glasglow, 01.06.1918 Letter to Teeplalty from Teeplay Teah, 4–5.

71 Testimony of Fridoline kazombiaze, M. Scott, In the face of fear: Documents relating to the appeal to the United Nations of the Herero and other South West African people against incorpo-

Frustrations after the First World War and the defeat of the Germans were not only held by the Herero. Many Africans began to search for an alternative future including the migrant laborers in the police zone.

Economic Challenges lead to New Solutions: Industrial and Commercial Workers' Union (ICU) and the United Negro Improvement Association (UNIA) in South West Africa

In the early 1920s, SWA's economic situation was particularly unstable. By 1921, Inflation was on the rise, and there were acute shortages of labor. The diamond mines saw a drastic decrease in their output as well as employment in 1921 and 1922 as the global diamond market slumped, making the economic situation of the Lüderitzbucht area more difficult.[72] Ovambo labor was, at least temporarily, hard to recruit. The newly created Consolidated Diamond Mines (CDM) which now controlled the SWA diamond fields, looked further afield for labor. Recruitment ranged from the Bechuanaland colony, and South Africa itself, specifically employing Xhosa and Basuto workers.[73] The overall numbers of these Southern African migrants to SWA's diamond fields in the 1920s would peak at around 2,818 Bechuana and Basuto workers in 1923. But these numbers were highly unstable and would decrease to 1,900 by 1924. 'Re-engagement' or signing up for new contracts after fulfilling the prior one was proving very low for both workers from Bechuanaland and the Union.[74] While the situation was looking unfavorable for heavy industry in the early 1920s, it was local workers, especially within the agricultural sector of the southern districts, that likely felt the economic blow hardest.

---

ration in the Union of South Africa and for the restitution of their tribal lands (Johannesburg: M. Scott), 1948, in Emmett, *Popular Resistance and the Roots of Nationalism in Namibia*, 86.

72 NAN, AP 4/1/2, South West Africa Report 1923, 8; the diamond production in SWA went from 606,423 Carats in 1920, to 171,321 in 1921, and bottoming out at 144,156 Carats in 1922. Output then began to rise in 1923 but would not attain 1920 levels by 1925, see chart of diamond mine production in SWA from 1909 to 1925, in NAN, AP 4/1/2, South West Africa Report 1925, 64.

73 CDM was created in the wake of WWI as a way of buying out most SWA German mine owners and bringing the mines under one company. It was the brain child of South African Ernest Oppenheimer who eventually was able to leverage his growing power to take control of the South African diamond mine behemoth De Beers; see Press, *Blood and Diamonds*, 201, 226–230; for contemporary details on the early creation of CDM see, NAN, AP 4/1/2, South West Africa Report 1922, 51.

74 NAN, AP 4/1/2, South West Africa Report 1924, 23.

In the Warmbad district, male workers were averaging about 15/- and females 10/- per month with food, drastically less than the mainly migrant men working in mine labor. While such low wages in the agricultural sector were not new, the bad economy exacerbated their plight. Instances in the districts of Gibeon and Maltahöhe were coming to light where white farmers, faced with drought and no market to sell their stock, were paying workers in IOUs that were not redeemed at the end of contracts. As a result, impoverishment of Africans in these districts was common.[75] Although premised by a snarky remark that the cost of living had gone up for everyone in SWA, Native Affairs Department of Lüderitzbucht summed up the situation for many Africans well in 1921 by writing:

> All he knows is that he has to pay perhaps 100% more for food and clothing than he did before the war, that though he may have received a 25% advance in wages he is more often hungry than before, and that it is probably the fault of the white man . . . .[76]

The harsh conditions referenced above had already led to push back by workers starting in 1920. In that year both local and migrant Africans began to join in a common purpose. As highlighted in the work of Lucien van der Walt, in May there was a large strike at the Charlottental diamond mine of around 250 Ovambo workers, and a handful of South Africans. It spread to other mines drawing in a variety of workers including some Kru, Nama and "coloured" people. Their strike was unsuccessful, and most Ovambo returned to work, while many of the migrants were deported. One South African who was not deported but banned from work on the diamond mines, would go on to be a key figure in the establishment of the Industrial and Commercial Workers' Union (ICU) in SWA, Jimmy La Guma.[77] He and other South Africans, as well as an Afro-Caribbean storekeeper, and a Nama man would be founding members of the Lüderitzbucht arm of the union. Later a branch would be opened in Keetmanshoop, and van der Walt notes ICU outposts in Walvis Bay as well as the diamond town of Elizabeth Bay by the mid-1920s.[78]

The organization had been founded in Bloemfontein, South Africa and was headquartered at Cape Town. It had a multi-ethnic makeup in South West Africa

75 NAN, AP 4/1/2, South West Africa Report 1924, 21–23.

76 NAN, ADM [152], C.248, Industrial Coloured Workers Union, Letter from the Native Affairs Department Lüderitzbucht to the Secretary of South West Africa, Lüderitzbucht, re: Native Unions. S.W.A., 30.5.1921.

77 Lucien van der Walt, "The ICU, the Mines and the State in South West Africa, 1920–1926: Garveyism, Revolutionary Syndicalism and Global Labour History," in *Labour Struggles in Southern Africa, 1919–1949 New Perspectives on the Industrial and Commercial Workers' Union (ICU)*, ed. David Johnson, Noor Nieftagodien, and Lucien van der Walt (Cape Town: HSRC Press, 2023), 10–12.

78 van der Walt, "The ICU, the Mines and the State in South West Africa, 1920–1926," 14.

but was primary led by South African workers in the protectorate. The organization's goals were clear as a charter document in SWA displays:

> The object of this Union shall be to protect and regulate the conditions of work in the trade and to promote the general and material welfare of the members of the Union by such means as
>
> a. Strong organization of all workers, male and female, (coloured and native) and to see that the Union undertakes a scheme of extending the I.C.U. throughout the Union of South Africa.
> b. To see that all females in industries are protected by the Trade Union Organisation by encouraging them to enrol in all branches of the I.C.U. and to help them obtain a living wage
> c. To see that the I.C.U. co-operates with the worker of other unions for the advancement of the whole working class.
> d. By co-operation insurance, sick and out of work benefits, old age pensions, and by such other means as the I.C.U. may from time to time determine.[79]

While the ICU focused on higher wages and better living conditions, it remained confined to a few locations in SWA. Further, it was primarily organized to improve the lives of those laboring in the larger industries such as mining and railway work. This meant that many other African laborers, including on farms, could not – at least directly – benefit from potential advances to be made by the ICU. Women, while explicitly mentioned in the document above, also benefited little as male workforces dominated the industries targeted for union membership. Further, starting with its arrival, the magistrate in Lüderitzbucht actively pushed to stop its spread by threatening the deportation of any South African members who were looking to recruit Ovambo laborers.[80]

The ICU had leadership dominated by Cape Workers, with John Declue, treasurer and representing SWA at the ICU Port Elizabeth 1921 conference, and William Andrianse, the SWA secretary of the union, being some of the most central figures in addition to La Guma.[81] The Cape Worker centric leadership was not surprising as the organization originated and was centered in the Union of South Africa. A 1922 Lüderitzbucht Native Affairs report explained participation in the ICU as follows: "The Capeboys and Cape Coloured people are, owing to their pecu-

79 NAN, ADM [152], C.248, Charter Document of the ICU in SWA, 3.

80 NAN, ADM [152], C.248, Industrial Coloured Workers Union, Letter from Magistrate of Lüderitzbucht to the Secretary of South West Africa, Activities of the Industrial & Commercial Workers Union, Lüderitzbucht, 5.1.1920.

81 NAN, ADM [152], C.248, Industrial Coloured Workers Union, Copy of article from the Eastern Province Herald, Port Elizabeth, Cape of Good Hope, 25.10.1921, Coloured and Native Workers. Conference of the I.C.U. Presidential Address. Riot Commemoration Service, 1; NAN, ADM [152], C.248, ICU letter from W. Adrianse to Clements Kadalie, 19.1.1922.

liar social status, bound to chafe under certain of our present laws, and the fact that they are, here, debarred from some of the privileges their class enjoys at the Cape, is an added grievance."[82] Although Cape Workers made up a large portion of the organization, the ICU also had some effect on pushing the new South African government to respond, at least officially, to grievances. In March of 1922, Native Affairs was pressured to launch a full inquiry into complains that the SWA chapters had brought to the 1921 ICU conference in Port Elizabeth.[83] Although the organization was an attempt to expand and protect African workers' rights in SWA from the early to mid 1920s, it clearly was limited in scope. Nevertheless, symbolically and in some ways tangibly, the ICU was important in the history of early, formalized African labor organization in SWA. The ICU membership also bled over to the UNIA and played a significant role in contributing to the Garveyite movement. Both shared similar goals and at their core were fighting for a betterment of the economic and societal position of Africans in South West Africa.

It was the UNIA, which came to the colony in the same year as the ICU, that melded local anti-colonial grievances and yearning for communal improvement with a global vision for African unity and liberation. It also had a larger support base than the ICU, gaining membership not just in the main settlements of the south, but across the colony and even in the rural farm areas. Whereas the ICU had a pre-ponderance of South African migrant representation in SWA, the UNIA had an outsized number of West African leaders and members in its SWA chapters. Among those in the UNIA were both Togolese and Kru. We have discussed how some Togolese in the late-German and post-war years were assimilating through their local businesses and marriage, and the same can be said of the Kru regarding relationships.[84] A 1920 report of West African men in Swakopmund reported that of the 16 from Liberia and the Gold Coast, 25 percent had wives or live-in female partners (most likely locals) and two of those couples had children.[85] Tellingly, an attached report on Kru in Walvis Bay for repatriation states that only one on the list of 21 "wishes to go."[86] Despite increasing challenges fac-

82 NAN, ADM [152], C.248, Industrial Coloured Workers Union, Confidential Letter from Native Affairs Lüderitzbucht to the Secretary of S.W. Africa at Windhoek, re: NATIVE UNIONS. S.W. AFRICA., 7.9.1922.

83 NAN, ADM [152], C.248, Industrial Coloured Workers Union, Untitled summary of grievances submitted by James De Clue of Lüderitz and the ICU more generally in relation to SWA, 2.

84 For more on the Togolese labor elite and their place in the late German and early South African SWA economy and society, see Chapter 4, "Alfred Kulivo and Togolese Entrepreneurs in the Colonial Ports."

85 NAN, SWAA [2233] A.494:2, 21.10.1920 Number of West Coast Boys in Swakopmund.

86 NAN, SWAA [2233] A.494:2, 21.10.1920 Number of Krooboys in Walfish Bay, for repatriation.

ing those living in SWA, the Kru seemed to see themselves progressively as part of the local population.

The Kru assimilation was mirrored in a government document from 1922 that specified that of the 39 Kru at the Windhoek 'location' for proposed repatriation, around a quarter had local wives. The women were also of varying ethnic background implying that Kru were becoming accepted in the broader SWA African community.[87] Certainly, increasing incorporation into local society melded with dim prospects of a prosperous life back in Western Africa drove the popularity of the Universal Negro Improvement Association amongst Kru in the region.

The UNIA had been created in Jamaica in August of 1914 only a few days after the First World War had begun. By 1916, its founder Marcus Garvey and the organization's main operations had moved to Harlem, New York City in the United States. It was a pan-Africanist movement centering around the betterment of people of African ancestry claiming, "Africa for Africans, at home and abroad!" The UNIA would become the largest black led organization in history and at its height had 300,000 dues paying members, a thousand chapters and maybe another million supporters around the world.[88] In South West Africa, its arrival was opportune.

In 1920, mounting political pressure in the Union of South Africa pushed the new administration in SWA into "removing the major inhibitions to the active exploitation of the colony. These changes, in turn, increased pressure on the indigenous population, accounting for increased resistance to the colonial state in the early 1920s."[89] On the heels of such policies that further disadvantaged Africans, Garveyism came to SWA. Soon, Kru were important members of its leadership. A 1921 Native Affairs letter on the UNIA reported "it seems that the Kroo Boys are amongst its most active members."[90] Exemplifying the position West Africans had in the organization, the group was referred to by Rhenish missionaries as the 'Monrovia' movement in SWA because of the prominence of Kru members as well as the fact that "the new ideology placed great expectations in the 'Republic in the North' (Liberia)."[91] Even more so than the ICU, Garveyism in the colony spanned

87 NAN, SWAA [2233] A.494:2, 22.05.1922 Return of Kroo Boys Residing in Location No. 1&2.

88 Robert Trent Vinson, *The Americans Are Coming! Dreams of African American Liberation in Segregationist South Africa* (Athens: Ohio University Press, 2012), 9.

89 Emmett, *Popular Resistance and the Roots of Nationalism in Namibia*, 90.

90 Letter from R.S. Cope, Officer in Charge of Native Affairs, Windhoek, to the Officer in Charge of Native Affairs, Lüderitz. 12.09.1921, from Robert A. Hill, ed., *The Marcus Garvey and Universal Negro Improvement Association Papers, Vol. IX: Africa for the Africans June 1921-December 1922* (Berkeley: University of California Press, 1995), 205.

91 Gregory Pirio, "The Role of Garveyism in the Making of Namibian Nationalism," in *Namibia 1884–1984: Readings on Namibia's History and Society*, ed. Brian Wood (London: Namibia Support Committee, 1988), 266.

ethnic divides with membership including not only Kru, but West Indians, Coloured people, Herero, Nama and Ovambo. Being black transcended all other identities.[92] It became a tool of grievance, with Herero and Ovambo joining Kru in using the UNIA to voice complaints against the new South African regime.[93]

By October 1921, the organization spread from Lüderitzbucht to Windhoek, then to other urban centers and lastly to the bush.[94] The movement initially grew through the region's railways and then by word of mouth via members to smaller African settlements. The ability for the UNIA to spread quickly and effectively was enhanced by West Africans and other members working for the railways. The shift in employment for many Kru in the colony from the harbors to the South African Railways, resulting from the prior war and change in colonial governance, was an important factor in Garveyism's expansion.

One group that had not been reached by the ICU, but as we discussed were acutely suffering in the early 1920s, were farm workers, who were likely willing members looking for change in a wide breadth of rural locations. Additionally, the increasing loss of Ovambo political independence as well as mass famine probably played a role to push Ovambo migrants into the organization. As membership spread, they often brought with them copies of the UNIA literature. This meant that literate workers could get news of the movement directly from the organization's mouthpiece, *Negro World*. The distribution of the UNIA's literature included at the colony's largest employer, the CDM diamond mines around Lüderitzbucht.[95]

The Universal Negro Improvement Association would have an important role in early-1920s SWA. Its effects were diverse, ranging from supplying the ideological framework for the development of subsequent Namibian nationalism, to petitioning the League of Nations for South West African self-governance.[96] But on a more local level, the organization helped improve members' lives, through initiatives such as help in cases of illness, or providing death benefits to members.[97] At the same time, the UNIA also spread rumors meant to galvanize support and proj-

92 Pirio, "The Role of Garveyism in the Making of Namibian Nationalism," 261.

93 Hill, *Africa for the Africans*, xlvii.

94 Pirio, "The Role of Garveyism in the Making of Namibian Nationalism," 262.

95 Pirio, "The Role of Garveyism in the Making of Namibian Nationalism," 261–262.

96 For a detailed analysis of the UNIA petitions to the League of Nations regarding SWA, see Douglas R. Jones, "'The League Will Not Ignore the Cry of the Negro Race for Justice': Marcus Garvey, the League of Nations and South-West Africa," *Journal of Southern African Studies* 48, no. 1 (January 2, 2022): 103–117; Hill, *Africa for the Africans*, xlvii; Intercepted Letter from Fitz Herbert Headly to Joseph Hailand, 14/11/22, 685.

97 *The Negro World* 22.11.1921 in Pirio, "The Role of Garveyism in the Making of Namibian Nationalism," 261.

ect a dream of a future unshackled from white colonial rule. This included the idea of eventual liberation of the colony by African Americans.[98]

The South African colonial government looked to suppress the movement in SWA. In referencing both the ICU and UNIA, Native Affairs in Lüderitzbucht stated in September of 1922, "[w]e are at present fighting the native union menace with ineffective weapons and I beg to submit the question of control or prohibition should be dealt with without delay."[99] Although the organizations were not banned, persecuting West Africans was seen as a way of weakening the UNIA in SWA; the administration stated that "they certainly have a bad effect on our aboriginals and are politically inclined."[100] The same document went on to state of the Kru in Lüderitzbucht, "I . . . recommend that they be encouraged to leave . . . . [I]n cases of proved crimes against them they should be deported . . . . I do not think that we could arbitrarily deport them all except in the case of criminals, but we should induce as many as possible to leave."[101] While this report noted that arbitrary deportation was at least not technically feasible, criminal records of West Africans in Windhoek from 1922 hint that many of their arrests were indeed arbitrary. Of the 19 Kru in Windhoek with criminal records for the year, over 40 percent were either for violation of curfew or 'location' regulations, possession of liquor, breach of the peace, or work absenteeism. These convictions were geared at controlling the African population and could likely be imposed almost at will by the state.[102]

Trying to push back against such government actions, in April of 1922 leaders of both the UNIA and the ICU in Lüderitzbucht met with the SWA Native Commissioner. They brought complaints of members suffering from false arrests, persecution, and censorship at the hand of the colonial state. The Native Commissioner largely wrote off the complaints as exaggerations or untrue, summing up his meeting notes by writing: "My general conclusion is that whilst most of the complaints are frivolous or exaggerated to support political aspirations and in some cases quite unfounded, there is room for improvement in such matters as . . . re-

---

98 Hill, *Africa for the Africans*, xlvii; Intercepted Letter from Fitz Herbert Headly to Joseph Hailand, 14.11.22 in Hill, 685; C.N. Manning, Native Commissioner of South West Africa, to Private Secretary in Hill, 455 fn. 4.

99 NAN, ADM [152], C.248, Industrial Coloured Workers Union, Confidential Letter from Native Affairs Lüderitzbucht to the Secretary of S.W. Africa at Windhoek, re: NATIVE UNIONS. S.W. AFRICA., 7.9.1922, 2.

100 NAN, SWAA [2233] A. 494/2, 06.05.1922 letter on the Kroo Boys and Other West African Natives by the Native Commissioner of S.W.A.

101 NAN, SWAA [2233] A. 494/2, 06.05.1922 letter on the Kroo Boys and Other West African Natives by the Native Commissioner of S.W.A.

102 NAN, SWAA [2233] A. 494/2, 05.08.20 Convictions recorded against Kroo-boys.

strictions against coloured persons trading within locations . . . [the] Sanitary system on [the] Luderitz Railway section . . . ."[103] While referencing two complaints that could be improved, the larger issues were disregarded, likely because the government clearly wanted to disempower and destroy both movements.

One path to this result was seen as kicking West Africans out of the colony, but they did not have grounds to repatriate even a sizable number of them from the colony because of their intermarriage with local women and most individuals' unwillingness to leave of their own volition. With these hurdles in place, the South West African Native Commissioner made clear that critical oversight of the community would be maintained. He recommended "that the Town Clerk be called upon to cause a roll of them to be framed, giving their names, the nature of their employment, their Hut numbers and stating whether they are married or single and whether they are holders of Hut licences or Lodgers permits."[104] While the state attempted to purge the colony of, or at least control, West Africans, it was rather fault lines within the African community that seem to have led to a decrease of Kru leadership within the local movement.

By 1922, the UNIA in SWA, which had operated as an amalgamation of both local and migrant Africans, with a strong representation of leadership of both Herero and Liberians, began to expel its West African leadership. As relayed by Pirio, a police report noted "that there was a 'friction' between the Liberian or Monrovian fraction and the Hereros in Windhoek, and subsequently the leadership of the Windhoek branch soon passed completely to Herero."[105] One can reasonably surmise that the stark contrast between the two groups' experiences under German colonialism may have had a hand in this eventual schism, especially as some West Africans had again found themselves in positions of local power, this time politically within the UNIA. Even as Kru leadership waned, South West African Garveyism with active West African participation, would continue to have a strong presence in the colony until the mid-1920s. However, by 1925 the UNIA along with the ICU in South West Africa had essentially met their end. Across the Atlantic in May of the same year, Marcus Garvey was sent to jail in the United States for

103 NAN, ADM [152], C.248, Industrial Coloured Workers Union, Letter from the Native Commissioner: South West Africa to the Secretary for South West Africa, Coloured and Native People, Luderitz: Alleged Grievances, 24.4.2022, 4.

104 NAN, SWAA [2233] A. 494/2, 31.03.1922 Letter on the Kroo-boys by The Native Commissioner of S.W.A.

105 Miscellaneous document, November 10, 1922, SWAGA A.50/32 in Pirio, "The Role of Garveyism in the Making of Namibian Nationalism," 264.

fraud following a failed appeal.[106] The movement in South West Africa and its leader thousands of miles away seemed to have met similar fates. With the UNIA's fall and the solidification of a strong new occupying government, the state now exercised effective control over the colonized population.[107]

The End of the 'Namibian Labor Corridors'

In this chapter I have argued that the First World War brought drastic change to the labor regime of South West Africa, both during the war and, most importantly, in the following decades. The three labor corridors that had been the backbone of the colony's economy starting with the war in 1904, workers from the Ovambo polities, South Africa, and West Africa, no longer defined the future of the colonial labor force. The 'Namibian Labor Corridors,' whereby migrants from regions not controlled directly by the colonial state made up the central pillars of the colony's economy, had ended with the First World War.

West Africans were forced to labor for the wartime German colonial state and military, while most South Africans and those from the Ovambo polities were sent home. In the post-war years, it became clear with the dissolution of the Ovambo polities and formal colonial control in northern SWA and southern Angola, that Ovambos would increasingly make up the sole labor corridor for migrant labor in South African controlled South West Africa. While individuals from both Bechuanaland and South Africa would make up sizable groups of migrants up until the mid-1920s, their numbers would soon fade. For West Africans in the colony, most lost their livelihoods and their assets in the war. While force-exiled Cameroonians looked for repatriation as soon as possible, many Togolese and especially Kru migrants increasingly integrated into local society. By 1920, South West Africa, while technically a League of Nations Mandate, had in reality gone from the center of the German empire to the periphery of the South African empire.

The post-war years brought further destabilization for the colony at large, from Spanish influenza, to inflation, and a weak economy in the early 1920s. The dire situation for many Africans during this period dovetailed with the spread of the Industrial and Commercial Workers' Union from South Africa, and the Garveyite movement from the United States. Both embodied the core goals of improv-

---

106 Ibrahim K. Sundiata, "The Garvey Aftermath: The Fall, Rise, and Fall," in *United States and West Africa- Interactions and: Interactions and Relations*, ed. Alusine Jalloh and Toyin Falola (New York: Boydell & Brewer, 2008), 77.

107 Emmett, *Popular Resistance and the Roots of Nationalism in Namibia*, 166.

ing the lives of Africans within the colony. The UNIA spread most widely and embodied a global vision of African unity, empowerment, and freedom from colonial rule. It evolved into a home-grown variant of Garveyism that placed local and migrant African political and economic enfranchisement at its center. West Africans helped spread the UNIA through their relatively new employment for the railways following the decline of the maritime industry. Eventually, inter-African tensions would, at least within certain chapters, lessen the leadership role of West Africans in the colony and by the mid-1920s the UNIA and ICU were essentially extinguished in SWA. A new future of an "Africa for the Africans!" in SWA had died.

The lives of other migrant Africans, however, did not disappear from the future of the region's history. In noting their continued presence in mid-century, Arthur Pickering, a Namibian whose family emigrated from the Caribbean to Lüderitzbucht in the early twentieth century, remarked that Lüderitzbucht's "location" in the 1940s was "very cosmopolitan," filled with people from Liberia, Ghana, Togo, Cameroon, Sierra Leone, and the Caribbean working in the fishing and canning industries.[108] In modern twenty-first-century independent Namibia, their ancestors can often only be perceived by unique surnames.

108 Arthur Pickering, Interview, March 22, 2018. One-on-one interview in Mr. Pickering's home with notes taken by hand.

Conclusion

This book has examined early Namibian history, from the 1890s under German colonialism, to the first decade of South African colonial rule in the 1920s, through the lens of migrant labor. While much of the historiography of this early period has focused on Germans, White South Africans, and African Namibian actors, migrants also played a central role. I have shown that rather than being colorful but inconsequential figures, the role of migrants is essential in understanding how early colonial Namibian society, economics, and politics functioned and evolved. Throughout the 1892 to 1925 period, migrants were important skilled and unskilled laborers, taking on jobs that included loading and unloading ships, building railway lines, running laundry businesses in settler towns, laboring on the diamond fields, and digging in the deep copper mines. While the later twentieth-century link between migrant contract labor, and the Namibian independence movement is well known and studied, migrants in the early 1920s were fundamental as political anti-colonial activists and leaders. They exercised these roles in the United Negro Improvement Association, a movement also known as Garveyism, as well as in the Industrial and Commercial Workers' Union.

In terms of sources, I brought together collections in a variety of languages from Southern and Western Africa, Europe, and North America to flesh out when possible, full life stories of migrants, from wage laborers to entrepreneurs. Assisting in this effort were many photographs, used when applicable, as valuable sources combined with written records. Further, I based large segments of my conclusions on the *Namibian Worker Database* constructed as part of my research project, that allowed for comparative analysis of workers across a diversity of backgrounds.

The chapters of this book followed a basic chronological progression from the late nineteenth century to the third decade of the twentieth century. The sections are connected via the overarching 'Namibian Labor Corridors' concept. This centers around a traumatic transformation in the demographics and economics of colonial Namibia that occurred starting in 1904/1905, when a major war erupted between the German empire, the Herero, and the Nama. It soon spiraled into a genocide undertaken by the Germans against the two later groups. As a result, the majority of labor in the colony became migrants, primarily recruited from three specific areas, forming corridors of circular labor migration between them and colonial Namibia. The corridors encompassed the following recruitment areas: one in West Africa, another in South Africa, and the third along the border between Namibia and Angola. In examining the 'Namibian Labor Corridors,' I also brought in connections between Namibia and labor regimes in South Africa, West Africa and beyond.

https://doi.org/10.1515/9783111374918-007

The first chapter, "Colonial Contact Zones: Power, Politics and Labor at Early Work Sites in German South West Africa 1892–1903," established a foundation for the book focusing on the early history of colonial labor and infrastructure development in the colony. In covering 1892 to 1903, it posited that labor sites in early colonial Namibia like the early Otavi mine around Tsumeb, the Swakopmund-Windhoek railway construction, and the foundation of Swakopmund and eventual construction of its mole, were 'contact zones' between local societies, migrant workers, and German imperialism. Through analyzing these 'contact zones' the reader came to understand broader changes in the colony as imperial actors attempted to assert more sway over the region and local Africans simultaneously attempted and often succeed at pushing back.

The second chapter, "The Human Infrastructure of the Namibian War: Origins of the 'Namibian Labor Corridors' in Warfare and Genocide 1904–1908," examined labor during the German imperial war and genocide against the Herero and Nama. We saw that 1904 was a tipping point for tensions in the colony as German imperialism increasingly gained more of a foothold and many African leaders simultaneously saw their power weaken. These tensions erupted in large-scale military conflict between the colonial power and Herero and Nama peoples.

The war meant that many local laborers fled colonial work sites and towns, just as the imperial military presence and troop numbers were increasing. They therefore had to progressively recruit abroad to support their large presence in the colony. Private employers contracted by the German government to build the Otavi railway, deemed essential for military supply and transport, initially attempted in 1904 to establish a European labor corridor, consisting mainly of Italian speakers from Italy and Austro-Hungary. However, in 1905 problems with strikes and general worker dissatisfaction led to an abandonment of this strategy.

Instead, labor demands were successfully filled with West African, and South African migrant labor during the conflict. I argue they became the 'human infrastructure' essential for the German military to transport, support, and supply troops in GSWA. These migrants were eventually joined by prisoner of war (POW) Herero and Nama forced laborers, including women and children. As the war came to an end by 1908, many Herero and Nama had been killed in a war that had become a genocide. The West and South African labor corridors, established during the conflict, would become increasingly important for the post-war colonial economy and society to function. During the war, and especially starting in 1908, they were also joined by Ovambo migrant workers, who made up the third and final labor corridor.

The third chapter, "Workers from the North: The Ovambo Labor Corridor 1905–1914," focused on Ovambo migrant workers in the settler region of Namibia both starting during the Namibian War until the beginning of World War One. I argued what I term the “Ovambo labor corridor” was the central pillar of the ‘Namibian Labor Corridors,’ making up the largest segment of workers during the post-war German colonial period. The chapter coincided with the opening of the copper mines of Tsumeb in 1906 and the discovery of diamonds in 1908 around Lüderitzbucht. Copper and diamond mines became the heart of the colonial economy, largely powered by Ovambo labor for the rest of the German colonial period and beyond. The chapter highlighted not only adult male workers, but also hereto unresearched aspects of Ovambo migrant labor in early colonial Namibia. That is namely the prevalence of child migrant labor throughout the Police Zone, as well as women workers in the north, especially at the Tsumeb copper mines. The chapter also looked at social life, as well as the importance of Ovambo migrants as consumers in the post-genocide colonial economy. While the importance of Ovambo labor during this period is without doubt, they were also joined by large numbers of migrants from the West and South African labor corridors who filled other essential roles in the colonial economy beyond being military auxiliaries.

“Privileged but Precarious West and South African Migrants: Labor Elite and Entrepreneurs, 1908–1914” was the fourth chapter, which covered a similar period to the previous chapter, while focusing on other groups of migrants. I argued that the West and South Africans became migrant elites in the GSWA economy, taking on average comparably higher paying roles that often required more skill than those filled by Ovambo laborers. Their elite status was the result of their pay as well as jobs, which included labor in train construction, as longshoremen, and even as business owners in the colonial ports.

The migrant elites’ unique place in colonial society was often at odds with increasingly strict racial laws in GSWA and meant that their position was precarious. The clearest example of this was the Wilhelmstal massacre, where over 12 South African train construction laborers were killed for protesting unacceptable working conditions. They came up against the limits of what according to the racialized colonial society was ‘allowed’ for migrant Africans in the colony. Even more well paid than most workers from South Africa, migrants from West Africa were the wealthiest Africans in the colony on average during the late German colonial period in Namibia. The last section of Chapter Four examined multiple life stories of these workers. Through these individual stories I highlighted their place within colonial society, including their relation to other migrant laborers, local Africans, and settlers. But the African migrant elite of GSWA largely lost their status with the eruption of World War One.

The fifth and last chapter of the book was titled “The End of the ‘Namibian Labor Corridors’: War, Pandemic, Unions, and Garveyism 1914–1925.” This chapter highlighted the end of what had been the ‘Namibian Labor Corridors’ through the disruption and chaos of World War One, the subsequent Spanish influenza pandemic, and the early years of South African rule in Namibia. At the beginning of the war many West Africans were forced into military auxiliary roles for the German army and in the years of the conflict lost large amounts of their assets. The South African migrant workers were sent home at the beginning of the war as well as those from the Ovambo polities.

The economy that restarted under South African occupational rule had increasingly no need for workers from West Africa, with Kru targeted for expulsion from the colony (although the government was not very effective in this endeavor). This was because the ports, and the skilled West African laborers who had been longshoremen, were less important to the South Africans, as trade with the former colonial metropole Germany completely stopped, and they connected the former German railways to their own. This facilitated imports from South Africa primarily by train, and these trans-colonial railway connections became the new primary artery of trade for the region under South African rule. Workers coming from South Africa, while continuing into the early 1920s were increasingly less central to the South African labor policy in Namibia. The new colonial government also preferred to have South Africans recruited to other mines considered central to the South African economy, such as the gold mines of Johannesburg or the diamond mines of Kimberly. Ovambo workers were clearly at the center of the new labor policy, making up more than 2/3rds of all migrant laborers in the first years of the South African occupation period. This coincided with the dissolution of the independence of the Ovambo polities, and the region coming under formal South African and Portuguese colonial rule around 1917.

I argued that this period of economic destabilization and new colonial occupation, led to the growth and expansion of the Industrial and Commercial Workers' Union (ICU) and the United Negro Improvement Association and African Communities League (UNIA), also known as the Garveyites, in colonial Namibia. Both fought for better working conditions and rights for Africans. Arguably the more successful of the two, the UNIA, became a cross-ethnic movement among a broad swath of Africans in the colony. As a global pan-African movement with origins in Jamaica and the United States, the UNIA spread anti-colonial ideas, and promoted African self-rule in colonies on the continent, including in South West Africa. A sizable portion of its leadership in South West Africa were West Africans, who had suffered economically in the post 1914 period, as well as Herero, who had experienced immeasurable atrocities in the war and genocide but were building back their identity and place in Namibian society. The chapter ended in 1925 with the slow dissolution of the UNIA and ICU in South West Africa largely due to colonial pressure and persecution, the formalization of colonial rule in 'Ovamboland,' as well as increasingly harsh rule from South Africa. The 'Namibian Labor Corridors' had come to an end. However, the foundations of the colonial, and eventual independent Namibian economy, constructed by migrant laborers in the early colonial period would last until the modern era.

I have importantly shown how very disparate peoples came to form the essential building blocks of a colonial economy. These actors were not mere pawns in a colonial labor network, but used, to greater or lesser extents, their agency to affect their life paths. Exploring these varying levels of agency included examining the reasons for why workers went to work in colonial Namibia, and what this says about other parts of Africa as well as Italian speaking Europe, where many migrants during this period came from. Further, I have explored the processes of worker recruitment, travel, the minutia of various forms of labor, social lives after work, and in certain cases the life trajectories of individuals. Migrant workers' possessions, from clothing, to instruments, and liquid assets were all important details examined throughout the book. Also, belief systems, family, sport, drinking, and games were essential to understanding what was significant to the migrants portrayed in this book.

In conclusion, I believe this work has added to the historiography of labor, economic and political history in Southern Africa, as well as contributed to bringing Namibian studies into the broader lens of 'Global Labor History.'

Figures

Figure 1 The 'Namibian Labor Corridors' 1892–1914 (Cartography by Bernard C. Moore) —— **5**
Figure 2 Estate File of Tango Mifango from the Ovambo Oukwanyama Polity. Note the cause of death is 'Spanish Influenza.' Files like this make up the majority of the Namibian Worker Database source material —— **14**
Figure 3 Approximate Boundaries of Concession Zone of the South West Africa Company, Ltd. The diagonal lines represent the area which had land concession rights as well. The yellow color represents mining and prospecting rights —— **29**
Figure 4 The 12-meter tall malachite hill (green hill) of Tsumeb. Although this photo was supposedly taken in the early 1900s, it may very well date from the early 1890s as Rogers did have a Kodak camera that may have been repaired during mining operations —— **36**
Figure 5 Map showing Walvis Bay and the Swakop River to the north —— **44**
Figure 6 Workers at the rock quarry for the mole —— **53**
Figure 7 D.S.W.A. Swakopmund. View from the mole. 63328 Verlag der Swakopmunder Buchhandlung G.m.b.H —— **54**
Figure 8 Italian workers on strike joined by black workers, likely Ovambo, to take a photo, circa 1904 —— **82**
Figure 9 Italian guesthouse in Swakopmund circa 1904–1905 —— **85**
Figure 10 Two Kru workers hired at Monrovia, Liberia aboard the steamer Entre Rios of the Hamburg-Südamerikanische Dampfschiffsgesellschaft in route to Swakopmund, GSWA —— **96**
Figure 11 Kru men working on deck. They were hired in Monrovia, Liberia on contract for the steamer Entre Rios of the Hamburg-Südamerikanische Dampfschiffsgesellschaft in route to Swakopmund, GSWA —— **99**
Figure 12 Using the steam crane to transport military horses from smaller vessels onto the mole in 1904. This photo does not portray the offloading of the Entre Rios but gives an idea of how animals were brought onto shore —— **102**
Figure 13 Kru workers offloading hay at Swakopmund in 1905 —— **104**
Figure 14 Herero forced laborers on the beach at Swakopmund, 1905–1906, pushing a train car; to the right of the women notice the tracks that Woermann-Linie installed specifically to take advantage of unskilled forced laborers for beach work —— **106**
Figure 15 Photo of a what are likely Woermann-Linie surf boats manned by Kru workers loading Herero prisoners from around 1905/1906 (note the completed wooden pier) —— **109**
Figure 16 An ox-wagon and German troops passing through the dry bed of the black Nossob ephemeral river in the Eastern theater of war in GSWA in 1904 —— **119**
Figure 17 Forced laborers loading train car in Swakopmund —— **126**
Figure 18 Approximate number of Ovambo Individuals in Settler region of GSWA 1908–1913. The graph begins in 1908 as comparable records from the previous years do not exist —— **135**
Figure 19 Districts in the Settler Zone with the Largest Ovambo Populations between 1908 and 1913. Statistics are from the first day of each year —— **136**
Figure 20 Map of the Ovambo polities, (Cartography by Bernard C. Moore) —— **137**

https://doi.org/10.1515/9783111374918-008

Figure 21 Ovambo migrants heading South and returning North through the Outjo train station in July 1910 — **138**
Figure 22 Tsumeb 1913: Ovambos on the way to the mine's labor office — **149**
Figure 23 Kasino Ovambo's pass and work book — **150**
Figure 24 Ovambo Workers recruited at Okaukuejo and Namutoni for contracts in the settler region between 1910 and 1914 — **152**
Figure 25 Ovambo men and boys on their way south on contract. As they are leaving Namutoni they are likely headed to work either in the copper mines of Tsumeb or a train construction project — **153**
Figure 26 Map of GSWA circa 1905 — **155**
Figure 27 Africans, likely including Ovambos taking the train in wagons also intended for cargo. Notice the woman with a head scarf facing to the right closest to the camera as well as the brakeman on the far right. Based on the two twin steam engines, this is likely the Swakopmund-Windhoek train line operating between 1902 and 1910 — **159**
Figure 28 Map of the diamond fields around Lüderitzbucht in 1910 — **164**
Figure 29 A troop of Ovambo workers searching for diamonds — **165**
Figure 30 Lüderitzbucht Diamond Fields Work Force April 1, 1912 to March 1, 1913, broken down by various African workers — **166**
Figure 31 Photo of Ovambo young men and boys working at diamond field Bayer — **167**
Figure 32 Labor on a larger diamond mine — **168**
Figure 33 Diamond field 'Unverhofft' of the Vereinigte Diamant Minen — **170**
Figure 34 Photograph of Ovambo (and likely Cape Workers) workers at the Tsumeb mine, around 1908 — **175**
Figure 35 Graph of African Workers at Tsumeb 1907–1910 — **177**
Figure 36 Ovambo and white workers laboring underground in the Tsumeb copper mines. They are building wooden supports to keep the tunnels from collapsing. Picture likely dates between 1906 and 1914 — **179**
Figure 37 Ovambo preachers, likely Ondonga in the early twentieth century — **183**
Figure 38 Above to the left we see a group of workers socializing around housing at Tsumeb during the first decades of the twentieth century. The photo to the right is a close-up of an okasandji from the late nineteenth-century Ovambo polities — **185**
Figure 39 Group of about 15 Ovambo migrants in Swakopmund. Some of the men are carrying calabashes, palm-leaf baskets, and what looks like okambulumbumbwa — **187**
Figure 40 Ovambo workers at the location at Bogenfels mine — **192**
Figure 41 Graph of Ovambo Workers Arriving at and Leaving the Lüderitzbucht Diamond Mines — **197**
Figure 42 Ovambo migrant workers at the Namutoni checkpoint on their return from contract — **200**
Figure 43 Map of the German colonial railways built between 1897 and 1912 (Cartography by Bernard C. Moore) — **208**
Figure 44 Approximate number of South African Individuals in the Settler region of GSWA from 1908–1913. The graph begins in 1908 as comparable records from the previous years do not exist — **213**

Figure 45 Group of train workers along the Lüderitz to Keetmanshoop railway. Based on the existence of trees and a well they are likely on the segment between Kubub and Keetmanshoop — **222**

Figure 46 Photo taken of two Cape Workers on the Nord-Südbahn construction in 1911. Based on the photo album chronology they are likely somewhere between 17 km and the construction of the line through the Auas Mountains — **226**

Figure 47 Photo of workers for Bachstein and Koppel laying the train line for the Nord-Südbahn through the Auas mountains — **227**

Figure 48 West Africans in GSWA 1908–1913 — **245**

Figure 49 Portraits in South African government documents of the former GSWA clerks, Paul Ayeboari (left) and Emmanuel Kwasi (right) — **251**

Figure 50 Advertisement for laundromat run by 'Alfred aus Togo und Alf. J. Mdingi' — **252**

Figure 51 Advertisement for 'Togo-Dampfwäscherei' (Togo Steamwasher) — **252**

Figure 52 Advertisements for various West African laundromats in GSWA — **253**

Figure 53 A 'Wedding Certificate' by Missionary Eich of the Rhenish Missionary Society who led the Swakopmund community — **258**

Figure 54 Approximate breakdown of migrant labor in SWA between 1915–1920 — **274**

Figure 55 Breakdown of Ovambo workers in the police zone from 1916–1920 during the martial law Period — **277**

Tables

Table 1 Death Registry statistics —— **111**
Table 2 Ovambo worker mortality at Tsumeb and Lüderitz for 1909, 1910, 1912 —— **194**

https://doi.org/10.1515/9783111374918-009

Primary Sources

Namibia

National Archives of Namibia (NAN)

NAN, ADM [238] SWAKOP 264/9 Claims of certain Krooboys and other Natives
NAN, ADM [152], C.248, Industrial Coloured Workers Union, South West Africa
NAN, ADM [211] 238, Natives Lüderitz
NAN, ADM [51] 675:5, Repatriation General
NAN, AP 4/1/2, South West Africa Report 1922
NAN, BCL [12], British Consul
NAN, BLU [011] B.G.L Band 4–5, Diamond mine African worker estate Files
NAN, BLU [027], E.1.A, Bezirksamt Lüderitzbucht, 1896–1915
NAN, BLU [146] G.5.a., Estate Inheritance. Coloured
NAN, BLU [168] Vol. 1, Death of Natives in the Diamond Area
NAN, BSW [107] UA 10/6, Death Register for Natives
NAN, BSW [57] XXII, Band II, Otavibahn
NAN, EST [788] 854 Estate of the Late Agide Giacomelli (Italian)
NAN, EVE [26] A.4.0 vol 3, Acta Italiener
NAN, GSW [372] D 245/05, *Akten des Kaiserlichen Bezirks-Gerichts zu Swakopmund*
NAN, NAUK CO 879/40: Resident Magistrate, Walvis Bay
NAN, NES [001] Native Estates
NAN, NES [002] Native Estates
NAN, NES [003] Native Estates
NAN, NES [004] Native Estates
NAN, NES [005] Native Estates
NAN, NES [006] Native Estates
NAN, NES [007] Native Estates
NAN, NLA [19] C.5, Handakten zum Nachlaß des verstorbenen Arbeiters Carlo Colla
NAN, OGW [68] *Generalia* XVI.2, *Kaiserliches Obergericht*
NAN, Photo 05040, *Kruneger ziehen tief im Wasser stehend ein Floss mit Pressheu heran*
NAN, Photo 25522. Provenance: A.0109, Stuhlmann
NAN, Photo 2346, Provenance: A.0898 Erinnerung an den Bau der Lüderitzbucht-Eisenbahn
NAN, Photo 24732, 'Kru Boys' by von Salzmann
NAN, Photo 24734, *'Wäscher an Bord des Entre Rios'* by von Salzmann
NAN, Photo 25521. Provenance: A.0109, Stuhlmann.
NAN, Photo 27000, Ovambo migrant workers, probably in Swakopmund, 1904/1905
NAN, Photo 28281, Ovambo migrant workers at the Namutoni checkpoint
NAN, Photo 23467, Date: 190?, Between 1906–1909, Provenance: A.0898 *Erinnerung an den Bau der Lüderitzbucht-Eisenbahn*, Remarks: Probably Lüderitzbucht railway construction
NAN, SPO [011] 2/0/0411, District-Commandant
NAN, SPW [57] 2/0/878, South African Police
NAN, SWAA [2233] A. 494/2, 05.08.20 Convictions recorded against Kroo-boys
NAN, Übersichtskarte des Diamantgebietes bei Lüderitzbucht, Block III, 1910
NAN, ZBU 2071 W.IV.I.3, *Medical treatment of workers*

https://doi.org/10.1515/9783111374918-010

NAN, ZBU 0162, A.VI.a.8 Vol. 1, Annual report of the native commissioner 1913–1914
NAN, ZBU 172 A.VI.d Vol. 1, Population Statistics Natives and Coloreds Main Statistics
NAN, ZBU 204, A IV w 2 Vol. 1. Publications specialia. Publications about the Protectorates
NAN, ZBU 2068 W.IV.i.8 Travel, food, and clothing for recruited Ovambo 1910–1913
NAN, ZBU 2068 W.IV.i.9 Travel, food, and clothing for recruited Ovambo 1910–1913
NAN, ZBU 2071 W.IV.I.2 Vol. 1, Ovambo Worker contract and obligations of the employer under the same, specialia, 1911–1914
NAN, ZBU 2071 W.IV.I.3, Medical treatment of workers, 1911–1912
NAN, ZBU 0162, A.VI.a.8 Vol. 1, Annual report of the native commissioner 1913–1914
NAN, ZBU 2063 W.IV.f.2, Native mine workers. Specialia 1912–1913

Scientific Society Swakopmund (SSS)

SSS (With the permission of Mr. Adolf Brock), unpublished Manuscript, E. Brock, *Reiserinnerungen, Afrikareise 10.11.1903–08.05.1904*
SSS, *Woermann-Linie Jahresbericht* (Swakopmund, 1916)
SSS, Woermann-Linie Jahresbericht 1913 (Swakopmund, 1913)

Archives of the Evangelical-Lutheran Church in the Republic of Namibia (ELCRN)

ELRCN, Windhoek, C.V.31, Gemeinde Chronik, Swakopmund

South Africa

Cape Town Archives (CA)

CA, NA 556, Correspondence Files 1903–1907
CA, NA 557, Correspondence Files, Papers relating to Native Labour Agents and native labour generally 1904–1907
CA, NA 612, Harbour Works, Swakopmund, 1901–3, Swakop Mouth Harbour Works
CA, NA 662 Part II, Compensation to Native Labourers, Native Estates
CA, NA 719, F473(ii), Papers relating to Native Labour, 1898–9, 1908–1910
CA, NA 727, Wages due to Labourers who died in German South West Africa 1905–1909

National Archives of South Africa (NASA)

NASA GG 275 4/24 Report by the Consul at Luderitzbucht on the treatment of natives by the authorities in German South West Africa
NASA GG 4/26 Collision between troops and Cape natives in German South West Africa
NASA, GG 275 4/21 Affray between troops and Cape boys in German South West Africa
NASA, GG 275 4/22 Affray in German SW Africa between Cape natives and troops
NASA, GG 275 4/19, Affray between Cape boys and German troops in German South West Africa
NASA, GG 275 4/24 Report by the Consul at Luderitzbucht on the treatment of natives by the authorities in German South West Africa

NASA, GG 276 4/26 Collision between troops and Cape natives in German South West Africa
NASA, GG 276 4/27, Collision between troops in German South West Africa and Cape Natives employed there
NASA, GG 276 4/45 Collision between German soldiers and Cape Natives at Wilhelmstal
NASA, GG 277 4/83, Collisions between German troops and Cape Natives at Wilhelmstal
NASA, GG 277 4/84, Collisions between German troops and Cape Natives at Wilhelmstal
NASA, GG 4/26 Collision between troops and Cape natives in German South West Africa
NASA, GG 606 File a. 33/3370/3: 'South West Protectorate Report of the Administrator for the Year, 1918'
NASA, GG 606 File D.B. 30/1723/9199: 'Report of the Administrator of the Protectorate of South West Africa, 1916'

Germany

Staats- und Universitätsbibliothek Bremen

Jahresbericht über die Entwickelung der Schutzgebiete in Afrika und der Südsee (Berlin: Mittler, 1906), HA 10 Ea 1502/10–1904/05, Einleitung

Bundesarchiv-Lichterfelde (BArch)

BArch R 1001/1482, Expedition der South-West-Africa-Company. – Reports of Mr. Matthew Rogers to the South West Africa Company
BArch, R 1001/1480, Expeditionen der South West Africa Company 1892 – 1896
BArch R 1001/1863, Häfen an der südwestafrikanischen Küste Juni 1886 – Sept. 1895
BArch, R 1001/1865a Hafenanlage in Swakopmund
BArch, R 1001/2089 Aufstände in Deutsch-Südwestafrika 1904
BArch, R 1001/3229, Arbeiterfrage und Arbeitsverhältnisse in Kamerun und Togo1886 – 1943
BArch, R 1002/865, Jacobs, N. N., Dr., Regierungsarzt 1905 – 1906
BArch, Photo N 881 – Streitwolf, Kurt.- Bildbestand / Fotograf(in): o. Ang., Deutsch-Südwestafrika.- Wandernde Ovambo-Arbeiter, 1900/1914 ca
BArch, R 8024/208, The South West Africa Company Limited, London – Berlin 1909 – 1914
BArch R 1001/9649, Bau und Betrieb von Eisenbahnen in den Kolonien. – Materialsammlung, 1907 – 1913

Bundesarchiv-Militärarchiv (BArch-MA)

BArch-MA, MSG 105/9, Zur Geschichte der deutschen Eisenbahntruppen, Die Verpflegungsschwierigkeiten im Groß-Namalande und die Eisenbahn Lüderitzbucht-Kubub; Schwabe, *Der Krieg in Deutsch-Südwestafrika 1904–1906*

Archiv- und Museumsstiftung der Vereinte Evangelische Mission (VEM)

VEM, RMG 1.631 b, B/c II 58, Ferdinand Lang, Band 2 1899–1919; 1942
VEM, RMG 2.503 a. Grootfontein (mit Otavi) , C/h 15 a, Vol. 1 1910–1946
VEM, RMG 2.509 a Lüderitzbucht C/h 23 a, Band 1 1904–1945

VEM, RMG 2.529 a C/h 46 a Tsumeb (mit Grootfontein, Gaup, Otavi), Band 1 1907–1939
VEM, RMG 2630 Mission conference in Ovamboland – Report from Wulfhorst, 2.10.05
VEM, RMG, Bericht Heinrich Vedders über die Situation der Afrikaner*innen in Swakopmund

Bildarchiv der Deutschen Kolonialgesellschaft, Universitätsbibliothek Frankfurt am Main (BADKGUBFM)

BADKGUBFM, Photo: A_00I_1330
BADKGUBFM, Photo 082-2990-195, Durchzug durch den Schwarzen Nossob, Sammlung Jean Bantz: Bahnfahrt von Swakopmund – Windhuk. Ostabteilung. D.S.W.Afr 1904
BADKGUBFM, Photo: A_00T_3096, *Gasthause der Italiener*
BDKGUFM, Photo: A_00H_1147, 1904, Swakopmund: Landung von Pferden bei der Mole
BADKGUBFM, Photo: A_00H_1192
BADKGUB, Photo PA02_013
BADKGUB, Photo A_00S_2995
BADKGUBFM, Photo 019-2146-15, Photographed by von farmer von Zanthier 53, Das Untersuchen des Feldes auf Abbauwürdigkeit
BADKGUBFM, Photo 019-2133-14, Photographer: Bayer, M., SWA 12 / Diamantenwüste Bayer. 57
BADKGUBFM, Photo 018-0212-09, K/R. Diamanten No 12 / No 9 / Bfu I 37 / Maschinelle Bearbeitung des Wüstensandes /lfd. No 170 / S.W.A.
BDKGUFM, Photo A_0MM_5619
BADKGUBFM, Photo 014-2183-08, Tsumeb Mine / Sortieren d. Erze
BDKGUFM, Photo A_0SS_7350, Tsumeb: Untertagebau, Abbau IV. Sohle, Lore auf Schienen
BADKGUBFM, Photo 068-2179-252, Geistliche schwarze Helfer im Ovamboland. Finnische Mission SWA, Fotograf: Neumeister, Otto
BDKGUFM, Photo 11478845, *Ovambo-Werft Bogenfels*

Reichstagsprotokolle

Verhandlungen des Reichstages, Bd.: 128. 1892/93, 55. Sitzung, 01.03.1893, Reichskanzler Graf von Caprivi, 1359
Verhandlungen des Reichstages, Bd.: 136. 1893/94, Berlin 1894, Aktenstück Nr. 48 (Denkschrift über das Ost- und Südwestafrikanische Schutzgebiet.), Landungsstelle an der Swakop-Mündung.
Verhandlungen des Reichstages, Bd.: 141. 1894/95, Berlin, 1895, Aktenstück Nr. 89 (Denkschrift, betreffend das Südwestafrikanische Schutzgebiet.), 494
Verhandlungen des Reichstages, Bd.: 159. 1897/98, Berlin, 8. Sitzung, Aloys Fritzen (Düsseldorf), 11.12.1898, 144
Verhandlungen des Reichstages, Bd.: 202. 1903/05, Berlin, 1905, 130. Sitzung, Dr. Arendt (Freikonservative Partei), 31.01.1905, 4133
Verhandlungen des Reichstages, Bd.: 202. 1903/05, Berlin, 1905, 131. Sitzung, Bebel (SPD), 01.02.1905, 4180–4181

Switzerland

Basler Afrika Bibliographien BAB
BAB, Annual Report of the Rhenish Mission Society 1901 (Barmen: Westdeutsche Druckerei, 1902)
BAB, Annual Report of the Rhenish Mission Society 1908 (Barmen: Westdeutsche Druckerei, 1909)
BAB, Annual Report of the Rhenish Mission Society 1910 (Barmen: Westdeutsche Druckerei, 1911)
BAB, BPA.159 1 Karl Exler, Photo Album "Andenken an D.S.W. Afrika"

Finland

The National Archives of Finland (NAF)
NAF, kotelo 986, Martti Rautanen Collection

Sweden

Vänersborgs Museum
Photo of Object VME00069, INSTRUMENT – Vänersborgs Museum, Sweden – CC BY. https://www.europeana.eu/de/item/916106/vbg_object_VME00069.

Great Britain

The University of Manchester, John Rylands University Library
19th Century British Pamphlets, Foreign and Commonwealth Office Collection, To the shareholders of the South-West Africa Company, Limited

USA

The Library of the University of Indiana at Bloomington
Wolfe W. Schmokel, "Liberia, Germany, Britain and the United States, 1905–1918" (unpublished paper, Burlington, VT, 1976), Frederick Dean McEvoy Collection, 1956–1979, Box 1, Publications and Manuscripts, Liberian Collections, Indiana University

MSU Libraries
Just, E. ca. 1910. German South West Africa. Africana Digital Collection, Gerald M. Kline Digital and Multimedia Center, MSU Libraries, https://archive.lib.msu.edu/DMC/Africana/MSS517/MSS517cc.pdf.

Newspapers / Magazines

Deutsche Kolonialzeitung (DKZ)
Deutschen Kolonialblatt
Windhuker Anzeiger (WA) / *Swakopmunder Zeitung / Deutsch-Südwestafrikanische Zeitung* (DSWAZ)
Cape Times
Windhuker Nachrichten (WN)
Lüderitzbuchter Zeitung (LZ)
Daheim

Websites

The 12-meter-tall malachite hill (green hill) of Tsumeb, ca. 1905, Tsumeb Museum, Unknown author, Public domain, via Wikimedia Commons, https://commons.wikimedia.org/wiki/File:1905_Tsumeb_Malachithuegel.JPG.

Golf Dornseif, "Waisen-Import und Dienstmädchen-Anwerbung für Südwest", http://www.golf-dornseif.de.

"Zwilling – Henschel 5376/1900," accessed January 26, 2022, http://www.heeresfeldbahn.de/lokomotiven/deutschland/zwilling/168.html

"Damara Und Namaqua Handelsgesellschaft MbH Vorgestellt Im Namibiana Buchdepot," accessed October 27, 2021, https://www.namibiana.de/namibia-information/who-is-who/organisationen/infos-zur-organisation/damara-und-namaqua-handelsgesellschaft-mbh.html

Interviews

Ilse Schatz, Interview, March 3, 2017. Windhoek, Namibia. Interview regarding her family, the history of Tsumeb, the copper mines, and labor. One-on-one interview (with her son present) in nursing home with notes taken by hand

Arthur Pickering, Interview, March 22, 2018. One-on-one interview in Mr. Pickering's home with notes taken by hand

Bibliography

Achmat, Zackie. "'Apostles of Civilised Vice': 'Immoral Practices' and 'Unnatural Vice' in South African Prisons and Compounds, 1890–1920." *Social Dynamics* 19, no. 2 (1993): 92–110.

Adick, Christel, and Wolfgang Mehnert. *Deutsche Missions- und Kolonialpädagogik in Dokumenten. Eine kommentierte Quellensammlung aus den Afrikabeständen deutschsprachiger Archive 1884 – 1914.* Frankfurt am Main: KO-Verl. für Interkulturelle Kommunikation, 2001.

Amenumey, D.E.K. "German Administration in Southern Togo." *The Journal of African History* 10, no. 4 (October 1969): 623–639.

Ammerman, Friedrich. "Wheels of Empire: The Otavi Railway and German Colonialism in South West Africa, 1882–1914." Master's thesis, Freie University, 2018.

Amupanda, Job Shipululo. *Diamond Warriors in Colonial Namibia: Diamond Smuggling, Migrant Workers and Development in Owamboland*. Basel, Switzerland: Basler Afrika Bibliographien, 2022.

Andrade, Gabriel E. "A Great Inspiration for Today's Vaccination Efforts: Biographical Sketch of Francisco Xavier Balmis (1753–1819)." *Journal of Medical Biography*, (2021): 183–188.

Apoh, Wazi, and Bea Lundt. *Germany and Its West African Colonies: "Excavations" of German Colonialism in Post-Colonial Times*. Münster: LIT Verlag, 2013.

Baltzer, Franz. *Die Kolonialbahnen mit besonderer Berücksichtigung Afrikas*. Berlin: Göschen, 1916.

Bauer, Gretchen. *Labor and Democracy in Namibia: 1971–1996*. Athens: Ohio University Press, 1998.

Bavendamm, Dirk and C. Woermann GmbH und Co. *150 Jahre C. Woermann. Wagnis Westafrika. Die Geschichte eines Hamburger Handelshauses 1837–1987.* Hamburg: Verl. Hanseat. Merkur, 1987.

Beckert, Sven and Dominic Sashsenmaier, ed. *Global History, Globally: Research and Practice around the World*. London: Bloomsbury, 2018.

Beese, Sebastian. *Experten der Erschließung: Akteure der deutschen Kolonialtechnik in Afrika und Europa 1890–1943*. Leiden: Brill Schöningh, 2021.

Beinart, William. "'Jamani' Cape Workers in German South West Africa, 1904–12." In *Hidden Struggles in Rural South Africa: Politics & Popular Movements in the Transkei & Eastern Cape, 1890–1930*, William Beinart and Colin Bundy, 166–191. Berkeley: University of California Press, 1987.

Beinart, William, and Colin Bundy. *Hidden Struggles in Rural South Africa: Politics & Popular Movements in the Transkei & Eastern Cape, 1890–1930*. London; Berkeley: University of California Press, 1987.

Beinart, William, and Colin Bundy. "Introduction: 'Away in the Locations.'" In *Hidden Struggles in Rural South Africa: Politics & Popular Movements in the Transkei & Eastern Cape, 1890–1930*, William Beinart and Colin Bundy, 1–45. Berkeley: University of California Press, 1987.

Bellucci, Stefano. "Transport." In *General Labour History of Africa: Workers, Employers and Governments, 20th–21st Centuries*, edited by Stefano Bellucci and Andreas Eckert, 195–219. Woodbridge: James Currey, 2019.

Bellucci, Stefano, and Andreas Eckert, eds. *General Labour History of Africa: Workers, Employers and Governments, 20th–21st Centuries*. Woodbridge: James Currey, 2019.

Bellucci, Stefano, and Andreas Eckert. "The 'Labour Question' in Africanist Historiography." In *General Labour History of Africa: Workers, Employers and Governments, 20th–21st Centuries*, edited by Stefano Bellucci and Andreas Eckert, 1–13. Woodbridge: James Currey, 2019.

Blackler, Adam A. "From Boondoggle to Settlement Colony: Hendrik Witbooi and the Evolution of Germany's Imperial Project in Southwest Africa, 1884–1894." *Central European History* 50, no. 4 (2017): 449–470.

Bley, Helmut. *Namibia under German Rule*. Windhoek: Namibia Scientific Society, 1996.

Boethke, R. *Die Verkehrstruppen in Südwestafrika*. Berlin: Mittler, 1906.

https://doi.org/10.1515/9783111374918-011

Brass, Tom, and Marcel van der Linden. *Free and Unfree Labour: The Debate Continues*. Bern: Peter Lang, 1997.

Brata, Aloysius Gunadi. “Exploring the Influence of Colonial Railways on Java’s Economic Geography,” 20. Munich Personal RePEc Archive, 2017.

Bravenboer, Brenda, and Walter Rusch. *The First 100 Years of State Railways in Namibia*. Windhoek: TransNamib Museum, 1999.

Bright, Rachel K. *Chinese Labour in South Africa: 1902–10 ; Race, Violence, and Global Spectacle*. Cambridge Imperial and Post-Colonial Studies. Basingstoke: Palgrave Macmillan, 2013.

Brockmann, Clara. *Briefe eines deutschen Mädchens aus Südwest*. Berlin: E.S. Mittler & Sohn, 1912.

Brooks, George E. *The Kru Mariner in the Nineteenth Century: An Historical Compendium*. Newark: Liberian Studies Association in America, 1972.

Brown, Carolyn, and Marcel van der Linden. “Shifting Boundaries between Free and Unfree Labor: Introduction.” *International Labor and Working-Class History* 78 (2010): 4–11.

Brown, Ernest D. “The Guitar and the ‘Mbira’: Resilience, Assimilation, and Pan-Africanism in Zimbabwean Music.” *The World of Music* 36, no. 2 (1994): 73–117.

Brown, George William. *The Economic History of Liberia*. Washington, DC: The Associated Publishers, Inc., 1941.

Bühler, Andreas Heinrich. *Der Namaaufstand gegen die deutsche Kolonialherrschaft in Namibia von 1904 bis 1913*. Frankfurt am Main: IKO – Verl. für Interkulturelle Kommunikation, 2003.

Burchard, Sophie. “Die Konstruktion eines rassifizierten weißen Weiblichkeitsideals in der Zeitschrift des Frauenbundes der Deutschen Kolonialgesellschaft: Kolonie und Heimat: Deutsche Kolonialgeschichte in ‘Deutsch-Südwestafrika’ im Kontext von Geschlecht, ‘Rasse’ und Sexualität.” Master’s thesis, Universität Wien, 2014.

Cardinall, A.W. “Aggrey Beads of the Gold Coast.” *African Affairs* 24, no. 96 (1925): 287–298.

Chikowero, Mhoze. *African Music, Power, and Being in Colonial Zimbabwe*. Bloomington: Indiana University Press, 2015.

Clarence-Smith, W.G., and R. Moorsom. “Underdevelopment and Class Formation in Ovamboland, 1845–1915.” In *Namibia 1884–1984: Readings on Namibia’s History and Society*, edited by Brian Wood, 175–189. London: Namibia Support Committee, 1988.

Comaroff, Jean, and John L. Comaroff. “Cattle, Currencies & the Politics of Commensuration on a Colonial Frontier.” In *The Political Economy of Everyday Life in Africa: Beyond the Margins*, edited by Wale Adebanwi, 35–71. Woodbridge: James Currey, 2017.

Conrad, Sebastian. *German Colonialism: A Short History*. Cambridge: Cambridge University Press, 2012.

Cooper, Allan D. “The Institutionalization of Contract Labour in Namibia.” *Journal of Southern African Studies* 25, no. 1 (1999): 121–138.

Cooper, Frederick. “Back to Work: Categories, Boundaries and Connections in the Study of Labour.” In *Racializing Class, Classifying Race: Labour and Difference in Britain, the USA and Africa*, edited by Peter Alexander and Rick Halpern, 213–235. London: Palgrave Macmillan, 2000.

Cooper, Frederick. *Decolonization and African Society: The Labor Question in French and British Africa*. Cambridge: University Press, 1996.

Cooper, Frederick. *On the African Waterfront: Urban Disorder and the Transformation of Work in Colonial Mombasa*. New Haven: Yale University Press, 1987.

Coplan, David B. “Erasing History: The Destruction of the Beersheba and Platberg African Christian Communities in the Eastern Orange Free State, 1858–1983.” *South African Historical Journal* 61, no. 3 (2009): 505–520.

Daughton, James Patrick. *In the Forest of No Joy: The Congo-Océan Railroad and the Tragedy of French Colonialism*. First edition. New York: W.W. Norton & Company, 2021.

DeLancey, Mark Dike, Rebecca Neh Mbuh, and Mark W. Delancey. *Historical Dictionary of the Republic of Cameroon*. Lanham: Scarecrow Press, 2010.

Deutsche Kolonialgesellschaft, ed. *Deutscher Kolonial-Atlas: mit illustriertem Jahrbuch*. Berlin: Reimer, 1905.

Deutscher Kolonial-Kalender und statistisches Handbuch. Berlin: Deutscher Kolonial-Verlag, 1909.

Deutsch-Südwestafrikanisches Adreßbuch: 1914. Swakopmund: A. Schulze, 1914.

Dierks, Klaus. *Namibian Roads in History: From the 13th Century till Today*. Frankfurt/Main: Selbstverlag des Institutes für Wirtschafts- und Sozialgeographie der Johann Wolfgang Goethe-Universität, 1992.

Dinklage, Max. *Liberia in seiner Bedeutung für Deutschlands Handel und zukünftige Versorgung*. Hamburg: Hamburg Boysen, 1918.

Dobler, Gregor. *Traders and Trade in Colonial Ovamboland, 1925–1990: Elite Formation and the Politics of Consumption under Indirect Rule and Apartheid*. Basel: Basler Afrika Bibliographien, 2014.

Dorward, David. "Arthur London, Chief Agent of Swanzy and Co: A Biography of Imperial Commerce on the Gold Coast." *African Economic History* 29 (2001): 61–77.

Drechsler, Horst. *Let Us Die Fighting: The Struggle of the Herero and Nama against German Imperialism (1884–1915)*. London: Zed, 1980.

Drechsler, Horst. *Südwestafrika unter deutscher Kolonialherrschaft: der Kampf der Herero und Nama gegen den deutschen Imperialismus, 1884–1915*. Berlin, DDR: Akademie-Verlag, 1966.

Drechsler, Horst. *Südwestafrika unter deutscher Kolonialherrschaft: Die großen Land- und Minengesellschaften*. Stuttgart: Steiner, 1996.

Duvall, Chris S. "Cannabis and Tobacco in Precolonial and Colonial Africa." *In Oxford Research Encyclopedia of African History. Oxford University Press, 2017.*

Eckardt, Paul. *Zwei Kriegsjahre beim südwestafrikanischen Train*. Berlin: Deutscher Kolonial-Verl., 1909.

Eckenbrecher, Margarethe von. *Was Afrika mir gab und nahm: Erlebnisse einer deutschen Ansiedlerfrau in Südwestafrika*. Berlin: E.S. Mittler & Sohn, 1907.

Eckert, Andreas. "Wage Labour." In *General Labour History of Africa: Workers, Employers and Governments, 20th–21st Centuries*, edited by Stefano Bellucci and Andreas Eckert, 17–44. Woodbridge: James Currey, 2019.

Eckert, Andreas. "Why All the Fuss about Global Labour History?" In *Global Histories of Work*, edited by Andreas Eckert, 3–22. Berlin: De Gruyter Oldenbourg, 2016.

Eckert, Andreas, and Jürgen Kocka. "Mission and Themes – Work and Life Course as Historical Problems. Perspectives of the International Research Center 'Re:Work.'" Accessed March 22, 2021. https://rework.hu-berlin.de/mission-and-themes.html.

Eckert, Andreas, and Marcel van der Linden. "New Perspectives on Workers and the History of Work: Global Labor History." In *Global History, Globally: Research and Practice around the World*, ed. Sven Beckert and Dominic Sashsenmaier, 145–162. London: Bloomsbury, 2018.

Eckl, Andreas E. "Konfrontation und Kooperation am Kavango (Nord-Namibia) von 1891 bis 1921." PhD dissertation, Universität zu Köln, 2004.

Eirola, Martti. *The Ovambogefahr: The Ovamboland Reservation in the Making: Political Responses of the Kingdom of Ondonga to the German Colonial Power, 1884–1910*. Rovaniemi: Ponjois-Suomen Historiallinen Yhdistys, 1992.

Eley, Geoff. "Foreward." In *The History of Everyday Life: Reconstructing Historical Experiences and Ways of Life*, edited by Alf Lüdtke, translated by William Templer. Princeton: Princeton University Press, 1995.

Emmett, Tony. *Popular Resistance and the Roots of Nationalism in Namibia, 1915–1966*. Basel: Schlettwein, 1999.

Epprecht, Marc. "The 'Unsaying' of Indigenous Homosexualities in Zimbabwe: Mapping a Blindspot in an African Masculinity." *Journal of Southern African Studies* 24, no. 4 (1998): 631–651.

Erichsen, Casper Wulff. "Forced Labour in the Concentration Camp on Shark Island." In *Genocide in German South-West Africa*, edited by Jürgen Zimmerer and Joachim Zeller, 84–99. Monmouth: Merlin Press, 2008.

"Etwas vom Bau der Nord-Südbahn in Südwest-Afrika." In *Süsserott's illustrierter Kolonial-Kalender*. Berlin: Wilhelm Süsserott, 1914.

Falk, Kurt. "Homosexualität bei den Eingeborenen in Südwestafrika." *Archiv für Menschenkunde* 1, (1925–1926): 202–214.

Few, Martha. "Epidemics, Indigenous Communities, and Public Health in the COVID-19 Era: Views from Smallpox Inoculation Campaigns in Colonial Guatemala." *Journal of Global History* 15, no. 3 (2020): 380–393.

Fitzpatrick, Matthew. "Population Policy and the Plantation Economy in German Samoa" (paper presented at the conference Colonial Capitalism in Action: The New Social and Economic History of German Colonialism, Hamburg, Germany, May 5–6, 2021).

François, Curt von. *Deutsch-Südwest-Afrika, Geschichte der Kolonisation bis zum Ausbruch des Krieges mit Witbooi (April 1893)*. Berlin: D. Reimer, 1899.

Freund, Bill. "Labor and Labor History in Africa: A Review of the Literature." *African Studies Review* 27, no. 2 (1984): 1–58.

Frost, Diane. *Work and Community among West African Migrant Workers since the Nineteenth Century*. Liverpool: Liverpool University Press, 1999.

Gabaccia, Donna R. "Worker Internationalism and Italian Labor Migration, 1870–1914." *International Labor and Working-Class History* 45 (1994): 63–79.

Galton, Francis. *The Narrative of an Explorer in Tropical South Africa: Being an Account of a Visit to Damaraland in 1851*. London: John Murray, 1853.

Gerwarth, Robert, and Erez Manela, eds. *Empires at War: 1911 – 1923*. Oxford: Oxford University Press, 2014.

Gewald, Jan-Bart. *Herero Heroes: A Socio-Political History of the Herero of Namibia 1890–1923*. Oxford: James Currey, 1999.

Gewald, Jan-Bart. "Mbadamassi of Lagos: A Soldier for King and Kaiser, and a Deportee to German South West Africa." *African Diaspora* 2, no. 1 (May 1, 2009): 103–124.

Gewald, Jan-Bart. "Near Death in the Streets of Karibib: Famine, Migrant Labour and the Coming of Ovambo to Central Namibia." *Journal Of African History* 44, no. 2 (2003): 211–239.

Gewald, Jan-Bart. "Ovita ovia Zürn – Zürn's Krieg." In *Namibia-Deutschland eine geteilte Geschichte: Widerstand, Gewalt, Erinnerung*, edited by Larissa Förster, Dag Henrichsen, Michael Bollig, and Klaus Schneider, 78–91. Munich: Edition Minerva, 2004.

Gewald, Jan-Bart. "The Issue of Forced Labour in the Onjembo: German South West Africa 1904–1908." *Itinerario: Journal of Imperial and Global Interactions* 19, no. 1 (1995): 97–104.

Gewald, Jan-Bart. "The Road of the Man Called Love and the Sack of Sero: The Herero-German War and the Export of Herero Labour to the South African Rand." *The Journal of African History* 40, no. 1 (1999): 21–40.

Giordano, Rosario, and Elisabeth Mudimbe-Boyi. *Belges et italiens du Congo-Kinshasa : récits de vie avant et après l'indépendance*. Paris: L'Harmattan, 2008.

Gordon, Robert J. "A Note on the History of Labour Action in Namibia." *South African Labour Bulletin* 1, no. 10 (April 1975): 7–17.

Gordon, Robert J. "Some Organisational Aspects of Labour Protests Among Contract Workers in Namibia." *South African Labour Bulletin* 4 (February 1978): 116–123.

Gordon, Robert J. "Variations in Migration Rates: The Ovambo Case." *Journal of Southern African Affairs* 3, no. 3 (1978): 261–294.

Gordon, Robert J., and Stuart Sholto Douglas. *The Bushman Myth: The Making of a Namibian Underclass*. Boulder: Westview Press, 2000.

Gründer, Horst. *Geschichte der deutschen Kolonien*. 7th ed. Paderborn: Ferdinand Schöningh, 2018.

Gunn, Jeffrey. "Homeland, Diasporas and Labour Networks: The Case of Kru Workers, 1792–1900." PhD dissertation, York University, 2019.

Gunn, Jeffrey. *Outsourcing African Labor: Kru Migratory Workers in Global Ports, Estates and Battlefields until the End of the 19th Century*. volume 4. Berlin: De Gruyter Oldenbourg, 2021.

Gustafsson, Kalle. "The Trade in Slaves in Ovamboland, ca. 1850–1910." *African Economic History* 33 (2005): 31–68.

Haak, Werner. *Tagebuchblätter aus Südwest-Afrika*. Berlin: Boll & Pickardt, 1906.

Hagen, Gunter Tronje. *Kurzes Handbuch für Neger-Englisch an der Westküste Afrikas unter besonderer Berücksichtigung von Kamerun*. Berlin: Dingeldey & Werres, 1908.

Hagens, W. "Der Togoneger als kaufmännischer Angestellter." *Koloniale Rundschau* 9 (1911): 570–571.

Harries, Patrick. "Symbols and Sexuality. Culture and Identity on the Early Witwatersrand Gold Mines." *Gender and History* 2, no. 3 (September 1990): 318–336.

Harries, Patrick. *Work, Culture, and Identity: Migrant Laborers in Mozambique and South Africa, c. 1860–1910*. London: James Currey, 1994.

Harris, Brent. "Photography in Colonial Discourse: The Making of ‚the Other' in Southern Africa, c. 1850–1950." In *The Colonising Camera*, edited by Wolfram Hartmann, Jeremy Silvester, and Patricia Hayes. Cape Town: University of Cape Town Press, 1999.

Hartmann, Wolfram. "Ondillimani! Ipumbu Ya Tshilongo & the Ambiguities of Resistance in Ovambo." In *Namibia under South African Rule: Mobility & Containment, 1915–46*, edited by Patricia Hayes, Jeremy Silvester, Marion Wallace, and Wolfram Hartmann, 263–304. Oxford: James Currey, 1998.

Hartmann, Wolfram. "Urges in the Colony. Men and Women in Colonial Windhoek, 1890–1905." *Journal of Namibian Studies: History Politics Culture* 1 (2007): 39–71.

Hartmann, Wolfram, Jeremy Silvester, and Patricia Hayes, eds. *The Colonising Camera: Photographs in the Making of Namibian History*. Cape Town: University of Cape Town Press, 1999.

Häussler, Matthias. *The Herero Genocide: War, Emotion, and Extreme Violence in Colonial Namibia*. New york: Berghahn Books, 2021.

Hayden, Christopher Ellis. "Of Medicine and Statecraft: Smallpox and Early Colonial Vaccination in French West Africa (Senegal -Guinea)." PhD thesis, Northwestern University, 2008.

Hayes, Patricia. "A History of the Ovambo of Namibia, c 1880–1935." PhD thesis, University of Cambridge, 1992.

Hayes, Patricia. "Order out of Chaos: Mandume Ya Ndemufayo and Oral History." *Journal of Southern African Studies Journal of Southern African Studies* 19 (1993): 89–113.

Helbig, Ludwig, and Werner Hillebrecht. *The Witbooi*. Windhoek: Cass, Longman Namibia, 1992.

Henrichsen, Dag. "'Damara' Labour Recruitment to the Cape Colony and Marginalisation and Hegemony in Late 19th Century Central Namibia." *Journal of Namibian Studies*, no. 3 (2008): 63–82.

Henrichsen, Dag. *Herrschaft und Alltag im vorkolonialen Zentralnamibia: das Herero- und Damaraland im 19. Jahrhundert*. Basel: Basler Afrika Bibliographien, 2011.

Henrichsen, Dag, Giorgio Miescher, Ciraj Rassool, and Lorena Rizzo. "Rethinking Empire in Southern Africa." *Journal of Southern African Studies* 41, no. 3 (2015): 431–435.

Herzog, Kai F. "Violence and Work: Convict Labour and Settler Colonialism in the Cape–Namibia Border Region (c.1855–1903)." *Journal of Southern African Studies* 47, no. 1 (2021): 17–36.

Hill, Robert A., ed. *The Marcus Garvey and Universal Negro Improvement Association Papers, Vol. IX: Africa for the Africans June 1921–December 1922*. Berkeley: University of California Press, 1995.

Hillebrecht, Werner. "The Nama and the War in the South." In *Genocide in German South-West Africa: The Colonial War of 1904–1908 and Its Aftermath*, edited by Jürgen Zimmerer and Joachim Zeller, 143–158. Monmouth: Merlin Press, 2008.

Hishongwa, Ndeutala S. *The Contract Labour System and Its Effects on Family and Social Life in Namibia: A Historical Perspective*. Windhoek: Gamsberg Macmillan, 1992.

Hishongwa, Ndeutala S. *Women of Namibia: The Changing Role of Namibian Women from Traditional Precolonial Times to the Present*. Stockholm: Förlaget By & Bygd, 1983.

Hofmeester, Karin, and Marcel van der Linden, eds. *Handbook Global History of Work*. München: De Gruyter Oldenbourg, 2017.

Hoog, Tycho van der. *Breweries, Politics and Identity: The History behind Namibian Beer*. Basel: Basler Afrika Bibliographien, 2019.

Isabel V. Hull. *Absolute Destruction: Military Culture and the Practices of War in Imperial Germany*. Ithaca: Cornell University Press, 2005.

Jäckel, Herbert. *Die Landgesellschaften in den deutschen Schutzgebieten. Denkschrift zur Kolonialen Landfrage*. Jena: Verlag von Gustav Fischer, 1909.

Jensen, Niklas Thode. "Safeguarding Slaves: Smallpox, Vaccination, and Governmental Health Policies among the Enslaved Population in the Danish West Indies, 1803–1848." *Bulletin of the History of Medicine* 83, no. 1 (2009): 95–124.

Jones, Douglas R. "'The League Will Not Ignore the Cry of the Negro Race for Justice': Marcus Garvey, the League of Nations and South-West Africa." *Journal of Southern African Studies* 48, no. 1 (January 2, 2022): 103–117.

Jung, John. *Chinese Laundries: Tickets to Survival on Gold Mountain*. Yin & Yang Press, 2007.

Kaiserlichen Statistischen Amt, ed. "XVIII. Die Schutzgebiete." *Statistisches Jahrbuch für das Deutsche Reich*. 1899 (1900): 215–220.

Kalb, Martin. *Environing Empire: Nature, Infrastructure, and the Making of German Southwest Africa*. New York: Berghahn, 2022.

Kalb, Martin. "Water, Sand, Molluscs: Imperial Infrastructures, the Age of Hydrology, and German Colonialism in Swakopmund, Southwest Africa, 1884–1915." *Environment and History* 26, no. 2 (2020): 175–206.

Karuka, Manu. *Empire's Tracks: Indigenous Nations, Chinese Workers, and the Transcontinental Railroad*. Berkeley: University of California Press, 2019.

Katjavivi, Peter H. *A History of Resistance in Namibia*. James Currey Publishers, 1988.

Katz, Elaine N. "The Underground Route to Mining: Afrikaners and the Witwatersrand Gold Mining Industry from 1902 to the 1907 Miners' Strike." *The Journal of African History* 36, no. 3 (November 1995): 467–489.

Kinahan, Jill. *Cattle for Beads: The Archaeology of Historical Contact and Trade on the Namib Coast*. Vol. 14. Windhoek: Namibia Archaeological Trust, 2000.

Kirby, P.R. "A Secret Musical Instrument, the Ekola of the Ovakuanyama of Ovamiloland." *South African Journal of Science* 38, no. 1 (1942): 345–351.

Kirch, Patrick Vinton, and Marshall Sahlins. *Anahulu: The Anthropology of History in the Kingdom of Hawaii, Volume 1: Historical Ethnography*. Chicago: University of Chicago Press, 1994.

Kleinöder, Nina. "Kolonialwirtschaft ohne Kolonien?: Deutscher Eisenbahnbau in Afrika im und nach dem Ersten Weltkrieg." In *1919 – Der Versailler Vertrag und die deutschen Unternehmen*, edited by Dieter Ziegler and Jan-Otmar Hesse, 311–342. De Gruyter Oldenbourg, 2022.

Kochhar, Rajesh. "Smallpox in the Modern Scientific and Colonial Contexts 1721–1840." *Journal of Biosciences* 36, no. 5 (2011): 761–768.

Kolonial-Wirtschaftlichen Komitee, ed. *Koloniales Hand- und Adreßbuch 1926–1927*. Berlin: Süsseroth, 1926.

Kreienbaum, Jonas. *"Ein trauriges Fiasko": koloniale Konzentrationslager im südlichen Afrika, 1900–1908*. Studien zur Gewaltgeschichte des 20. Jahrhunderts. Hamburg: Hamburger Edition, 2015.

Kreienbaum, Jonas. "Friedrich von Lindequist, koloniale Konzentrationslager und transimperiales Lernen." *Revue d'Allemagne et des pays de langue allemande*, 2016, 75–88.

Kreienbaum, Jonas. "'Wir sind keine Sklavenhalter' – Zur Rolle der Zwangsarbeit in den Konzentrationslagern in Deutsch-Südwestafrika (1904–1908)." In *Lager vor Auschwitz. Gewalt und Integration im 20. Jahrhundert*, edited by Christoph Jahr and Jens Thiel, 68–83. Berlin: Metropol-Verl, 2013.

Kreplin, Emil, and Friedrich Knacke. *Die deutschen Diamanten und ihre Gewinnung*. Berlin: Reimer, 1914.

Krüger, Gesine. *Kriegsbewältigung und Geschichtsbewusstsein: Realität, Deutung und Verarbeitung des deutschen Kolonialkriegs in Namibia 1904 bis 1907*. Göttingen, DE: Vandenhoeck & Ruprecht, 1999.

Krüger, Gesine. "Writing in Images: Aspects of Mission Photography in Southern Africa." In *Hues between Black and White: Historical Photography from Colonial Namibia 1860s to 1915*, edited by Wolfram Hartmann, 241–258. Windhoek: Out of Africa Publishers, 2004.

Kuhn, Gary. G. "Liberian Contract Labor in Panama, 1837–1897." *Liberian Studies Journal* 6, no. 1 (1974): 43–52.

Kuhn, Philalethes. *Die Herero*. Berlin: Reimer, 1907.

L'Ange, Gerald. *Urgent Imperial Service: South African Forces in German South West Africa, 1914–1915*. Rivonia: Ashanti Publishers, 1991.

Lawrance, Benjamin Nicholas. "Most Obedient Servants." *Cahiers d'études Africaines* 40, no. 159 (January 1, 2000): 489–524.

Legassick, Martin. "The Frontier Tradition in South African Historiography." In *Economy and Society in Pre-Industrial South Africa*, edited by Shula Marks and Anthony Atmore, 12: 44–79. London: Longman Group, 1972.

Leutwein, Theodor. *Elf Jahre Gouverneur in Deutsch-Südwestafrika*. Berlin: E.S. Mittler & Sohn, 1908.

Levinson, Olga. *Diamanten im Sand: das wechselvolle Leben von August Stauch*. Windhoek: Kuiseb-Verl, 2007.

Likuwa, Kletus Muhena. "Colonialism and the Development of the Contract Labour System in Kavango." In *Re-Viewing Resistance in Namibian History*, edited by Jeremy Silvester, 105–126. Windhoek: University of Namibia Press, 2015.

Likuwa, Kletus Muhena. "Continuity and Change in Gender Relations within the Contract Labour System in Kavango, Namibia, 1925–1972." *Journal of Southern African Studies* 47, no. 1 (2021): 79–92.

Likuwa, Kletus Muhena. *Voices from the Kavango: A Study of the Contract Labour System in Namibia, 1925–1972*. Basel: Basler Afrika Bibliographien, 2020.

Likuwa, Kletus Muhena, and Napandulwe Shiweda. "Okaholo: Contract Labour System and Lessons for Post Colonial Namibia." *Mgbakoigba: Journal of African Studies* 6, no. 2 (2017): 26–47.

Linden, Marcel van der. "Globalizing Labour Historiography – The IISH Approach," 14. Amsterdam: International Institute of Social History, 2002.

Linden, Marcel van der. "The Promise and Challenges of Global Labor History." *International Labor and Working-Class History* 82 (2012): 57–76.
Linden, Marcel van der. *Workers of the World: Essays Toward a Global Labor History*. Leiden: Brill, 2008.
Linden, Marcel van der, and Jan Lucassen. *Prolegomena for a Global Labour History*. Amsterdam: International Institute of Social History, 1999.
Lindner, Ulrike. *Koloniale Begegnungen: Deutschland und Großbritannien als Imperialmächte in Afrika 1880–1914*. Frankfurt am Main: Campus Verlag, 2011.
Lindner, Ulrike. "Transnational Movements between Colonial Empires: Migrant Workers from the British Cape Colony in the German Diamond Town of Luderitzbucht." *European Review of History* 16, no. 5 (2009): 679–695.
Loth, Heinrich. "Zu den Anfängen des Kampfes der Arbeiter Südwestafrikas gegen den deutschen Imperialismus." *Wissenschaftliche Zeitschrift der Karl-Marx-Universität Leipzig, Gesellschafts und Sprachwissenschaftliche Reihe*, no. 3 (1961): 351–356.
Löytty, Sakari. "People's Church – People's Music." PhD thesis, Sibelius Academy, DocMus, 2012.
Lüdtke, Alf. "'Alltagsgeschichte': Verführung Oder Chance? Zur Erforschung Der Praxis Historischer Subjekte." *Göttinger Jahrbuch*, 1986, 183–200.
Lunn, Jon. *Capital and Labour on the Rhodesian Railway System: 1888–1947*. Basingstoke: Macmillan, 1997.
Lyon, William Blakemore. "From Labour Elites to Garveyites: West African Migrant Labour in Namibia, 1892–1925." *Journal of Southern African Studies* 47, no. 1 (2021): 37–55.
Lyon, William Blakemore. "Namibian Worker Database." CSV, Data set. Berlin: edoc-Server Open-Access-Publikationsserver der Humboldt-Universität, 2024. https://doi.org/10.18452/28347.
Lyon, William Blakemore. "The South West Africa Company and Anglo-German Relations, 1892–1914." Master's thesis, Cambridge University, 2015.
Mans, Minette. *The Changing Faces of Aawambo Musical Arts*. Basel Southern Africa Studies 11. Basel: Basler Afrika Bibliographien, 2017.
Mark-Thiesen, Cassandra. *Mediators, Contract Men, and Colonial Capital: Mechanized Gold Mining in the Gold Coast Colony, 1879–1909*. Rochester: University of Rochester Press, 2018.
Mark-Thiesen, Cassandra. "The 'Bargain' of Collaboration: African Intermediaries, Indirect Recruitment, and Indigenous Institutions in the Ghanaian Gold Mining Industry, 1900–1906." *International Review of Social History* 57, no. S20 (2012): 17–38.
Marquardt, Gary. "Open Spaces and Closed Minds : A Socio-Environmental History of Rinderpest in South Africa and Namibia, 1896–1897." PhD thesis, University of Wisconsin-Madison, 2007.
Martin, Jane. "Krumen 'Down the Coast': Liberian Migrants on the West African Coast in the 19th and Early 20th Centuries." *The International Journal of African Historical Studies* 18, no. 3 (1985): 401–423.
Martino, Enrique. "Touts and Despots: Recruiting Assemblages of Contract Labour in Fernando Pó and the Gulf of Guinea, 1858–1979." PhD thesis, Humboldt University, 2016.
Martino, Enrique. *Touts: Recruiting Indentured Labor in the Gulf of Guinea*. Berlin: De Gruyter Oldenbourg, 2022.
Matthias. Häussler. *Der Genozid an den Herero: Krieg, Emotion und extreme Gewalt in "Deutsch-Südwestafrika."* Erste Auflage. Genozid und Gedächtnis. Weilerswist: Velbrück Wissenschaft, 2018.
Mbenzi, Petrus Angula. "Renaming of Places in Namibia in the Pre-Colonial, Colonial and Post-Colonial Era: Colonising and Decolonising Place Names." *Journal of Namibian Studies* 25 (2019): 71–99.

Mbuende, Kaire. *Namibia, the Broken Shield: Anatomy of Imperialism and Revolution*. Malmö: Liber, 1986.

McKeown, Adam. "Global Migration, 1846–1940." *Journal of World History* 15, no. 2 (2004): 155–189.

McKittrick, Meredith. "The 'Burden' of Young Men: Property and Generational Conflict in Namibia, 1880–1945." *African Economic History*, no. 24 (1996): 115–29.

McKittrick, Meredith. *To Dwell Secure: Generation, Christianity, and Colonialism in Ovamboland*. Portsmouth: Heinemann, 2002.

Medick, Hans, and David Warren Sabean, eds. "Introduction." In *Interest and Emotion: Essays on the Study of Family and Kinship*, 1–8. Cambridge: Cambridge University Press, 1984.

Michelle R. Moyd. *Violent Intermediaries: African Soldiers, Conquest, and Everyday Colonialism in German East Africa*. New African Histories. Athens: Ohio University Press, 2014.

Miescher, Giorgio. *Namibia's Red Line: The History of a Veterinary and Settlement Border*. New York: Palgrave Macmillan, 2012.

Millard, Joan. "Grass-Roots Pioneers of Transvaal Methodism." *Missionalia* 17, no. 3 (1989): 188–198.

Mistry, S.D. "Ethnic Groups of Indians in South Africa." *South African Medical Journal = Suid-Afrikaanse Tydskrif Vir Geneeskunde* 39, no. 31 (1965): 691–694.

Mitchell, J. Alexander. "Plague in South Africa: Perpetuation and Spread of Infection by Wild Rodents." *The Journal of Hygiene* 20, no. 4 (1921): 377–382.

Mokopakgosi, B.T. "German Colonialism in Microcosm: A Study of the Role of Concessionaire Companies in the Development of the German Colonial State in Namibia, 1890–1915." PhD thesis, University of London, 1988.

Moodie, T. Dunbar, Vivienne Ndatshe, and British Sibuyi. "Migrancy and Male Sexuality on the South African Gold Mines." *Journal of Southern African Studies* 14, no. 2 (January 1988): 228–256.

Moodie, T. Dunbar, and Vivienne Ndatshe. *Going for Gold: Men, Mines, and Migration*. Berkeley: University of California Press, 1995.

Moore, Bernard C. "Namibia Report on Concession Companies up to 1920." ERC Project, Political Economy of African Development. Windhoek, Namibia, 2021.

Moore, Bernard C. "Smuggled Sheep, Smuggled Shepherds: Farm Labour Transformations in Namibia and the Question of Southern Angola, 1933–1975." *Journal of Southern African Studies* 47, no. 1 (January 2, 2021): 93–125.

Moore, Bernard C., Stephanie Quinn, William Blakemore Lyon, and Kai Herzog. "Balancing the Scales: Re-Centring Labour and Labourers in Namibian History." *Journal of Southern African Studies* 47, no. 1 (2021): 1–16.

Moorsom, Richard. *Underdevelopment and Labour Migration: The Contract Labour System in Namibia*. Bergen: Chr. Michelsen Institute, 1997.

Musambachime, M. Chambikabalenshi. "'Kapitohanga: The Disease That Killed Faster than Bullets': The Impact of the Influenza Pandemic in the South West Africa Protectorate (Namibia) from October 1918 to December 1919." Basel: Basler Afrika Bibliographien, 2000.

Muschalek, Marie. *Violence as Usual: Policing and the Colonial State in German Southwest Africa*. Ithaca: Cornell University Press, 2019.

Namhila, Ellen Ndeshi. *Kaxumba kaNdola: Man and Myth: The Biography of a Barefoot Soldier*. Basel: Basler Afrika Bibliographien, 2005.

Namhila, Ellen Ndeshi. *Native Estates: Records of Mobility across Colonial Boundaries*. Basel: Basler Afrika Bibliographien, 2017.

Nampala, Lovisa T., and Vilho Shigwedha. *Aawambo Kingdoms, History and Cultural Change: Perspectives from Northern Namibia*. Basel: Schlettwein, 2006.

Nampala, Lovisa Tegelela. *Infrastructures of Migrant Labour in Colonial Ovamboland, 1915 to 1954*. Basel: Schlettwein, 2023.

Nasson, Bill. *Abraham Esau's War: A Black South African War in the Cape; 1899 – 1902*. Cambridge: Cambridge Univ. Pr., 1991.

Nasson, Bill. "Moving Lord Kitchener: Black Military Transport and Supply Work in the South African War, 1899–1902, with Particular Reference to the Cape Colony." *Journal of Southern African Studies* 11, no. 1 (1984): 25–51.

Ndakalako-Bannikov, Martha. "Changing Dresses: Owambo Traditional Dress and Discourses on Tradition, Ethnicity, and National Identity in Namibia." *Journal of Folklore Research* 57 (2020): 73–110.

Ngavirue, Zed. *Political Parties and Interest Groups in South West Africa (Namibia): A Study of a Plural Society*. Basel: Schlettwein, 1997.

Ngwenya, Barbara Ntombi. "The Development of Transport Infrastructure in the Bechuanaland Protectorate 1885–1966." *Botswana Notes and Records* 16 (1984): 73–84.

Nujoma, Sam. *Where Others Wavered: The Autobiography of Sam Nujoma*. London: Panaf Books, 2001.

Oelschlager, Vanita. *The Gandy Dancers: And Work Songs from the American Railroad*. Akron: VanitaBooks, 2015.

Oestermann, Tristan. *Kautschuk und Arbeit in Kamerun unter deutscher Kolonialherrschaft 1880–1913*. Industrielle Welt. Cologne: Böhlau Verlag, 2023.

Olorunfemi, A. "West Africa and Anglo-German Trade Rivalry 1895–1914." *Journal of the Historical Society of Nigeria* 11, no. 1/2 (1981): 21–35.

Olusoga, David, and Casper W. Erichsen. *The Kaiser's Holocaust: Germany's Forgotten Genocide and the Colonial Roots of Nazism*. London: Faber and Faber, 2011.

Ọmọsini, Olufẹmi. "Railway Projects and British Attitude Towards the Development of West Africa, 1872–1903." *Journal of the Historical Society of Nigeria* 5, no. 4 (1971): 491–507.

Onselen, Charles van. *Chibaro: African Mine Labour in Southern Rhodesia 1900–1933*. London: Pluto Press, 1980.

Onselen, Charles van. *New Babylon, New Nineveh: Everyday Life on the Witwatersrand 1886–1914*. Johannesburg: Jonathan Ball, 2001.

Onselen, Charles van. "Reactions to Rinderpest in Southern Africa 1896–97." *The Journal of African History* 13, no. 3 (1972): 473–488.

Onselen, Charles van. *The Night Trains: Moving Mozambican Miners to and from the Witwatersrand Mines, 1902–1955*. Oxford: Oxford University Press, 2021.

Ortloff, Hermann. *Die Landungsverhältnisse an der Küste Deutsch-Südwestafrikas*. Berlin: Verlag von Dietrich Reimer, 1902.

Otavi-Minen-Aktiengesellschaft. *Die Geschichte der Otavi-Minen-AG: 1900–2000; ein ereignisreiches Jahrhundert*. Otavi Minen AG, 2000.

Pallaver, Karin. "A Recognized Currency in Beads. Glass Beads as Money in Nineteenth-Century East Africa: The Central Caravan Road." In *Money in Africa*, edited by Catherine Eagleton, Harcourt Fuller, and John Perkins, 20–29. London: The British Museum Press, 2009.

Pirie, Gordon. "Railways and Labour Migration to the Rand Mines: Constraints and Significance." *Journal of Southern African Studies* 19, no. 4 (1993): 713–730.

Pirio, Gregory. "The Role of Garveyism in the Making of Namibian Nationalism." In *Namibia 1884–1984: Readings on Namibia's History and Society*, edited by Brian Wood, 259–267. London: Namibia Support Committee, 1988.

Pool, Gerhardus. *Eisenbahnen in Deutsch-Südwestafrika, 1897–1915*. Edited by Rolf-Reinhard Henke. Translated by Kuno Budack. Windhoek: Namibia Wissenschaftliche Gesellschaft, 2009.

Pratt, Mary Louise. *Imperial Eyes: Travel Writing and Transculturation*. London: Routledge, 2009.
Prein, Philipp. "Guns and Top Hats: African Resistance in German South West Africa, 1907–1915." *Journal of Southern African Studies* 20, no. 1 (1994): 99–121.
Press, Steven. *Blood and Diamonds: Germany's Imperial Ambitions in Africa*. Cambridge: Harvard University Press, 2021.
Preußen/Großer Generalstab. *Die Kämpfe der deutschen Truppen in Südwestafrika. 1, Der Feldzug gegen die Hereros / auf Grund amtlichen Materials bearb. von der Kriegsgeschichtlichen Abteilung I des Großen Generalstabes*. Vol. 1. Berlin: Mittler, 1906.
Quiring, Erich. "Die Eisenbahnen Deutsch-Südwestafrikas und ihre Bedeutung für die wirtschaftliche Entwicklung der Kolonie." PhD thesis, Friedrich-Alexander-Universität, 1911.
Rich, Jeremy. *A Workman Is Worthy of His Meat: Food and Colonialism in the Gabon Estuary*. Lincoln: University of Nebraska Press, 2009.
Richardson, Peter. *Chinese Mine Labour in the Transvaal*. London: Palgrave Macmillan, 1982.
Rohrbach, Paul. *Deutsche Kolonialwirtschaft. 1, Südwest-Afrika*. Berlin: Buchverlag der "Hilfe," 1907.
Roland, Bude, Klaus Fricke, and Martin Murray. *O&K Dampflokomotiven. Lieferverzeichnis 1892–1945*. Buschhofen: Verlag Railroadiana, 1977.
Ross, Robert. *A Concise History of South Africa*. Cambridge, UK: Cambridge University Press, 2011.
Ross, Robert. *Clothing: A Global History*. Cambridge: Polity, 2008.
Rubel, William. *Bread: A Global History*. London: Reaktion Books, 2011.
Salzmann, Erich von. *Im Kampfe gegen die Herero*. Berlin: Dietrich Reimer, 1905.
Samarin, William J. *The Black Man's Burden: African Colonial Labor On The Congo And Ubangi Rivers, 1880–1900*. Boulder: Westview Press, 1989.
Sander, A.D. *Die Rinderpest und ihr Einfluss auf die wirtschaftlichen Verhältnisse in Deutsch-Sudwestafrika*. Berlin: Hermann Paetel, 1897.
Sander, Ludwig. *Geschichte der Deutschen Kolonial-Gesellschaft für Südwest-Afrika: von ihrer Gründung bis zum Jahre 1910; in zwei Bänden*. Vol. 1. 2 vols. Berlin: Reimer, 1912.
Schaller, Dominik J. "'Every Herero Will Be Shot' Genocide, Concentration Camps, and Slave Labor in German South-West Africa." In *Forgotten Genocides: Oblivion, Denial, and Memory*, edited by René Lemarchand, 51–90. Philadelphia: University of Pennsylvania Press, 2011.
Schatz, Ilse. *Tsumeb zu O.M.E.G.'s Zeiten*. Namibia: S.N. Publishing Company, 1997.
Schnorbus, Heidi and Otavi-Minen-Aktiengesellschaft, eds. *Die Geschichte der Otavi-Minen-AG: 1900–2000; ein ereignisreiches Jahrhundert*. Frankfurt am Main: Brönners Druckerei Breidenstein, 2000.
Schueler, Judith. *Materialising Identity the Co-Construction of the Gotthard Railway and Swiss National Identity*. Technology and European History Series 1. Amsterdam: Aksant, 2008.
Schuler, Monica. "Kru Emigration to British and French Guiana, 1841–1857." In *Africans in Bondage. Studies in Slavery and the Slave Trade. Essays in Honour of Philip D. Curtin on the Occasion of the Twenty-Fifth Anniversary of African Studies at the University of Wisconsin*, edited by Paul E. Lovejoy, 155–201. Madison, Wisconsin, University of Wisconsin Press, 1986.
Schürmann, Felix. "Ships and Beaches as Arenas of Entanglements from Below: Whalemen in Coastal Africa, c. 1760–1900." *InterDisciplines. Journal of History and Sociology* 3, no. 1 (2012): 25–47.
Schwabe, Kurd. *Der Krieg in Deutsch-Südwestafrika 1904–1906*. Berlin: Weller, 1907.
Schwabe, Kurd. *Mit Schwert und Pflug in Deutsch-Südwestafrika*. Berlin: Ernst Siegfried Mittler und Sohn, 1899.
Scott, John L. "British Concentration Camps of the Second South African War (The Transvaal, 1900–1902)." Master's thesis, Florida State University, 2007.

Scotto, Giulia. "Colonial and Postcolonial Logistics." *Footprint: Delft Architecture Theory Journal* 23 (2018): 69–86.

Siefkes, Martin. "Einführung in das Tagebuch des Johannes Spiecker während des Herero-Nama-Aufstands in Deutsche Südwestafrika." In *Mein Tagebuch: Erfahrungen eines deutschen Missionars in Deutsch-Südwestafrika 1905–1907*, edited by Lisa Kopelmann and Martin Siefkes, 7–38. Berlin: Simon Verl. für Bibliothekswissen, 2013.

Siiskonen, Harri. *Trade and Socioeconomic Change in Ovamboland, 1850–1906*. Helsinki: SHS, 1990.

Silvester, Jeremy. *My Heart Tells Me That I Have Done Nothing Wrong: The Fall of Mandume*. Windhoek: Discourse, 1995.

Silvester, Jeremy, ed. *Re-Viewing Resistance in Namibian History*. Windhoek: UNAM Press, 2015.

Silvester, Jeremy, and Jan-Bart Gewald, eds. *Words Cannot Be Found: German Colonial Rule in Namibia: An Annotated Reprint of the 1918 Blue Book*. Sources for African History, v. 1. Leiden: Brill, 2003.

Simone, AbdouMaliq. "People as Infrastructure: Intersecting Fragments in Johannesburg." *Public Culture* 16, no. 3 (2004): 407–429.

Smith, Leonard V. "Empires at the Paris Peace Conference." In *Empires at War: 1911 – 1923*, edited by Robert Gerwarth and Erez Manela, 254–277. Oxford: Oxford University Press, 2014.

Söhnge, Paul Gerhard. *Tsumeb, a Historical Sketch*. Windhoek: Committee of the S.W.A. Scientific Society, 1976.

Spiecker, Johannes. *Mein Tagebuch: Erfahrungen eines deutschen Missionars in Deutsch-Südwestafrika 1905–1907*. Edited by Lisa Kopelmann and Martin Siefkes. Berlin: Simon Verl. für Bibliothekswissen, 2013.

Spies, S.B. *Methods of Barbarism?: Roberts and Kitchener and Civilians in the Boer Republics, January 1900-May 1902*. Cape Town: Human & Rousseau, 1977.

Spinage, Clive. *Cattle Plague: A History*. New York: Springer US, 2003.

Stals, E.L.P. *Duits-Suidwes-Afrika na die Groot Opstande: 'n studie in die verhouding tussen owerheid en inboorlinge*. Pretoria: Die Staatsdrukker, 1984.

Steinmetz, George. *The Devil's Handwriting: Precoloniality and the German Colonial State in Qingdao, Samoa, and Southwest Africa*. Chicago Studies in Practices of Meaning. Chicago: University of Chicago Press, 2007.

Stejskal, James. *The Horns of the Beast: The Swakop River Campaign and World War I in South-West Africa, 1914–15*. Warwick: Helion Limited, 2014.

Strassegger, Regina. "Die Wanderarbeit der Ovambo während der deutschen Kolonialbesetzung Namibias. Unter besonderer Berücksichtigung der Wanderarbeiter auf den Diamantenfeldern in den Jahren 1908 bis 1914." PhD thesis, Karl-Franzens-Universität Graz, 1988.

Sullivan, Jo Mary. "The Kru Coast Revolt of 1915–1916." *Liberian Studies Journal* 14, no. 1 (1989): 51–71.

Sundiata, Ibrahim K. *From Slaving to Neoslavery: The Bight of Biafra and Fernando Po in the Era of Abolition, 1827–1930*. Madison: University of Wisconsin Press, 1996.

Sundiata, Ibrahim K. "The Garvey Aftermath: The Fall, Rise, and Fall." In *United States and West Africa-Interactions and: Interactions and Relations*, edited by Alusine Jalloh and Toyin Falola, 75–89. New York: Boydell & Brewer, 2008.

Sundiata, Ibrahim K. "The Rise and Decline of Kru Power: Fernando Po in the Nineteenth Century." *Liberian Studies Journal* 6, no. 1 (1975): 25–41.

Sunseri, Thaddeus. "The Baumwollfrage: Cotton Colonialism in German East Africa." *Central European History* 34, no. 1 (2001): 31–51.

Swanzy, Henry. "A Trading Family in the Nineteenth Century Gold Coast." *Transactions of the Gold Coast & Togoland Historical Society* 2, no. 2 (1956): 87–120.

Thomsen, Hermann. *Deutsches Land in Africa*. Munich: Verlag der Deutschen Alpenzeitung, 1911.

Tischler, Julia. *Light and Power for a Multiracial Nation: The Kariba Dam Scheme in the Central African Federation*. Basingstoke: Palgrave Macmillan, 2013.

Todzi, Kim Sebastian. *Unternehmen Weltaneignung: der Woermann-Konzern und der deutsche Kolonialismus 1837–1916*. Hamburger Beiträge zur Geschichte der kolonialen Globalisierung. Göttingen: Wallstein Verlag, 2023.

Tönjes, Hermann. *Ovamboland; Land, Leute, Mission. Mit besonderer Berücksichtigung seines grössten Stammes Oukuanjama*. Berlin: M. Warneck, 1911.

Tonkin, Elizabeth. *Narrating Our Pasts the Social Construction of Oral History*. Cambridge,: Cambridge University Press, 1999.

Tracey, Andrew. "The System of the Mbira." *African Music* 10, no. 1 (2015): 127–149.

Turrell, Robert Vicat. *Capital and Labour on the Kimberley Diamond Fields, 1871–1890*. Cambridge: Cambridge University Press, 1987.

Uth, Max Rud. *Im Sattel und Ochsenwagen: Erlebnisse und Beobachtungen in Deutsch-Südwest-Afrika*. Fulda: Uth, 1907.

Vedder, Heinrich. *Kurze Geschichten aus einem langen Leben*. Verlag d. Rhein. Missions-Gesellschaft, 1953.

Vellut, Jean-Luc. "Les bassins miniers de l'ancien Congo belge : essai d'histoire économique et sociale (1900–1960)." *Les cahiers du CEDAF*, no. 7 (1981): 1–70.

Vietor, Johann Karl. "Die Arbeiterfrage in den deutschen Kolonien." In *Sonderabdruck aus den Verhandlungen des Deutschen Kolonialkongresses 1902*, 519–526. Berlin: Verl. Kolonialkriegerdank, 1902.

Vinson, Robert Trent. *The Americans Are Coming! Dreams of African American Liberation in Segregationist South Africa*. Athens: Ohio University Press, 2012.

Vito, Christian G. De, and Anne Gerritsen, eds. *Micro-Spatial Histories of Global Labour*. Cham: Palgrave Macmillan, 2018.

Voeltz, Richard A. "The European Economic and Political Penetration of South West Africa, 1884–1892." *The International Journal of African Historical Studies* 17, no. 4 (1984): 623–639.

Wägli, Bruno. "Dampf in Südwest: Eisenbahnbau zur Kolonialzeit in Deutsch-Südwestafrika." Bachelor Research Paper, Universität Freiburg, 2008.

Wallace, Marion. *A History of Namibia from the Beginning to 1990*. Oxford: Oxford University Press, 2013.

Walt, Lucien van der. "The ICU, the Mines and the State in South West Africa, 1920–1926: Garveyism, Revolutionary Syndicalism and Global Labour History." In *Labour Struggles in Southern Africa, 1919–1949 New Perspectives on the Industrial and Commercial Workers' Union (ICU)*, edited by David Johnson, Noor Nieftagodien, and Lucien van der Walt, 2–17. Cape Town: HSRC Press, 2023.

Wedekind, Klemens. *Impfe und herrsche. Veterinärmedizinisches Wissen und Herrschaft im kolonialen Namibia 1887–1929*. Göttingen: Vandenhoeck & Ruprecht, 2020.

White, Luise. *The Comforts of Home: Prostitution in Colonial Nairobi*. Chicago: University of Chicago Press, 1990.

Wilkins, Mira. "Multinational Enterprise to 1930: Discontinuities and Continuities." In *Leviathans: Multinational Corporations and the New Global History*, edited by Alfred D. Chandler and Bruce Mazlish, 45–79. Cambridge: Cambridge University Press, 2005.

Yekani, Minu Haschemi. "'Inder und Chinesen werden unsere Kolonie nicht in die Höhe bringen.' Arbeit, Klima, und der 'Rase' Diskurs in Tansania (1885–1914)." In *"Deutsche Arbeit": kritische Perspektiven auf ein ideologisches Selbstbild*. Göttingen: Wallstein Verlag, 2018.

Zeller, Joachim. "'Ombepera i Koza – the Cold Is Killing Me: A history of the concentration camp at Swakopmund (1904–1908)." In *Genocide in German South-West Africa: The Colonial War of 1904–1908 and Its Aftermath*, edited by Jürgen Zimmerer and Joachim Zeller, 64–80. Monmouth: Merlin Press, 2008.

Zimmerer, Jürgen. *German Rule, African Subjects: State Aspirations and the Reality of Power in Colonial Namibia*. Translated by Anthony Mellor-Stapelberg. New York: Berghahn, 2021.

Zimmerer, Jürgen. *Von Windhuk nach Auschwitz? Beiträge zum Verhältnis von Kolonialismus und Holocaust*. Münster: LIT Verlag, 2011.

Zimmerer, Jürgen, and Joachim Zeller. *Genocide in German South-West Africa: The Colonial War of 1904–1908 and Its Aftermath*. Monmouth: Merlin Press, 2008.

Name Index

Amupanda, Job Shipululo 133
Andrade, Gabriel E. 161

Beckert, Sven 10–11
Beinart, William 117, 120, 129, 179, 205, 212–213, 218, 237, 239–241
Bellucci, Stefano 10, 72, 115
Bley, Helmut 8, 20–21, 58, 60, 62, 70
Brooks, George E. 45, 48, 90, 92, 97

Cooper, Allan D. 9
Cooper, Frederick 7, 115

Dinklage, Max 90–91, 93
Dobler, Gregor 73, 133, 141–142, 205–206
Drechsler, Horst 8, 20–21, 26, 28, 59, 108

Eckert, Andreas 10–12, 72, 115
Eckl, Andreas E. 155, 276
Edvinsson, Rodney 2
Eirola, Martti 2, 22, 138, 140, 145–146
Emmett, Tony 9, 262, 270–271, 286, 290

Falk, Kurt 189
Frost, Diane 97–98, 248

Galton, Francis 30
Gerritsen, Anne 12–13
Gewald, Jan-Bart 9, 20, 24, 35, 60, 69, 81, 110, 127, 129, 264, 266, 268, 273
Gordon, Robert J. 37, 152–153, 155, 172, 178, 198
Gründer, Horst 25
Gunn, Jeffrey 48–49, 91

Haak, Werner 48
Hagen, Gunter Tronje 250
Hagens, W. 250
Halpern, Rick 7
Harries, Patrick 117, 189, 195
Harris, Brent 16, 96
Hartmann, Wolfram 15–16, 21, 189
Häussler, Matthias 69–70, 87
Hayes, Patricia 15–16, 133, 139, 178, 189, 275–276
Henrichsen, Dag 8, 27, 30, 62, 226, 262
Hillebrecht, Werner 95
Hull, Isabel V. 70, 123

Kalb, Martin 43, 50, 53, 57, 71, 209
Kocka, Jürgen 12
Kreienbaum, Jonas 108, 128
Krüger, Gesine 15, 110
Kuhn, Philalethes 60

Legassick, Martin 19
Leutwein, Theodor 59, 61–62, 69–70
Likuwa, Kletus Muhena 9, 16, 134, 185, 276
Lindner, Ulrike 118, 162, 204–205, 212, 240, 247
Lüdtke, Alf 12

Maherero, Samuel 69
Mark-Thiesen, Cassandra 20, 90, 142, 169
McKittrick, Meredith 22, 134
Miescher, Giorgio 3, 19, 59, 147
Mokopakgosi, B. T. 20, 25–26, 28, 35, 77, 134, 145, 151
Moodie, T. Dunbar 181, 189
Moorsom, Richard 9, 133
Muschalek, Marie 55, 172

Namhila, Ellen Ndeshi 9, 13, 15
Nampala, Lovisa T. 9, 133, 141, 154
Nasson, Bill 115–116

Oestermann, Tristan 90–92, 204, 248, 250
Olorunfemi, A. 90–91
Ortloff, Hermann 43, 50, 53

Pirio, Gregory 286–287
Ponzi, Carlo (Charles) 89
Pratt, Mary Louise 19
Press, Steven 134, 162–163, 165, 195

Schatz, Ilse 22, 174, 179–180, 193
Schwabe, Kurd 46–47, 103, 220
Siiskonen, Harri 2, 22, 139
Silvester, Jeremy 8, 15–16, 35, 81, 127, 129, 273, 275–276
Simone, AbdouMaliq 71

https://doi.org/10.1515/9783111374918-012

Spiecker, Johannes 143–144, 178
Strassegger, Regina 9, 134, 144, 147, 150, 152, 154, 156, 160, 167
Swanzy, Henry 256

Tjiseseta, Manasse 31–33, 62, 125
Todzi, Kim Sebastian 9, 89, 93, 107, 147
Tonkin, Elizabeth 16

Uth, Max Rudolf 48–49, 55–56

van der Linden, Marcel 10–11, 72
van Onselen, Charles 11, 60, 117, 142, 160, 188–189, 193, 195, 253
Vedder, Heinrich 107–109
Vito, Christian G. De 12–13
Voeltz, Richard A. 29
von François, Curt 36, 43–44, 46
von Salzmann, Erich 78, 96–102
von Trotha, Lothar 69–77, 114, 145, 220

Walt, Lucien van der 283
White, Luise 191
Wilkins, Mira 76
Witbooi, Hendrik 36, 43, 46, 63, 95

Zarossi, Luigi 77–80, 86–89
Zeller, Joachim 8, 95, 108–110
Zimmerer, Jürgen 8, 95, 109–110, 146, 218, 235, 237, 240

Subject Index

African migrant elite
– defining 205–207
– First World War 202, 260
– high pay and skilled jobs 202
– martial law period 278
– non-Kru West Africans 205
– racial and economic barriers 203
– recruiting Indian/Chinese migrants 203–205
– religion 240–243
– social life 244
– sports 243–244
– and white settlers 203
Alltagsgeschichte 12

Baster 66–68, 118, 243
Bayer diamond field 167–168
beer consumption 55–57, 188
"Blue Book" report 273
boeremeal 157
Bogenfels mine 191–192

Cameroonian exiles
– economic stability 269
– men, German military service 268
– wages 265–266
– war compensation claim 267–268
– women 268–270
– work type 266
Cape wagon drivers. *See* wagon drivers
Cape Worker recruitment/migration, railway construction
– demand 213, 216
– free movement, workers 219
– 'French' 215
– hiring 215
– income 219
– Namibian War 219
– Native Affairs in Cape Town 217
– Okiep copper mines 217
– pay scale 215–216
– permission, local authorities 216
– Port Nolloth 216
– Rand Mines 218
– travel to GSWA 214

Consolidated Diamond Mines (CDM) 282, 287
copper mine. *See* Tsumeb mines, Ovambo workers

death registry for natives 110–111, 113
Deutsche Kolonialgesellschaft für Südwestafrika (DKGfSWA) 25, 28, 47, 54, 61, 95
diamond mines 1–3
– African workforce 166–167
– alcohol 188
– Bayer 167–168
– Bogenfels 191–192
– Itere's death 170–173
– larger, labor on 168–169
– Lewala, Zacharias 162
– Lüderitzbucht, arriving and leaving 196–197
– map of diamond fields 163, 164
– searching by hand 165–166
– six-month contracts, Lüderitzbucht 148
– transporting workers 74
– weather 152
– Unverhofft 169–170
– wages 151
– water and food provisions 195
– workers clothes 154
– workers health 192–193
disease outbreaks 38–39
DKGfSWA. *See Deutsche Kolonialgesellschaft für Südwestafrika* (DKGfSWA)

Entre Rios ship life, Kru workers
– adolescent males 97
– German shipmates, interactions 101
– Hamburg-Südamerikanische Dampfschiffsgesellschaft 96
– hiring workers 98
– labor recruitment process 98
– listening to gramophone, soldiers 100–101
– offloading process 101–103
– photographs 96–99
– selling goods 97
– transporting horses 100, 102–103
– washing and ironing 99, 100
– Woermann's operations 98

https://doi.org/10.1515/9783111374918-013

First World War 3, 7, 17, 203, 240, 259, 290
- economic and social change 260
- labor elite 71
- Liberia, economic collapse to 279
- South African rule 132, 263–265
- Spanish influenza 17, 279–282
- UNIA 286

German South West Africa (GSWA) 1, 19–20
- contract work 19–23
- economic change 19–20
- Herero communities 19–23
- infrastructure and economic investment 24–26
- Lüderitz, Adolf 23–24
- map of 155
- Oukwanyama and Ondonga 22
- settler farmer population 21
Global Labor History (GLH) 10–11
green hill, Tsumeb 35–36

Industrial and Commercial Workers' Union (ICU)
- leadership 284–285
- membership 285
- Port Elizabeth, conference in 285
- and UNIA 285–290, 295
- wages and living conditions 284
Italian workers
- assets of 87–88
- challenges 80
- Colla, Carlo (life story) 84–87
- dietary habits 83
- interactions with African laborers 81
- Otavibahn construction 75–76
- slave-like conditions, Herero forced laborers 82
- on strike 82–83
- tensions between Germans and Italians 83–84
- *Trattoria Internazionale* guesthouse 84–85
- work and strikes 78–80

Karibib-Windhoek line, Wilhelmstal massacre
- bi-colonial investigation 229
- building issues, Cape Workers 232
- investigations 236–237
- Ovambo and Cape Workers 229
- recruitments 230–231, 239
- soldier-workers 234–235
- South African business and political pressure 239, 240
- Transkei workers 230, 232–233
- Union investigation 238
- violence 235–238
- wages issue 231–233
- worker contracts 231
Koloniale Bergbaugesellschaft (KBG) 2–3, 149, 167
Kru workers
- alien natives 270
- challenges, South African rule 270–273
- daily realities of 90
- German military, operations 95
- *Hans Woermann* 93–94
- Herero forced laborers 105–107
- Herero prisoners, *Woermann-Linie* surf boats 108–109
- human infrastructure 92, 113
- Liberian-German economic relations 90–91
- *Lüderitzbucht-Gesellschaft L. Scholz & Co* 95
- non-forced laborers, fatalities of 112
- outbreak of war 90
- strike 93
- waning status 278
- wartime workforce 94
- *Woermann-Linie* 91–94
- wood pier construction 94
- working conditions, free laborers 105

labor question (in Southern Africa) and outbreak of war
- 'Colonial Congress' meeting 115
- Rand mines 116–117
- shortages 115
- Transkei and Western Cape 117–118
- wages 116, 117
labor studies 9–10
longshore workers, Swakopmund
- DKGfSWA 47
- Kru workforce 45, 47–49
- steamers and surf boats 45
- and Walvis Bay 43–44, 46
- *Woermann-Linie* steamer 45

micro-spatial historical method 12–13
mole construction, Swakopmund
- European workers 50–51

- housing demand 54
- Kru workforce 57
- 'old guard' of German workers 53
- Ovambo and Herero workers 52
- punishments 55
- racism and segregation 55
- rock quarry 52–53
- South African War 51
- water supply 54

'Namibian Labor Corridors' 4–5
- European Labor Corridor 75–89
- free and unfree labor 72
- Herero and Nama communities 69
- homelands 74
- labor dynamics 73
- migrant labor/workers, demands 70, 71
- mineral extraction 261

Namibian Worker Database 13–15, 292
Native Estate Files (NES) 13–15

Otavi mines, SWACO expedition
- African leaders and mine management 37
- compensation 34–35
- concession zone, boundaries of 28, 29
- copper products 30
- disease outbreaks 38–39
- Herero and cattle herds 27
- local building techniques 33–34
- negotiations with Tjiseseta 31–33
- strike 39–42
- Topnaar 30–31
- Tsumeb, green hill 35–36
- types of work 38–39

Oukwanyama Kingdom 138, 143, 145, 275, 276
Ovambo migrant laborers 132, 263
- beads 142–143
- Bogenfels mine 191–192
- contract and recruitment process 139–162
- conversion to Christianity 141
- historiography 133
- Kasino 149, 150, 156
- tobacco usage 142
- tradable commodities 143–144
- traditional symbols, wealth 141
- train journey 157–160
- travel times 156

Ovambo preachers 182–184

photography 15–16
- Kru workers 96–99
- südbahn construction project 222
- of tsumeb mines, Ovambo workers 175

Police Zone/settler region 3, 22
Ponzi scheme 89
Portuguese natives 276, 278

railway construction projects 207–208
- Cape Worker migration 216–219
- Cape Worker recruitment 213–216
- DKEBBG and Bachstein-Koppel 210–211
- hybrid project management 209
- map of 208
- South African employment 212–213
- Südbahn 210, 219–224
- Windhoek-Keetmanshoop line 210, 224–228

Rand mines 116–117, 218–219, 239
recruitment process, Ovambo migrants
- contracts, negotiating/signing 147–148
- farmers 150–151
- Finnish missionaries 146
- firms 147
- Hereroland 146
- medical examination 148
- at Namutoni and Okaukuejo 147, 151, 152
- Otavi Bahn construction 145
- passes 146–147
- transport infrastructure 146
- wages 149–151
- work sites, arrival 147

red line 146, 147

salvage colonialism 25
sexually transmitted diseases (STDs) 189
smallpox vaccinations 161–162
South African National Party (SAP) 219
South West African Company (SWACO) 21, 26, 61, 63, 68. *See also* Otavi mines, SWACO expedition
Spanish influenza 3, 14, 17, 262, 279–282

Südbahn construction project 219–220
- Baiweg 220
- costs for 224
- funding 224
- Keetmanshoop extension 221
- military transport 220
- photography 222
- physical challenges of labor 221
- work conditions 220–221
- workers at rest 222–223
SWACO. *See* South West African Company (SWACO)
Swakopmund
- construction, Swakopmund-Windhoek railway 58–68
- longshore workers 42–49
- mole, building 49–58
Swakopmund-Windhoek railway construction 50, 58
- additional supplies 63
- adverse climactic conditions 64
- African rinderpest panzootic 58–60
- *Baiweg* ox-wagon transport 60–61
- challenges 67, 68
- conditions, black workers 65–66
- contracts 62
- Damara labor 62–63
- food scarcity and malaria outbreak 64
- Herero herds 59–60
- labor development 67–68
- 'Otjimbingwe Petition' 67
- project's recruitment agreements 62
- salary variation, white and black workers 64–65
- SWACO 61
- temporary white migration 63
- traditional ox-wagon routes 58
- transports, Baster oxen-wagons 66–67
- typhus outbreak 64
- working conditions 64

Tango Mifango, NES file 13–14
Togolese entrepreneurs 249–250, 256
- assets 259
- business success 256
- clerks 251–252
- complex identity 257
- consumption patterns 257–258
- economic success 255–256
- English speakers, West Africans 250
- experiences 249, 259
- First World War 259
- *Heimathaus* (homeland house) 253, 254
- laundromats, advertisements 250–253
- "Max und Wilhelm aus Togo" 255
- and Mdingi, Alfred J. 250, 256–257
- *Togo-Dampfwäscherei* (Togo Steamwasher) 252–254
- wedding certificate 258–259
Tsumeb mines
- black workers 178, 180
- child labor 174–176
- contracts 174
- female surface workers 176
- graph of African workers 177
- local missionaries 178
- OMEG 151–153, 173–174
- Otavibahn train line 174
- photograph of 175
- weather 152
- white workers 178–179

United Negro Improvement Association (UNIA) 262, 285–291, 295

vaccinations 161–162
Vereinigte Diamanten Minen (VDM) 2

wagon drivers 114–115
- concentration camps 128–129
- contracts 121–122, 124
- experiences 122–125
- forced laborers, loading train 126–127
- human infrastructure 118
- labor question and outbreak of war 115–118
- ox-wagon and German troops 118–120
- recruitment operations 120–121
- treatment 124, 127–129
- working with recruiters 121

West African entrepreneurs and skilled workers 244–245
- Dares, Pieter and Kru 246–249
- economic roles 245
- German Cameroon 246
- Kulivo, Alfred and Togolese 249–260
West African Labor Corridor. *See* Kru workers
Windhoek-Keetmanshoop line (Nord-Südbahn) 224–225
- Cape Workers, Auas mountains 225–227
- Hendricks, Johannes 226–228
- Ovambo workers 225
World War One (WWI). *See* First World War